IFIP Advances in Information
and Communication Technology 298

IFIP – The International Federation for Information Processing

IFIP was founded in 1960 under the auspices of UNESCO, following the First World Computer Congress held in Paris the previous year. An umbrella organization for societies working in information processing, IFIP's aim is two-fold: to support information processing within its member countries and to encourage technology transfer to developing nations. As its mission statement clearly states,

> *IFIP's mission is to be the leading, truly international, apolitical organization which encourages and assists in the development, exploitation and application of information technology for the benefit of all people.*

IFIP is a non-profitmaking organization, run almost solely by 2500 volunteers. It operates through a number of technical committees, which organize events and publications. IFIP's events range from an international congress to local seminars, but the most important are:

- The IFIP World Computer Congress, held every second year;
- Open conferences;
- Working conferences.

The flagship event is the IFIP World Computer Congress, at which both invited and contributed papers are presented. Contributed papers are rigorously refereed and the rejection rate is high.

As with the Congress, participation in the open conferences is open to all and papers may be invited or submitted. Again, submitted papers are stringently refereed.

The working conferences are structured differently. They are usually run by a working group and attendance is small and by invitation only. Their purpose is to create an atmosphere conducive to innovation and development. Refereeing is less rigorous and papers are subjected to extensive group discussion.

Publications arising from IFIP events vary. The papers presented at the IFIP World Computer Congress and at open conferences are published as conference proceedings, while the results of the working conferences are often published as collections of selected and edited papers.

Any national society whose primary activity is in information may apply to become a full member of IFIP, although full membership is restricted to one society per country. Full members are entitled to vote at the annual General Assembly, National societies preferring a less committed involvement may apply for associate or corresponding membership. Associate members enjoy the same benefits as full members, but without voting rights. Corresponding members are not represented in IFIP bodies. Affiliated membership is open to non-national societies, and individual and honorary membership schemes are also offered.

Vashek Matyáš
Simone Fischer-Hübner
Daniel Cvrček
Petr Švenda (Eds.)

The Future of Identity in the Information Society

4th IFIP WG 9.2, 9.6/11.6, 11.7/
FIDIS International Summer School
Brno, Czech Republic, September 1-7, 2008
Revised Selected Papers

Springer

Volume Editors

Vashek Matyáš
Petr Švenda
Masaryk University, Faculty of Informatics
Botanicka 68a, Brno 602 00 , Czech Republic
E-mail: {matyas, svenda}@fi.muni.cz

Simone Fischer-Hübner
Karlstad University, Department of Computer Science
Universitetsgatan 2, 651 88 Karlstad, Sweden
E-mail: simone.fischer-huebner@kau.se

Daniel Cvrček
Brno University of Technology
Bozetechova 2, Brno 612 66, Czech Republic
E-mail: dancvrcek@gmail.com

CR Subject Classification (1998): D.4.6, K.6.5, C.2.0, H.2.7, K.4.4

ISSN 1868-4238
ISBN-13 978-3-642-24231-1 Springer Berlin Heidelberg New York

springer.com

Softcover reprint of the hardcover 1st edition 2009

Typesetting: Camera-ready by author, data conversion by Scientific Publishing Services, Chennai, India
Printed on acid-free paper SPIN: 12720286 06/3180 5 4 3 2 1 0

Preface

What constitutes an identity, how do new technologies affect identity, how do we manage identities in a globally networked information society? The increasing diversity of information and communication technologies and their equally wide range of usage in personal, professional and official capacities raise challenging questions of identity in a variety of contexts.

The aim of the IFIP/FIDIS Summer Schools has been to encourage young academic and industry entrants to share their own ideas about privacy and identity management and to build up collegial relationships with others. As such, the Summer Schools have been introducing participants to the social implications of information technology through the process of informed discussion.

The 4th International Summer School took place in Brno, Czech Republic, during September 1–7, 2008. It was organized by IFIP (International Federation for Information Processing) working groups 9.2 (Social Accountability), 9.6/11.7 (IT Misuse and the Law) and 11.6 (Identity Management) in cooperation with the EU FP6 Network of Excellence FIDIS and Masaryk University in Brno. The focus of the event was on security and privacy issues in the Internet environment, and aspects of identity management in relation to current and future technologies in a variety of contexts.

Following the holistic approach advocated by the involved IFIP working groups and by the FIDIS Network of Excellence, a diverse group of participants ranging from young doctoral students to leading researchers in the field engaged in discussions, dialogues and debates in an informal and supportive setting. The interdisciplinary, and international, emphasis of the Summer School allowed for a broader understanding of the issues in the technical and social spheres.

On the first five days (September 1–5), all topical sessions started with introductory lectures by invited speakers, followed by parallel workshops and seminars in the afternoons. The workshops consisted of short presentations based on the contributions submitted by participating PhD students, followed by active discussions. The weekend program (September 6–7) featured practical hands-on security and privacy workshops, namely, a local version of the "Capture The Flag" exercise.

Contributions combining technical, social, ethical or legal perspectives were solicited. Keynote speeches provided the focus for the theme of the Summer School – Historic Perspectives on Software Security and Privacy, Wireless Security and Privacy, Multilateral Security for Reputation Systems, Ambient Law, ePassport Security, Virtual Communities and Social and Legal Aspects, Mobile Identity Management, Security Standards and Privacy Management, Mass Surveillance and Data Retention as well as Anonymity and Censor-Free Publishing – and the contributions from participants enhanced the ideas generated by the keynote speeches. The Summer School was a very successful event. More than 50 delegates from 20 countries actively participated. We succeeded in initiating intensive discussions between PhD students and senior acclaimed researchers from different disciplines.

These proceedings include both keynote papers and submitted papers that were accepted by the Program Committee, and presented at the Summer School. The review process consisted of two steps. In the first step, contributions for presentation at the Summer School were selected based on reviews of submitted short papers by the Summer School Program Committee. The second step took place after the Summer School, when the authors had an opportunity to submit their final full papers addressing discussions at the Summer School. The submissions were reviewed again, by three reviewers each, and those included in these proceedings were carefully selected by the International Summer School Program Committee and by additional reviewers according to common quality criteria.

It is our pleasure to thank the members of the Program Committee, the additional reviewers, the members of the Organizing Committee as well as all the speakers. Without their work and dedication, this Summer School would not have been possible. Last but not least, we owe special thanks to Microsoft Research, FIDIS and IFIP for their financial support.

February 2009

Vashek Matyáš
Simone Fischer-Hübner
Daniel Cvrček
Petr Švenda

The Future of Identity in the Information Society - Challenges for Privacy and Security, FIDIS/IFIP Internet Security and Privacy Summer School

September 1–7, 2008, Brno, Czech Republic
http://www.buslab.org/SummerSchool2008/

General Chair

Vashek Matyáš	Masaryk University, Czech Republic

Program Committee Co-chairs

Simone Fischer-Hübner	Karlstad University, Sweden
Daniel Cvrček	University of Cambridge, UK

Program Committee

Geoff Busby	Independent Consultant, UK
David-Olivier Jaquet-Chiffelle	Berne University of Applied Sciences, Switzerland
George Danezis	Microsoft Research Cambridge, UK
Penny Duquenoy	Middlesex University, UK, IFIP WG 9.2 Chair
Mark Gasson	Reading University, UK
Dieter Gollmann	Technische Universität Hamburg-Harburg, Germany
Marit Hansen	Independent Center for Privacy Protection, Kiel, Germany
Dogan Kesdogan	Siegen University, Germany
Kai Kimppa	University of Turku, Finland
Mathias Klang	IT University/University of Göteborg, Sweden
Elisabeth de Leeuw	Ordina, The Netherlands, IFIP WG 11.6 Chair
Ronald Leenes	Tilburg University, The Netherlands
Marc van Lieshout	TNO, The Netherlands
Javier Lopez	University of Malaga, Spain
Leonardo Martucci	Karlstad University, Sweden
Steven Murdoch	University of Cambridge, UK
Lexi Pimenidis	Siegen University, Germany
Kai Rannenberg	Goethe University Frankfurt, Germany, IFIP TC11 Chair
Zdeněk Říha	Masaryk University, Brno, Czech Republic
Jozef Vyskoč	VaF, Slovakia

Diane Whitehouse	The Castlegate Consultancy, UK
Louise Yngström	Stockholm University/KTH, Sweden
Albin Zuccato	TeliaSonera, Sweden

Additional Reviewer

Rose Mharie Åhlfeld	Skövde University, Sweden

Local Organizing Committee

Petr Švenda (Chair)	Masaryk University, Czech Republic
Jan Krhovják	Masaryk University, Czech Republic
Marek Kumpošt	Masaryk University, Czech Republic
Václav Lorenc	Masaryk University, Czech Republic
Kamil Malinka	Brno University of Technology, Czech Republic
Andriy Stetsko	Masaryk University, Czech Republic
Jiří Kůr	Masaryk University, Czech Republic

Table of Contents

Challenges of Emerging Technologies

Privacy-Enhanced and Anonymous Applications

Business and Organisational Perspectives

Privacy Awareness and Individual Control

Anonymity Attacks and Analysis

Software Security – The Dangers of Abstraction

Dieter Gollmann

Hamburg University of Technology, Hamburg, Germany
diego@tu-harburg.de

Abstract. Software insecurity can be explained as a potpourri of hacking methods, ranging from the familiar, e.g. buffer overruns, to the exotic, e.g. code insertion with Chinese characters. From such an angle software security would just be a collection of specific countermeasures. We will observe a common principle that can guide a structured presentation of software security and give guidance for future research directions: There exists a discrepancy between the abstract programming concepts used by software developers and their concrete implementation on the given execution platform. In support of this thesis, five case studies will be discussed, viz characters, integers, variables, atomic transactions, and double linked lists.

1 Introduction

Once upon a time, computer security was about access control, with authentication and authorisation as its fundamental components [12]. Internet security was about communications security. Strong encryption was the main tool to solve problems in this area. Today, attackers send malformed inputs to networked applications to exploit buffer overruns, or to perform SQL injection, cross-site scripting (XSS), or cross-site request forgery (XSRF) attacks. Access control and encryption are of little help to defend against these current threats.

Lesson: Security is a moving target.

Software security has become our main challenge. Software is secure if it can handle intentionally malformed input [11]. Networking software is a popular target as it is intended to receive external input and as it involves low level manipulations of buffers. Mistakes at that level can allow an attacker to circumvent logical access controls by manipulations at a "layer below" [9]. Web applications are a popular target. They are intended to receive external input and are written by a multitude of authors, many of whom have little security expertise.

1.1 Security and Reliability

Reliability deals with accidental failures that are assumed to occur according to some given probability distribution. The probabilities for failures are given first; then the protection mechanisms are constructed and arguments about their efficacy can be made. To make software more reliable, it is tested against typical usage patterns.

V. Matyáš et al. (Eds.): The Future of Identity, IFIP AICT 298, pp. 1–12, 2009.

It does not matter how many bugs there are, it matters how often they are triggered.

In SQL injection attacks and the like, the attacker picks the inputs – and their probability distribution – with the aim to penetrate security controls. In security, the defender has to move first; the attacker picks his input to exploit weak defences. To make software more secure, it has thus to be tested against "untypical" usage patterns, but there are typical attack patterns.

Lesson: Measures dealing with failures that are governed by given probability distributions address reliability issues rather than security issues.

Think twice about using reputation or "trust" for security! These approaches extrapolate future actions from past behaviour and do not capture strategic decisions by truly malicious attackers.

2 Dangers of Abstractions

When writing code, programmers use elementary concepts like character, variable, array, integer, list, data & program, address (resource locator), or atomic transaction. These concepts have abstract meanings. For example, integers are an infinite set with operations 'add' and 'multiply', and a 'less or equal' ordering relation. To execute a program, we need concrete implementations of these concepts.

Abstraction hides "unnecessary" detail and is a valuable method for understanding complex systems. We do not have to know the inner details of a computer to be able to use it. We can write software using high level languages and graphical methods. Anthropomorphic images explain what computers do (send mail, sign document). Software security problems typically arise when concrete implementation and abstract intuition diverge. We will explore a few examples:

- Characters
- Integers
- Variables (buffer overruns)
- Atomic transactions
- Double linked lists

2.1 Characters

To demonstrate the pitfalls when handling characters, we take a look at a failure of a standard defence against SQL injection attacks[1]. In SQL, single quotes terminate input strings. In a typical SQL injection attack, the malicious input

[1] See `http://shiflett.org/blog/2006/jan/addslashes-versus-mysql-real-escape-string`; a similar problem in earlier versions of WordPress is discussed in `http://www.abelcheung.org/advisory/20071210-wordpress-charset.txt`

a) SELECT * FROM users WHERE passwd = ' password '

b) SELECT * FROM users WHERE passwd = ' ' OR '1=1' '

Fig. 1. Constructing SQL queries from strings, dashed boxes represent user input; case a) shows intended use; case b) is a SQL injection attacks that forces the WHERE clause to evaluate to true

contains a single quote followed by code segments picked by the attacker. When SQL statements are constructed by piecing together strings, some taken from the user input, others from the application issuing a database query, a single quote in user input can change the logical structure of the database query (Fig. 1 a)). Thus, attackers may be able to issue data base queries not envisaged by the application writer (Fig. 1 b)). As a countermeasure, the application could check user inputs and add a slash before any single quote encountered.

GBK (Guo Biao Kuozhan) is a character set for Simplified Chinese. In GBK, `0xbf27` is not a valid multi-byte character. When processed as single-byte characters, we have `0xbf` followed by `0x27`, a single quote. Adding a slash in front of the single quote gives `0xbf5c27`, but this happens to be the valid multi-byte character `0xbf5c` followed by a single quote. The single quote has survived!

Lesson: An operation may have different effects when observed at different levels of abstraction.

2.2 Integers

In mathematics integers form an infinite set with addition, multiplication, and a "less or equal" relation. On a computer system, integers are represented in binary. The representation of an integer is a binary string of fixed length (precision), so there is only a finite number of "integers". Programming languages have signed and unsigned integers, short and long (and long long) integers. The operations on these data types follo9w the rules of modular arithmetic. With unsigned 8-bit integers we have $255 + 1 = 0$, $16 \cdot 17 = 16$, and $01 = 255$. With signed 8-bit integers we have $127 + 1 = -128$ and $-128/-1 = -1$.

In the following loop, the counter i has the value 2^k after the k-th iteration. At the level of the mathematical abstraction, the value of i will always be strictly greater than 0 and the loop would be infinite.

```
int i = 1;
while (i > 0)
{
i = i * 2;
}
```

Unsigned n-bit integers represent integers modulo 2^n. Hence, the value of i after n iterations is $2^n \bmod 2^n = 0$; there will be a carry-overflow and the loop will terminate. For signed integers, the carry-bit will be set after $n-1$ iterations and i takes the value -2^{n-1}.

In mathematics, the inequality $a + b \geq a$ holds for all $b \geq 0$. Such obvious "facts" are no longer true at the implementation level. Integer overflows can in turn lead to buffer overruns. Consider the following code snippet (from an operating system kernel system-call handler):

```
char buf[128];
combine(char *s1, size_t len1, char *s2, size_t len2)
{
if (len1 + len2 + 1 <= sizeof(buf)) {
    strncpy(buf, s1, len1);
    strncat(buf, s2, len2);
    }
}
```

Two character strings are concatenated and stored in a 128-bit buffer. In C, strings are zero-terminated so the program includes a check that should make sure that the buffer is large enough to hold both strings and the terminating zero. However, for 32-bit integers `len2 = 0xFFFFFFFF` results in `len2` $+ 1 = 0$. If `len1` does not exceed the length of the buffer, the buffer will be written to while the number of bytes written can exceed the length of the buffer. The fact that computer integers do not behave like proper integers has led to vulnerable code more than once.

> *Lesson: Many programmers appear to view integers as having arbitrary precision, rather than being fixed-sized quantities operated on with modulo arithmetic [1].*

More information on integer overflows and on C libraries that properly handle finite precision integer arithmetic can be found e.g. in [11].

2.3 Variables

Variables are used in the abstract specification of algorithms. In the abstract specification we might denote the data type of a variable but we are not concerned with its actual representation. A buffer is the concrete implementation of a variable. If the value assigned to a variable exceeds the size of the allocated buffer, memory locations not allocated to this variable are overwritten. If the memory location overwritten had been allocated to some other variable, the value of that other variable can be changed. An attacker could change the value of a protected variable A by assigning a deliberately malformed value to some other variable B.

Unintentional buffer overruns crash software, and have been a focus for reliability testing. Intentional buffer overruns are a concern if an attacker can modify security relevant data. Attractive targets are return addresses specifying next method to be executed and security settings.

Historic Perspective. Since the contribution by Aleph One [15], buffer overruns have been extensively studied in the literature on software security, see e.g. [11,17,8]. We leave a detailed treatment of buffer overrun attacks to these sources and only give a brief historic perspective. Our first example from the 1980s relates to Digital's VMS operating system. The login procedure had the option of logging in to a particular machine by entering

username/DEVICE =<machine>.

In one version of VWS the length of the argument *machine* was not checked. A device name of more than 132 bytes overwrote the privilege mask of the process started by login. Users could thus set their own privileges. Our second example is the Morris worm from 1988 that exploited a buffer overrun in the fingerd daemon [7].

Lesson: Buffer overruns predate Windows.

For a recent case of a buffer overrun attack, we refer to a heap-based buffer overrun in μTorrent 1.6 allowing remote attackers to execute arbitrary code via a torrent file with a crafted announce header (CVE-2007-0927). μTorrent is a widely used lightweight torrent client. There is no automatic patching system and many of its users are "security-unaware" and do not use – or even disable – anti virus software. Hence, this case could have a higher damage potential than some operating system vulnerabilities.

Lesson: Buffer overrun attacks are moving to the application layer.

Defences against buffer overrun attacks come in various shapes. When developing code in la language like C, be careful and check how much you are writing to a buffer. The integrity of the return address can be protected by canaries [6] or by split control and data stacks [13,18]. The latter defences maintain the logical separation between code and data in the machine architecture. Shellcode insertion on the stack can be prevented by making the stack non executable. Finally, you can leave memory management to others and use a type safe language like Java.

Storage Residues. Buffer overrun attacks overwrite sensitive variables. There is a dual security problem, viz a process reading variables that it not yet had assigned a value to. In a multi-process system, several processes are running at the same time but only one is active. When a new process becomes active it gets access to resources (memory positions) used by the previous process. This is known as *object reuse*. *Storage residues* are data left behind in the memory area allocated to the new process. This is a security problem if sensitive data have been left. Operating systems thus usually allow a process only to read from memory it has written to.

To illustrate we summarize the Sun tarball story [10]. A *tarball* is an archive file produced by the `tar` utility. Some time in 1993 it was discovered that tarballs produced under Solaris 2.0 contained parts of the password file. The following explanation emerged. The `tar` utility copied material in 512-byte blocks from disk to archive in a read/write cycle using a buffer. This buffer was not zeroed before data was read in. Thus, there could be a storage residue; if the last chunk of the file did not fill the buffer the previous content was read out. These memory positions happened to always hold a part of the password file.

This behaviour was caused by the following sequence of actions. During the read/write cycle `tar` looked up information about the user running the program. Therefore `/etc/passwd` was put on the heap. After checking the user the buffer for `/etc/passwd` was freed, but not zeroed. *tar* happened to be the next program getting this memory space, so memory residues were still there. The problem had not occurred in previous versions because the check of the user had happened earlier in the program. While fixing a bug, some code was removed and the vulnerability was exposed.

Are storage residues always a problem? Not so long ago, during a code review of Linux sources a read of an uninitialized variable was discovered in OpenSSL code. The offending line was commented out. After some delay in time, it was observed that the OpenSSL key generation algorithm produced predictable keys; the uninitialized variable had intentionally been used to provide randomness.

Lesson: In security, there are no correct answers.

2.4 Atomic Transactions

A *race condition* occurs when multiple transactions access shared data in a way that the overall results depend on the sequence of accesses. This can happen when multiple processes access the same variable. In multi-threaded processes, as in Java servlets, race conditions can occur between threads in a process.

A transaction is *atomic* if it is either executed in its entirety or if it has no effect at all. Access to a protected resource is fitting example for a transaction that should be executed atomically. The operating system first checks whether the access request is permitted; only in case of a positive outcome will the resource be made available to the requestor. If an attacker could change an essential parameter, e.g. a pointer to the resource, between those two steps, she could get access to a resource other than the one the initial check was performed for. Time-of-check-to-time-of use (TOCTTOU) is a well known security issue, as are `access()/open()` races in Unix [2].

For our illustrating example, we go further back in time to CTSS, one of the early time-sharing operating systems. One morning, users logging on to this system had the password file shown as the message of the day. The explanation was a race condition [5]. On CTSS, every user had a unique home directory. When a user invoked the editor, a scratch file with fixed name SCRATCH was created in this directory. At some point in time, the system was modified so that several users could work concurrently system manager. Later, the following occurred.

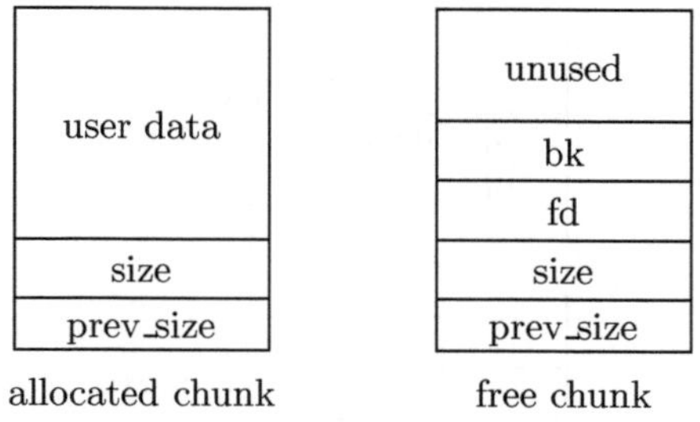

Fig. 2. Chunks in Doug Lea malloc

1. System manager *A* starts editing the message of the day, so SCRATCH in the system manager's directory contains this message.
2. System manager *B* starts editing the password file; now SCRATCH in the system manager's directory holds the password file.
3. System manager *A* saves the message of the day from SCRATCH, displaying the password file.

To defend against attacks exploiting race conditions enforce atomicity, e.g. through locks, so other processes are prevented from changing security relevant parameters. For more information on race conditions, on methods for scanning code for such vulnerabilities, and on possible countermeasures, see e.g. [4,14,3,16]. Finally, note that in Java it is the programmer's task to deal with race conditions by suitable synchronization of concurrent accesses.

2.5 Double-Linked Lists

There exist attacks more sophisticated than simple buffer overruns that exploit features of Unix memory management to overwrite arbitrary pointers. Our explanations will be based on Doug Lea malloc. Memory is divided into chunks. A chunk contains user data and control data. The control data include a boundary tag that gives the size of the chunk and the size of the previous chunk in memory. Chunks are allocated with `malloc()` and deallocated with `free()`. Free chunks are placed in bins. A bin is a double linked list, where chunks are ordered in increasing size. Free chunks contain boundary tags and forward and backward pointer to their neighbours in the bin (Fig. 2).

The size of a chunk is given in bytes, but chunk sizes are always multiples of 8 bytes. Thus, the three least significant bits of size are not used and have been designated for control flags:

- `0x1`: PREV_INUSE – indicates that the previous chunk in memory is free;
- `0x2`: IS_MAPPED
- Some libraries also use the third bit.

There should be no adjacent free chunks in memory. Hence, when a chunk is freed and a neighbouring chunk is free, both chunks are coalesced into a single chunk. Chunks are taken out of a bin with the `unlink` utility:

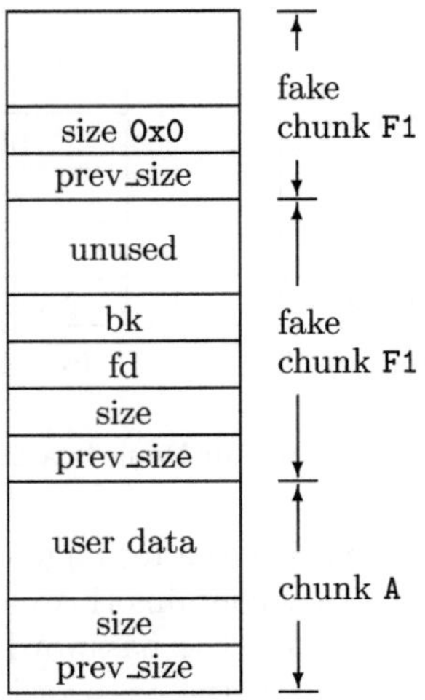

Fig. 3. Exploiting unlink after a buffer overrun

```
#define unlink(P, BK, FD)
{
[1] FD = P->fd;
[2] BK = P->bk;
[3] FD->bk = BK;
[4] BK->fd = FD;
}
```

`unlink` saves the pointers in chunk `P` to `FD` and `BK`. It then updates the backward pointer of the next chunk in the list: the address located at `FD` plus 12 bytes (offset of the `bk` field in the boundary tag) is overwritten with value stored in `BK`. Finally, the forward pointer of the previous chunk in the list is updated.

To demonstrate how `unlink` can be used to overwrite arbitrary pointers, we sketch a hypothetical buffer overrun attack [8]. Assume chunk `A` has a buffer overrun vulnerability; `A` is allocated. The attack is launched by overwriting the adjacent chunk `B` with fake chunks. These fake chunks are constructed so that there seems to be a free chunk next to `A` (Fig. 3).

Now free chunk `A`. The PREV_INUSE flag in chunk `F2` had been set so that `F1` is marked as free. `A` will be coalesced with the adjacent 'free' chunk and the fake chunk `F1` will be unlinked. Running `unlink(F1,FD,BK)` will add a 12 byte offset to the address given as the `fd` pointer in `F1`, overwriting this address with the value given as the `bk` pointer in `F1`. The attacker controls the values in `F1` and thus can overwrite a pointer of her choice with a value of her choice.

It is not necessary to have a buffer overrun to exploit `unlink`. To see how, we have to take a closer look at `free()`. Memory is deallocated with `void free (void *ptr)` where `*ptr` must have been returned by a previous call to `malloc()`, `calloc()` or `realloc()`. If `ptr` is null, no operation is performed.

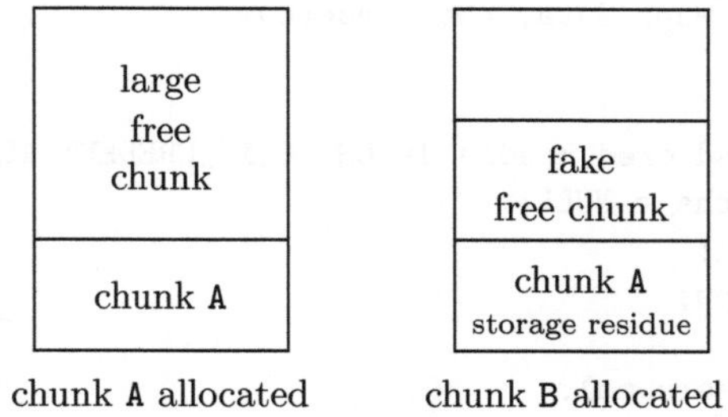

Fig. 4. Double free vulnerability

The behaviour is undefined if `free(ptr)` has already been called. Exactly this situation is the root of so-called *double-free vulnerabilities.*

Double free attacks exploit programs where memory is deallocated without setting the respective pointer to null. They only work if current memory usage is favourable to the attacker, but of course attackers can make their own luck. The vulnerable program allocates a memory block `A` that has to be adjacent to free memory (Fig. 4 left). When `A` is freed, forward or backward consolidation will create a larger block. Then the attacker allocates a larger block `B` hoping to get space just freed. In this case, a fake free chunk is written into `B` adjacent to the storage residue of `A` (Fig. 4 right). When `free(A)` is called again, consolidation with the fake chunk will overwrite a target address in the way described above. Double free vulnerabilities have been found in zlib (CA-2002-07), MySQL, Internet Explorer, Linux CVS, and MIT Kerberos 5.

Uninitialized memory corruption is a similar attack method. An exploitable vulnerability has been reported for the Heimdal FTPD server (CVE-2007-5939). In the code given in figure 5 `ticketfile` is declared but not initialized[2]. If `pw` is equal to null the program will jump to label `fail` and the uninitialized `ticketfile` will be freed. In this case the behaviour of `free()` is undefined and the attacker can try to manipulate the memory layout so that `free()` is applied to a pointer suitably prepared by the attacker.

We could treat double free and uninitialized memory corruption vulnerabilities as control flow problems. In the first case, memory deallocation is not performed completely; in the second case, memory allocation has not been completed before the memory is freed. The problems can be removed by tidying up memory allocation and deallocation.

We could also try to make `unlink` more secure. This utility is intended for taking elements out of a double linked list. The attacks violate this abstraction applying `unlink` to chunks that are not part of a double link list. As a defence – implemented e.g. in glibc 2.3.5 – one could check that the argument of `unlink` is part of a double linked list and meets other assumptions of Doug Lea malloc.

[2] See `http://archives.neohapsis.com/archives/fulldisclosure/2007-12/0175.html`

```
int gss_userok(void *app_data, char *username)
{
...
  if (data->delegated_cred_handle != GSS_C_NO_CREDENTIAL) {
    krb5_ccache ccache = NULL;
    char* ticketfile;
    struct passwd *pw;

    pw = getpwnam(username);

    if (pw == NULL) {
      ret = 1;
      goto fail;
    }

    ...

    fail:
    if (ccache)
    krb5_cc_close(gssapi_krb5_context, ccache);
    free(ticketfile);
  }
...
}
```

Fig. 5. Code segment from Heimdal FTPD

- check for membership in a double linked list locally with `!(p->fd->bk == p->bk->fd == p)`.
- Check if the first element in the bin is the one being added.
- Check if chunks are larger or equal to minimal size (16 bytes) and smaller than the memory allocated up to now.

3 Conclusion

Software security is not just about buffer overruns, and we have only just scratched the surface. There is more to it than just discrepancies between source code and object code, take integer overflows as an example. There are no quick fixes like avoiding unsafe C functions or by writing code only in type safe languages. Indeed, software security cannot be solved entirely at the level of the programming language. Programmers can make logical errors when the implementations of the abstractions they are using behave in unexpected ways. When security research tries to get ahead of the next reported vulnerability, it might well systematically compare programming concepts with their implementations.

When a problem area becomes known, tools and libraries can help dealing with the issues arising, but these tools and libraries have to be used. It is a technical challenge to develop useful and efficient tools. It is an organisational and motivational challenge to get those tools adopted. This challenge is not made easier by the fact that the focus of attacks is moving from operating systems to applications. Cross-site scripting was the at number one in the 2007 OWASP Top Ten Vulnerabilities[3]. In the CVE database, cross-site scripting was at number one in 2005, and SQL injection at number two in 2006. There are better chances reaching the software experts writing systems code than reaching the many application experts writing application code.

Final lesson: Security research will stay in business ...

References

1. Ashcraft, K., Engler, D.: Using programmer-written compiler extensions to catch security holes. In: Proceedings of the 2002 IEEE Symposium on Security and Privacy, pp. 143–159 (2002)
2. Bishop, M., Dilger, M.M.: Checking for race conditions in file accesses. Computing Systems 9(2), 131–152 (1996)
3. Borisov, N., Johnson, R., Sastry, N., Wagner, D.: Fixing races for fun and profit: How to abuse atime. In: 14th USENIX Security Symposium, pp. 164–173 (2005)
4. Chen, H., Wagner, D.: MOPS: an infrastructure for examining security properties. In: 9th ACM Conference on Computer and Communications Security, pp. 235–244. Springer, Heidelberg (2002)
5. Corbato, F.J.: On building systems that will fail. Communications of the ACM 34(9), 72–81 (1991)
6. Cowan, C., Pu, C., Maier, D., Walpole, J., Bakke, P., Beattie, S., Grier, A., Wagle, P., Zhang, Q., Hinton, H.: StackGuard: Automatic adaptive detection and prevention of buffer-overflow attacks. In: Proceedings of the 7th USENIX Security Symposium, pp. 63–78 (1998)
7. Eichin, M.W., Rochlis, J.A.: With microscope and tweezers: An analysis of the Internet virus of November 1988. In: Proceedings of the 1989 IEEE Symposium on Security and Privacy, pp. 326–343 (1989)
8. Foster, J.C.: Buffer Overflow Attacks. Syngress Publishing, Rockland (2005)
9. Gollmann, D.: Computer Security, 2nd edn. John Wiley & Sons, Chichester (2006)
10. Graff, M.G., van Wyk, K.R.: Secure Coding. O'Reilly & Associates, Sebastopol (2003)
11. Howard, M., LeBlanc, D.: Writing Secure Code, 2nd edn. Microsoft Press, Redmond (2002)
12. Lampson, B., Abadi, M., Burrows, M., Wobber, E.: Authentication in distributed systems: Theory and practice. ACM Transactions on Computer Systems 10(4), 265–310 (1992)
13. Lee, R.B., Karig, D.K., McGregor, J.P., Shi, Z.: Enlisting hardware architecture to thwart malicious code injection. In: Hutter, D., Müller, G., Stephan, W., Ullmann, M. (eds.) Security in Pervasive Computing. LNCS, vol. 2802, pp. 237–252. Springer, Heidelberg (2004)
14. Lhee, K.-s., Chapin, S.J.: Detection of file-based race conditions. International Journal of Information Security 4(1-2), 105–119 (2005)

[3] See `http://www.owasp.org/index.php/Top_10_2007`

15. Aleph One: Smashing the stack for fun and profit. Phrack Magazine, 49 (1996)
16. Uppuluri, P., Joshi, U., Ray, A.: Preventing race condition attacks on filesystem. In: SAC 2005 (2005) (invited talk)
17. Viega, J., McGraw, G.: Building Secure Software. Addison-Wesley, Boston (2001)
18. Xu, J., Kalbarczyk, Z., Patel, S., Iyer, R.K.: Architecture support for defending against buffer overflow attacks. In: Proceedings of the EASY-2 Workshop (2002)

History of Privacy*

Jan Holvast

Holvast & Partner, Privacy Consultants, NL - Landsmeer,
The Netherlands
henp.holvast@wxs.nl

Abstract. Discussion on privacy issues is as old as mankind. Starting with the protection of one's body and home, it soon evolved in the direction of controlling one's personal information. In 1891, the American lawyers Samuel Warren and Louis Brandeis described the right to privacy in a famous article: it is the right to be let alone. In 1967 a new milestone was reached with the publication of Alan Westin's Privacy and Freedom when he defined privacy in terms of self determination: privacy is the claim of individuals, groups, or institutions to determine for themselves when, how, and to what extent information about them is communicated to others.

History of privacy makes clear that there is a strong relationship between privacy and the development of technology. The modern discussion started with the use of cameras and went on to include the development and use of computers in an information society in which personal data on every individual is collected and stored. Not only is it a great concern that privacy is eroding but also that we are entering a surveillance society. This loss of privacy seems to be even more the case since the protection of privacy is strongly dependant upon the political will to protect it. Since 9/11, however, this political will world-wide is oriented more toward the effective and efficient use of technology in the battle against criminality and terrorism than it is toward protecting privacy. Therefore it is time to re-evaluate the use of technology and the protection of privacy. It is not only privacy that is at stake but above all democracy.

Keywords: Data protection, information, information technology, information society, privacy, self regulation, surveillance society, vulnerability.

1 Introduction

"The good news about privacy is that eighty-four percent of us are concerned about privacy. The bad news is that we do not know what we mean." The figures Anne Branscomb [1] mentions are still true for most countries in the Western hemisphere, and the reason for not knowing what we are talking about is primarily because many

* This contribution is an elaboration of a more lengthy article in Karl de Leeuw and Jan Bergstra (Eds), The History of Information Security: A Comprehensive Handbook. Elsevier: 2007.

V. Matyáš et al. (Eds.): The Future of Identity, IFIP AICT 298, pp. 13–42, 2009.

authors on privacy issues are writing about different aspects of privacy. Some are referring to the need for privacy; whereas, others are referring to the right to privacy, the invasion of privacy, the functions of privacy, or even the (legal) protection of privacy. In this paper, we start with the need for privacy and attempt to unravel the confusion within that issue. Thereafter, we will give an overview of the concept of privacy, an interpretation of that discussion, and a way of looking at privacy. In addition we will examine the function of privacy in order to clarify the importance of privacy (protection).

The third chapter is devoted to the attacks on privacy starting with the first publicly discussed cases in 1361 and then focusing on the development during the 20th century until the present day. This chapter makes clear how strong the relationship is between privacy discussion and technology, in particular information technology as it is called now. It shows the double face of technology, which can help people to master problems and simultaneously can influence people and their conduct in a negative way. An example of these technologies is the Radio Frequency Identity (RFID). As a pacemaker, the RFID is helpful but as a chip under the skin it can become a tool for tracing all movement of an individual. Another example is ambient technologies which will be present in almost all households in the Western hemisphere.

For some time, there have been ways to protect privacy. In many countries, this protection is included in a country's constitution, and in some cases privacy protection is deliberately translated into privacy and data protection laws. The legal systems are, however, not always the same. In this work, we will make a distinction between comprehensive legislation (omnibus laws) and sectoral laws which are intended to protect a particular part of society or areas such as communication technology. In addition to legal measures, self-regulation is used, in particular by industry in the form of codes of conduct or codes of practice. More and more technology itself is used as a means of protection. Security measures are examples but also the often discussed but less implemented Privacy-Enhancing Technologies (PETs) are examples of using technology itself in the protection of privacy. In addition, publicity after privacy has been invaded in an unacceptable way is an important tool of protection, although in an indirect way. We will give some famous examples.

Returning to the issue of privacy, we will explain how privacy is often invaded. Information has two important characteristics: it is power and it is money. These two reasons drive the collecting, storing, and using of information in the current way that it does. It is also the explanation for the omnipresence of information technology. Everywhere humans walk, sleep, and talk, technology is present. And as humans are increasingly adept at data producing, more and more traces of our daily life will be gathered and known by others, both in government and in industry. Countermeasures will be politically defined, and their power relations given in order to see that not all privacy will be able to be protected. Consequently, we must conclude that we are increasingly going to live in a surveillance society in which almost everything about our lives will be known. The consequences of this new society are until now unknown while sociologists seem to have no interest in this new society.

2 Privacy

2.1 The Need for Privacy

Humans have always had a need for privacy. The privacy issue can already be seen in the writings of Socrates and other Greek philosophers [2], when a distinction is made between the 'outer' and the 'inner', between public and private, between society and solitude. Although private life sometimes was seen as an antisocial behaviour, periods of retirement normally were accepted. There always has been a kind of conflict between "the subjective desire for solitude and seclusion and the objective need to depend on others" [3, p. 5].

An important change took place with the colonization of America. It appears that issues of privacy were brought along from Europe. The ownership or possession of land in the New World furnished a secure base for the privilege of privacy. Because of the distance between homesteads, in the view of David Flaherty [4], physical privacy became a characteristic of everyday life, and the home itself became the primary place of privacy. The home is still seen in that way since the home is a personal castle, which emphasizes the idea that privacy is related to wealth. Historically, poverty and the home meant less privacy, particularly where families share common dwellings with almost no physical separation.

Nowadays it is generally accepted that everybody has a need for privacy, although the way it is appreciated differs from culture to culture and from person to person. At the same time it is clear that a need for privacy can never be absolute and must be balanced against other needs, for example the need for fighting terrorism, criminality, and fraud. As we will then see, the discussion on privacy primarily is a political discussion about the way the distinct individual and societal interests can be balanced.

2.2 The Concept of Privacy

In the most fundamental form, privacy is related to the most intimate aspects of being human. Throughout history privacy is related to the house, to family life, and to (personal) correspondence. This relation can be seen as a way of controlling a situation. Since the 14th through the 18th century, people went to court for eavesdropping or for opening and reading personal letters. Since the end of the 19th century, the emphasis shifted more toward personal information with the same intention that is, to control one's own information.

The general discussion on privacy started shortly after the Second World War in the United States. Numerous publications were devoted to the issue of privacy. In these publications attention primarily is paid to a description of the concept of privacy and to the developments of techniques invading privacy, in particular the computer which is seen as primarily responsible for privacy invasion. These publications culminated in the founding in 1962 of the Project *The Impact of Science and Technology on Privacy*. The project was developed between 1962 and 1966 by the Special Committee on Science and Law of the Association of the Bar of the City of New York. Director of Research was Alan Westin who published extensive details of the results in the Columbia Law Review and in his book *Privacy and Freedom* and laid a profound base for the later discussion [5], [6], [7].

In almost all publications from that period, three words are used in relation to privacy: freedom, control, and self-determination [8], [9], [10], [11], [12], [13], [14] [15]. The concept of privacy is defined in almost the same way as it was in 1891 by Warren and Brandeis. Privacy is described as a right to be let alone and a right of each individual to determine, under ordinary circumstances, what his or her thoughts, sentiments, and emotions shall be when in communication with others. Because of the advancement in technology, privacy becomes an ever growing concern. These characteristics of privacy are repeated and elaborated by numerous authors in the beginning of the 1960s.

In his *Privacy and Freedom*, Alan Westin summarizes the discussion and defines privacy based on all of these points. "Privacy is the claim of individuals, groups, or institutions to determine for themselves when, how, and to what extent information about them is communicated to others. Viewed in terms of the relation of the individual to social participation, privacy is the voluntary and temporary withdrawal of a person from the general society through physical or psychological means, either in a state of solitude or small-group intimacy or, when among larger groups, in a condition of anonymity or reserve" [7, p. 7]. Since 1967, there has almost not been a publication on this subject in which this definition is not presented.

As can be seen from the literature on the subject, two dimensions of privacy can be distinguished: a relational one and an informational one. The first deals with the relation one has to other people, for example controlling who may enter the domestic environment or who is allowed to touch one's body. These aspects sometimes are described as territorial privacy and bodily privacy [14]. The informational dimension is related to the collection, storing and processing of (personal) data.

Common to both dimensions of privacy is the need to maintain control over personal space, the body, and information about oneself; however, it is clear that in certain situations, loss of control is even more important, for example when people lose their consciousness due to an accident. Control can, then, be described in the form of two aspects of freedom: being free to ... and being free from.... The first is the more active part. Within certain borders, humans prefer being free to do what they wish and not be hindered by others or experiences from the past. The second is being free from being watched or eavesdropped on. In both situations the central idea is the concept of self-determination. Although these two freedoms sound rather absolute, it is clear that 'within certain borders' does mean that in all these situations we are depending on others, our neighbours, our co-citizens, and other people. Living in a community means by definition involved with others. But it means at the same time that we must have some free space or sense of freedom since otherwise we would be prisoners of society.

In the writer's view, privacy can be described as the individual's right to self-determination, within certain borders, to his home, body, and information. Although the word 'right' suggests otherwise, the concept of privacy is much more politically determined than legally. This position is more clearly demonstrated by the changing climate of opinions since 9/11. Personal data, such as Passengers Name Records is now made available for governmental use without much debate. A comparable situation shows the discussion on the retention of communication traffic data for at least half a year in order to trace back potential terrorist who have used electronic means of communications. It shows how due to a sudden event the balance between a need for privacy and the need for information can change fundamentally. It is not the right itself that is being discussed but rather the amount of privacy that is remained after the government satisfies its need for information. As we will increasingly see, the technical means for collecting and storing information are increasing in an enormous way.

2.3 The Functions of Privacy

It is almost impossible to describe the various ways in which the functions of privacy were seen in the past. Alan Westin has given a comprehensive description of these earlier functions in his study 'Privacy and Freedom' [7, p. 330-338]. He distinguishes among the four functions of privacy which are still important in modern life.

The first is a need for personal autonomy, which is vital to the development of individuality and the consciousness of individual choice in anyone's life. Privacy is equally important as it supports normal psychological functioning, stable interpersonal relationship, and personal development. Privacy is the basis for the development of individuality.

In the second place we need privacy as a form of emotional release. Life generates such strong tensions for the individual that both physical and psychological health demand periods of privacy. It supports healthy functioning by providing needed opportunities to relax, to be one's self, to escape from the stresses of daily life, and to express anger, frustration, grief, or other strong emotion without fear of repercussion or ridicule. The consequence of denying opportunities for such privacy can be severe, ranging from increased tension and improvident expression to suicide and mental collapse.

A third function is that of self-evaluation and decision making. Each individual needs to integrate his experiences into a meaningful pattern and to exert his individuality on events. Solitude and the opportunity for reflection are essential for creativity. Individuals need space and time in which to process the information which is coming to them in an enormous amount. Privacy allows the individual the opportunity to consider alternatives and consequences to act as consistently and appropriate as possible.

A fourth function is the need for a limited and protected communication, which is particularly vital in urban life with crowded environments and continuous physical and psychological confrontations. The value of privacy recognizes that individuals require opportunities to share confidences with their family, friends and close associates. In short privacy is creating opportunities for humans to be themselves and to stay stable as a person.

Unfortunately since Westin's 1968 study, little attention has been paid to these four functions, and it is still unclear how a significant threat to one's privacy affects psychological growth. Scientists know too little about how people respond under constant surveillance. A concern, however, is that people may become more conformist as they suppress their individuality [15]. On matters related to employees, more information is available. Barbara Garson in *The Electronic Sweatshop* states that there is some empirical prove that for clerical workers whose keystrokes are counted by the minute or airline clerks whose figures are posted daily, electronic monitoring has been linked to pain, stress, and serious disease. Medical reasons then have been some help in limiting the monitoring of employees [16].

3 Privacy under Attack

Literature and court cases show that for a very long time, in one way or another, privacy has always been perceived as attacked. At first the attack on privacy was done by persons with whom individuals have a close contact, such as neighbours and people living in the same village or colony. Later attacks were also accomplished by governmental agencies, industry, or the press. In this chapter we will make a distinction between past situation which lasted until the 1980s and the present situation which covers from the 1980s until 2008 as well as the future situation of which we already now have clear indications of new methods of privacy surveillance.

Although these three periods are distinctive from each other, it is not to say that they can be separated one from the other. An important characteristic of the use of information and information technology is that it is a cumulative process. The beginning of one period does not at all mean that the previous period has concluded. The contrary is the case as, for example, photography and computer uses for privacy invasion show. Many of the earlier techniques are combined with new, even more powerful techniques.

In this overview of (technical) attacks, this contribution will strongly rely on past literature and court cases from the United States since most publications dealing with these discussions and incidents of privacy are published in that country. For the present and future situation, we will use international references, including web-pages. These sources will show that attack on privacy is becoming not only an international but a global problem.

3.1 Use of Information in the Past

Almost all authors on privacy start the discussion with the famous article *The Right to Privacy* of Samuel Warren and Louis Brandeis in the *Harvard Law Review* of December 15, 1890 [17]. Although the effects of this article can not be underestimated this starting point does not mean that there have been no discussions on the invasions of privacy before 1890. As Westin shows in his publications, in the fifteenth century the word 'privacy' was already used in England and historical research shows that colonists in New England were respecting privacy in relation to an individual's home, family, and even written communication. Hixson [3] shows that there was opposition against the first U.S. census as early as 1790, although the government required little more than enumeration of persons, both slave and free. This opposition resulted in instructions to census takers in 1840 that individual returns be treated as confidential. It was feared that the citizen was not adequately protected from the danger that private affairs or the secrets of family would be disclosed to the neighbours.

3.1.1 Trespass

As we have seen, the home and its related physical privacy were, from the beginning, the form of privacy that most vehemently was protected. It is not astonishing that the first cases brought to court had to deal with intrusions of the home, in particular by eavesdropping. Electronic Privacy Information Center (EPIC) cites James Michael who shows that in 1361 the Justices of Peace Act in England provided for the arrest of peeping toms and eavesdroppers. In 1765, British Lord Camden, striking down a warrant to enter a house and seize papers wrote "We can safely say there is no law in this country to justify the defendants in what they have done; if there was, it would destroy all the comforts of society, for papers are often the dearest property any man can have" [14, p. 5]. The law of trespass and the constitutional protection of unreasonable search and seizure in the United States as formulated in the Fourth Amendment were interpreted as protections against official and unofficial intrusions.

3.1.2 Correspondence

In addition to the home, personal mail was seen as a part of private life in need of special protection. Long before this protection was generally accepted, in particular by the use of the telegraph, the first incidents about invasion of reading personal mails are known. One story is from 1624 [3]. Plymouth Plantation was the scene for what Hixson mentions as the first recorded invasion of privacy. Governor William Bradford learned of a plot against the leadership of the small colony. He had intercepted several incriminating letters written by two newcomers and sent to friends in England. When the two men denied any conspiracy the governor produced the letters and asked them to read the content aloud. The men expressed outrage that their private correspondence had been intercepted but did not comply further since they had no legality on which to stand.

3.1.3 The Press

Curiosity has always been an enemy of privacy and is a foible that has stimulated privacy invasion and on which newspapers have exploited individual privacy on a commercial basis. Already in 1873 the first complaints were uttered against the way journalists were using interview techniques. President Cleveland expressed dislike of the way the press treated him on occasion, especially when some journalists followed him and his bride on their honeymoon trip in 1886. Also E.L. Godkin wrote at the end of the 19th century that the chief enemy of privacy in modern life is the curiosity shown by some people about the affairs of other people [3, p. 29].

Although it is not known how far Warren and Brandeis were influenced by Godkin, generally the discussion on the attack on privacy starts with the famous article of these two lawyers, published in 1890 in the *Harvard Law Review* under the title *The Right to Privacy* [17]. The reason for publication grew out of a specific situation. The *Saturday Evening Gazette,* which specialized in 'blue blood items' reported activities of Warren and his wife in lurid details. Warren, together with Louis D. Brandeis, was the first to start a fundamental discussion on his rights not to have his thoughts, statements, or emotions made public without his consent. Since the publication of this famous article, no contribution of the issue of privacy fails to mention it.

3.1.4 Instantaneous Photography

In their article Warren and Brandeis not only blame the press but also recent inventions and business methods like instantaneous photographs. In combination with the newspaper business, these business methods and new technologies invaded sacred personal and domestic precincts. As predicted in the famous Warren and Brandeis article, these numerous mechanical devices would be the source for 'what is whispered in the closet shall be proclaimed from the housetops' [17, p. 134].

Since 1890, however, the relationship to the use of technical means is apparent. Already mentioned in the article of Warren and Brandeis, the use of instantaneous photographs makes possible publication for various purposes without the consent of an individual. A classic type of invasion of privacy is the use without consent of a person's picture to promote a product. The initial test was *Roberson v. Rochester Folding Box Co.,* which startled the New York legal world [18]. A local milling company decided to use a photo of Abigail Rochester, a charming and attractive girl at the time, to promote their product. For that reason the brilliant slogan *The Flour of the Family* was used and, together with the photo, placed in numerous stores, warehouses, and saloons. Abigail claimed a 'right of privacy' and brought suit for the sum of $15,000. The New York Court denied the suit, by a 4-3 decision, saying that her claim held no right on grounds that it was yet unknown to common law what had been infringed.

This decision excited much amazement and strongly influenced later court cases, in particular three years later *Pavesich v. New England Life Insurance Co.* In that court case, Paolo Pavesich's picture was used, also without his consent, by a life insurance company for an advertisement. The photograph showed a healthy man (Pavesich) who did buy a life insurance policy, in contrast to a sick man who did not and presumably could not make such an 'invaluable' purchase for his future security. In the picture of Pevasich there was a legend underneath: "In my healthy and productive period of life I bought insurance in the New England Life Insurance Co. of Boston Massachusetts, and today my family life is protected." Pavesich had, in fact, never purchased such a life insurance, nor made any such statement as quoted. He found the advertisement distasteful and brought suit for $25,000 damages. In this case the right of privacy was unanimously accepted. The Court found the insurance company subject to damages for invading the privacy of Pavesich [18, p. 99]. It was a strong precedent for precisely one aspect of personal privacy: the unauthorized use of an individual's picture.

3.1.5 Wiretapping

An extremely important and much cited case has been *Olmstead v. United States* in 1928 [19]. In this case wiretapping equipment was used by the police as a way of obtaining evidence. However, the complaint was not accepted by five of the nine justices because there had been no actual entry into the houses and nothing tangible had been taken. So the search and seizure amendment did no apply. Even more important than the decision, however, was the dissent of Justice Brandeis, the co-author of the article *The Right to Privacy* in Harvard Law Review. In his view, this case indicated that the privacy of the man had been invaded, that is "the right to be let alone – the most comprehensive of rights and the right most valued by civilized men."

Brandeis' reasoning was adopted only forty years later in the *Katz v. United States* case. Federal authorities used electronic listening devices attached to the outside of a telephone booth used by one Charles Katz, whom the authorities suspected of violating gambling laws. Even though the property was not invaded the court found that this method of collecting evidence infringed on the Fourth Amendment's rights of Katz. In the view of the court, the constitution protects whatever seeks to be preserved as private. What is most remarkable about this case is the interpretation of what is private within the meaning of the Fourth Amendment. In the view of Justice Harlan private can be defined by the individual's actual, subjective expectation of privacy and the extent to which that expectation was one that society is prepared to recognize as 'reasonable'. This interpretation has since been used in many cases related to homes, business, sealed luggage, and packages. At the same time it is also often criticized and seen to be of limited value since it is restricted to government invasion of privacy and does not apply to objects controlled by third parties such as bank records. Above all, this case is dependent upon what society's expectation of what invasion of privacy is, which is a serious disadvantage since whatever the public views as reasonable tends to evolve more slowly than does information technology [20].

3.1.6 Psychological Testing and Lie Detectors

Around the 1960s, it was not the single collection of data by means of photography and technical devices that worried people but the mass collection of data with the help of psychological testing, lie detectors, and attitude scales used by social scientists. Not only are these techniques criticized but in particular the philosophy behind the use of them. In his *The Organization Man* William H. Whyte [21] expects that social sciences will become more and more a type of social engineering, the goal of which is to adapt a society to one in which all problems will be solved. In a cynical moment, Whyte promoted a kind of Universal Card with an individuals' fingerprint, IQ, and several other personal characteristics attached. To his astonishment the proposal was not criticized but strongly endorsed.

Another criticism came from Vance Packard [22]. In his *The Hidden Persuaders* he shows the strong relationship between techniques that detect hidden personal emotions and feelings and the way this data is used for advertisement.

As a criticism not only of the techniques as discussed but the social sciences in general, Oscar Ruebhausen and Orville Brim [23] are the first to make clear that the development of social research proves that ethical and legal rules are necessary and most especially regulations that allow for the expressed consent of the individual who is willing to cooperate. Nowadays the use of these techniques, in particular that of the lie detector and questionnaires are still criticised.

3.1.7 Computer as a Black Box

At this same point in discussion of privacy rights, a new development was added, that is how the computer could be used as a primary data storage device. Large scale storage of data as well as the processing and exchange of data between organizations are now possible. The computer as a data giant has been seen as frightening by several authors. Numerous publications have appeared with thrilling titles that warn of gigantic invasions of personal privacy, for example *The Assault on privacy: Computers, Data Banks and Dossiers* [24], and *The Data bank Society* [25]. The emphasis is in this issue is on computers and databases, that is huge collections of data processed by electronic means.

At the end of the 1970s, a new dimension—telecommunication—was added to the discussion. Telecommunication in combination with informatics was referred to as telematics. It is not only the processing of data which is frightening but above all the distribution of the data to unknown recipients. The combination of computer and telecommunications led, in turn, to a 'tele'-hype of what the future might bring about in society, such as tele-education, tele-work, tele-medication and tele-papers. The future is the human home in which individuals communicate with the outside world exclusively by way of the television. It is a brave new world in which privacy will be strengthened since the home will become even more than ever a castle but at the same time privacy can be attacked by all traces that remain from that type of communication.

3.2 Present Use of Information Technology

3.2.1 Video Surveillance

Surveillance video cameras are increasingly being used throughout the public arena [26]. In almost all cities of the western world walking around means being recorded and it is expected that this surveillance will be expanded in the next years by improved technology, by centralizing the surveillance, and by the unexamined assumptions that cameras are providing security.

Cameras in some countries are being integrated into the urban environment in ways similar to the integration of the electricity and water supply at the beginning of the last century [27]. The CCTV market in an increasing way integrated into technologies, such as the internet, face recognition software, and law enforcement databases is enjoying an uninterrupted growth. CCTV's power is substantially increasing, and it has features that include night vision, computer assisted operations, and motion detection facilities.

3.2.2 Biometric Identification

Biometrics[1] is the science and technology of measuring and statistically analyzing biological data. In information technology, biometrics refers to technologies for measuring and analysing human body characteristics such as fingerprints, eye retinas and irises, voice patterns, facial patterns, and hand measurements, especially for authentication and identification. Biometrics involves comparing a previously captured, unique characteristic of a person to a new sample provided by the person. The biometric information is used to identification or verification of a persons to find out whether they are who they claim to be. This process can mean an attack on one's privacy when the collection takes place without consent or permission and without transparency about the purpose for which this data is used.

3.2.3 Genetic Data

There is an increase in DNA-analysis for medical testing research and for investigative purposes which are incorporated into routine health [26, p.5] testing. Unlike other medical information, genetic data is a unique combination difficult to be kept confidential and extremely revealing about us. Above all it is easy to acquire since people constantly slough off hair, saliva, skin cells, and other trails containing our DNA. No matter how hard we strive to keep our genetic codes private, we are always vulnerable to the use of it. The data collected tells about our genetic diseases, risk factors, and other characteristics. For the financial services companies, it would

[1] http://whatis/techtarget.com/definition7

be useful to be able to assess risks on the basis of genes patterns that can indicate an individual's future potential susceptibility to illness and diseases. A specific problem with genetic data is that an individual who discloses his or her genetic information also discloses the genetic data of his or her relatives.

3.2.4 Identity Theft

Identity theft is one of the fastest growing types of fraud. Identity theft is the use of another person's financial identity through the use of the victim's identity information. This information includes a person's name, address, date of birth, social security number, credit card numbers, and checking account information. Elbirt [28] makes a distinction is sometimes made between identity theft and identity fraud. Identity theft occurs when someone is using one's personal information to impersonate him or her to apply for new credit accounts in his or her name. Identity fraud involves an unauthorized person using one's credit card number from an existing account to make purchases. Seen from the consequences for the individual, theft normally refers to both.

One of the increasing forms is phishing by which thieves on the internet pose as legitimate account managers for credit card companies and financial institutions and ask for personal information under the guise of account verification or maintenance [29]. An even more aggressive form is pharming, a word play on farming and phishing. Pharming is an attack aiming to redirect a website's traffic to another (bogus) website. This website duplicates the look and feel of a bank or other sensitive website. Via this bogus website criminals try to steal, for example, account information.[2]

3.2.5 Data Warehousing and Data Mining

Datawarehousing is the collation of (personal) data into huge, queriable repositories in such a way that they allow analysis of all data related to a particular person. This data is collected in order to make data mining possible, which is a statistical technique enabling analysis of the data in order to find patterns and relations which are nor expected nor predictable. In this way new patterns can be discovered or can confirm already suspected relationships. A famous example is the data mining that marketers show that fathers who buy diapers often pick up beer at the same time. The link prompted some stores to stock the seemingly unrelated items at the same aisle so even more fathers would reach for beer. The underlying expectation is forming profiles of groups of people that make behaviour predictable, for example potential terrorists or criminals.

3.2.6 Chip or Smart Cards

A chip or smart card is a credit card size device with an embedded microprocessor(s), capable of storing, retrieving, and processing a tremendous amount of information related to one person. This person is obliged to wear and use this card in all contacts he or she has with the distributor or distributors of the cards, since combinations of applications are likely. Examples of these cards are the modern driver license, passport, medical cards, and loyalty cards. The content of the card can be read by making contact with a reader or in a contactless way as is used on public transport.

---

[2] http://en.wikipedia.org/wiki/pharming

3.2.7 Global Positioning System (GPS)

With the rapid growth of wireless communications, such as mobile phones, the use of the Global Positioning System and the related Location Based Services (LBS) is increasing. The GPS is a system of 24 well-placed satellites that orbit the Earth and make it possible for people with ground receivers to pinpoint their geographic location. The location accuracy is anywhere from one hundred to ten meters for most equipment. A well-known application is the use of GPS in automobiles to order to pinpoint precisely a driver's location with regards to traffic and weather information. By using mobile telephones it is rather simple to detect the place where the mobile is by using network based technology and/or handset bases technology. By using the cell of origins method the telephone, once connected, is communicating his position regularly. In this way the user of the telephone can always be traced, as in the case of International Mobile Subscription Identity (IMSI), which collects the signals of mobile telephones and can identify the content of the communication. Another use also based on tracing is electronic monitoring as an alternative for imprisonment in certain cases.

3.2.8 Internet

Internet is the most fruitful area for data collection in modern times. It is quite possible to collect tremendous amounts of data on almost all users of the internet without their knowledge. Using search engines like Google makes clear how elusive the internet is becoming. Although it is at the same time a mighty instrument in the hands of the consumer or citizen for improving his or her knowledge, it is also an instrument for contacting these individuals. The combination of cookies and spam shows in which ways the internet can be used for advertising purposes. A cookie is a piece of information unique to a user that the user's browser saves and sends back to a web server when the user revisits a website. Cookies form a specific part of the more general area called spyware which extracts information from an individual without the user's knowledge or consent. The purpose of spyware is to gain access to information, to store information, or to trace the activities of the user. Cookies allow the server to link information entered by users on different web pages and keep a consistent state of the user's session. The registration information is stored on the server and if it's part of a cookie it contains a limited subset of this.

This information in the form of an email address can be used for advertising purposes in the form of spam, which is hundreds of unsolicited junk emails that contain advertising or promotional messages and sent to a large number of people or even to one person at the same time [30]. Spam, therefore, can be described as the electronic distribution of large amounts of unsolicited emails to individuals' email accounts. Spam email is definitely distinctive from the traditional direct mailings in that the costs for such massive mailings fell to the sender. The cost of sending mail through conventional means is very real, including postage costs all paid by the sender. On the other hand, costs of sending bulk emails are very small. It is the fact that emails can be sent at low costs and in great quantities that attracts direct marketers and other companies to use spam emails for advertisements.

3.2.9 Key Logger

A key logger application records the key strokes an individual enters on a computer keyboard [14, p. 39]. Key stroke loggers can be employed to capture every key pressed on a computer keyboard, including information that is typed and deleted. Such devices can be manually placed by law enforcement agents on a suspect's computer or installed remotely by placing a virus on the suspect's computer that will disclose private encryption keys. The question of legitimacy of these methods arose in the case of *United States v Scarfo* where a key logger was placed in order to capture an individual's PGP encrypted password. The existence was confirmed by the FBI. The key logger did not need physical access to the computer in order to accomplish the desired task of capturing private information.

3.2.10 Radio Frequency Identification (RFID)

Use of the RFID is advancing rapidly and, in a sense, is the successor of the chip card. In a similar way, RFID tracks and traces objects and subjects easily. One of the most well known applications is a yellow tag tracing cows in countries of Western Europe. RFIDs are smart tags which make it possible to follow exact movements of the objects wearing it. It is in a type of successor of the barcode with the most important difference being that a barcode is identifying a type of product whereas the RFID is identifying each distinct product. An RFID label consists of two parts: a microchip and an antenna. The chip contains data about the product and a unique code by which the product can be identified. The antenna makes it possible for that data to be sent to a receiver; therefore, one of the most important differences from past applications is that the tag can be read from a distance without the wearer of the tag being knowledgeable of the tracing.

This tag can be attached to a product (cow) but can also be implanted under the skin. In the summer of 2004, the RFID application became well known in bars of Barcelona, Spain and Rotterdam, The Netherlands where visitors had the possibility to have an RFID-chip implanted under their skin. This chip recognized people as they entered a bar, knew their preferences for drinks, and knew the bank accounts to be charged for paying the drink bills. This RFID-chip was used during the football World Championship in Germany so that on every entrance billet, an RFID-chip was attached thus each visitor could be identified and, in case of incidents, be arrested. In Japan the RFID is sometimes part of a whole system of sensors and communication techniques forming an Ubiquitous Network Soceity.

3.2.11 Wireless Networking

Wireless networking has already been in use for several years in the form of Wi-Fi that is, Wireless Fidelity. Wi-Fi was intended to be used for mobile computing devices, such as laptops; however, it is now used increasingly for other applications, including Internet Access, gaming, and basic connectivity of consumer electronics such as television and DVD-players.

A new development in the field of wireless networking is Bluetooth. Bluetooth is an industrial specification for wireless personal area networks (PANs)[3]. It provides a

[3] http://en.wikipedia.org/wiki/Bluetooth

way to connect and exchange information between devices like personal digital assistants (PDAs), mobile phones, laptops, PCs, printers, and digital cameras by way of a secure, low cost, globally available short range frequency. The range of Bluetooth depends upon its power class which covers one to one hundred meters; it also includes a low-cost microchip in each device.

This flexibility is making Bluetooth vulnerable to interceptions, and the most serious flaws of Bluetooth security may be the disclosure of personal data. Research from the University of Tel Aviv in Israel has detected that Bluetooth can be cracked, and these findings have been published in the *New Scientist*. The researchers have shown both active and passive methods for obtaining the PIN for a Bluetooth Link. The passive attack would allow a suitably equipped attacker to eavesdrop on communication. The active method makes use of a specially constructed message that must be inserted at a specific point in the protocol to repeat the pairing process. After that the first method may be used to crack the PIN.

3.3 Technical Use in the Future

3.3.1 Ambient Technology

In a sense, the RFID-chip is a significant part of a development process called ambient technology or, as it is sometimes referred to, as pervasive or ubiquitous computing. Ambient intelligence is an intelligence system that operates in a surrounding environment, a trend brought about by a convergence of advanced electronic, and particularly wireless, technologies and the internet [31]. These ambient devices are not personal computers, but very tiny devices, either mobile or embedded, in many objects, including cars, tools appliances, clothing, and consumer goods in such a way that they become an everyday part of life and reacting to our behavior as well as participating our human needs.[4] Used in refrigerators they can remind us to use the oldest products and once the item is used automatically adding it to our shopping list. The vacuum cleaner can also be started without human intervention once dust density becomes too high. Utilities are able to monitor the performance of home appliances, sending repairmen or replacements before they break down. Local supermarkets can check the content of customers' refrigerators and make out a shopping list for customers. From desktop computers, office workers can check up on children at home [32].

3.3.2 Neurolinguistics

Neurolinguistics is based on the fact that different people are processing information differently [33]. So, for example, there is a difference between male and female brains with the female brains taking more notice of more cues within a piece of communication and using colors, imagery, and graphics much more to interpret meaning compared to male brains. Combined with other technologies a NBIC convergence takes place: combination of nanotechnology, biotechnology, information technology and cognitive science.

---

[4] http://searchnetworking.techtarget.com/sDefinition

Neurolinguistics uses knowledge on how information processing styles differ in order to target consumers. It can be used to detect different responses to car designs and to evaluate television commercials. This type of use is called neuromarketing: seeing how different people respond to advertising and other brand-related messages by seeing brain responses.

3.3.3 Memetics

The science of memetics has recently attracted significant attention [33]. A meme is an idea that is passed from one human generation to another. It is the cultural and sociological equivalent of a gene, the basic element of biological inheritance. In contrast to genetics, a meme acts not vertically through the generations but horizontally. They work as a viral contagion. A good example of the principle is how it is difficult not to start yawning if others are yawning or not applaud when others start to applaud. It is speculated that human beings have an adaptive mechanism that other species don't have. Humans can pass their ideas from one generation to the next, allowing them to surmount challenges more flexibly and more quickly than through the longer process of genetic adaptation and selection. Examples of memes include the idea of God and other forms of belief.[5]

It is believed that changing memes means a change in personality, for example when anti-depressants are used. Therefore it is a concern that others can use memes to influence human behaviour and influence humans both in commercial areas and in political campaigns. The influence might be an unconscious one that might be most enduring if installed at an early stage. In relation to memes it is feared that marketers can use it to infect consumers with a mind virus that is not recognised consciously but which suddenly results in joining a fad or fashion.

3.3.4 Grid Technology

A new way of living will evolve as the internet morphs into 'the grid'. Wireless tags will be embedded in nearly every object, and even people, linking humans and machines together as 'nodes' on a single global network. By tying all computers together into a single grid, this system will allow any one computer to tap the power of all computers. It is a sort of fourth wave bringing together the power of mainframes, PCs, and the Internet. This grid system will be able to link companies, consumers, and governments together. Biochips might be able to send real-time heart readings to cardiologists by way of the grid. "A smart chip in your convertible could allow the manufacturer to track both the car and your driving habit. A digital double of your car might even be parked on the grid, where your mechanic could watch it for engine trouble or the police could monitor your speeding" [34, p. 67]. The endless streams of data are too voluminous for human engineers to track. The grid therefore will have to be self-managing, self-diagnosing, and self-healing, telling people when things go wrong and instructing us on how to fix them. At the moment there seems to be only one problem: software to make the grid secure does not yet exist. It is said that in a highly networked world the 'castle' model of security with firewalls will not work.

---

[5] http://whatis.techtarget.com/definition

4 The Protection of Privacy

4.1 Introduction

As we have already noted, the first protections of privacy came from the citizen himself or from relatives. During the Middle Ages this picture stayed almost the same. However with the rising intrusion of governments into private lives, assistance against privacy intrusion required the help of others, legal legislation, and the addition of self-regulation. Later technical instruments like security measures and PET were added.

EPIC distinguishes four models of privacy protection [14, p. 3]:

- Comprehensive laws: a general law that governs the collection, use, and dissemination of personal information by both the public and the private sector. An oversight body then ensures compliance.
- Sectoral laws: rules in favour of specific laws, governing specific technical applications, or specific regions, such as financial privacy.
- Self-regulation, in which companies and industry establish codes of conduct or practice and engage in self-policing.
- Technologies of privacy: with the development of available technology-based systems it becomes possible for individuals to protect their privacy and security.

Although there will always be distinctions between countries and cultures in how these four measures will be emphasized, it seems clear that the countries which will protect the data most efficiently will probably use all four of the models simultaneously to ensure data protection.

As can be seen from the formulation in this model, emphasis will be on data protection. Nonetheless it is necessary to make the distinction between privacy protection and data protection. The first is a general protection historically oriented towards the home, family life, and correspondence while the latter will emphasis the informational dimension.

4.2 Comprehensive Laws and Regulatory Agents

The legal interpretation of privacy depends on the way the concept is used. As we have seen, two dimensions can be distinguished: a relational and an informational one. With respect to the relational privacy there has been a long tradition in Europe and in the United States. In terms of protecting data, the regulation is nascent. In 1971 the first privacy act, The Data Protection Act, took effect in the State of Hesse (Germany); shortly thereafter, Sweden and the United States passed privacy legislation. Subsequently, privacy protection has become a part of many constitutions, with the exception of the United States where the protection must be derived from amendments. This paper will start with a short overview of the situation in the United States followed by a more extensive treatment of the situation in Europe.

4.2.1 Privacy Protection

Although the United States is the country where most of the earliest discussions have taken place, privacy protection has never had a base in the U.S. constitution. An important characteristic of the American constitution, which went into effect in 1789, is that in general it has a negative formulation. The U.S. constitution does not oblige the government to protect but rather to refrain from taking actions. In that sense and in an indirect way, people are protected against government actions. Although more or less all constitutional freedoms are related to privacy, this type of privacy right is not explicitly mentioned in the Constitution. In particular it must be derived from three amendments: the First, Fourth, and Fourteenth.

The First Amendment protects the freedom of expression, religion, and assembly. The freedom of expression assures the unfettered interchange of ideas for the bringing about of political and social change by the public [19].

The Fourth is centered on the prohibition of unreasonable search and seizure. As can be understood from the history in the United States, it has two deeply rooted concerns: that its citizens' property is protected from seizure by the government and that its citizens' home and person be protected from warrantless and arbitrary searches. This very amendment is the much used, but still unclear, concept of 'reasonable expectation of privacy' which was introduced by Justice Henson in the famous court case *Olmstead vs. US*.

The Fourteenth Amendment guarantees due process and nondisclosure of personal information. As this language is more in line with the informational dimension of the computer age, we will treat this amendment in relation to data protection.

Although there has been some form of legal privacy protection for some time now based on case law, international recognition of privacy as a human right can be traced back to the period immediately following the Second World War. Recognition of this particular right emerged as a response to some of the abuses perpetrated by fascist regimes before and during the war. The Universal Declaration of Human Rights was adopted on 10 December 1948 by the United Nations general Assembly. In article 12 the territorial and communications privacy is protected. It states: "No one should be subjected to arbitrary interference with his privacy, family, home or correspondence, nor to attacks on his honour or reputation. Everyone has the right to the protection of the law against such interference or attacks." It was the first international instrument to deal with this right to privacy. As it was in the form of a resolution of the General Assembly it was not legally binding.

In 1950 the European Convention for the Protection of Human Rights and Fundamental Freedoms was drafted. Article 8 of the Convention is still one of the most important international agreements on the protection of privacy: "Everyone has the right to respect for his private and family life, his home and his correspondence." At the same time the second paragraph of the article makes clear that this right to privacy is not absolute. Interference by a public authority is allowed when such is necessary in accordance with the law and is necessary in a democratic society in the interest of national security, public safety, and the economic well-being of the country, for the prevention of disorder or crime, for the protection of health and morals or for the protection of the rights and freedoms of others. With this formulation three zones of privacy are defined, that is private and family life, home, and correspondence, although correspondence is very narrowly related to the secrecy of letters.

This Convention has a legal mechanism for its enforcement through the European Commission. It is legally binding on each state that ratifies it and must be put into effect in its domestic laws. This Convention has inspired many countries to create and formulate national laws and constitutions for the protection of privacy that went further than the requirements of this Convention as was already the case in the United States in the First, Fourth, and Fourteenth Amendments. In particularly the notion of correspondence has been deepened.

4.2.2 Data Protection

Although the protection of personal data is dealt with in the Fourteenth Amendment this turned out to be increasingly insufficient in an age in which information became an important force. Therefore in 1974 the Privacy Act was enacted which enforces agencies to process data fairly and limits the disclosure of individual records. The Privacy Act protects in full American tradition primarily against governmental processing of data. In the private sector the emphasis is on self-regulation combined with specific sectoral laws. A few examples out of numerous ones are the Children's Online Privacy Protection Act (COPPA) of 1998, the Fair Health Information Practice Act of 1997, and the Fair Credit Reporting Act of 1997.

As we have seen since the 1960s, the relationship between privacy and the use of data has become closer as has the awareness that this form of privacy should be protected. In addition to the domestic laws on data protection, in 1981 a special Convention was devoted to the use of personal data: the Convention for the Protection of Individuals with Regard to Automatic Processing of Personal Data [35]. In this convention some general guidelines were formulated with regard to data processing and were elaborated in approximately twenty recommendations for specific fields, such as police, medical data, and statistical data.

These guidelines are in large part are based on the principles of data protection formulated by the Organisation for Economic Co-operation and Development (OECD) which outlines protection is equated to privacy protection [36]. Curiously, the OECD is endorsing the protection of privacy on the one hand, yet they are promoting these principles because there is a danger that disparities in national legislation could hamper the free flow of personal data across the frontiers. Restrictions of these flows could cause serious disruption in important sectors of the economy, such as banking and insurance. For that reason these principles can be seen as guidelines that enhance fair and good practices more than they enhance privacy protection. Nevertheless they have had a big influence on all data protection legislation in Europe and elsewhere.

These Principles are:

Collection Limitation Principle: There should be limits to the collection of personal data and any such data should be obtained by lawful and fair means and, where appropriate, with the knowledge or consent of the data subject.

Data Quality Principle: Personal data should be relevant to the purposes for which they are to be used, and, to the extent necessary for those purposes, should be accurate, complete, and kept up-to-date.

Purpose Specification Principle: The purposes for which personal data are collected should be specified not later than the time of data collection and the subsequent use limited to the fulfilment of those purposes or such others as are not incompatible with those purposes and as are specified on each occasion of change of purpose.

Use Limitation Principle: Personal data should not be disclosed, made available or otherwise used for purposes other than those specified in accordance with the specified purpose except: (1) with the consent of the data subject or (2) by the authority of law.

Security Safeguards Principle: Personal data should be protected by reasonable security safeguards against such risks as loss or unauthorised access, destruction, use, modification, or disclosure of data.

Openness Principle: There should be a general policy of openness about developments, practices, and policies with respect to personal data. Means should be readily available of establishing the existence and nature of personal data, and the main purposes of their use, as well as the identity and usual residence of the data controller.

Individual Participation Principle: An individual should have the right: (1) to obtain from a data controller, or otherwise, confirmation of whether or not the data controller has data relating to him; (2) to have communicated to him, data relating to him (i) within a reasonable time; (ii) at a charge, if any, that is not excessive; (iii) in a reasonable manner; and (iv) in a form that is readily intelligible to him; (3) to be given reasons if a request made under subparagraphs (1) and (2) are denied, and to be able to challenge such denial and (4) to challenge data relating to him and, if the challenge is successful, to have the data erased, rectified, completed or amended.

Accountability Principle: A data controller should be accountable for complying with measures which give effect to the principles stated above.

These principles, however, have not been implemented in legislation in all member states of the European Union in the same way. Therefore the fear of hampering the free flow of information remained. In the beginning of 1990 an effect was made to harmonize legislation within the EU. It resulted in a European Directive on Data Protection [37].

This directive enshrines two of the oldest ambitions of the European integration project: the achievement of an Internal Market (the free movement of personal information) and the protection of fundamental rights and freedoms of individuals. It is stated that both objectives are equally important. The status of such a directive is that it binds member states to the objectives to be achieved, while leaving to national authorities the power to choose the form and the means to be used to implement these objectives.

The directive applies to the public and private sector and covers the processing of personal data by both automated and manual means. Processing includes any operation or set of operations which is performed on personal data, which mean all information relating to an identified or identifiable natural person. This directive elaborates in a way the general OECD principles operationally. These principles are formulated relating to data quality and criteria are given for making data processing legitimate. Special attention is paid to special categories of processing of data of what formerly was called sensitive data: personal data revealing racial or ethnic origin, political opinions, religious or philosophical beliefs, trade-union membership, and the processing of data concerning health or sex life. Processing of data relating to offences, criminal convictions or security means may be carried out only under the control of official authorities, with suitable specific safeguards, or as provided under national law. The controller, that is to say the one who determines the purpose and means of processing is obliged to inform the data subject about the purpose of the processing, except where he already has the information. As already is written into the principles, the data subject has the right of access to his own data as well as the right to rectify, erase or block the processing of data in case the data are not correct or not up to date.

All member states are obliged to comply with the directive and to implement the principles in national laws. With the implementation the member states shall provide that one or more public authorities are responsible for monitoring the application with its territory of the provision. Regarding the transfer of data to third countries (countries outside the European Union) there is the strict rule that this transfer may take place only if the third country in question ensures an adequate level of protection, judged as such by the European Commission. If this level is missing, additional measures have to be taken either in conformity with the directive or in the form of contractual clauses. One of them is the so-called Safe Harbour Principles formulated by the Federal Trade Commission (FTC) in the United Sates.

4.2.3 Regulatory Agents

An essential aspect of any data or privacy protection is oversight. In most countries with a comprehensive law or an omnibus data protection, there is a data commissioner, sometimes in the person of an ombudsman. Under the Directive 95/46/EC, it is an obligation to have such a data commissioner.

Under article 21 of this directive, all European Union countries, including the new ones, must have an independent enforcement body. These agencies are given considerable power: governments must consult the body when they draw up legislation relating to the processing of personal data; the bodies also have the power to conduct investigations and have a right of access information relevant to these investigations; they may impose remedies such as ordering the destruction of information or ban processing and start legal proceedings, hear complaints, and issue reports. The official is also generally responsible for public education and international liaison in data protection and data transfers. They have to maintain a register of data controllers and databases. They also are represented in an important body at the European Union level through article 29 Working Group which issues reports and comments on technical and political developments.

4.3 Sectoral Laws

As we have seen, the recommendations based on the Strasbourg Convention form a kind of sectoral legislation in addition to a more comprehensive legislation. In 1997 a special European directive was adopted which is specifically related to the protection of privacy in the telecommunication sector [38]. The development of more advanced digital technologies, such as the Integrated Services Digital Networks (ISDN) gave rise to specific requirements concerning the protection of personal data. Meanwhile this directive is repealed and replaced by a directive on privacy and electronic communications [39]. In addition to Directive 95/46/EC which formulates general principles of data protection, this directive is oriented towards the use of new advanced digital technologies in public communications net works, in particular the internet.

The new Directive is a response to two developments that addresses the idea that the private sphere must be protected in a more advanced way. The first is the development of so-called spyware, web bugs, hidden identifiers, and other similar devices that can enter the user's terminal unawares. Such devices, for instances cookies, should be allowed only for legitimate purposes and with the knowledge of the user concerned. These cookies may, for example, only be used for analyzing the effectiveness of website designs and advertising and in verifying the identity of users engaged in on-line transactions. Users should therefore have the opportunity to refuse to have a cookie or similar device stored on their terminal equipment.

The second development is unsolicited communications. In the EC directive, safeguards are provided against the use of unsolicited communications for direct marketing purposes in particular by means of automated calling machines, telefaxes, e-mail, and SMS messages. For these forms of communications the prior explicit consent of the recipient must be obtained before such communications are addressed to them; in short the user must opt in for these communiqués to be legitimate. The only exception is the use of electronic contact details for the offering of similar products or services by the company that has obtained these contact details. The customer should be informed about this use and be given the opportunity to refuse such usage or to opt out.

This directive, then, is meant not only to protect the privacy of the consumer, it allows also for the retention of traffic and location data of all people using mobile telephones, SMS, landline telephones, faxes, e-mails, chatrooms, internet, and any other electronic communication devices. The traffic data include all data generated by the conveyance of communications on an electronic communications network, and location data is the data indicating the geographic position of a mobile telephone user, like the GPS. The contents of communications are not covered by these measures.

4.4 Protection by Technical Means

Related to technological instruments, Charles Raab [40] makes a distinction among the following:

- *Systemic instruments* which are produced by engineers who design the network, the equipment, the computer code, or the technical standards and protocols;

- *Collective instruments,* which result from government policies, such as policy applications in which government and business builds privacy protection into a technical systems for goods and services, such as the development of a public key encryption infrastructure;
- *Instruments of individual empowerment,* required for explicit choices by individuals, such as encryption instruments, devices for anonymity, filtering instruments, and the Platform for Privacy Preferences (P3P)

4.4.1 Systemic Instruments

The systemic approach regulates to the technical rules embedded within the network architecture. The technical standards and protocols as well as the default settings chosen by system developers set threshold information privacy rules. They define the capabilities of networks to invade or protect privacy. As an example anonymous internet use may be built into the network structure just as surveillance tracking may be built into the network. Cookie management options are developed to allow users greater control over such tracking. Joel Reidenberg [41] calls this kind of regulations the *Lex Informatica.*

4.4.2 Collective Instruments

One example of these instruments is a measure which becomes well known under the name Privacy Enhancing Technologies (PET's). The basic idea behind PET was developed by David Chaum, who published an article in *Communications of the ACM* on security without identification [42]. Although this article and other publications of Chaum got a lot of publicity, the real breakthrough came when the data protection authorities of The Netherlands and Canada published two reports on Privacy-enhancing Technologies [43].

PET's are a coherent system of ICT[6] measures that protect privacy by eliminating or reducing personal data or by preventing the unnecessary or undesirable processing of personal data without losing the functionality of the information system. Eliminating personal data means that adequate measures are taken to prevent identification of a person. Direct and indirect identifiers are removed in such a way that a person can no longer be identified. Reducing personal data means that although identification is possible it is made more difficult and is only allowed in a controlled context, for example by using a Trusted Third Party (TTP). In both situations the starting point is that personal data are not always needed and that the necessity of the personal data must be proved. If that is not possible, either the data is made anonymous or a so-called Identity Protector is used, which converts the actual name to a pseudo-identity.

A very old application of this kind of technology is data security. Data or information security means that a coherent package of measures is taken and maintained for securing the collection and processing of information. These measures are related to availability (information must always be available for the legitimate user), exclusiveness (information may only be used by authorized persons), and integrity (information must be in accordance with reality and be reliable, correct, and up to date). To be accurate as to which types of measures are needed, a risk analysis is

[6] Information and Communication Technology.

necessary in which the importance of information is measured as well as the consequences in case the information gets lost. These measures enclose all people and all means that are necessary for data processing. A concrete plan is made including all technical and organizational measures that should be taken, regarding the costs, the state of the technique, and the risks of the processing. Well known security measures are firewalls, which protect against unauthorised access, the use of passwords, and the authorization for the users of information.

4.4.3 Instruments of Individual Empowerment

One peculiar application of PET is offering the individual the means and measures for empowering his own control over the processing of his personal data. It deals with instruments that can be chosen by the individual to enhance his control over the processing and distribution of his data. Sometimes these instruments are called add-ons and well known examples are the cookie killers, the proxy servers, anonymous remailers, and the Platform for Privacy Preferences.[7] A good example of such an instrument in relation to the internet is the system MUTE, developed by Jason Rohrer [44], in which random access strings are used. Each time a computer (node) is connected with a P2P network that uses software to facilitate the sharing of music, a new IP-address is generated, making it extremely difficult to track the user.

Another example of this type of protection is the research done after PISA: Privacy Incorporated Software Agent. PISA is a specific application of the Intelligent Software Agent Technologies (ISATs). PISA enables the user to control the quality of input of the consumer or the citizen in e-commerce or e-government transactions and communications for protection against loss of control over personal information. A much discussed disadvantage for the protection of privacy is that agents need to maintain a perfect profile of their users in order to know one's likes and dislikes, habits and personal preferences, contact information about friends and colleagues, or the history of websites visited, and many other electronic transactions performed.

4.5 Protection through Bad Publicity

During the last years a strong form of protection has come from the media which publish regularly on all types of misuse of data. In some cases, the public outcry has demonstrated the significant role of the media in informing consumers and facilitating a popular response. The media then highlights not only the effectiveness of protests but also the potential for the technologies such as e-mail and general internet usage in order for disclosure of information to be used to protect privacy.

In Stockholm a discussion started on February 10, 1986 when the newspaper *Dagens Nyheter* intensified its coverage of the Metropolit study [45]. Metropolit Projects in Copenhagen, Oslo, and Stockholm were initiated based on the same concept. All males born in these three cities were registered from birth certificates by way of regular medical investigation. Age tests, as well as psychological tests, home surveys on military service, and family particulars were carried out. The different files were all identified with a personal identification number which made linkage possible. Discussion of one specific research project rapidly escalated into a general

[7] See f.e. www.anonymizer.com, www.zeroknowledge.com, www.privada.com

outcry against micro data research methods. The strongest criticism was leveled at the fact that many variables were merged into databases from other sources as well as from paper documents. A subsequent judicial examination proved that no illegal activities had taken place, and that neither data laws nor any other instruction or legal provision had been contravened. Despite the fact that Statistics Sweden had not been in any way involved in the project, the affair had a strong negative influence on the public attitude towards social research in general and Statistics Sweden in particular.

In 1991 Lotus Development Corporation and Equifax abandoned plans to sell Households a CD-ROM database containing names, addresses, and marketing information on 120 million consumers, after they received 30.000 calls and letters from individuals asking to be removed from the database. More recently, Lexis-Nexis, has changed plans for P-tracks, a service that provides personal information about virtually every individual in America to "anyone willing to pay a search fee of eighty-five to hundred dollars" [20, p. 104/105]. The database includes current and previous addresses, birth dates, home telephone numbers, maiden names, and aliases. Lexis was also providing social security numbers but stopped in response to a storm of protest and is honouring the requests of anyone who wishes to be deleted from the database.

So found the Vons chain of supermarkets in Los Angeles [46] itself the recipient of unwelcome front page publicity when it allegedly used data contained in its store-card database to undermine a damages claim from a shopper. The shopper claimed that he slipped on spilt yogurt in the store, shattering his kneecap, but said that when he filed a suit for damages, he was advised by the store's mediator that his club card records showed him to be a frequent buyer of alcohol.

5 Analysis

Analysis of the use of personal data shows how important information is becoming and shows the omnipresence of technique, probably resulting in a surveillance society.

5.1 Importance of Information

Information is becoming more and more important since it has two characteristics: information is *money* and information is *power*. Although these two characteristics partly are in parallel with the distinction between the private and public sector, a cross fertilization appears quite often. The private sector is not only interested in money but very often in an influence, as can be seen in the power that insurance companies wield. In addition, the public sector is also interested in influencing people and in money. These two characteristics, then, make it clear that in contrary to general opinion, privacy is not a true juridical issue, but in fact a political one. Making money and having power are not wrong; however, the way such influence is used, and perhaps over-reach, can create problems.

Several tools are used for collecting and analyzing personal information: database marketing, relationship marketing, permission marketing, and loyalty programs which all help marketers to find the information they crave. When these collection techniques combine with data warehousing and data mining tools, individual information security can be at risk. Database marketing is also known as one-to-one marketing, whereas permission marketing acknowledges the need of permission from customers before approaching them with advertising messages, which can stand as one solution to the problem. The philosophy behind this approach is that customers are willing to release personal information if they can profit by doing so, as seen with loyalty cards. The consequence is that direct marketers fill mailboxes; relationship marketers ask for more and more information; telemarketers call home at dinner time; and spam is a highly used tool for advertisement.

Getting and using power is again a question of balancing several interests and balancing the means and the political choices. Political choices mean that choices are made in which the privacy is protected as much as is possible. The impetus for information as a means to knowledge and power became visible after the dramatic attacks of terrorists on September 11, 2001. These policy changes were not limited to the United States but also involved most other countries with increasing surveillance powers and minimizing oversight and due process requirements. The use of new technologies were incorporated and included which in turn permitted governments to use these powers and formalize its roving powers. In general, the result was a weakening of data protection regimes, an increase in data sharing, and an increase in profiling and identification [14, p. 25-27] of individuals.

As we have seen, information is power and since the terrorist attacks in New York, Madrid, and London this type of power over citizens is becoming more and more a reality. Information is seen as one of the most important weapons in the battle against terrorism and crime. Measures like the introduction of Passengers Name Records (PNR) and the long retention of traffic communication data make clear that politics in one way or another will win. Data commissioners talk about balancing the interests of privacy protection and the protection of security, but it is clear that one can not speak of a real balance. Laws are used to accept means and measures of data collection which were never accepted without the current political agendas. The introduction of CCTV, the use of internet data, and the exchange of data among all western countries are clear examples of this untoward development.

Long before the attack of 9/11 intelligence agencies from America, Britain, Canada, Australia, and New Zealand jointly monitored all international satellites telecommunications traffic by a system called 'Echelon', which can pick specific words or phrases from hundreds of thousands of messages. In 2000 it was publicly revealed that the America's FBI had developed and was using an internet monitoring system called 'Carnivore'. The system places a personal computer at an internet service provider's office and can monitor all traffic data about a user, including e-mail, and browsing. It gives governments, at least theoretically, the ability to eavesdrop on all customers' digital communications.

5.2 The Omnipresence of Technique

Compared with approximately one hundred years ago, the situation has changed dramatically. From an incidental intrusion by humans into each other's lives and, rarely, having the technical means to find out too much, society now has the technical means and capacity of collecting individual data to a serious level. Since technique is omnipresent and, as an old sociological wisdom says, humans are a data producing animal, all tracks and traces left behind by human beings can be and are collected. As we have seen, since information is money and power government and industry are using almost all means at their disposal for this data collection regime.

It is, however, not only the omnipresence of technique which is frightening but also the sheer lack of awareness of its usage. One of the most impressive examples is the way data can be collected from the internet. Cookies and more general spyware are used to collect data without our knowledge. And this lack of transparency increases once data are used. Although in many case we know the purpose of the use, we do not always know for sure whether the actual use is as indicated. Responsible for this lack of transparency in data mining is making clear the distinction between data and information. Data is a collection of details or facts which, as such, are meaningless; however, when those details or facts are placed in a context which makes data usable, serious information can be gleaned. Depending upon the placement-context, the same data can be transformed into different information.

The classical example is the speed of a car. Saying that a car is driving at a speed of forty miles does not mean anything. Depending upon the context, for example in a city or on a highway, the information can be interpreted quite differently: in a city, forty miles per hour can be too fast, especially in a school zone during school in-take hours but on a highway, forty miles per hour may be too slow and seriously jeopardize the flow of traffic.

Another example is the supermarket which introduces loyalty cards and asks patrons to fill in a form in which the sex of the owner of the card and the sex of his of her partner must be filled in. Although it was said that the provided data would only be used for contacting the owner or his or her partner, it is clear that the data can also be used for detecting homosexual relations. Numerous other examples make clear the importance of the distinction between data and information. Knowing for what purpose *data* are used does not mean that for the same purpose the *information* would be used.

5.3 Surveillance

The omnipresence of technique and the acceptability of politics and the law to collect, store, and use almost all personal data is making the information society a surveillance society. Simultaneously the number of techniques is increasing so intrusion of privacy is inevitable. Distinct authors [47], [48], [26], agree that surveillance might create conformist actions. People will keep their records clean and will avoid controversial or deviant behaviour, whatever their private views and intentions might really be.

But it is not only surveillance that matters, it is the fact that we are on the way to a *riskless* society in which more and more the policy is oriented toward avoiding risks and errors produced by human beings. Personal data is used for determining the amount of risk a person forms in the eyes of government and industry. In government these figures are used for political reasons, in industry for discriminating between the good and bad consumer. It is this use which makes a consumer into a glass-consumer, in a manner of speaking, for whom there is a deep concern for unfair exclusion, unfair targeting, and unfair discrimination [49].

6 Lessons Learned of?

Starting with the more general discussion on privacy in 1891 with the publication of Warren and Brandeis *The Right to Privacy* we will pose the question if we have learned from the developments and incidents. The answer must be: yes and no. For making this clear three periods must be distinguished.

The first is the period between 1891 end the beginning of the 70's of last century. This period can be described as the period of growing awareness of the importance of privacy and privacy protection. Many articles and books on privacy are published in which this importance is stressed cumulating in Alan Westin's *Privacy and Freedom.*

The second period –from the beginning of the 70's till the beginning of the 21th century- can be described as the period of taking measures ending in the implementation of the European Directive on Data Protection, not only in the European countries but in almost all technological advanced countries. Together with the establishing of data protection authorities a kind of legal protection is suggested. Unfortunately this legal protection is overemphasised, in particular by the data protection authorities, and seen as the only best solution for a political problem.

This becomes obvious in the third period which starts at the beginning of this century. In this period the incident of 9/11 is of overriding importance. It makes clear how information can be used in the battle against fraud, criminality and terrorism. It at the same time shows the weakness of legal regulation as these regulation can simple be overruled by legislation in favour of order and law. It shows again how the protection of privacy is a political issue that can not be solved by only legal means. In that sense it is stimulating that the young generation, as for example present at the Summerschool in Brno, was not so much looking at the legal solution as well on technical solutions, like security and anonymity. It was even more stimulating that they went back to the basis, the articles of David Chaum published in the beginning of the 90's of the last century. He in my view is the real Godfather of the philosophy that in a period in which the stress is on the use of information for almost all purposes the path to anonymity is an important solution. In that sense legal people have learned less form the past, the technical people seemingly the more.

7 Conclusions

The legal measures, and the way political decisions are taken, make clear that data protection is passive. The consumer or citizen plays almost no significant role in the process. It is the government (laws) and industry (laws and self-regulation) who define the way and amount of protection. A more active role can be played when the consumer or citizen is allowed to use technical means, but also in this case it is politics and government who determines when and how these techniques may be used.

It is the government that wants to control the use of information and refuses to strengthen the position of the individual. For that reason, almost all emphasis is on reactive control of privacy predicaments. If some form of participatory control is given, it is always given under the restriction that in the end it is the government who has the ultimate control. Only in relation to industry does the role of the consumer become legally empowered regarding the use of cookies and spam. At the same time industry is used as a source of information. Traffic and location data must be stored longer then is necessary and must be given to a government in case of suspicion of terrorist actions.

Not only are these techniques empowering governments but they also become legal as has been seen in the case of the Patriot's Act in the United States and the Regulation of Investigatory Powers Act in the United Kingdom. The same development can be seen at the Directive on Privacy and Electronic Communications, which opens the possibility to enact from domestic laws the retention of traffic and location data. Most especially, these developments strongly suggest vigilance. Information as a means of power and legislation as legitimizing power are dangerous instruments in the hands of unethical politicians who are missing the necessary checks of balances of a democracy. In that case not only is privacy at stake but above all so is democracy. It is time to revisit the use of technology, the law, and the role consumers have in this serious issue. A positive sign comes from the British National Consumer Council in its publication *The Glass Consumer, Life in a Surveillance Society* [50]. Although the title sounds pessimistic, the book ends optimistically with the NCC's agenda and recommendations for the future.

References

1. Branscomb, A.W.: Who Owns Information? From Privacy to Public Access. Basic Books, New York (1994)
2. Moore Jr., B.: Studies in Social and Cultural History. M.E. Sharpe, Inc., Armonk (1984)
3. Hixson, R.F.: Privacy in a Public Society. Human Rights in Conflict. Oxford University Press, Oxford (1987)
4. Flaherty, D.H.: Privacy in Colonial New England. University Press of Virginia, Charlottesville (1972)
5. Westin, A.F.: Science, Privacy and Freedom: Issues and Proposals for the 1970's. Part I; The Current Impact of Surveillance on Privacy, Disclosure, and Surveillance. Columbia Law Review 66, 1003–1050 (1966)
6. Westin, A.F.: Science, Privacy and Freedom: Issues and Proposals for the 1970's. Part II, Balancing the Conflicting demands of Privacy, Disclosure, and Surveillance. Columbia Law Review 66, 1205–1253 (1966)
7. Westin, A.F.: Privacy & Freedom. The Bodley Head, London (1967)
8. Bates, A.: Privacy – A Useful Concept? Social Forces 42, 429–435 (1964)
9. Brenton, M.: The Privacy Invaders. Coward-McCann, Inc., New York (1964)
10. Harisson, A.: The Problem of Privacy in the Computer Age, an annotated bibliography. The Rand Corporation, Santa Monica (1967)
11. Jourard, S.M.: Some Psychological Aspects of privacy. Law and Contemporary Problems 31, 307–319 (1966)
12. Kalven Jr., H.: The Problem of Privacy in the Year 2000. Daedalus 93, 876–882 (1967)
13. Konvitz, M.R.: Privacy and the Law: a Philosophical Prelude. Law and Contemporary Problems 31, 272–281 (1966)
14. EPIC, Privacy & Human Rights, An international Survey of Privacy Laws and Developments. Electronic Privacy and Information Centre and Privacy International, Washington (2002)

15. The Economist, Move over, Big Brother, The Economist Technology Quarterly, 26 (December 2, 2004)
16. Garson, B.: The Electronic Sweatshop, How Computers Are Transforming the Office of the Future Into the Factory of the Past. Penguin Books, New York (1988)
17. Warren, S.D., Brandeis, L.D.: The Right to Privacy. In: Adam Carlyle Breckenridge, The Right to Privacy, pp. 133–153. University of Nebraska Press, Lincoln (1970)
18. Mayer, M.F.: Right of Privacy. Law Arts Publishers, Inc., New York (1972)
19. Zelermyer, W.: Invasion of Privacy. Syracuse University Press (1959)
20. Cate, F.H.: Privacy in the Information Age. Brooking Institution Press, Washington (1997)
21. Whyte, W.H.: The Organization Man. Penguin Books, Middlesex (1956)
22. Packard, V.: The Hidden Persuaders. Penguin Books, Midddlesex (1964)
23. Ruebhausen, O.M., Brim Jr., O.G.: Privacy and Behavioral Research. Columbia Law review 65, 1184–1211 (1965)
24. Warner, M., Stone, M.: The Data Bank Society. Organizations, Computers and Social Freedom. George Allen and Unwin Ltd., London (1970)
25. Miller, A.: The Assault on Privacy: Computers, Dossiers and Data Banks. The University of Michigan Press, Ann Arbor (1971)
26. Stanley, J., Steinhardt, B., Monster, B., Chains, W.: The Growth of an American Surveillance Society. American Civil Liberties Union, New York (2003)
27. Davies, S.: Big Brother at the Box Office, Electronic Visual Surveillance and the Bog Screen. In: Proceedings of the 21th International Conference on Privacy and Personal Data Protection, Hong Kong, pp. 151–160 (1999)
28. Elbirt, A.J.: Who are You? How to Protect Against Identity Theft. IEEE Technology and Society Magazin, 5–8 (2005)
29. Cavoukian, A.: Identity Theft Revisited: Security is Not Enough. Information and Privacy Commissioner, Ontario (2005)
30. Erbschloe, M., Vacca, J.: Net Privacy, A Guide to developing and implementing an ironclad ebusiness plan. McGraw-Hill, New York (2001)
31. Duquenoy, P., Masurkar, V.: Surrounded by intelligence .... In: Duquennoy, P., Fisher-Hübner, S., Holvast, J., Zuccato, A. (eds.) Risks and Challenges of the Network Society, pp. 121–134. Karlstad University Studies, Karlstad (2004)
32. The Economist, The surveillance society, May 1 (1999)
33. Evans, M.: The data-informed marketing model and its social responsibility. In: Lace, S. (ed.) The Glass Consumer, Life in a surveillance society, pp. 99–132. National Consumer Council (2005)
34. Foroohar, R.: Life in the grid. In: Newsweek, pp. 64–67, September 16-23 (2002)
35. Council of Europe, Convention for the Protection of Individuals with Regard to Automatic Processing of Personal Data, European Treaty Series No. 108, Strasbourg (1982)
36. OECD, Guidelines on the Protection of Privacy and Transborder Flows of Personal Data, Paris (1981)
37. Directive 95/46/EC of the European Parliament and the Council of 24 October 1995 on the protection of individuals with regard to the processing of personal data and the free movement of such data, Official Journal of the European Communities, 281/31-50 (1995)
38. Directive 97/66/EC of the European Parliament and the Council of 15 December 1997 concerning the processing of personal data and the protection of privacy in the telecommunications sector, Official Journal of the European Communities, 24/1-8 (1998)
39. Directive 2002/58/EC of the European Parliament and the Council of 12 July 2002, concerning the processing of personal data and the protection of privacy in the electronic communication, Official Journal of the European Communities, 201/37-47 (2002)

40. Raab, C.: Regulatory provisions for privacy protection. In: Lace, S. (ed.) The Glass Consumer, Life in a surveillance society, pp. 45–67. National Consumer Council (2005)
41. Reidenberg, J.: Technologies for Privacy Protection. Paper presented at the 23rd Internation Conference of Data Protection Commissioners, Paris (2001)
42. Chaum, D.: Security without identification: Transaction Systems to make big brother obsolete. Communications of the ACM 28, 1020–1044 (1985)
43. van Rossem, H., Gardeniers, H., Borking, J., Cavoukian, A., Brans, J., Muttupulle, N., Magistrale, N.: Privacy-enhancing Technologies, The path to anonymity, vol. I and II. Registratiekamer, The Netherlands & Information and Privacy Commissioner, Ontario, Canada (1995)
44. Grodzinsky, F.S., Tavani, H.T.: Verizon vs the RIAA: Implications for Privacy and Democracy. Paper presented at ISTAS 2004, International Symposium on Technology and Society, Globalizing Technological Education (2004)
45. Brantgärde, L.: Swedish trends in Data Protection and Data Access. In: de Guchteneire, P., Mochmann, E. (eds.) Data protection and data access, pp. 105–122. North-Holland, Amsterdam (1990)
46. Computer Business Review (June 2001)
47. Burnham, D.: The Rise of the Computer State. The threat to our Freedoms, our Ethics and our democratic Process. Random House, New York (1983)
48. Flaherty, D.: The Emergence of Surveillance Societies in the Western World: Toward the Year 2000. Government Information Quarterly 4, 377–387 (1988)
49. Hall, H.: Data use in credit and insurance: controlling unfair outcomes. In: Lace, S. (ed.) The Glass Consumer, Life in a surveillance society, pp. 157–186. National Consumer Council (2005)
50. Lace, S. (ed.): The Glass Consumer, Life in a surveillance society. National Consumer Council (2005)

Applied Ethics and eHealth: Principles, Identity, and RFID

Diane Whitehouse[1] and Penny Duquenoy[2]

[1] The Castlegate Consultancy, 27 Castlegate, Malton, North Yorkshire, England YO17 7DP, UK
[2] Middlesex University, UK
diane.whitehouse@thecastlegateconsultancy.com, P.Duquenoy@mdx.ac.uk

Abstract. The social and ethical implications of contemporary technologies are becoming an issue of steadily growing importance. This paper offers an overview in terms of identity and the field of ethics, and explores how these apply to eHealth in both theory and practice. The paper selects a specific circumstance in which these ethical issues can be explored. It focuses particularly on radio-frequency identifiers (RFID). It ends by discussing ethical issues more generally, and the practice of ethical consideration.

Keywords: Applied principles, consent, convergence, eHealth, ethics, health, identity, identity management, privacy, RFID, security.

1 Introduction

The growing range of information and communication technologies (ICT) that is available, and its diverse uses in different capacities, whether personal, professional, informal or formal, raises a number of interesting – indeed challenging – questions about human identity. As the June 2008 conference organised by the Centre for Ethics and Technology, Delft, Netherlands, suggested:

> *Access, rights, responsibilities, benefits, burdens and risks are [now] apportioned on the basis of identities of individuals. These identities are formed on the basis of personal data collected and stored and manipulated in databases. This raises ethical questions, such as obvious privacy issues, but also a host of identity related moral questions concerning (the consequences of) erroneous classifications and the limits of our capacity for self-presentation and self definition.*
>
> *http://www.ethicsandtechnology.eu/* Accessed 16 June, 2008

The aim of this paper is to demonstrate the tight relationship between ethics and current technologies against the background of the eHealth domain. The paper is based on contributions to two International Federation for Information Processing (IFIP) summer schools, held in 2007 and 2008. These concentrated on issues relating to ethics, identity, and identity management in the Information Society. eHealth, as a particular case study, raises a number of issues relating to identity and therefore provides a useful context for investigation.

V. Matyáš et al. (Eds.): The Future of Identity, IFIP AICT 298, pp. 43–55, 2009.

To introduce the key issues of ethical debate, the paper progresses as follows. It outlines the relationship between identity, health, eHealth, and ethical issues. It describes the development of eHealth, particularly in Europe. A brief introduction to ethics sets the stage for a general discussion on eHealth and ethics. An overview of the ethical principles that inform the healthcare sector comes next. These principles are applied to the healthcare setting. Ethical dilemmas that surround a particular technology used in the eHealth area are introduced – radio frequency identifiers (RFID). The issues at stake relate principally to privacy, security, and consent. Finally, a broad set of conclusions are formulated.

The context, evidence and examples that are described are generally those of the European scene. This is the authors' location and tends to be their area of particular interest. Clearly, however, these issues are not uniquely European, they are global. In this sense, we fully recognise the achievements of e.g. the World Health Organisation and the World Bank in terms of eHealth policy development and implementation. In a growingly international ('flat') world, how we handle the provision of healthcare for the benefit of peoples in all parts of the globe may be about to change substantially [39].

2 Identity, Health, and eHealth

Identity relates to people's personal conceptions of themselves and the different ways in which others view them (as a patient, for example, or conversely as a doctor/expert). Identity is fundamental to the carrying-out of healthcare: it enables the identification of types of disease which citizens or patients experience, and their degree of wellbeing; it can help define the stage in the lifecycle at which patients are, and the disease grouping into which they fit. These characteristics may even enable eventually more effective *triage*, the process of "the assignment of degrees of urgency to wounds or illnesses to decide the order of treatment of a large number of patients or casualties" [28]. Today, technology-based equivalents and mechanisms to support these processes can include the out-of-hours telephone, email, and Web-based facilities available in some countries (e.g., the National Health Service (NHS) Direct (NHS Direct) service in England).

Thus, identity and identification can influence the appropriate form of treatment given to citizens/patients. In this broader sense, identity plays a role in organisational management in terms of who gets treatment, who delivers it, and how healthcare overall is managed. The traditional, and changing, power relations among the various participants in the health arena also influence these choices.

eHealth today forces a high degree of focus on identity, because technology intervenes increasingly in the various processes involved in the understanding of and provision of healthcare. ICT mediates between the practitioner and the patient, and may have considerable influence on organisational practice. Increasing convergence is taking place, both in terms of the technologies associated with health/eHealth practice and in relation to the diminishing degrees of separation between difference areas of health activity: whether the wellness industry, primary care, secondary care, clinical research, rehabilitation, care, and pharmaceutical practice.

Hence, what needs to occur is the correct identification of the patient; the specific health professional(s) involved; and the particular institution. Sound and secure methods of identifying human beings are needed so that appropriate analysis, diagnosis, treatment, and follow-up can be given correctly and confidentially to the individuals concerned. Appropriate files need to be linked and integrated [20] and data management practices implemented. This maintenance of correct data and identification methods is fundamental to the ethical practice of healthcare (discussed in sections 4.1 and 4.2).

Good data management, however, is not only to be considered in respect of ethics and identity. Other ethical issues that are pertinent to eHealth are associated with the personalisation and the degree of intimacy of the particular technology. Examples include technology implants; genetic analysis; and the uses to be made of health data [24,33,37].

Clearly Radio Frequency Identification (RFID) offers a possible solution to identifying people, products, and services throughout the health sector. However, it is also evident that there are social and ethical concerns which might mitigate or at least modify its widespread use [2,17,25].

3 eHealth – Definition and Background

What precisely is eHealth? A number of definitions are available in the academic literature and in policy-related materials [6,8,14,26,27]. In this context, we have chosen to focus on one of the more pragmatic and applied definitions. This well-known description was included in the text of the eHealth action plan [6, p4]:

> *[eHealth] describes the application of information and communications technologies across the whole range of functions that affect the health sector.*

eHealth has alternatively been referred to as medical informatics or medical information systems, clinical informatics or clinical information systems, health informatics or health information systems, or information and communication technologies for health [12].

Historically, eHealth constitutes a journey with many milestones. ICT for health has been developing for over four decades – in Europe, for two. In the European Union, in the late 1980s, the early foundations of eHealth were laid; pilot studies were co-financed by the small number of countries which was composed of the originating members of the second stage of the European Union. From the 12 states at that era, the Union has now grown to 27 members. From an initial funding of €20 million in 1988, the investment in this particular domain of research and development expanded tenfold in the Sixth Framework Programme. The Commission is now co-financing the Seventh Framework Programme that extends throughout the period, 2007 to 2013. The amount of financing provided by the Commission dedicated to eHealth in this Framework Programme is expected to be well over €200 million. Its emphasis is on fields of research activity such as personalised health (health information systems that support healthcare for individuals), patient safety, and work on the model of the "virtual physiological human" (the bringing together of very large databases that can merge clinical, genomic, and environmental data so as to predict and describe the health status of individuals much more effectively).

However, it is not only research in eHealth that is of importance. eHealth has become an area for strong policy development with the formulation of a seven-year plan for policy convergence [6]. 2008 has been a key year for eHealth in Europe, in this sense. In the context of patient mobility, cross-border health services, and eHealth interoperability, a Proposal for a Directive and a Recommendation have already been adopted [9,11]. A policy document on telemedicine was published in the same year [10].

There is much current emphasis on the actual deployment and application of eHealth. eHealth is perceived as a key enabler of good healthcare, and a means of reinforcing the Union's common values and goals for its health systems. Two-thirds of the Member States believe that their health policy priorities can be supported by eHealth. Not only does every European Member State now possess its own eHealth road map or action plan, but all the States are now building their own initiatives to apply eHealth systems, services, and applications. While there are many commonalities among the 27 States, there is, nevertheless, considerable disparity among them with regard to their stages of innovation and how they are putting eHealth into practice [16]. This 2007 overview shows that the principal, common eHealth services in European countries all have relevance for ethical concerns such as the quality of care and the importance of access to care of the patient/citizen. Of the six eHealth domains which most Member States are introducing, building, and using, the three technical areas are infrastructure, electronic health records or cards, and interoperability (Ibid, p13-15).

On two recent occasions, the Member States have committed themselves to work together on eHealth[1]. This engagement is paralleled by the practical developments of the European Commission's Competitiveness and Innovation Framework Programme (CIP) Information and Communication Technologies Policy Support Programme (PSP) (also known as the CIP PSP). This scheme supports the practical advance and integration of information and communication technologies use in their public sector domains among the Member States. In eHealth, the ministries of health, eHealth competence centres, and industry in 12 Member States focus on electronic health data (health records/medication records or "patient summaries") and ePrescribing.[2]

Finally, European and international industries are paying a renewed interest in the eHealth market. Many elements of the relevant industries are endeavouring to work together on a number of eHealth-related initiatives: one example is Continua Health Alliance[3]. In late 2007, the European Commission also launched a platform known as the Lead Market Initiative. This initiative emphasises the notion of the public sector as a driver of technological innovation and potential industrial growth – eHealth is one of the six domains to which attention is paid [8].

What next for eHealth in Europe as a whole is fast becoming one of Europe's biggest challenges.

4 Ethics and Its Application

Ethics constitutes a branch of moral philosophy, of which there are several schools of thought and action and a host of ethical theories. The consideration of ethics and ethical theory in relation to human behaviour is known as *normative ethics*, in contrast to

---

[1] See the conference declarations of two high-level (Ministerial) conferences in 2007 and 2008: http://ec.europa.eu/health-eu/news/ehealth/ehealth2007_en.htm and http://www.ehealth2008.si/ Accessed 8 January 2009.

[2] See http://www.epsos.eu/

[3] See http://www.continuaalliance.org/home/

more abstract discussions on morality (i.e. meta-ethics). In the context of this paper, we are interested in normative ethics which is the practical application of ethics. In recent years, different ethical theories have been used to assess the ethical implications of ICT. Two of the most common theories used are Kantian ethics and utilitarian ethics (otherwise known as consequentialism).

Briefly summarised, Kant argues that human will motivates moral action, but that the will can only motivate itself from a rational foundation [21]. Accordingly, rationality implies autonomy (i.e. self-determination) and rational argument dictates that all human beings must be equal. These positions give rise to two propositions: to treat humanity always as an end in itself and never as a means to an end; and to act only on those principles (maxims) which at the same time one would desire to be a universal law. Kant specified: "Act only on that maxim which you can at the same time will to be a universal law" [21, p421].

Utilitarian ethics is located in the domain of 'consequentialist' ethics where the principles of moral actions are considered as being based on their consequences. The principle of utility ('utility principle') is that right actions bring the greatest happiness (determined as being either of the highest value or of the least harm) to the greatest number of people. One of the difficulties with this theory is that the consequences of actions cannot be predicted.

Ethical theories are useful as a point of departure to enable people to make appropriate choices and to act accordingly. They provide people with a form of toolkit that can enable them, at any moment in time and in any specific context – complete with its own criteria and constraints – to understand the particular moral position taken and the reasoning which underpins a specific moral choice.

These two theories have led to two distinct positions. In the first, there is a consideration of human autonomy and respect for others; in the second, a basis for deciding (and assessing) a course of action focused on the greatest benefit. In the following section, we consider principles that have been derived from these essential 'goods' and which have been applied to the practice of medicine, the field of health and, more recently, the combined fields of eHealth (i.e., medicine or health and ICT). The more applied the field, the more the ethical questions leap out and demand answers. The technologies involved add yet at least another layer of complexity to the issues involved.

4.1 eHealth and Ethics

Identity is an increasingly important issue for many fields of public sector services. In just one of these sectors – eHealth, a growing number of challenges relating relate to identity and identity management. It is always useful to view a hypothetical issue within an ethical domain in terms of practical examples. eHealth provides a realistic illustration of a number of ethical questions.

Ethics is fundamental to all fields of human concern. Issues relating to privacy, confidentiality, informed consent, and so on, can be seen as intrinsic to the health sector. They affect people often when they are at their most vulnerable. The health sector – and eHealth as a support mechanism that is implicitly part of it – can be considered as being based fundamentally on ethical notions; it is replete with ethical dilemmas.

eHealth is of particular interest and preoccupation not only because it provides a means of supporting people's health (and health issues are based on moral or ethical imperatives), but also because of the questions that surround the technologies that are increasingly associated with healthcare and care provision.

A popular ethical framework that underpins the field of biomedical ethics [3] was first proposed some 20 years ago in 1989. The framework is described as a "set of mid-level principles mediating between high-level moral theory and low-level common morality" [19]. The four basic principles laid out are of non-malfeasance; beneficence; a respect for autonomy; and justice and equity. These four are described below:

- *Non-malfeasance*

Non-malfeasance means, of course, to 'do no harm' or *primum non nocere* – which lies at the very basis of all medical care. Aspects of non-harm may relate to increasing the quality of healthcare, and reducing its risk (hence, quality and safety).

- *Beneficence*

Beneficence means promoting wellbeing, increasing its level of safety (rather than just reducing risk), and protecting people. It is a more pro-active approach to health-care. It too can be said to concentrate on aspects that relate to quality and safety.

- *Respect for autonomy*

Autonomy may relate to that of the health professional or to that of the particular citizen/patient whose health is at stake. It seems to have a relationship to the potential access to healthcare; as does the principle of justice and equity which follows.

- *Principle(s) of justice/equity*

These access-related principles have been especially strong in healthcare provision and management in Europe over the past sixty-year period.

These four notions are clearly of importance. Their implications are explored in detail in [12]. They match closely the ethical concepts of the two theories – Kantian and utilitarian – discussed in section 4. To do no harm and to promote wellbeing correspond to the notion of least harm or the greatest happiness (the utility principle). Respect for autonomy and principles of justice/equity relate to the theories of Kant.

An adaptation of unpublished work developed in [30] enables us to focus on some of the notions implicit in these four ethical principles, and to understand at the same time that there are further issues which require our attention, matters which relate to the economy and sustainability of health and healthcare.

With eHealth, the overall aim would be to create a balance of access ('A'), quality ('Q'), and economy (effectiveness and/or efficiency) ('E') ('AQE') in the particular health system or service. However, is the AQE relationship really an equilateral triangle? Or do its dimensions change at different points of time and in diverse circumstances? What happens when one adds the notions of provision and continuity (which may also affect quality), and safety (associated with quality or, indeed, with security) to the mix? Economy is surely closely related to principles of both the greatest good and at the same time respect for autonomy. Conceptually, are Kantian and utilitarian principles opposites or is a merger of the two possible (cf. implicitly [22])? Certainly, the economic aspects and the business models that underpin eHealth are likely to take on a far higher prominence than was previously the case [8]. However, so too, under conditions of economic crisis, may altruism, benevolence, and voluntarism.

The abundant late 20th century distribution of labour as support to healthcare may well have to pass on, away, and down – over the next decades – from specialists to generalists and, indeed, to citizens and patients themselves (e.g. [39,40]. The economics and re-organisation of healthcare may require serious consideration.

4.2 Applied Principles in eHealth

High-level principles can be brought to bear on specific areas of application. Codes of ethics provide the ethical foundation for many organisations, particularly professional bodies. The ICT industry encompasses a range of disciplines that include electronic engineering, computer science, and information management. The ethical principles of these professions fall usually into groupings that state that they protect the public interest, uphold the standards of the specific profession, promote knowledge transfer, and require a commitment to personal integrity. Of direct relevance in this case are the "rules of conduct" for Health Informatics Professionals drawn up in the United Kingdom under the auspices of the Health Informatics Committee of the British Computer Society. They recognise the role played by ICT in the field of medicine [22].

The complexity of modern society and communities of work mean that the ethics of specific occupations (e.g. their codes of ethics, behaviour, or practice) need to be given careful consideration when each meet in realms of collaborative or cooperative practice. In eHealth, a wide range of different occupations and professions may converge e.g. clinicians, researchers, insurers, and pharmacists. Similar tensions may face small organisations (or scopes) when merged with larger ones.

The fundamental ethical principles laid down by [22], follow those outlined in section 4.1. They are the: Principle of Autonomy; Principle of Equality and Justice; Principle of Beneficence; Principle of Non-Malfeasance; and the Principle of Impossibility. (This last principle relates to the assumption that it must be possible to meet the rights and duties that are expressed by the previous three statements.) These principles are transposed into concrete and practical uses that are aligned with the responsibilities of Health Informatics Professionals. The professional has "a duty to ensure that appropriate measures are in place that may reasonably be expected to safeguard: The security of electronic records; The integrity of electronic records; The material quality of electronic records; The usability of electronic records; The accessibility of electronic records." (Ibid, p14).

These five characteristics of electronic records are regarded by Health Informatics Professionals as important so as to achieve further progress in healthcare. Each of them describes a state of usefulness that could be compromised as a result of technical mediation: these are the possible 'crisis points' of technically-mediated patient information. Presenting patient information can be construed as providing "the correct information at the right time, to the right people"; it is the basis for a strong ethical foundation to eHealth [13]. This is not an easy task given the increasingly complex interactions implied by eHealth.

5 Applying an Ethical Framework to a Particular Technology in a Specific Setting: RFID

Ethical issues may differ depending on various aspects of eHealth – research, policy, deployment or implementation. The ethical issues may also be different according to the specific technology to which they apply. It is therefore important to choose a frame (i.e., framework) or approach to the ethical stance to be taken: a frame that can remain reasonably standard yet can still be applied flexibly according to the particular circumstance under investigation. It is also a priority to maintain a process-related view of ethics, and to search continuously for the kinds of setting in which the ethics of behaviour may be explored and/or debated.

Given contemporary developments in the field of ICT, it is perfectly possible to select numerous examples of technologies that pose ethical challenges. Such technologies affect many fields, and are almost completely ubiquitous. Health services are rapidly expanding their use of ICT, especially to respond to the considerable challenges they face contemporarily. Among these technologies is the very specific field of RFID. Recent articles highlight the privacy and security issues at stake in both the United States and Europe in relation to RFID [1], and with more specific attention to health [2,17,25].

"Radio frequency identification (RFID) is a technology that allows automatic identification and data capture by using radio frequencies" [7]. It can allow "automatic identification of objects, animals or people by incorporating a small electronic chip on its "host". Data is *[sic]* stored on this chip and can then be "read" by wireless devices, called RFID readers."[4] Such devices can be active, passive, or semi-passive. Today more and more practical industrial products are available that are enlarging RFID's implementation and application, including in the health domain. We take, and understand, RFID to be one of the many eHealth applications currently available on today's market.

The framework we have developed in this paper enables us to pursue further the ethical questions at stake when dealing with eHealth. So too do the three papers presented at the 2007 IFIP summer school that dealt with RFID. We do not, however, explore more widely the various other articles available on this subject (such as [1,2,17,25].

First, we deal with our own approach to the problem domain; then, we expose the thinking of the three separate sets of investigators present at the 2007 summer school.

5.1 Introducing a Frame

To examine the ethical issues that might arise from RFID, we consider the fundamentals of the specific technology and its relationship to the 'ethical entity' – which in the case of health is a human being (although it could also be an animal). RFID means that there is a small device that stores data that can be communicated to a receiver for a designated purpose. The device is incorporated on – and even, on occasions in – its host (e.g. a health professional, a product such as a medical device such as a prosthesis, a

[4] See http://ec.europa.eu/information_society/policy/rfid/about_rfid/index_en.htm Accessed 20 September, 2008.

pharmaceutical product, or a physical piece of clinical or hospital equipment). The ethically challenging characteristics of RFID are that it is a small (possibly unseen) form of ICT that is attached in some way to someone or something which transmits information using a range of radio frequencies. We have said above that it allows "automatic identification and data capture" – identification of what is an ethically pertinent question. It could be simply the device, it could be a person, it could be a condition, or it could be all three.

Relating the use of RFID to the principles of non-malfeasance; beneficence; autonomy; and justice/equity can facilitate ethical decision-making. In any use of RFID that is under consideration in the eHealth domain, the following kinds of questions emerge. Is anyone harmed (most particularly the patient, but we should always consider other people too)? Does the technology promote wellbeing (i.e., does it protect the patient from harm or keep the patient safe)? Does the use of the device promote justice and equity (or, conversely, does it enable discrimination and inequality)? Section 5.2 illustrates some concerns with RFID that may challenge these principles.

5.2 Outlining Some Empirical Evidence

Internationally, there is much current interest in the social and ethical considerations that relate to RFID (see e.g., [7,17,25,29]). However, the three groups of researchers whose ideas on RFID on which we rely more substantially are three sets of researchers at the 2007 IFIP summer school; they are listed here in alphabetic order: Hansen & Meissner [18]; Kumar [23]; and van Lieshout & Cool [36].

The matter of greatest concern to all three sets of researchers was that of privacy. They raised questions about precisely what aspects of personal privacy may be, at least potentially, contravened by RFID. For example, privacy can be challenged through the particular type of RFID technology that is used, and by the circumstances in which it is used – including the degree of informed consent permitted or rendered possible: such notions of consent can even be provocatively fluid [33]. Privacy (i.e., confidentiality) and consent are key ethical principles in the health domain.

Interesting insights can be drawn with regard to the use of RFID technology from the field of bio-metrics: it can enable foresight into how far the notion of invasive RFID can be stretched (cf. [18]). In terms of the degree of potential exploitation of possibilities that surround RFID, there are a number that raise ethical concerns including: the unauthorised reading of tags; real-time tracking of individuals; the use of data for purposes other than those originally specified; the profiling and monitoring of both people and behaviour (all four of these issues relate to notions of contravention of privacy or confidentiality); and the combining of personal data (which may accelerate or enlarge all of these possible threats/preoccupations). All of the above issues would compromise severely ethical standards of identity management in the health sector.

Two of the three sets of authors [18] and [36] assessed the possible contravention of privacy legislation in Europe as it is based within the European Data Privacy Directive; following the principle of subsidiarity, this legislation is applied with a different range of depth and intensity in the various European Member States. Subsidiarity implies that in European Union law, the Union may only make laws where Member

States agree that the action of individual countries is not sufficient. Such law, however, needs to be applied by the individual Member States using ways and means that are appropriate to them at their local level.

An in-depth exploration of the legal aspects of eHealth in relation to privacy (but also in respect to certain elements of commercial and liability law) is explored in European Commission [16] and [34]. The policy conclusions of this, latter, 2006-2007 Legally eHealth study emphasise the need to review legal uncertainties in data protection, product liability, and competition law, to disseminate more adequately legal knowledge and consumer protection issues, and to create eHealth information infrastructure guidelines.

Both articles [18] and [36] acknowledge that potential technological solutions may be introduced as countermeasures to privacy contravention. The latter also identify the role that self-regulation may play as a possible countermeasure to invasion of privacy – on the part of members of both the manufacturing and retailing industry. As a topic, however, this latter area of self-regulation received proportionally less attention and depth of analysis.

In addition to the concept of privacy intervention, [23] covers briefly a range of other possibly unethical uses of RFID. On the one hand, he highlights the separate notions of cyber-racism and/or domination, and the creation of deliberate shifts in people's perception, memory, and identity. On the other hand, he approaches in more detail the possibility that RFID may have various health effects or side-effects.

6 Conclusions

Clearly, ethics is important and it matters. Ethics is much more than simply theory; ethics is also about the influence it has on our behaviour and on our day-to-day practice. It is not just about what we as human beings think, it is about what we act out and what we do. Ethical principles can have a huge influence on the policy or political stances and directions that groups and individuals take. A first approach, as a result of this knowledge, is to be informed about what ethical stances and principles are in general. A second is to understand how they apply to specific fields – in this case, eHealth.

The ethics of eHealth may well bring individual welfare into harsh contrast and even conflict with that of the greatest good. We are reminded of the notion that technologies often offer the opportunity to undertake actions and explore possibilities that had previously not been considered – simply because 'we can', whereas we may always consider that there are always things that one should *not* do [38].

There can also be many tensions, pressures, and contentions between principles and behaviours, and between different interpretations and specific ethical stances. Most ethical questions require more profound thought and deliberation. Ethics is therefore also a process. One of the sponsoring organisations of this series of summer schools, IFIP, has for more than a decade placed considerable emphasis on the creation of *fora* for dialogue – what it calls 'spaces for discussion' (an argument put forward again in [4]).

While only the single service sector of eHealth (and the role played in it by RFID) was selected for discussion in this paper, the implications for identity and for ethics of various ICT applications warrant further study – especially as technologies converge [5,35]. eHealth has, of course, the potential to offer interesting insights, but so do other industrial or service sectors such as eGovernment and eInclusion.

Our recommendation is to start from the field in which you are, the particular area that concerns you, and to consider the ethical implications of the technology or technologies with which you work.

Acknowledgements

A certain compatibility may be found between our work and that of Els Soenens [31,32]. Feedback and input from the discussions held with attendees at both the 2007 and the 2008 IFIP summer schools are warmly appreciated. So too are the comments and encouragements of three anonymous 2008 reviewers. The helpful insights of colleagues Chris Zielinski of the World Health Organisation and Marc Griffiths of The Castlegate Consultancy are equally recognised. Final responsibility for the content and orientation of the paper remain with the two authors.

References

1. Albrecht, K.: How RFID tags could be used to track unsuspecting people. Scientific American (August 2008)
2. Bacheldor, B.: AMA issues ethics code for RFID chip implants. RFID Journal (July 17, 2007)
3. Beauchamp, T., Childress, J.F.: 5th edn. Oxford University Press, Oxford (2001)
4. Berleur, J., Burmeister, O., Duquenoy, P., Gotterbarn, D., Goujon, P., Kaipainen, K., Kimppa, K., Six, B., Weber-Wulff, D., Whitehouse, D. (eds.): Ethics of Computing Committees. Sug-gestions for Functions, Form, and Structure. IFIP-SIG9.2.2. IFIP Framework for Ethics of Computing (September 2008)
5. Bibel, W.: Converging Technologies in the Natural, Social and Cultural World. Special Interest Group for the European Commission via an Expert Group on "Foresighting the New Technology Wave" (2004)
6. COM (2004)356 final e-Health – making healthcare better for European citizens: An action plan for a European e-Health area. European Commission, Luxembourg (30.4.2004)
7. COM(2007)96 final Radio Frequency Identification (RFID) in Europe. Steps towards a policy framework (2007)
8. COM(2007) 860 final A lead market initiative for Europe (21.12.2007)
9. COM(2008) 414 final Proposal for a Directive on the application of patients' rights in cross- border healthcare (2.7.2008)
10. COM(2008) 489 final (2008) Telemedicine for the benefit of patients, healthcare systems and society (2.11.2008)
11. COM(2008) 3282 final (2008) Commission recommendation of 2nd July 2008 on cross-border interoperability of electronic health record systems (2.7.2008)
12. Collste, J.: Applied Ethics and ICT-systems in Healthcare. In: Duquenoy, P., George, G., Kimppa, K. (eds.) Ethical, Legal, and Social Issues in Medical Informatics. Medical Information Science Reference (IGI Global) (2008)
13. Duquenoy, P., George, C., Solomonides, A.: Considering Something ELSE: Ethical, Legal and Socio-Economic Factors in Medical Imaging and Medical Informatics. In: Special Issue: The International Conference MIMI 2007 on 'Medical Imaging and Medical Informatics' August 14-16, 2007, Beijing, China. Müller, H., Gao, X., Luo, S. (Guest Editors) Computer Methods and Programs in Biomedicine 92(3), pp. 227–237. Elsevier Ireland Ltd. (2008), ISSN0169-2607

14. Eng, T.R.: The eHealth Landscape: A Terrain Mapping of Emerging Information and Communication Technologies in Health and Health Care. The Robert Wood Johnson Foundation (2001)
15. Eysenbach, G.: What is e-health? J. Med Internet Res. 3(2), e20 (2001)
16. European Commission: eHealth priorities and strategies in European countries. Office for Official Publications of the European Communities, Luxembourg (2007)
17. Foster, K.R., Jaeger, J.: The Murky Ethics of Implanted Chips. IEEE Spectrum Online (March 2007)
18. Hansen, M., Meissner, S.: Identification and Tracking of Individuals and Social Net-works using the Electronic Product Code on RFID Tags. In: Fischer-Huebner, S., Duquenoy, P., Zuccato, A., Martucci, L. (eds.) IFIP International Federation for Information Processing. The Future of Identity in the Information Society, vol. 262, pp. 143–150. Springer, Boston (2008)
19. Holm, J.: Review of Beauchamp and Childress (2001). J. Med. Ethics 28, 332 (2002)
20. Joosten, R., Whitehouse, D., Duquenoy, P.: Putting identifiers in the context of eHealth. In: Fischer-Huebner, S., Duquenoy, P., Zuccato, A., Martucci, L. (eds.) IFIP International Federation for Information Processing. The Future of Identity in the Information Society, vol. 262, pp. 389–403. Springer, Boston (2008)
21. Kant, I.: Grounding for the Metaphysics of Morals, translated by James W. Hackett Publishing Company, Ellington (1981)
22. Kluge, E.-H.: A Handbook of Ethics for Health Informatics Professionals. Health Informatics Committee, British Computer Society, London (2003)
23. Kumar, V.: Implantable RFID Chips: Security versus Ethics. In: Fischer-Huebner, S., Duquenoy, P., Zuccato, A., Martucci, L. (eds.) IFIP International Federation for Information Processing. The Future of Identity in the Information Society, vol. 262, pp. 151–157. Springer, Boston (2008)
24. Mordini, E.: Biometrics, Human Body, and Medicine: A Controversial History. In: Duquenoy, P., Carlisle, G., Kimppa, K. (eds.) Ethical, Legal, and Social Issues in Medical Informatics. Medical Information Science Reference (IGI Global) (2008)
25. Michael, M.G., Fusco, S.J., Michael, K.: A Research Note on Ethics in the Emerging Age of UberSurveillance (Überveillance). Computer Communications 31(6), 1192–1199 (2008)
26. Oh, H., Rizo, C., Enkin, M., Jadad, A.: What is eHealth (3): A Systematic Review of Published Definitions. J. Med. Internet Res. 7(1), e1 (2005)
27. Pagliari, C., Sloan, D., Gregor, P., Sullivan, F., Detmer, D., Kahan, J.: What is eHealth (4): A Scoping Exercise to Map the Field. J. Med. Internet Res. 7(1), e9 (2005)
28. Pearsall, J. (ed.): The New Oxford Dictionary of English. Oxford and. Oxford University Press, Oxford (2001)
29. Perakslis, C., Wolk, R.: Social Acceptance of RFID as a Biometric Security Measure. IEEE Technology and Society Magazine (Fall 2006)
30. Purcarea, O., Iakovidis, I., Healy, J.-C.: Access, quality, and economy of eHealth. Unpublished manuscript submitted to the American Journal of Telemedicine (2003)
31. Soenens, E.: Identity management systems in healthcare: the issue of patient identifiers. In: Matyáš, V., et al. (eds.) The Future of Identity in the Information Society. IFIP AICT, vol. 298. Springer, Heidelberg (2009)
32. Soenens, E., Leys, M.: FIDIS deliverable: D4.11 eHealth identity management in several types of welfare states in Europe, 31.3.2008 (2008)

33. Timmins, N.: Electronic medical records a step closer. Financial Times (2008), http://www.ft.com/cms/s/0/ff2823e8-85d0-11dd-a1ac-0000779fd18c.html?nclick_check=1 (accessed January 8, 2009)
34. van Doosselaere, C., Wilson, P., Herveg, J., Silber, D.: eHealth ...but is it legal? Eurohealth 13(2), 1–4 (2007)
35. van Lieshout, M.: Social and Ethical Dimensions of Converging Technologies. Draft proposal for a IFIP-related conference (draft– in preparation) (2008)
36. van Lieshout, M., Cool, L.: Privacy implications of RFID: An assessment of threats and opportunities. In: Fischer-Huebner, S., Duquenoy, P., Zuccato, A., Martucci, L. (eds.) IFIP International Federation for Information Processing. The Future of Identity in the Information Society, vol. 262, pp. 129–141. Springer, Boston (2008)
37. Warwick, K., Cerqui, D.: Prospects for Thought Communication: Brain to Machine and Brain to Brain. In: Duquenoy, P., Carlisle, G., Kimppa, K. (eds.) Ethical, Legal, and Social Issues in Medical Informatics. Medical Information Science Reference (IGI Global) (2008)
38. Weizenbaum, J.: Computer Power and Human Reason: From Judgment to Calculation. W.H. Freeman, San Francisco (1976)
39. Whitehouse, D.: Preface. In: Duquenoy, P., Carlisle, G., Kimppa, K. (eds.) Ethical, Legal, and Social Issues in Medical Informatics. Medical Information Science Reference (IGI Global) (2008a)
40. Whitehouse, D.: The increasing role of eHealth for better specialist care in Europe. In: Building on solid foundations to improve specialist healthcare for European citizens. UEMS 50th anniversary conference, Brussels, April 18, pp. 55–59. UEMS, Brussels (2008b)

Identity Management Systems in Healthcare: The Issue of Patient Identifiers

Els Soenens

Vrije Universiteit Brussel, Center for Law, Science, Technology and Society Studies*
Pleinlaan 2, 1050 Brussels, Belgium
Els.Soenens@vub.ac.be

Abstract. According to a recent recommendation of the European Commission, now is the time for Europe to enhance interoperability in eHealth. Although interoperability of patient identifiers seems promising for matters of patient mobility, patient empowerment and effective access to care, we see that today there is indeed a considerable lack of interoperability in the field of patient identification. Looking from a socio-technical rather than a merely technical point of view, one can understand the fact that the development and implementation of an identity management system in a specific healthcare context is influenced by particular social practices, affected by socio-economical history and the political climate and regulated by specific data protection legislations. Consequently, the process of making patient identification in Europe more interoperable is a development beyond semantic and syntactic levels. In this paper, we gives some examples of today's patient identifier systems in Europe, discuss the issue of interoperability of (unique) patient identifiers from a socio-technical point of view and try not to ignore the 'privacy side' of the story.

Keywords: eHealth, interoperability, (unique) patient identifiers, identity management, privacy.

1 eHealth and the Need to Identify Patients

Clearly, the urge to identify patients is not something new or exclusive to the domain of eHealth. The importance of correct patient identification for reasons of 'delivery of care, administrative processes, support services, record keeping, information management, and follow-up and preventive care' has been recognized well before eHealth came into the picture [19]. Nevertheless the issue got renewed attention in the light of the idea of eHealth.

* The homepage of this interdisciplinary research group (under directorship of Prof. S. Gutwirth) can be accessed via http://www.vub.ac.be/LSTS

V. Matyáš et al. (Eds.): The Future of Identity, IFIP AICT 298, pp. 56–66, 2009.

eHealth[1] envisions efficient and authorized access to medical data in order to develop patient mobility[2], patient empowerment[3] and enhanced quality of care for citizens. eHealth reflects the idea that Information and Communication Technologies (ICT's) facilitate the access to medical data from various sources on an almost permanent scale. This means that, when necessary, healthcare organizations must be able to exchange and receive medical information about a specific patient. Thus, in order to facilitate the development of eHealth services and applications across Europe, interoperability of patient identification system is crucial [14]. However, when the use of a patient identifier eases the linking of (medical and other) information from several sources to a unique citizen, privacy could be at stake. In other words, whereas correct and easily available patient information is essential to healthcare delivery, it could also entail the risk of breaking off patient safety[4]. The European Commission acknowledges this 'double sword', as can be seen in the recently adopted Communication and proposal for a Council Recommendation on patient safety [21].

Summarized, one can observe at least three important requirements of patient identification systems in an (European) eHealth area: First of all, patients should be *uniquely* identified. Unique identification implies that there is an indisputable association between the medical data and a single individual. Secondly, *interoperable exchange* of patient identifiers (and medical data) should be considered essential. Finally, *privacy and patient safety* should be respected. For the EU, it is crucial that patient identification systems should not endanger the protection of patients' privacy and confidentiality. But aren't these requirements mutually exclusive? Doesn't the use of unique and interoperable patient identification schemes actually impede the protection citizen's privacy?[5]

---

[1] eHealth in Europe implies the use of information and communication technologies to facilitate safe and efficient healthcare delivery, citizen empowerment, patient mobility, easy access to care and the development of an European market for eHealth applications: [2].

[2] Patient mobility can be seen in the light of the 'European strive for free movement of citizens and goods. In the context of health care, the free movement refers both to the freedom of citizens to easily and safely seek for health care abroad as well as to the free movement of health data in Europe (under legal-technical restrictions)': [1].

[3] It is the idea 'to empower patients with a sense of ownership of their own health care, and to improve communication between patients and clinicians': [22:32]. Patient empowerment reflects the idea that healthcare seekers must be able to make their own choices about treatments. As such, patients become 'active consumers of healthcare': [22]. Recently, the International Council on Medical and Care Compunetics (ICMCC) launched the term *'Patient 2.0 Empowerment'* which underlines the use of ICT: 'the active participation of the citizen in his or her health and care pathway with the interactive use of Information and Communication Technologies.': see http://www.epractice.eu/document/5162.

[4] In the EU patient safety is understood as 'freedom for a patient from unnecessary harm or potential harm associated with healthcare': see http://ec.europe.eu/health-eu/care_for_me/patient_safety/index_en.htm.

[5] The participants of the 2008 PhD Event (Greece) of the FIDIS project (The Future of Identity in the Information Society) had an interesting discussion about this issue. Some participants, under which lawyers, were convinced of the fact that exchange of interoperable patient identifiers between healthcare contexts is by definition at odds with privacy protection, while others believed that it should be possible to exchange patient information (including identifiers) and still uphold assurance of privacy protection of individuals.

We will argue that they are not. However it certainly calls for a delicate and complex balancing exercise from the countries of the European Economic Area (EEA).[6]

It is the aim of this paper to explore promising solutions for patient identification in today's European eHealth context, taking into account the three requirements summed up above. We start with a non-exhaustive overview of the state of art of patient identification systems across Europe (section 2). We draw on the results reported in deliverable D4.11 of the Network of Excellence 'The Future of Identity in the Information Society' (FIDIS) [1].[7] Secondly we stress that it is feasible to look at the development and implementation of interoperable patient identification systems as a complex issue combining various technical, social, economical and legal aspects and dimensions (section 3). Thirdly, the requirement of unique identification is focused on. In section 4, we explore existing approaches to uniquely identify patients. Finally, we highlight some of the prospects of patient identification systems that are privacy-friendly and feasible in a cross-border eHealth context (section 5).

2 State of Art Anno 2008

Several EU projects (such as Artemis 'A Semantic Web Service-based P2P Infrastructure for the Interoperability of Medical Information Systems' [3] or RIDE 'A Roadmap for Interoperability of eHealth Systems' [4]); studies [1] [5] and European Commission documents [14] recently indicated a huge variety in the state of art of patient identifiers across Europe. In general differences relate to the reach of the patient identification schemes (hospital specific, national or regional), the purpose of the patient identifier (billing, statistical and/or medical purposes) as well as to the specific content and structure of the identifier (e.g. Social Security Number (SSN) as patient identifier or as building block for one or more unique health care number(s)).

Another major difference between patient identifier systems is that they can be designed to be implemented in one specific healthcare institution or on the contrary, the systems can cover a whole area or nation. In Germany patient identification typically depends on the specific identification system of the hospital [1] whereas national patient identification schemes are implemented in e.g. Denmark, Finland, the Netherlands and the United Kingdom (UK) [5]. In Italy and Spain regional identification schemes exist [6] [1]. However in the latter country, the National Health Service

[6] Justification: Often, the policy documents on eHealth of the European Commission not only address the Member States of the European Union, but also other countries of the European Economic Area (EEA). Especially in the context of cross-border healthcare and interoperability in eHealth, it is important to take into account these EEA countries.

[7] The FIDIS D4.11 study was based on information received from FIDIS partners about their home nations (in 2007). As a result the examples in [1] are mainly limited to the following countries: Belgium, Germany and Hungary, Finland, Norway, Spain, The Netherlands. However, when relevant, practices of other (EEA) countries found in literature, are presented as well (e.g. France). Because of this non–exhaustive approach, we suggest interested readers to look into the results of EU projects such as 'A Roadmap for Interoperability of eHealth Systems' (RIDE) (http://www.srdc.metu.edu.tr/webpage/projects/ride/modules.php?name=Deliverables) and 'A Semantic Web Service-based P2P Infrastructure for the Interoperability of Medical Information Systems' (Artemis) (http://www.srdc.metu.edu.tr/webpage/projects/artemis/home.html) to find more detailed information about other countries.

(NHS) personal identification code links the various system-specific personal identification codes of citizens [1].[8]

There are also major differences that relate to the scope of the identifier used. The (unique) identifier can be used for healthcare related matters only or it can be used for affairs that transcend healthcare. Out of the surveyed countries in the FIDIS study, we found that only the UK use unique national patient identifiers which are specific for the domain of health care [1] [5]. Currently, the British health numbers are still used both for administrative (billing) and medical reasons [5]. Contrary to the UK, some countries use a patient identifier that is not specifically designed for healthcare matters only. In Norway, Sweden and the Netherlands, national citizen identifiers are used to identify patients.[9] Identity management systems in healthcare can be based on the Social Security Number (SSN) as well. This is e.g. still the case in Belgium, where the diversity in patient identification systems is 'solved' in practice by the use of the SSN.[10] In Switzerland, there is a unique identification number for electronic records, which is upon now based on the social security number.

This short non-exhaustive overview of approaches in patient identification systems in Europe not only reveals the huge diversity between regions and/or countries but simultaneously confirms the need for actions by Member States of the EU or by other countries of the EEA to facilitate interoperability in the field. In the following section we emphasise the need to look beyond the technical aspects of the issue of interoperability by addressing a socio-technical point of view.

3 Interoperability of Patient Identifiers on a European Level

The socio-historical context has changed since eHealth came into the European picture. In the past, the need for interoperability was never so urgent and thus it made

[8] See regulation RD 183/2004 which regulates the individual health card: 'The regulation was approved in order for all NHS beneficiaries to have a unique personal identification code that would provide good service and would permit obtaining the appropriate medical information at every point of the public health system. The assignment of the NHS personal identification code is realised at the moment of the inclusion of the relative data to every citizen in the database protected by the NHS, developed by the Ministry of Health, and acts as the link for the different autonomous personal identification codes that every person may be assigned during his/her life': [1].

[9] In Norway they use control numbers. A control number is 'a national person identifier that is commonly used as the index key for medical records': [3]. In the Netherlands the Citizen Service Number (BSN) an unique identification number used throughout the public sector, is recently introduced as personal patient number.

[10] In Belgium, 'there is no common patient identification scheme used by GP (general practitioners, sic.) or hospitals. Many medical software applications introduce their own proprietary identifiers. Such schemes are generally limited to the assignment of a random number, which only guarantees uniqueness within that particular application. In practice, the identification issue is solved through the comparison of administrative information and often inclusion of the INSS. Belgian's Unique Social Security Number (INSS) is an extension of the national numbering scheme': [8]. On several occasions in the past, the Belgian privacy committee contemned the national practice and called for a 'unique patient identification number specifically dedicated to the processing of personal information regarding healthcare': [8].

perfect sense for institutions to develop their own software and (privacy-friendly) context-specific patient identifiers [4]. Today however, in several aspects, interoperability has become a condition sine qua non for eHealth [7].

From a technical point of view, both semantic and syntactic interoperability[11] are vital. There must be agreed upon a common understanding about patient identifiers and technical standards and platforms must be developed so that patient identifiers can be exchanged in secure ways and provide authorised cross-border access to patient information. From an economical point of view, interoperability of patient identifiers facilitates free movement of people and data smoothing the progress of a European Health Information Space. For business, the 'potential value of recognizing and taking advantage of trends and opportunities in the interoperable exchange of health information among disparate entities is enormous' [4]. From the social point of view, interoperability of patient identification makes it easier for citizen to receive healthcare (at home or abroad) and facilitates public health research and epidemiological studies. From a legal point of view, rules and regulations about interoperability are important to smooth the progress of eHealth business and to avoid legal disputes e.g. about access rights.

The question is thus: How to make patient identification interoperable between organisations and even regions or nations? Although a lack of interoperability in the field is perceived (see section 2), it is without doubt that the topic is getting attention by the EU. Acknowledging the diversity in systems, the necessity for interoperability with regard to eHealth as well as the wish to develop a European Health Information Space by 2015, the European Commission recently launched a recommendation to enhance interoperability in eHealth [14]. The recommendation asks Member States of the EU as well as countries of the EEA to work together, to discuss good practices and to develop a European dynamic in order to make patient identification in Europe more interoperable [14]. These efforts are in line with the Action Plan for a European eHealth Area [10]. In order to find a global and common approach to patient identifiers in Europe, the EU suggests looking at recent developments in the field of standardization[12] and in the context of the European Health Insurance Card.

We argue that interoperability of cross-border patient identification systems (whether on the institutional, the sub-national or supra-national level) should be regarded as a complex issue, in which technical, economical, social, legal and normative aspects all influence the process. Or as the European Commission stated: 'the notion of *eHealth interoperability* used here is not only the technical definition of the term that relates to connecting systems and exchanging information, but also seeks to

[11] 'Syntactic interoperability (which we term as messaging layer), involves the ability of two or more systems to exchange information. Syntactic interoperability involves several layers: network and transport layer (such as Internet), application protocol layer (such as HTTP or email), messaging protocol and message format layer (such as ebXML messaging or SOAP), and the sequencing of the messages. Semantic interoperability is the ability for information shared by systems to be understood at the level of formally defined domain concepts': [9].

[12] In Europe, CEN TC251 (The European Committee for Standardization, Technical Committee for Health Informatics), CENELEC (Comité Européen de Normalisation Electrotechnique) and ETSI (European Telecommunication and Standardisation Institute) are working on the domain. These three organisations received a standardisation mandate from the EC [16]. The HISA, EHCRA and Health Level Seven (HL 7) standards are considered as highly useful (see e.g. [17]).

recognise the concept of connecting people, data, and diverse health systems, while particularly taking into account the relevant social, political, regulatory, business/industry, and organisational factors.' [14]. Looking from such a point of view, the creation of a system for cross-border identification of patients across Europe is perceived as a tremendous task: 'it could even be argued that the technical requirements for eHealth interoperability are the easy part of the challenge' [20].

It is especially important to take into account the fragmentized and multi-dimensional character of the issue for the reason that the organization of patient identification is subject to the subsidiarity principles of the European Union.[13] The interoperability process starts from bottom–up, taking into account good practices selected out of existing identification systems in healthcare institutions and regions. However, these systems must be seen as the result of specific needs and practices in a particular socio-historical context.

The efforts to enhance interoperability should of course take into account the existing data protection requirements as well as the specific underlying normative attitudes of healthcare system, the role of insurance companies, the existing approaches in the field of identity management etc.[14] For example in some countries, due to legal and socio-historical reasons, there exists no national identification number (Germany, Hungary) whereas in other countries such as Norway, Sweden or Turkey a national personal identifier is common and often used as an index key for medical records [3].

Rather than creating a whole new method to identify patients throughout Europe, the European Council suggests allowing Member States to maintain their own (national, regional) patient identification number systems. Only at a later stage, interoperability should be developed at the European level. An alternative solution would be to create a European Patient Identifier (EPI), which can easily and safely be used for matters of cross-border healthcare delivery and European public health statistics and which would be interoperable with existing national health identifiers [5].[15]

In this section we mainly focused on the examples mentioned in the FIDIS deliverable [1] but of course there are a lot of other efforts going on in the field of eHealth interoperability that relate to patient identification. Leaving aside the necessity of interoperability, eHealth applications and services count on unique identification of patients.

4 Unique Identification of Patients

In the context of eHealth, patient identifiers must be able to *uniquely identify* citizens across healthcare organizations. Unique identification is essential for integration of information across healthcare contexts, for creating a long-life view of one's health and for the development of a Health Information Space. Patient identifiers can either be unique or not. The former are permanently assigned and unique across the entire

---

[13] According to the Article 8 (7) Data Protection Directive 95/46/EC, Member States have the duty 'to determine the conditions under which a national identification number or any other identifier of general application may be processed'.

[14] Although it is very interesting to investigate in further detail how specific healthcare and insurance models influence patient identification systems, this falls outside the scope of the paper.

[15] See further section 5.

(cross-border) healthcare environment whereas non-unique patient identifiers depend on the healthcare provider, the system or/and the time [19]. Examples of unique patient identifiers are e.g. the SSN and biometric identifiers. As seen in the previous sections, the SSN is indeed often used to uniquely identify patients. This poses privacy questions (see also next section). But what if a Member State opposes the use of such a unique health identifier for each citizen in Europe? Interestingly, unique identification can be done by using a unique identifier or alternatively by the use of non-unique identifiers. The Artemis project developed a 'Patient Identification Process (PIP) Protocol' suitable for cross-border for interoperability without the need to use unique identifiers [3].[16] This PIP protocol provides a solution for locating and accessing prior clinical records facilitating continuity of care, an aspect that is likely to become very important in the healthcare sector. The HL7 MPI mediation standard can be mentioned as another example of unique identification of patients without using unique identifiers [19].

In any case, throughout the process of creating interoperable identifiers that uniquely identify patients, important choices influencing the privacy side of the story are made. In the following section we discuss this topic.

5 What about Privacy?

Without doubt, patient identifiers are 'essential but also privacy-invasive tools of eHealth' [1]. Privacy can be at risk if interoperable patient identifier systems facilitate exchange and access of sensitive information. However, Hippocrates' Oath still remains and is reflected in today's privacy framework (e.g. in the Directive 94/46 EC).[17] Existing privacy regulatory frameworks ensure the protection of personal data and define the conditions under which processing of personal data is allowed.

We argue that privacy protection of patients is depending on administrative, technical, legal, social and organizational measures. Regarding security, there should be a differentiation between the identification function and access control function (for audit trails and /or preventive actions). The design of the patient identifier should be content free and irreversible to guarantee anonymity. Finally, staff and user training seem to be absolutely preconditional for privacy [19].

In the following several concrete suggestions for privacy-friendly patient identification systems are made. First of all, privacy-friendly patient identification schemes must be able to assure that citizens have individual control over who uses their data and for what purposes. It is therefore suggested by [12] that 'voluntary, patient-controlled system of unique identifiers is the only way to ensure acceptable levels of safety and accuracy when exchanging medical information through an electronic national network'. However, unique identifiers have the potential to link data from electronic health records with other data sources. Especially the use of the Social Security Number (SSN) as a patient identifier can imply serious privacy risks. When using the SSN as a patient identifier,[18] health related data can easily be linked with other personal information, creating a bearing surface for profiling practices.

[16] For more information we refer to the Artemis deliverables: [18].
[17] For a detailed overview of legal aspects of eHealth, we refer to [11].
[18] As is the actual practice in Belgium and Switzerland.

We therefore suggest not the use the SSN as a direct patient identifier to provide access to information in medical records. However, the SSN can be used as the basis for the creation of a unique patient identifier but only when irreversibility and thus anonymity is guaranteed. By using a 'double hashing method' (a first coding from SSN to health identification number (for health portal) and a second one (for data processing shelter) [6]), the privacy risks can be minimized. This is so because there is an irreversible transformation of the SSN. This approach has been proposed by the Belgian HEPI GO project. Interestingly, two test phases were planned: first a 'primary HEPI' which is not 100% anonymous will be implemented, whereas in the second phase they want to use a 'secondary HEPI' (using pseudonyms and Trusted Third Parties to guarantee the anonymity of the citizen/patient) [8].[19] The double hashing method has also been suggested by [6] for interoperable yet privacy-friendly patient identification numbers in France.[20] As a thumb of rule, reversible encryption techniques should be avoided when using the SSN as a patient identifier [5]. The approach of Quantin et al. ensures factual interoperability at the European level by including a family–component in the hashed SSN [6].[21] This is very important for realizing a Health Information Space in Europe and for public health research and epidemiological studies in general. The approach could facilitate the use of a Unique European Health Identifier in compliance with the existing data protection framework. The already mentioned approach developed by the Artemis project also shows that it is possible to have interoperable unique patient identification that allows undirected searches for patient records without violating data protection requirements [3].

It has also been suggested that a high level of confidentiality of the medical data in electronic patient files can be reached by differentiating the access modalities of various actors (healthcare providers, administrative levels, public bodies, insurances). This could be done by separating the overall unique patient identifier into several unique identifiers that are purpose–specific. This means e.g. that administrative levels use a purpose-specific identifier which allows them to see only the information necessary for billing purposes and not the medical information [1].

---

[19] Recently however the Belgian privacy commission permitted the classic SSN to be used as a means of obtaining access to citizens' medical data through the Belgian eHealth platform. The commission's new position represents a 180-degree turn on its previous stance; it may jeopardize the current level of privacy protection of Belgian citizens [13].

[20] Method utilizing a derived social security number with the same reliability as the social security number. We show the anonymity techniques classically based on unidirectional hash functions (such as the secure hash algorithm (SHA-2) function that can guarantee the security, quality, and reliability of information if these techniques are applied to the Social Security Number). Hashing produces a strictly anonymous code that is always the same for a given individual, and thus enables patient data to be linked. Different solutions are developed and proposed in this article. Hashing the social security number will make it possible to link the information in the personal medical file to other national health information sources with the aim of completing or validating the personal medical record or conducting epidemiological and clinical research. This data linkage would meet the anonymous data requirements of the European directive on data protection.': [6]. See also [15] and [16].

[21] The Hashed SSN alone can not provide enough input for the creation of a European Health Information Space. See [6].

Also, content-free patient identification numbers are useful against privacy – intrusions. In other words, no information about the sex, age or place of birth of the patient should be revealed by the patient identification number [5]. For example, Switzerland will introduce a new social security number (after July 2008). This number will no longer entail sensitive information - it will be a totally random number.

6 Conclusion

In the context of eHealth, (unique) patient identifiers are critical but also privacy - invasive tools. Actually, a lot of efforts are made to discuss good practices and to develop a common understanding and vision about interoperability of patient identifiers in Europe. Although the time seems right for European Member States to develop more interoperability between patient identification systems, evidence shows that the road is still long.

Accepting the fact that existing patient identification systems in healthcare institutions, regions or nations should be seen as a particular outcome of specific socio-economical, legal and historical circumstances, it is without doubt that there are a lot of other aspects besides semantic and syntactic interoperability that have to be dealt with. For example: Do Member States want to use something as a (unique) European Patient Identifier for medical purposes? How to create interoperability between national patient identifiers if not all countries are used to have unique identifiers for citizens and some legislations explicitly prohibit this? Alternatively, interoperable solutions that do not rely on the use of unique national identifiers are proposed.

Interoperability of patient identification systems is crucial for realizing the prospects of eHealth at the individual level as well as at the community level. During the process of making patient identifiers in Europe interoperable, important choices have to be made. This will have consequences (even unintended) on the future use of medical data. We therefore believe it is essential to strive for interoperable solutions to uniquely identify patients throughout Europe that ensure strong privacy guarantees.

Acknowledgement

Research done by the author was funded by FIDIS (Future of Identity in the Information Society, Network of Excellence, FP 6 of the European Union, www.fidis.net) for FIDIS deliverable 4.11, edited by Soenens and Leys (2008).

The author thanks the participants of the FIDIS/IFIP Summer School 2008 to whom a draft version of this paper was presented for their feedback and insightful questions.

References

1. Soenens, E., Leys, M. (eds.): eHealth identity management in several types of welfare states in Europe. FIDIS Deliverable D4.11 (2008), http://www.FIDIS-project.eu

2. Wilson, P., Lessens, V.: Rising to the challenges of eHealth across Europe's regions. Report of the High Level Conference on eHealth, Malaga (2006), http://ec.europa.eu/information_society/activities/health/docs/events/ehealth2006malaga/ehealth2006rising_challenges_ehealth_europe_regions.pdf
3. Eichelberg, M., Aden, T., Thoben, W.: A Distributed Patient Identification Protocol based on Control Numbers with Semantic Annotation. Int'l Journal on Semantic Web & Information Systems 1(4), 24–43 (2005), http://www.srdc.metu.edu.tr/webpage/projects/artemis/publications/ijswis_eichelberg.pdf
4. RIDE: Publishable Final Activity Report D1.1.6 (2008), http://www.srdc.metu.edu.tr/webpage/projects/ride/deliverables/D1.1.6RIDEPublishableFinalActivityReport-v1.1.doc#_Toc189556115
5. Quantin, C., et al.: Unique Patient Concept: a key choice for European epidemiology. International Journal of Medical Informatics 76, 419–426 (2007)
6. Quantin, C., et al.: Building Application-Related Patient Identifiers: What Solution for a European Country. International Journal of Telemedicine and Applications 2008, article ID 678302, 5 pages (2008), http://www.hindawi.com/GetArticle.aspx?doi=10.1155/2008/678302&e=cta
7. High Level Group on Health Services and Medical Care: Report from the High Level Group to the Employment, Social Affairs, Health and Consumer Protection Council on 6-7 December 2004. HLG/2004/21 FINAL (2004)
8. HEPI-GO Project Belgium: Final Project Report (2006)
9. Dogac, A., et al.: Key Issues of Technical Interoperability Solutions in eHealth and the RIDE project. eHealthNews.EU Portal (2007), http://www.ehealthnews.eu/images/stories/pdf/ride.pdf
10. European Commission: eHealth making healthcare better for European citizens. COM(2004)356 final (2004)
11. European Commission: Legally eHealth. Putting eHealth in its legal European Context (Study report prepared by Van Dosselaere C. et al.) 14–16 (2008)
12. Medical News Today: Creation Of Voluntary Unique Patient Identifiers For Exchanging Electronic Health Records Called For. Medical News Today (December 2007), http://www.medicalnewstoday.com/articles/91766.php
13. De Morgen: Vragen rond privacy bij eHealth (30/05/2008)
14. European Commission: Recommendation of 2nd July 2008 on cross-border interoperability of electronic health record systems (COM(2008)3282 final) (2008), http://ec.europa.eu/information_society/activities/health/docs/policy/20080702-interop_recom.pdf
15. Quantin, et al.: Proposal of a French Health Identification Number Interoperable at the European Level. In: Medinfo Proceedings of the 12th World Congress on Health (Medical) Informatics; Building Sustainable Health Systems, pp. 503–507 (2007)
16. European Commission, DG Enterprise and industry: Standardisation mandate addressed to CEN, CENELEC and ETSI in the field Of Information and Communication Technologies. M/403 (2007), http://www.ict.etsi.fr/Activities/Documents/Mandate403_eHealth.pdf

17. Patient identity in eHealth: Project fact sheet 'patient identity in eHealth. Exchange of good practices in eHealth' (2005), http://ec.europa.eu/information_society/activities/health/docs/studies/patientehealth-fp6book.pdf
18. Artemis: Building interoperability into medical information systems, http://www.srdc.metu.edu.tr/webpage/projects/artemis/publications/istresults.doc
19. Appavu, S.I.: Analysis of Unique Patient Identifier Options. Final Report prepared for the Departement of Health and Human Services (1997), http://www.ncvhs.hhs.gov/app0.htm
20. European Commission: Connecting eHealth Services. Europe's Information Society Portal, http://ec.europa.eu/information_society/activities/health/policy/interoperability/index_en.htm
21. European Commission: Press Release 'Commission takes steps to promote patient safety in Europe', IP/08/1973, December 15 (2008)
22. Stroetmann, K.: Final project report Deliverable 5.3 in the framework of the eHealth ERA project (September 2007)

A Survey on Transparency Tools for Enhancing Privacy*

Hans Hedbom

Dept. of Computer Science Karlstad University Karlstad, Sweden
Hans.Hedbom@kau.se

Abstract. This paper provides a short survey on transparency tools for privacy purposes. It defines the term transparency tools, argues why they are important and gives examples for transparency tools. A classification of transparency tools is suggested and some example tools are analyzed with the help of the classification.

1 Introduction

At our department we are involved in EU research projects (among them FIDIS [9], PRIME [6] and PrimeLife [12]) aiming at understanding the consequences to privacy for a user[1] in a networked world and at constructing concepts and tools that can help a user to regain control over her personal sphere. One goal of these projects is to increase the possibilities that a person has to know what really happens with her personal data, i.e. what data about her are collected and how they are further processed, by whom, and for what purposes. This is important in order to judge if the data are processed in a legal manner and whether they are correct. The concept usually used to describe these properties is the notion of transparency. Consequently, one of our goals is to develop tools and concepts for increased transparency. As a first step to reach this goal and to get an idea of what has been done in the area and the current state of the art, a short survey of transparency tools for privacy purposes has been conducted. In this process we have also tried to find a way of categorizing these tools. Even though we realize the great importance legal, social and economical tools, frameworks and

* Part of the research leading to these results has received funding from the European Community's Seventh Framework Program (FP7/2007-2013) under grant agreement n 216483. The information in this document is provided "as is", and no guarantee or warranty is given that the information is fit for any particular purpose. The above referenced consortium members shall have no liability for damages of any kind including without limitation direct, special, indirect, or consequential damages that may result from the use of these materials subject to any liability which is mandatory due to applicable law.

[1] We imply that "user" and "end user" throughout this paper are also data subjects in the system.

V. Matyáš et al. (Eds.): The Future of Identity, IFIP AICT 298, pp. 67–82, 2009.

sanctions play in the transparency area[2], the focus of the survey has been on technical tools. This paper describes the results of the survey.

2 Why Transparency Tools?

In todays Internet environment, information on individuals tend to get collected and revealed to a number of different actors. The distributed nature of the World Wide Web and services like e-shopping, e-health, on line community services and e-government makes it hard for a user to keep track on where information about her is stored, to whom it is handed out and for what purposes it is used. This situation will be even worse with the advent of so called intelligent environments or AmI environments which are highly distributed networks of sensors and computers gathering information on their environments and possibly trying to adopt the environments to a users preferences. Some authors have argued [16,13] that in these environment the traditional privacy paradigm of concealment (i.e. controlling the access to (or even the existence) and distribution of personal data) does no longer hold or is impossible to maintain. Instead they claim that the main focus must be on controlling the proper use of the data. In order to do this a user must be able to get information on how her personal data is used and possibly from which sources it originated. To achieve this type of control transparency tools play an important role. Transparency is a legal privacy principle, which also can be derived from the EU Data Protection Directive 95/46/EC [10]. When a data controller is requesting personal data from a data subject, the data controller must inform the data subject about her identity (name and address), the purposes of data processing, the recipients of the data and all other information required to ensure the processing is fair ([10] Art. 10) The data subject has the right to access all data processed about her, to demand the rectification, deletion or blocking of data that is incorrect or is not being processed in compliance with the data protection rules ([10]Art. 12). The users right to access also includes the right to obtain knowledge of the logic involved in any automatic processing of data concerning her. Even though there is no legal requirement that users can exercise their rights on line, we believe that such a state of affairs would be beneficial for all parts involved and could also make the process more administratively efficient.

3 The Scope of the Survey

In order to define the scope of the survey and to understand what we are examining we need to define what we mean by a transparency tool for privacy purposes. First of all, transparency as such can be required for more than privacy purposes e.g. different types of audit and control to make sure that company finances are in order or that procedures and processes are managed and used in an appropriate

[2] Even though there exists technical tools for transparency we believe many of them require additional legal tools or technologies such as reputation systems and black lists in order to be fully effective. This is because there is limited use in getting the information if the person involved cannot act against the service if the promises are broken or her personal data is misused in some way.

manner and of course there exists tools to aid in those cases. In this survey we have limited ourselves to consider tools that have the objective to help the user to enhance her privacy. Thus, we focus on transparency tools for enhancing privacy. So, what is a transparency tool for privacy purposes then? FIDIS [9] has in its deliverable D7.12 [5] defined a concept called Transparency Enhancing Technologies (TETs). Their provisional definition of TETS is literally [5]:

"Type A: legal and technological instruments that provide (a right of) access to data processing, implying a transfer of knowledge from data controller to data subjects, and/or

Type B: legal and technological instruments that (provide a right to) counter profile the smart environment to 'guess' how one's data match relevant group profiles that may affect one's risks and opportunities, implying that the observable and machine readable behaviour of one's environment provides enough information to anticipate the implications of one's behaviour."

However, their vision on TETs is for tools that make it possible for individuals to assess how profiles will be used on them and to be able to judge how different actions will influence the outcome of this profiling. In our view this definition is too narrow considering the implications of the word transparency. Further, since we do not consider legal tools the definition is too wide in that sense.

In [7], Hansen defines transparency tools as follows: "When dealing with personal data and privacy, transparency tools are tools which can provide to the individual concerned clear visibility of aspects relevant to these data and the individuals privacy." This definition is, we believe, too narrow since it only takes into account the end user and not entities that act on behalf of user's or in the interest of the user to increase the user's privacy such as data protection officers.

Based on the definitions above and on the classification on privacy mechanisms given in [13] we would like to give the following definition on transparency tools for privacy purposes (please note that by a proxy acting on behalf of the user we also include organizations authorized by other entities than the user to protect the privacy interests of the user) : A transparency tool for privacy purposes is a technological tool that has one or more of the following characteristics:

- gives information on intended collection, storage and/or data processing to the data subject, or a proxy acting on the behalf of the data subject, in order to enhance the data subject's privacy;.
- provides the data subject, or a proxy acting on the behalf of the data subject, with access to stored data and/or to logic of data processing in order to enhance the data subject's privacy;.
- provides counter profiling capabilities for a data subject, or a proxy acting on behalf of the data subject, in order to 'guess' how her data match relevant group profiles that may affect her risks and opportunities, implying that the observable and machine readable behavior of her environment provides enough information to anticipate the implications of her behavior.

To lessen the scope further we have excluded technologies that we deem as enabler technologies such as policy languages, obligation management and transfer protocols from the survey. Thus, technologies like P3P [15] and EPAL [4] are not considered in the survey even if they would be considered as a tool by themselves. However, tools that use these technologies and make them more accessible for the user are included.

4 The Privacy Risks of Transparency Tools

Transparency tools as such cannot only help the user to increase her privacy but could also if improperly designed actually be a severe privacy threat to the user. The reason for this is that since some of them give a lot of information to the user about her personal data and in some cases limited control over this data people masquerading as the user also will get this information and this control. Some of the transparency tools that provide information on how data has been processed, such as TAMI, also require the services side to keep extensive logs on user data and processing, which as such might be privacy-sensitive. Thus, systems that use these types of transparency tools need to have good access control mechanisms and routines to not turn the tool into a privacy threat. This in turn implies that there must be mechanisms in place to guarantee that data is only handed out and controlled by either the user concerned or somebody authorized by the data controller. In a networked environment with a lot of users this can be a complex and costly system to implement and manage.

5 An Attempt for a Classification

For designing privacy enhanced systems it is helpful to have a classification that can be used in order to compare different tools or choose the right tool for the system. Since we want to compare and analyze the tools in this survey we need some characteristics as parameters that can help us in this process. Because of this we will, in this section, describe a brief classification of transparency tools based on a number of characteristics that we believe are important to take into consideration. Please note that since we are in reality talking about two types of activities, i.e. data storage and processing, some tools might fall under different category regarding the data stored and regarding access to processes.

5.1 Possibilities of Control and Verification

One of the more interesting aspects of a transparency tool is how much control and verification on the process of gathering and processing personal information is given to the user. This gives an indication on how much the user/proxy can learn about the actual processing and also get a view on what is really stored about her. Roughly this parameter is divided into three categories.

1. **Promises:** In this case the user gets information on what the data controller promises to do or not to do with the data in the future. This category encompasses the tools that will present, or in other ways give access to, the privacy policy or other types of commitments from the gathering side in a more or less user-friendly manner, but give no on line or automatic way for the user/proxy to verify these claims.

2. **Read only:** In this case the user or her proxy can get access to information on what processing the data actually has gone through up to a specific point in time and/or to the stored personal data itself in a read only manner. This category could be combined with the "Promises" category either in the tool itself or by using another tool to retrieve/store the privacy policy to be fully effective. This is because we believe that the privacy policy negotiated with the data controller (in combination with applicable laws) is needed in order to make a sound judgment on whether a privacy violation has occurred or not.
3. **Interactive:** In the interactive category the tools, in addition to the properties in 2), have the ability to let the user or her proxy actively influence the stored data and/or the processing of the data in some way according to legal requirements or agreed on policies. This category could also be subdivided into "Fully Interactive" and "Partly Interactive" depending on whether the user can use the tool to manipulate all stored data and/or processing or just parts of it.

5.2 Target Audiences

Transparency tools can also be categorized according to their expected audience (i.e the users of these tools). In essence these could be divided into professionals and non-professionals (i.e. people that professionally do audits for privacy protection and the data subjects whose personal data is processed and stored). In the following we will call these categories Auditors/Proxies respective Data Subjects. Of course users and professionals come "in many shapes and sizes" and could probably be divided into further levels, e.g. beginners, intermediate, experts and so on and tools made for Auditors/Proxies could certainly be used by Data Subjects and vice versa. However, in this classification we will concentrate on the high level differences that one might expect between tools for these two target audiences and the properties that one would expect to find in a tool for the specific audience.

1. **Tools for Data Subjects:** Tools for data subjects are expected to have a high level of "user friendliness". In the transparency case this will generally mean that the information is presented in an easy to understand manner and that the privacy implications of different choices and actions are explained so that the data subject understands what she is doing and what consequences her action will have. In order to achieve this, these tools usually limit the information that is presented by using predefined choices and filters with limited customization and try to find alternative ways (e.g. icons or graphs) of presenting complex information properties. Tools for users are also expected to have a high degree of automatisation when it comes to interpreting policies or finding privacy violations. Finally, one would expect these tools to give advice on how to proceed or who to contact in case of privacy violations or questions.
2. **Tools for Auditors/Proxies:** Tools targeted towards Auditors/Proxies do not necessarily produce output that is presented or explained in a way that is supposed to be read or understood by non-professionals. One would also

expect these types of tools (especially if they are used for audits) to be transparent in themselves (i.e. to produce their own logs and audit trails) in order to get an understanding in how they have been used and on what data decisions are based on. Finally, these types of tools might give direct access to data or processes that are outside of what a Data Subject would be allowed to access or expected to handle or understand.

5.3 Scope

Another categorisation parameter is the amount of privacy information that the tool can make accessible to the user. From a privacy perspective this will give an indication on what level of transparency the tool offers and what a user can expect to gain by using the tool and from a security perspective it will help to judge the amount of information that could be revealed or compromised if the tool is compromised. We have chosen to call this aspect "the scope" of the tool and divided it into four levels. These levels are constructed from a user view and are based on what answer the tool is expected to give on the hypothetical question "Please give me all info that x has on me and how x has handled that information"

1. **Service Scope:** The tool will give transparency to information stored and processed by a single service.
2. **Organizational Scope:** The tool will give transparency to information stored and processed by a single organization.
3. **Conglomerate Scope:** The tool will give transparency to information stored and processed by a conglomerate of organizations (e.g. multiple governmental offices or big corporations).

5.4 Trust Requirements

Many solutions have requirements in order to achieve trust on the data controller side. With trust in this case we mean the level of assurance that a user can have that the data controller behaves as expected and that she does not try to cheat or deceive the user (e.g. by not following the negotiated privacy policy). These trust requirements can be either directly expressed in the solution or implicitly presented due to assumptions on the operation environment or the technology used. The levels we have chosen for the trust requirements are strictly speaking not a classification but rather consist of a number of high level trust components. This means that a solution can require more than one of the components described below. The ideal situation is when the user does not need to place any trust in the data controller at all in order to protect her privacy, thus the less trust needed the better it is. In the list of components below we do not discuss the technical, legal, social or economical means in order to implement the component since there are a number of ways of solving this. The high level trust components are the following:

1. **Trusted Server:** The server environment used in the solution is assumed to behave in a trusted manner. This generally means that enough mechanisms

to prevent or deter the server from cheating are implemented on the server side. Thus, we have to expect that the server behaves as expected and in a fair manner. Note that this notion also works in a p2p environment since a p2p connection at any point in time and for any transport direction can be divided into a client/ server relationship: In essence this means that both sides are a potential server and thus both fall under the same assumptions that are put on the server side.
2. **Trusted Third Party:** In this case the solution requires that parts of the responsibilities and functions in the solution are taken over by an impartial third party component. This component guarantees that even if one of the parties tries to cheat or violate negotiated policies, one can trust that the solution as a whole will continue to behave in a fair and trusted manner.
3. **Trusted Client:** The client environment used in the solution is assumed to behave in a trusted manner. This generally means that enough mechanisms to assure to a certain level that the client is not compromised or under the control of an attacker are present and that the client does not release data in an uncontrolled manner. Generally, one could infer that a solution that does not itself try to protect the data it uses on the client side is assuming a trusted client environment.
4. **No trust needed:** The solution itself is designed in such a manner that it, in some way, prevents (or makes it exceedingly hard for) the server and the client from cheating or misbehaving. This is achieved without the use of an external trusted third party to guarantee the trustworthiness of the solution.

5.5 Information Presented

In a sense transparency is all about achieving a balance of information. Because of this, it is valuable to know what type of information can be gathered and presented by the tool. Information of interest is not only personal data stored and processed by the data controller and the logic of the processing, but also information about the data controller herself (or rather the service provider or organization she represents). Such information need not necessarily be acquired from the data controller but can be harvested from other information sources. We have chosen to classify the type of information into three categories. Note that these categories are not orthogonal but rather complementary:

1. **Required information:** The tool gathers and presents information that a service provider has to provide according to the Law (in a EU context this would e.g. be national laws based on the EU Data Protection Directive 95/46/EC Art. 10 [10] (type of data processed, identity of the controller, for what purposes,)).
2. **Extended information:** The tool gathers and presents information given or harvested from the service provider that is not legally required but that increases the transparency for the user in a privacy context.
3. **Third party information:** The tool gathers and presents information given or harvested from other sources than the service provider that increases the

transparency for the user in a privacy context. This might e.g. be privacy seals, whether the service provider is blacklisted, reputation systems or security breach reporting systems.

5.6 Other Aspects

There are other aspects that could be interesting when comparing solutions but more from a designer/implementer perspective than from a user/provider perspective. In this section we will mention them briefly.

Technologies Used. The technology used in and by the tool probably plays an important part in both making the tool economically feasible and getting a widespread use. Standard protocols, languages and frameworks tend to mean that less work is needed to integrate the tool in new as well as legacy systems. Concerning technologies used we would like to differ between three high level aspects: Communication, Information retrieval and Infrastructure Requirements. Regarding communication the interesting aspects from our view point are the standards used and since many Internet services today are based on different web standards we would like to suggest a classification into three categories: predominately Web Standards, predominately non-web Standards and predominately proprietary solutions. The question of information retrieval is more or less a question of sophistication of the tool i.e. does it just retrieve the my stored data or can I get more information and will directly reflect in the possibilities of control and verification properties and scope properties that can be achieved by the tool. This aspect is not so much a categorization but rather a list of possible capabilities or technologies used e.g. data mining, transaction logging and direct storage access. Finally the Infrastructure Requirements are usually reflected in the trust requirements of the tool and might result in specialized hardware, software and architectural components being needed for e.g. trusted computing.

Security Requirements. As mentioned before transparency tools might impose security risks. Exactly how severe this risk is or what security requirements are needed is probably hard to judge looking at the tool itself since this also depends on the data being processed and the implementation of the tool. We will not elaborate these issues much further but rather list some aspects that will influence the security requirements of the solution. The list is not meant as an exhaustive list, but rather mentions the more important aspects that, from a transparency perspective (in a privacy context), influence the requirements. Normal server (and client) security practices and tools should be evaluated and used to secure the tool as one would do for any other application.

1. **Sensitivity of data:** The more sensitive the data is the higher the requirements on how they can be handled and who can get access to it. The consequences of a privacy violation can also be considered to be more severe for sensitive data. In many cases it can be hard to judge if the data is sensitive or not since the sensitivity is dependent not only on the data itself but

also on the data processing purposes and the context in which it is processed and stored.

2. **Concentration of data:** The higher the concentration of data, i.e. the larger the amount of identifiable information about an individual the tool has access to, the higher the privacy impacts are if the data is compromised.
3. **Ease of access:** The easier it is to get access to a transparency service and the more well known it is the better it is from a usability perspective. However, one would also expect well known and easy accessible services to be more prone to attacks especially if they contain information of value for potential attackers.

6 Examples of Transparency Tools

In this section we will give an overview of different types of transparency tools that are either available, under development or suggested in research papers. We also elaborate on the differences and commonalities of the example tools and classify them according to the classification given in section 5. Please note that the amount of space given to any specific solution is not meant in any way to reflect the importance of that tool.

6.1 The TAMI Project

TAMI [16] is a project at MIT/CSAIL laboratory aimed at creating a Transparent Accountable Data Mining (TAMI) system. The idea is to use technology present in (or developed in connection with) the Semantic WEB efforts. In connection with this it is part of a bigger project aimed towards making the WEB policy aware. The current descriptions of TAMI is highly geared towards law enforcement agencies and other governmental agencies using data mining to find evidence or other information about persons.

In [16] Weitzner et al. identify three distinct classes of rule violations that could occur in connection with data mining.

Adverse actions premised on factual incorrect antecedents.

Impermissible sharing of data beyond the collecting organization.

Adverse actions premised on interference from data where the data, while factually correct and properly in the possession of the user, is used for an impermissible purpose.

The TAMI system is designed to detect these types of violations and consists of a set of general-purpose interference components:

I. The Inferencing Engine: Used to analyze available data and to assess compliance with relevant rules.

II. The Truth Maintenance System: A persistent store fed by 1 and used to assess reliability of inferred results and to record justifications and proof antecedents.

III. Proof Generator: Used to construct proofs that adverse actions and critical transactions are justified by facts and permissible under applicable rules.

Using these components it is possible to construct an audit trail that can be used to trace the sources of a decision and also see if the data has been used and handled in a correct manner.

The TAMI system is still under development and does in the state described by [16] use XML and RDF in N3 format for data sources and transaction logs and N3 logic to express rules and policies. As far as we know there is no practical implementation of the TAMI system.

Looking at TAMI first we can easily infer that it is not primarily meant to be what we classified as a tool for data subjects but rather is meant as an Auditor/Proxy tool. Since it is based on information mined from different data sources without sending the usage policy to the data subject or inform the data subject on what data is gathered it can be considered as a pure "read only" system regarding the data and a "combination of read only and promises system" regarding the processing of the data since the proof-engine will give information on what processing rules that were used. The scope of the tool is hard to judge since it currently is only a research system and in itself has the potential to fall into any of the scope categories dependent on which sources it takes its data feeds from. Regarding the trust requirement one can derive that it does not really trust its clients (data sources) since it stores where the information comes from and where this source got it from i.e. the origin of the data and based on this it judges the trustworthiness of the data. However, as far as we can judge, the system as a whole requires a trusted server since there are still ample opportunities for the server to cheat regarding policies and data that is feed into the proof engine. Since the tool is aimed primarily as an audit tool one might argue that the auditor might act as a trusted third party and thus prevents the server from cheating. There is also the fact that the tool as it is currently described is meant for law enforcement and one might argue that these types of organizations are assumed to be trusted to play by the rules as default (at least in a democracy). Finally, since the primary purpose of TAMI is to act as an audit-trail for law enforcement and to be used in court we would argue that it presents legally required information and in some sense extended information since it presents the originating sources of the information.

6.2 Privacy Bird

Privacy Bird [1] is a browser plug-in that helps people to decide if the web pages they enter are compliant with their own privacy preferences. At the heart of the plug-in is a P3P policy interpreter and tools for constructing P3P privacy preferences in a user friendly fashion. When installed it will manifest itself as a bird icon in the browser that have different colors depending on how well the web servers P3P policy compares to the users preferences. If the policies match the users preferences the bird will be green, if they do not match, it will be red and if the web server does not have a policy it will be yellow. Different sounds are associated with the different states of the bird and can be used to further enhance the awareness of the user. It is also possible to get more information on the policy of the web server by using menus that turn up when the bird is clicked. This is information on what in the server policy that did not match the user policy, a summary of the server policy in human readable form, contact information to the web page owner and links to the full privacy policy of the web server.

Regarding privacy bird, one can deduce that it is definitely a "Promises" tool aimed at users. It has limited functionality and does not store transactions or promises and thus it is not usable as a Auditor/Proxy tool. Based on the discussion above, one could also infer that the tool really needs a trusted server if it is to be considered as a transparency tool. Regarding the scope it depends on the policy described but generally we would consider this as having a service scope. The information presented by privacy bird is strictly legally required since it only presents the privacy policy of the service.

6.3 The PRIME Project

PRIME [6] has been a European project that aimed at developing tools and concepts for privacy enhanced identity management systems. Within the project a proof of concept prototype was developed. This PRIME prototype consists of a PRIME-enabled server side that communicates with the PRIME enabled user side components. For PRIME-enabled web applications, a plug-in has been developed that will give access to the different tools developed by PRIME. Among those tools, four are interesting from a transparency perspective: The "Send Personal Data?" Dialog, the concept of PrifPrefs (privacy preferences), the Assurance Control Function (ACF) and the DataTrack. Below we will discuss each of these tools. The ACF has the main purpose of assuring the trustworthiness and integrity of the PRIME server. It performs this duty by using sub components to check whether the service provider is blacklisted or has a privacy seal and to verify the integrity of the hardware and the prime code. Since the tools are currently prototype tools and still further developed within the scope of the PrimeLife project we will describe their intended functionality and not the functionality actually implemented at this point.

The "Send Personal Data?" Dialog is in essence a policy aware automatic form filler that issued to obtain informed consent from the user for the disclosure of her personal data to a services side. The "Send Personal Data?" Dialog is following the approach of multi-layered privacy notices as suggested by the Art.29 Working Party [11]. When data needs to be sent to the server it will pop up and present the privacy policy of the web server and also help the user decide what privacy implications the data will have. The policy is presented to the user on a purpose by purpose manner acting as an interactive form filler wizard. It will start by asking the user which PrifPref she wants to use in this specific case. PrifPrefs are privacy preferences stored at the user side describing basically what data or types of data the user is willing to communicate and for what purposes those data may be collected and used. These privacy preferences can be bound to a web service (recipient), a pseudonym or a combination of these or they could be generally applicable based on a desired level of privacy. There are predefined PrifPrefs for anonymous usage and minimal data release. Based on the PrifPref the "Send

Personal Data?" Dialog will present the information the server wants purpose by purpose indicating if the data asked for and the purpose specified conforms with the stated PrifPref. The user can get more information on why and how the requested data violates her chosen PrifPref and possible consequences if the user decides to send the data anyway. If the actual data to use is stored in the PrifPref it is automatically filled in the form otherwise the user is asked to provide the information. If new information or new purposes are added to the selected PrifPref in this process the user can save this as a new PriPref for later use.

The Data Track is a view handler towards a history data base. The purpose of the tool is to let the user keep track of what data she has disclosed and to whom. The data is basically presented in two different ways. One view is a table with the different receivers of the data, how many times data has been sent out to this receiver and the dates of the different receiver sessions. By double clicking on a row in the table the receiver can get a more detailed view on exactly what data was sent during this session and the privacy policy that was agreed on when the transfer was performed. The other view is based on a card metaphor where the data are presented as a deck of cards that can be browsed through. The cards basically contain the same information as a table row with the addition of three buttons. These buttons are used for communication with the web server that the cards relate to and are used to either interactively (if the server has the ability) or in an offline manner request, the deletion of data, correction of data or access to the data that the server currently has stored about the user. The idea here is to make it easy for the user to exercise her legal rights towards the data controller. When double clicked, the card view will display the same detailed information as mentioned for the table view above. The Data Track also includes search functionality so that the user more easily can find answers to questions such as in what sessions certain information was given or what information a specific receiver has on the user.

The PRIME project tools in their current state of implementation are also to be considered as a "Promises" tool. However, the storage capabilities and the tracking of transactions makes it possible to verify and to some extent prove privacy violations if data or logs are apprehended. By implementing the transparency capabilities planned (service data access and secure logging on the server side) the data track would end up as a "interactive" tool both regarding the processing and storage of data. The PrifPrefs by themselves are just a tool for constructing privacy preferences and cannot be seen as a transparency tool. However, in connection with the "Send Personal Data?" Dialog and the local Data Track database it could be used to inform the user about what the collected data is used for and whether the services side really requests only the minimal amount of data from the user for the purposes of a requested service. As with TAMI the scope of the tool is dependent on the data sources used which in the data track case depends on the search capabilities of the data track and the data stored there. However in its current prototype implementation we would argue that it has a service scope.

Concerning the trust requirement the PRIME solution in its ideal implementation does not require a trusted server for the transparency services. However, the current prototype does require a trusted server and there are other parts of the PRIME solution that require trusted third parties (e.g. identity providers, black list providers and privacy seal granting authorities). Regarding the information presented the tool will present legally required information through the data track and the "Send data dialog" and third party information through the ACF.

6.4 Privacy Evidence

In a couple of articles (e.g [13]) Sackmann et al. discuss an approach based on what they call privacy evidence. The key components in this system is a secure logging facility and an automated privacy audit component to give the user information on how well a system fulfills the promised (or user provided) privacy policy. The general work-flow of the system is the following:

1. The data subject delivers her privacy policy to the system.
2. The data subject interacts with the system in some way and every action of the system is logged to a secure log file.
3. The data subject can inspect the logs with a specific low view tool that will provide the record that belongs to the respective data subject.
4. The log view created by the tool can be sent to an automatic audit facility that compares the log view with the provided privacy policy and construct privacy evidence. These give the user an indication of whether there has been any violation against the policy.

Central to this setup are, besides the policy language, three components: the secure log, the log view and the automated audit facility. The secure log used is a file of encrypted log entries where hash chains are used to make sure that the logs integrity is not tampered with and for key generation to insure forward security. Further some user identification information is used to create the keys for the encrypted entries, so that only entries related to a specific data subject are readable by that data subject (further details are given in [Sackman06]). The log view is constructed by traversing this file entry by entry and it constructs the view based on the identifier of the data subject. Finally, the automated audit is performed by constructing a violation set (i.e the set of rules describing violations of the rules described in the policy). This violation set is then compared with the log view and any match in this comparison process constitutes a violation of a policy rule.

Classifying Privacy Evidence we can first conclude that it is a "read only" tool regarding processing and as far as we can judge a "promises" tool regarding the stored data. This is however dependent on how extensive the logging is and what goes into the log's. Given the right log instructions, it might be a "read only" tool in the stored data area as well. It is also developed as a tool for data subjects. Concerning the scope it is dependent on how it is deployed, but because of the intensive logging needed it is hard to see that it would scale well to anything but a service scope. Concerning the trust classification the solution in its current state requires both a trusted server and a trusted third party. The information given is also dependent on the implementation but will, dependent on the legal context, be either required or extended.

6.5 The Amazon Book Recommendation Service

It is debatable whether this tool really falls under the scope of the survey. However we have chosen to include it since it is an example of customer influenced profiling.

Zwick et al. [17] discuss the Amazon book suggestion service as an example of a service where the customers can directly influence their user profile. As an Amazon customer it is possible to subscribe to a book recommendation service. This service will recommend different books to you based on your previous purchase. By clicking a link in the recommendation a window will appear. This window tells you which of your previous purchases were used to generate the recommendation. The user can then choose whether she wants to remove any of the "input" purchases from her profile so that it is not used as a base for recommendations any more.

The Book Recommendation Service is a tool for data subjects and a partially interactive tool regarding processing, but gives almost no information regarding stored data. Despite this it will give a very limited insights into the processes or the profiles used. Thus, we believe that the user has minimal capabilities as a customer to influence the result. She will only know that a specific input generated a specific result, but not why and how or even how the different input parameters relates to each other when multiple purchases are used to generate a result. Nevertheless, it is a good start since it makes part of the profile visible to the user. Regarding scope it has a service scope. Given the trust requirements there are implicit trusted server requirements to guarantee fairness since the data subject currently has no choice but to trust that Amazon actually behaves. The information given will, dependent on the legal context, be either required or required and extended.

6.6 Other Solutions

Of course there exist other transparency solutions than the once described in the example. However, due to space limitations in the paper we have chosen to just briefly mention some of them in this section. Concerning web services the Norwegian government gives its citizens the ability to see data stored on them by connected governmental offices through the "minside" web portal [14] similar portals are discussed or planed in other European countries. Regarding keeping track of transaction (i.e. similar responsibilities as part of the PRIME data track) "iJournal" [2], a part of Mozilla Privacy Enhancement Technologies (MozPETs) and "iManager" [8] for use with PDAs and mobiles should be mentioned. Microsoft CardSpace [3] also have some transaction tracking capabilities.

7 Conclusions

In the paper we have given an overview on transparency tools for enhancing privacy. We have given a definition on what we consider such a transparency tool and discussed and suggested a number of parameters that can be used to classify and compare implemented and suggested solutions for transparency tools. Finally, we have given a short analysis and comparison on some example solutions. The conclusion that can be drawn from this survey, taking both the example solutions and the referred solutions are the following:

On the control and verification side there are very few tools that can be classified as "interactive" (i.e. have the ability to let the user/proxy actively influence the stored data and/or the processing). This could be due to the fact that many companies see the information as a big asset and that it is necessary to have a very well developed identity management system and a good access control in order to not turn that type of functionality into both a privacy and a security risk. And thus they are reluctant to provide this type of service on line, but rather stick to manually based and analog methods for the service.

Regarding trust, all the actually implemented solutions and some of the suggested solutions do require (or assumes) a trusted server and some of them also require (or assume) some form of trusted third party. The reason for this might be the problems of practically implementing and maintaining a trusted computing environment and the lack of standards and requirements regarding privacy and privacy auditing. However, according to our experience, many companies and service providers behave in a responsible and fair manner since they are usually dependent on a good reputation in order to be profitable.

Most of the presented or referred solutions, as far as there is a possibility to make a judgment, have a service scope. However, there is one notable exception to this in the referred solution. This exception is the "minside" web service that in our opinion has a "Conglomerate Scope" or at least,as far as we know, has the intention to have this when it is fully implemented.

Acknowledgment

This work has partially been done within the scope of the European network of excellence FIDIS (www.fidis.net), PRIME (www.prime-project.eu) and PrimeLife (www.primelife.eu). The author would also like to thank Simone Fischer-Hbner, Stefanie Poetzsch, Marit Hansen and the participants of the FIDIS/IFIP summer school 2008 for helpful comments and discussions on this paper. Further I would like to thank the participants in the upcoming FIDIS D 7.12 deliverable working group for interesting and helpful discussions on transparency tools. FIDIS receives research funding from the European Unions Sixth Framework Program and the Swiss Federal Office for Education and Science. PRIME has received has received funding from the European Unions Sixth Framework Program and PrimeLife receives funding from the European Community's Seventh Framework Program.

References

1. Privacy Bird, http://www.privacybird.org
2. Brckner, L., Voss, M.: Mozpets – a privacy enhanced web browser. In: Proceedings of the Third Annual Conference on Privacy and Trust (PST 2005), Canada (2005)
3. Chappell, D.: Introducing windows cardspace. Technical report, Windows Vista Technical Articles (2006)
4. World Wide Web Consortium. Enterprise privacy authorization language (epal 1.2). W3C Member Submission (November 2003)
5. Hildebrant, M. (ed.): D 7.12: Biometric behavioural profiling and transparency enhancing tools. FIDIS Deliverable (work in progress)
6. Fischer-Hbner, S., Hedbom, H. (eds.): Deliverable d14.1.c framework v3. PRIME Project Deliverable (March 2008)
7. Hansen, M.: Marrying transparency tools with user-controlled identity management. In: Proceedings of Third International Summer School organized by IFIP WG 9.2, 9.6/11.7, 11.6 in cooperation with FIDIS Network of Excellence and HumanIT, Karlstad, Sweden (2007)
8. Jendricke, U., Gerd tom Markotten, D.: Usability meets security– the identity-manager as your personal security assistant for the internet. In: Proceedings of the 16th Annual Computer Security Application Conference (2000)
9. FIDIS (Future of Identity in the Information Society), http://www.fidis.net
10. European Parliament. Directive 95/46/ec of the european parliament and of the council of 24 october 1995 on the protection of individuals with regard to the processing of personal data and on the free movement of such data. Official Journal, L 281/31– L 281/39 39 (October 1995)
11. Article 29 Data Protection Working Party. Opinion on more harmonised information provisions. 11987/04/EN WP 100 (November 2004)
12. PrimeLife, http://www.primelife.eu/
13. Sackmann, S., Strker, J., Accorsi, R.: Personalization in privacy-aware highly dynamic systems. Communications of the ACM 49(9) (September 2006)
14. Min Side, http://www.norge.no/minside
15. W3C. The platform for privacy preferences 1.0 (p3p1.0) specification (April 2002)
16. Weitzner, J., Abelson, H., Berners-Lee, T., Hanson, C., Hendler, J., Kagal, L., McGuiness, D.L., Sussman, G.J., Waterman, K.: Transparent acountable data mining: New strategies for privacy protection. Computer Science and Artificial Intelligence Laboratory Technical Report MIT-CSAIL-TR-2006-007, Massachusetts Institute of Technology, Cambridge, MA, USA (2006)
17. Zwick, D., Dholakia, N.: Whose identity is it anyway? consumer representation in the age of database marketing. Journal of Macromarketing 24, 31 (2004)

When Spiders Bite: The Use, Misuse, and Unintended Consequences of "Silent Information"

Thomas P. Keenan

Professor, Faculty of Environmental Design, University of Calgary,
Calgary, Alberta Canada
keenan@ucalgary.ca

Abstract. Spiders are the workhorses of the Internet, silently (and almost invisibly) traversing the online world, 24 hours a day, looking for information that may be of interest to someone. It is being archived, organized, and sold, usually without the knowledge or consent of the subject of the information. Serious consequences are starting to appear, such as the withdrawal of three candidates from the October 2008 Canadian Federal election because of previous online indiscretions. While these were intentional if mis-guided postings, information made available without our consent can have equally devastating effects. Advances in artificial intelligence, as well as the increasing tendency to post more and more information, such as videos, will make the gathering, aggregation, and republishing of this "silent information" an increasingly important issue that must be addressed from the technical, social, ethical and legal perspectives, and sooner rather than later.

Keywords: Privacy, identity, profiling, data mis-use, tagging.

1 The Elephant in the Room

Well intentioned privacy experts, such as Canada's Privacy Commissioner, spend a great deal of ongoing effort [1] discussing the rules that should govern the collection and use of personally identifiable information. Despite cross-cultural differences, there is general agreement on the duty of companies and governments to handle personal information with great care.

Canada's *Personal Information Protection and Electronic Documents Act,* (PIPEDA) which received Royal Assent on April 13, 2000, requires that "an organization may collect, use or disclose personal information only for purposes that a reasonable person would consider are appropriate in the circumstances."

European countries are even more advanced in regulating the use of personal data, stemming in part from historical factors such as the Holocaust, "when the Nazis used public and church records to identify Jews to be rounded up and sent to concentration camps" [2] and manifested in national laws inspired by the landmark The European Union Directive on Data Protection of 1995 [3].

Even in the United States, which has a reputation of being less concerned about corporate invasion of privacy, and relatively more concerned about such action by

V. Matyáš et al. (Eds.): The Future of Identity, IFIP AICT 298, pp. 83–91, 2009.

governments, [2] credit bureaus are highly regulated and required to disclose information they hold on a person upon proper request. Many jurisdictions, notably the state of California, have enacted laws in the last five years mandating that breaches of private information be disclosed in writing. All of these are good and useful policies, but they generally refer to information collection and use that a person already knows about.

They are therefore missing the proverbial "elephant in the room."

In real life, vast amounts of personally identifiable information are being harvested, informally, in a variety of ways, in many jurisdictions, with no real consent of the subject. In many cases the subject of the information is unaware of the collection, and certainly not fully informed as to the ultimate destination of the information. This paper will confine itself to information that winds up on the Internet, partly because that medium has become the dominant way in which such information is shared, and also because, frankly, there is no way to really know what information is being collected and shared behind closed doors, though the author's previous paper [4] hints at the extent of government snooping projects such as CARNIVORE.

That paper, as well as an excellent study by Jones and Soltren, [5] demonstrated that social networking sites such as MySpace, Facebook and Nexopia are treasure troves of information about people that, with little difficulty, can be tied back to them. The privacy policies of such sites generally confer ownership of all content to the site operator, and provide little opportunity to effectively retract information, beyond simply deleting it and hoping for the best. Technical factors, such as the ease with which a digital photo can be copied off such sites, make any idea of "recalling your information" completely infeasible. You can virtually assume that if you post it, it will be copied by someone or archived somewhere.

The dominant automated technology for trolling the Internet for information is a robotic computer program called a "web crawler," or more commonly a "spider." Because computing power, storage, and bandwidth have become so inexpensive, it is now feasible for these agents to continually traverse the Internet, collecting whatever information they are directed to amass, copying it from webpages and other sources onto a company's own computers. Just as living spiders can inflict a painful or even fatal bite, the information gathered by computer spiders can cause harm by revealing personal or corporate data that was not intended to be shared. The damage is further complicated by the near impossibility of regaining control of that information once it has been harvested by a spider.

In addition to being easy to collect, information has become relatively easy to process into actionable intelligence. Artificial intelligence programs for extracting useful information and patterns from data have names like Adaptive Fuzzy Feature Map, (American Heuristics Corporation), PolyAnalyst 6.0. (Megaputer Intelligence Inc), and FactSpotter (Xerox). There are also companies that offer data mining as a professional service.

These existences of these programs and services provide a clue to the motivation of those who set spiders loose on the Internet. Just as biological spiders search for food and bite when threatened; these companies and individuals see economic advantage in collecting, organizing, using and selling the data that has been casually left around by others.

2 What Is "Silent Information"?

There is no word that comes to mind (at least in the English language) to precisely describe personal information that is available to others without the subject's explicit knowledge and/or consent. The closest would probably be Clarke's work [6] on "profiling" but that relates to the different problem of making inferences about someone, while silent information is already linked to a specific person.

As just one provocative example, USA/Israel-based Zoom Information Inc. (www.zoominfo.com) collects, without obtaining consent, a variety of information from mentions in newspaper articles, publicly posted presentations, etc. Just as Google's spiders prowl the Internet, looking for information to index, this company's robotic probes seek information that can be attached to an individual's profile. As of October 15, 2008, they claim to have information on over 44 million people and more than 4 million companies. Much of it is incomplete and incorrect. Most people do not even realize they are listed there. Yet ZoomInfo stays in business because some of their information is unique and so valuable in the business context (for example, senior executives and their contact information) that people will pay $99 US/month for access to it.

One could argue that posting a PowerPoint presentation that shows my job title as "Professor" is giving tacit permission for someone to put my name and that title into a database and sell access to it. However, I was also, to my chagrin, listed on ZoomInfo as Chairman of the Board of a US defense contractor, based on an erroneous name-based inference by the company's software.

Sometimes, the results of a ZoomInfo search are bizarre and even hilarious. The current Prime Minister of Canada, Stephen Harper, was listed for a period of time on this site with the job title "Reluctant Leader" and his company shown as "the Conservative party" simply because those terms appeared in a newspaper article about him. To be fair, there is a mechanism to "claim your profile" and correct errors, but the Honorable PM has not yet done so as of this writing.

Another source of potential embarrassment is the website DiplomacyMonitor.com, which archives press releases by the many countries for 90 days. Sometimes governments have been known to pull press releases off their official websites, but they remain readable at this site. There are also "whistleblower" sites such as www.wikileaks.org, which says it specializes in "source documents were classified, confidential or censored at the time of release."

During the Canadian federal election campaign, which culminated in the October 2008 vote, several candidates were forced to withdraw when embarrassing facts about them surfaced on the Internet.

Justin West, who was running for the New Democratic Party (NDP) in a riding in British Columbia, withdrew from the race after images of him swimming in the nude, which were over a decade old, were found on the Internet. Conservative Chris Reid was forced out because of evidence that he had made extremist comments on a personal blog. NDP hopeful Dana Larsen had to step down when a video of him smoking marijuana was found online. Past indiscretions simply never go away in the digital world.

More poignant and personal examples arise from companies such as ChoicePoint, a LexisNexis company which sells "comprehensive credentialing, background screening, authentication, direct marketing and public records services to businesses and nonprofit organizations." It goes far beyond credit information, which in the US is regulated under the Fair Credit Reporting Act. For example, this company gathers data by sending people into courthouses to copy out court records.

One woman (in a personal communication with the author) said she had trouble obtaining credit because of this company's refusal to include the full details of a Small Claims Court appearance she made (in which she was actually the plaintiff). The company has admitted to other blunders involving private information, at least one on a massive scale. In a Form 8-K regulatory filing with the US Securities Exchange Commission dated March 4, 2005, the company reported that "based on information currently available, we estimate that approximately 145,000 consumers from 50 states and other territories may have had their personal information improperly accessed." A Nigerian national named Olatunji Oluwatosin pleaded "no contest" to identify theft charges arising from this data breach, and was sentenced to ten years in prison. ChoicePoint was fined $10M US.

2.1 A Difficult but Necessary Definition

For the purposes of this paper, "silent information" is defined as **"**person-linked information which is deliberately collected and distributed without the subject's explicit understanding and consent to the full range of its ultimate use.**"**

The "person" could be a real human being, a company, a login name, a Second Life avatar, etc. This linking may be "explicit" (personally identifiable information is included) or "implicit" (it is possible to deduce the subject's identity). This would therefore exclude aggregated or demographic data, which is frequently being sold, except where the sample size is so small as to effectively disclose the identity of the subject.

Another dimension relates to the authoritativeness of the linking of data item A to person B. ZoomInfo, as discussed above, often mis-attributes data to people who have similar names, so it would generally be less authoritative than, for example, an official driver's license database.

Clearly the subject of "profiling" is closely related to "silent information." Even if it is not personally identifiable, the collection of data on a group of people can be used to take measures that may affect them. So, for example, Google provides aggregated data on the movies that are viewed by college students. This can be used by movie distribution companies to plan advertising campaigns to maximize their profits. While not, strictly speaking, an invasion of privacy, the net effect is some manipulation of behavior imposed upon a group that is, quite probably, unaware of how this is happening.

"Location-based marketing", in which for example SMS messages are sent to a user as he or she walks by a store, takes this one step further, leading people to wonder, "How did they know I would enjoy a latte right now?" The key point is not the intrusiveness of such a technique, but the fact that its operation is not transparent to the person being targeted.

2.2 What Is Consent?

The most challenging part of this definition is probably the phrase "without the subject's explicit understanding and consent." Precisely what does that mean? Is having accepted a posted privacy policy sufficient evidence of understanding and consent? Probably not.

Such policies are usually ignored. Khosrow-Pour's study [7] of over 261 US business graduate students, found high awareness (77.4% had "seen a privacy policy statement") but also low interest (54.4% said they had not "read a privacy policy statement"). Another study [5] of Facebook-using students at MIT, Harvard, NYU and the University of Oklahoma found 91% had not read the site's Terms of Service and 89% had "never read the privacy policy."

In addition, having plowed through a statement crafted in legal language does not imply understanding the full implications. For example, what if you have agreed to post something on website A and it is then harvested and posted on website B without your knowledge? The author was called by someone who objected that a memorial tribute she had written at a funeral home's website had been posted on another site "without my consent". She had basically lost control of this writing once it was posted online, and it didn't "feel right" to her.

The "rules of engagement" when it comes to the re-use of information posted online are often hazy because it is impossible to predict all the possible ways in which information could be re-purposed, now and in the future. In fact, information that may seem to have no or very slight privacy implications may well become very intrusive in the future. Consider, for example, the blood samples routinely taken from babies when they are born. In some places, these have been archived for decades and, now, with modern technology, they could suddenly become a treasure trove of DNA information.

2.3 What Is "Deliberate vs. Accidental Disclosure?"

There are certainly breaches that happen without the consent of the site operator. Ample illustration of this came in the August 2008 "Facebook virus" crisis, in which someone was able to send messages to Facebook users that appeared to be from their "Friends" on the system. The goal was to get victims to download and execute the "codecsetup.exe" file which installs the GAMPASS virus. The unauthorized use of the profile photos of "Friends" conferred credibility to the attack, and was a triumph of social engineering against Facebook users, who have been characterized as "notoriously naïve when it comes to security awareness" [8].

A 2007 study by Sophos PLC [9] revealed that 41% of Facebook users contacted at random divulged personal information to a fictitious person, created for the study. At the same time a Facebook spokesperson estimated that less than 20% of users have changed their privacy settings from the default.

Site operators like Facebook can be victim of their own internal errors, even in the absence of malicious outsiders. Sophos reported in July 2008 that personal data on 80 million Facebook users was compromised because "a security slip-up by the website during the process of a public beta test of its new design for members' profiles left birth date information exposed"[10]. Facebook quickly fixed the problem.

One might argue that at least Facebook users took some voluntary action to post their information, such as real birth date, even if their intention for its use was not properly respected. An even clearer case of accidental disclosure happened at Columbia University. On June 10, 2008, the Vice President responsible for Student Auxiliary & Business Services wrote individual letters [11] to a large group of people, noting that "one archival database file containing the housing information of approximately 5,000 current and former undergraduate students was found on a Google-hosted website" and that "your name and Social Security number were included in the file". While these students were probably aware that this information was in the hands of their university, they certainly never expected it to be found on the public Internet.

Accidents like this will happen, and the laws and policies to deal with them are still evolving, both in government legislation and in court cases. The author [12] suggested a mechanism which would provide monetary compensation to victims of identity theft if it could be linked back to gross negligence on the part of a company that held information on them, and in fact that is exactly how the TJX data breach is being handled, with up to $30 US in compensation being offered as compensation to most self-declared victims. (see www.TJXsettlement.com.)

2.4 Technical Issues Affecting Silent Information

It should be noted that website operators, Internet service providers, etc. may need to make use of user-posted information for purely technical reasons such as backups and system optimization, or to comply with lawful requests from appropriate authorities, including the removal of inappropriate content. Most jurisdictions, and certainly Canada in its PIPEDA act [1] make allowances for this.

One of the simplest forms of "silent information" is the website that sent you to another place on the Internet. While the designers of the original Internet Protocol suite probably never anticipated the extent of interest in your navigation history, it has become a "hot topic" because of its value in e-commerce settings, i.e. to pay the site that drives traffic to a commercial site.

There is no universal mechanism for keeping track of who really was visited an open website (one that does not require account/password type authentication) beyond recording the IP address and the referrer link. This mechanism is laid out in RFC2616 (July 1999) updated by RFC 2817 (May 2000). However, IP addresses are of limited utility and can be spoofed by knowledgeable users. Therefore, website operators turn to other mechanisms.

Cookies (strings of data left on a computer by a website to facilitate tracking on subsequent visits) have been identified as potential privacy violation and explicitly addressed, e.g. in the 2002 European Union telecommunication privacy directive [13] which requires the user be informed of the attempt to store a cookie and given the option to refuse it. Outside of Europe, cookies are still routinely set, though most browsers can be configured to refuse or challenge them.

Web bugs (usually small e.g. 1x1 pixel images, which require downloading from a server) are another tracking technique that can log whether web pages are being read and if so by what IP address. This is useful to spammers, e.g. for identifying "live" email addresses, and for other marketing purposes. Some email clients are counteracting this technique by asking explicitly for permission to download images.

3 Legal, Ethical, Policy and Social Issues

Non-technical policy questions abound in this area. Who owns information that has been harvested online? What rights do people have to get it corrected? How does this play out in a cross-border situation? What is the legal status of deliberately planted "dis-information"? They are just starting to be addressed in the courts. In July, 2008 a UK judge awarded 22,000 GBP to a man who was the victim of "Facebook libel" because of a fraudulent and malicious profile created by others [14]. Lawyers are even being told to analyze their clients' online presence and to review any blogs and emails before their opponents can raise them in court [15].

In a case that is still before the Canadian and US courts, a person has posted a photograph of the leader of a Canadian organization with the comment "This person should be killed." There is a significant difference between the laws in those two countries regarding whether or not this is "protected speech" (e.g. under the First Amendment to the US Constitution), "hate speech", or an incitement to commit a criminal act.

Another fascinating development is the move to link an individual's DNA information to other personal information held in databases. DNA is collected by law in many jurisdictions from those convicted or even accused of crimes. It is also surrendered voluntarily for purposes such as paternity testing. Google has invested in at least two companies (Navigenics and 23andMe) that work in this area. DNA provides a non-refutable, highly authoritative validation of identity. Once a link is made between a person's DNA and online persona, the concept of online anonymity becomes essentially moot.

Even without DNA linking, it has been shown, for example by George Danezis at the FIDIS/IFIP Summer School in Brno in September, 2008, that assumptions about gaining true anonymity by the use of "anonymizer" programs such as Tor (available at www.torproject.org) may well be unfounded. In addition, information that is now effectively anonymous, or of little interest, can easily be saved and processed in the future, with greater computing power and superior algorithms, leading to a retroactive breach of privacy.

Should we have expectations of privacy in the online world? Do we? At least one study [16] suggests that bloggers have abandoned any notion of privacy. The move to "open source" content provides further evidence of a trend towards freer dissemination of information. Just as philosophers and lawyers needed to define a community standard for obscenity 50 years ago, perhaps we will need an understanding about what is "reasonable privacy" in the near future.

4 Information Tagging – At Least a Partial Solution

The inability of some of the largest media companies in the world to prevent piracy of their movies and music gives a clue as to how difficult it would be to actually keep track of the spread and possible misuse of one's personal information. Just as someone can sneak a video camera into a movie theatre or concert, if one can display information on a screen, it's possible to capture and re-enter it manually, obliterating any attempt to control it. But it's still worth trying.

Let's consider a very restricted problem – tracking where your "Facebook profile photo" may have migrated online. You could "watermark" it visibly, noting that you do not authorize further distribution. There is also steganography software that will allow you to put invisible codes into the image to help in identifying it. Europol already administers [17] a database of the checksums of images used in child pornography investigations to assist in subsequent cases.

But how would you know where to look for your photo? We may be getting close to a solution for that. It turns out that several companies, notably Google [18] and Idée Inc. [19] are working on "visual search engines" to help content owners track images by visual identification, even if the image has been altered, e.g. by Photoshop. The latter company's TinEye project is now in a public beta trial, but as of August, 15, 2008, only accesses 701 million images so a visual search using my Facebook profile photo didn't show any proliferation. However, Hillary Clinton's photo popped up as being copied in 22 different places as strange as www.thisisbigbrother.com.

5 The Future

Should personal information be explicitly "tagged" for its acceptable use? How would we even anticipate those uses? Several commentators have noted that the very act of tagging information, e.g. "this is my driver's license number, please do not mis-use it" invites the abuse that it is trying to prevent. Even saying "this is confidential" provides a temptation to some people to snoop. Indeed, the very foundation of "whistle-blower sites" like www.wikileaks.org relates to people's very natural curiosity about things that they are not supposed to see.

One way in which tagging may have value is in the legal enforcement of rights to information such as our photographs. Although the holders to music and movie copyrights have had a difficult time enforcing their rights, it is definitely true that putting a label on information indicating that it is not simply "there for the taking" provides useful legal support in acting against those who have appropriated the information. Still, as noted in a previous paper, [4] the most popular places people are posting information generally assert that they own the information posted there. So the creator, of, say, a Facebook profile photo, might not actually be able to do much if that image was mis-used.

Perhaps we should just follow the precautionary principle and never make something available online which might come back to hurt us? Doing that would greatly limit our "online presence" and perhaps still fail to protect us effectively. It seems clear that some combination of technical, legal, ethical and educational measures will be needed to preserve the public's confidence in both personal privacy and freedom to communicate.

References

1. Privacy Commissioner of Canada, Privacy Act Reform, http://www.privcom.gc.ca/legislation/pa/pa_reform_e.asp (accessed August 14, 2008)
2. Sullivan, B.: 'La difference' is stark in EU, U.S. privacy laws, http://www.msnbc.msn.com/id/15221111/ (accessed August 14, 2008)
3. http://www.cdt.org/privacy/eudirective/EU_Directive_.html (accessed August 15, 2008)
4. Keenan, T.: On the Internet Things Never Go Away Completely. In: Fischer-Hübner, et al. (eds.) The Future of Identity in the Information Society, pp. 37–50. Springer, Boston (2008)

5. Jones, H., Soltren, H.J.: Facebook: Threats to Privacy, http://groups.csail.mit.edu/mac/classes/6.805/student-papers/fall05-papers/facebook.pdf (accessed August 15, 2008)
6. Clarke, R.: Profiling: A Hidden Challenge to the Regulation of Data Surveillance, http://www.anu.edu.au/people/Roger.Clarke/DV/PaperProfiling.html (accessed August 15, 2008)
7. Khosrow-Pour, M. (ed.): Technologies For Commerce and Services Online, p. 103. IGI Global (2008)
8. Arrington, M.: Elaborate Facebook Worm Virus Spreading, http://www.techcrunch.com/2008/08/07/elaborate-facebook-worm-virus-spreading/ (accessed August 15, 2008)
9. Sophos, PLC, http://www.sophos.com/pressoffice/news/articles/2007/08/facebook.html (accessed August 14, 2008)
10. Sophos PLC, http://www.sophos.com/pressoffice/news/articles/2008/07/facebook-birthday.html (accessed August 15, 2008)
11. Wright, S.: Personal letter dated June 10, 2008, sent to Columbia University students
12. Keenan, T.: When Disclosure Becomes Spam – The Apparent Failure of Well Intentioned Privacy Policies and Legislation and How to Fix Them. In: Proceedings, 49th Annual Conference of the Western Social Science Association, Calgary, AB (2007)
13. http://eurlex.europa.eu/smartapi/cgi/sga_doc?smartapi!celexapi!prod!CELEXnumdoc&lg=en&numdoc=32002L0058&model=guichett (accessed August 15, 2008)
14. Richards, J.: Fake Facebook profile victim awarded 22,000 GPB, http://technology.timesonline.co.uk/tol/news/tech_and_web/article4389538.ece (accessed August 15, 2008)
15. Menzies, K.B.: Perils and possibilities of online social networks: has your client been networking on Facebook or MySpace? If so, you need to know about it - because your opponent will. In Trial 44(7), p. 58
16. Viégas, F.B.: Bloggers' Expectations of Privacy and Accountability: An Initial Survey, Media Laboratory, Massachusetts Institute of Technology, http://jcmc.indiana.edu/vol10/issue3/viegas.html (accessed August 15, 2008)
17. Leyden, J.: http://www.theregister.co.uk/2003/04/14/us_gov_builds_huge_child/ (accessed August 15, 2008)
18. Beet TV, http://searchengineland.com/080715-084529.php (accessed August 15, 2008)
19. Personal communication, Leila Boujnane, CEO, Idée Inc., Banff, Alberta (June 7, 2008)

Data Retention and Anonymity Services
Introducing a New Class of Realistic Adversary Models

Stefan Berthold, Rainer Böhme, and Stefan Köpsell

Technische Universität Dresden,
Faculty of Computer Science,
01062 Dresden, Germany
{stefan.berthold,rainer.boehme,stefan.koepsell}@tu-dresden.de

Abstract. The recently introduced legislation on data retention to aid prosecuting cyber-related crime in Europe also affects the achievable security of systems for anonymous communication on the Internet. We argue that data retention requires a review of existing security evaluations against a new class of realistic adversary models. In particular, we present theoretical results and first empirical evidence for intersection attacks by law enforcement authorities. The reference architecture for our study is the anonymity service AN.ON, from which we also collect empirical data. Our adversary model reflects an interpretation of the current implementation of the EC Directive on Data Retention in Germany.

1 Introduction

In the absence of anonymising technology, every computer connected to the Internet communicates with a unique address. So online users can be identified by the address of their communication device and the time of activity. The objective of anonymity services is to hide the relation between individual users and addresses from the users' communication partners and, with certain technologies, also from possible eavesdroppers on the communication links. However, by using an anonymity service, Internet users forward (part of) their traffic to the anonymity service, which such obtains all information necessary to re-identify anonymised users. Therefore, in principle, every anonymity service should be constructed in a way to delete this information as soon as possible in order to protect itself from becoming a target for adversaries who are interested in de-anonymising Internet users. This was valid until lately.

Recent legislation in the European Union, and particularly in Germany, requires anonymity services to store this sensitive data for months before it can be deleted. This is understood as a necessary trade-off between the interest of data protection and law enforcement: anonymity services are susceptible to be abused for criminal activities. In such cases, anonymity should indeed be revocable (though other means than data retention have been proposed to achieve this end [1,2]).

V. Matyáš et al. (Eds.): The Future of Identity, IFIP AICT 298, pp. 92–106, 2009.

In common terms of the literature on privacy and anonymity, deanonymisation by means of data retention can be considered as kind of attack. In contrast to other typically studied attacks on anonymity services, here the capabilities of the adversary are determined by law. This opens up a remarkably clear insight into what is in and what is out of control of the adversary and thus outlines a pretty specific adversary model. The characteristics of this kind of adversary model are different from common models in the relevant literature. The centre of interest has shifted from whether the adversary is *able to snoop or infer* private data to the extent the anonymity service is *obliged to retain (and provide on request)* the data. Obviously, any party that has (unauthorised) access to the data falls under this adversary model.

Thus, data retention regulations may mark a turning point for the design and the analysis of anonymity services. The question we will face in future is about how much anonymity is legally achievable under attacks that make use of retained data. And, correspondingly, one challenge will be to adapt current anonymity services or construct new ones with appropriate features to resist these attacks or mitigate their (side-) effects.

This introductory paper on the new class of legally defined adversary models can only focus on selected specific aspects, namely mix networks and intersection attacks. More specifically, we study the advantage which the adversary may gain from data that has been retained in line with the legal framework in Germany. The mix reference implementation for our study is AN.ON, an anonymity service which has been developed at TU Dresden and has been running successfully on the Internet for years. To quantify the impact of the attacks, simulations have been conducted based on data which has been gathered from a part of the broad AN.ON user community,[1] who gave their consent to participate in our study. Our main result is that dummy traffic, though not always a strong measure against arbitrary adversaries, is strikingly helpful against the law-abiding adversaries.

The paper is structured as follows. Section 2 recalls very briefly the essential principles of anonymity services. In Section 3, we give our interpretation of the current legislation. In the absence of case law, we take this interpretation as a base for the following sections. It also defines the adversary model for the rest of the paper. In Sections 4 and 5, we describe the cross-section attack and the intersection attack. We expect that these two attacks are most likely to be mounted on retained data in order to compromise or revoke the anonymity of AN.ON users. In Section 6, we describe the setup of our study to measure the potential of intersection attacks using retained data. The results of this study are presented in Section 7. In Section 8, we extend intersection attacks to the case of uncertainty of the adversary about the connection between two observable events (existing versions of the attacks assume full certainty). Finally, Section 9 concludes the paper and points to further generalisations and research topics of interest against the backdrop of the new class of realistic adversary models.

---

[1] The number of AN.ON users can only be estimated, but not finally determined. AN.ON by default does not store data that allows to distinguish different users.

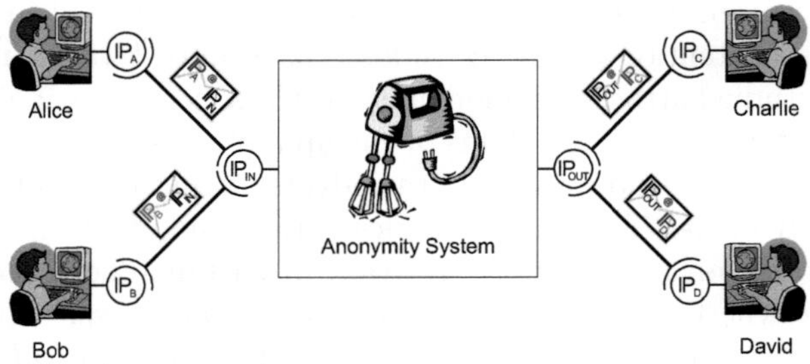

Fig. 1. Anonymity service modelled as "black box" which replaces IP addresses of forwarded messages

2 Anonymity Services in a Nutshell

For the purpose of our study, we can understand an anonymity service as a "black box" which acts as a proxy (cf. Fig. 1). Users redirect their network traffic through the proxy in order to achieve anonymity. For instance, browsing the web without revealing the identity is a common application of anonymity services. In this context, we understand anonymity as the obfuscation of all relations that let an outsider, the adversary, learn about the links between incoming and outgoing proxy traffic. Consequently, the adversary would not be able to determine the persons who are exchanging messages through the proxy, if anonymity is preserved. This should even hold if the adversary eavesdrops the data on all communication links of the proxy. Anonymity can be achieved by a combination of cryptography and data handling methods, such as padding, reordering, delaying etc. [3]

3 Legal Background

The directive 2006/24/EC (data retention directive) "on the retention of data generated or processed in connection with the provision of publicly available electronic communication services or of public communication networks", passed by the European parliament on March 15th, 2006, sets the legal framework of data retention for the European Union member states. According to the directive, the member states have to "bring into force the laws, regulations and administrative provisions necessary to comply with this directive by no later than 15 September 2007" [2006/24/EC]. The goal of the directive is to strengthen the success of law enforcement in the area of Internet-related crime and, more generally, whenever electronic communication is involved in criminal activities. The need for directive emerged from the fact that data about past communication relations is already unavailable when criminal offences come to trial, in which evidence from the communication relations could be helpful. Data on communication relations can provide indications about the person who accessed a specific website or who called a specific telephone, for instance.

Germany reacted to the data retention directive and adapted several laws [4]. With respect to anonymity services on the Internet, the changes of the Telecommunications Act are most significant [5]. This act defines in detail what kind of data has to be stored for various types of communications providers, including telecommunication companies like fixed-line or mobile phone providers and Internet service providers (ISPs). The act defines a retention period of six months. It anticipates services like anonymity services, which are in the first place contradictory to the law enforcement goals. In order to prevent any information gap, the Telecommunications Act declares in §113a 'Retention of Data':

> '(6) Those, who provide telecommunication services and thereby alter data which have to be stored according to this law, have to store the original data and the new data as well as the time of the alteration.'[2]

Anonymity services can be understood as proxy servers. The idea behind such proxies is briefly described in Section 2. In terms of sentence (6) of §113a of the Telecommunications Act the proxy, that is the anonymity service, replaces the IP addresses of senders and receivers with the proxy IP address in order to relay messages (cf. Fig. 1 above) and 'thereby alters data which have to be stored' according to the law. Consequently, anonymity services in principle have to store possibly identifying information about their users.

An urgent question is which data exactly has to be logged by anonymity services such as AN.ON in order to comply with the data retention law. In §113a, the Telecommunications Act distinguishes several types of services and defines for each service the sort of data to be stored. The closest match for AN.ON is 'Internet Service Provider' (ISP). According to the Telecommunications Act, an ISP has to log the IP address of a user, a unique identifier of the connection, and the period of time in which this assignment was valid. In combination with sentence (6), this means that the anonymity service has to log the replacement of IP addresses only, but nothing more, particularly no 'identifiers' of higher layers, such as TCP port numbers etc. Besides, consulted lawyers argue that only the replacement of source IP addresses (but not destination IP addresses) are allowed to be retained. They justify their assessment with sentence (8) of §113a: '... data about retrieved Internet pages must not be retained.' The lawyers also conclude that logging is allowed only for IP packet flows in upstream direction, that is only for packets from the user to the service, for instance a web server, but not for downstream packets.[3] In fact, the effective interpretation of the law remains uncertain until the German Federal Supreme Court makes a final decision. For

[2] Note that the quotations of the Telecommunications Act are unofficial translations of the official law in German. The authors are not aware of any official translation of the current version of the Telecommunications Act. The former version (of 22 June 2004) is available in English (online at: `http://www.bmwi.de/BMWi/Redaktion/PDF/Gesetz/telekommunkationsgesetz-en`).

[3] This is due to the fact that in a bidirectional communication, upstream and downstream are linakble. Thus logging of downstream source addresses implies logging of upstream destination addresses–which is prohibited by law.

this study, we assume that our interpretation is correct.[4] Thus, we can derive that anonymity services have to log the replacement of the original source IP address whenever an IP packet is forwarded from a user to a server. In other words, the anonymity service has to log the time and source IP address of *every* IP packet it receives from a user.

4 Cross-Section Attack

In this section, we study a very simple attack that could be mounted on retained data. This is at the same time the foundation for the intersection attack which will be introduced in Section 5. Looking from the perspective of law enforcement, the reply to the typical law enforcement request, "To which person was IP address $\mathrm{IP}_{\mathrm{out}}$ assigned at time t?" (Q_1), would include all retained source IP addresses for time t. We will refer to these IP addresses by the symbol $\mathcal{S}(t)$, that is, we consider $\mathcal{S}(t)$ denoting the set of retained IP addresses at time t.

The number of elements in $\mathcal{S}(t)$ can be understood as a measure of anonymity, as for instance in [7].[5] Critics of this way of measuring anonymity mention (rightly so) that the probability distribution of all elements in $\mathcal{S}(t)$ is not necessarily uniform [8,9]. However, we know that the best case from the perspective of law enforcement would be, if $\mathcal{S}(t)$ contains one element only. This is also the worst case for anonymity by any measure. The size of $\mathcal{S}(t)$ depends on two parameters: (a) on the extent of use of the anonymity service and (b) on the resolution of the timestamp t. Note that the timestamp is not specified in greater detail by law.

We have quantified the activity of users[6] of our AN.ON system in order to get a better idea of $\mathcal{S}(t)$ and its size. To keep the task manageable, we decided to log the start and end time of *anonymous channels* only. The alternative would have been to log all incoming IP packets, but that would be rather expensive. In AN.ON, anonymous channels are the basic end-to-end communication vehicle, similar to a TCP/IP connection.

We found that nearly half of all channels lasted no more than one second, so we assume that analysing the channel activities leads to a good approximation of the actual size of $\mathcal{S}(t)$. Fig. 2 shows the results of the quantification at the 'Dresden–Dresden' cascade of our AN.ON system.[7] The red dots depict the total number of users logged in, regardless if they were active or idle. The black dots show the number of users with at least one open channel. For both aggregations,

---

[4] Other interpretations of the law can be found in the literature, e.g. in [6] the authors assume that: "the German legislation requires operators of anonymisers to link all incoming and outgoing messages and store this relation."

[5] The literature often refers to $\mathcal{S}(t)$ as the "anonymity set".

[6] When we speak about 'users' (e.g. number of users, activity of users etc.), we mean established connections to the AN.ON system. It is not possible to tell how many different human beings are behind them.

[7] Our AN.ON system is based on mix cascades. A cascade is a fixed chain of anonymity service servers (called mixes). Users may freely choose the cascade they want to use.

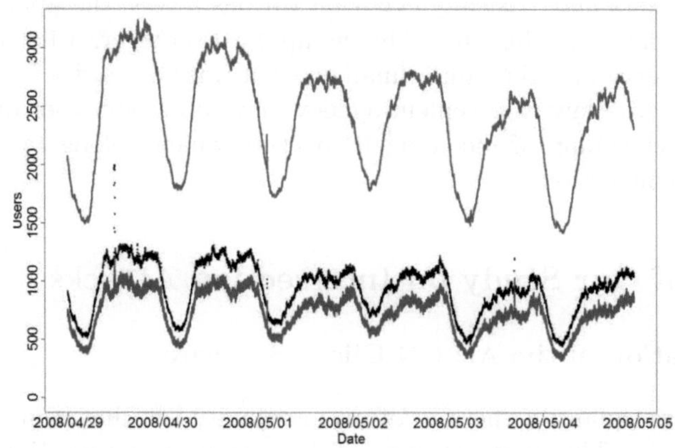

Fig. 2. Curves showing the total number of users logged in (red), the number of users which have an open channel within a given minute (black) and the number of users with an open channel within a given second (blue)

a time resolution of *one minute* was used. For comparison, the blue dots depict a setting which is similar to the black dots, but with a time resolution of one second.

Observe that the size of $\mathcal{S}(t)$, cf. Question Q_1, has never fallen below 400 between 29th of April 2008 and 5th of May 2008. That is, even when resolving a Q_1 request, a law enforcement agency would still have to investigate at least 400 users to identify the person they are looking for. As we see in Fig. 2, the accuracy of the time resolution (seconds vs. minutes, that is blue vs. black dots) is less important in practice than the overall usage rate of the anonymity service.

5 Intersection Attack

A single request for $\mathcal{S}(t)$, that is the set of all retained users at a single point in time, might not be sufficient to narrow down the number of suspects to a reasonable small set, as we have seen in the previous section. Thus, a law enforcement agency could request the sets of online users for *several* points in time. With these sets, the agency would be able to mount an intersection attack [10] which, in theory, drastically narrows down the set size. Intersection attacks, however, require that the requested points in time are related to events that are linkable to one and the same target person. For the sake of simplicity, we assume that each event is related to exactly one point in time. Thus, a newly formulated request of a law enforcement agency would be "To which person was IP address IP_{out} assigned at times t_1, t_2, and t_3?" (Q_2). If the law enforcement agency possesses a priori knowledge that one and the same target person is responsible for the events of interest observed at t_1, t_2, and t_3, then this person (or rather her identifier) belongs to the intersection of $\mathcal{S}(t_1) \cap \mathcal{S}(t_2) \cap \mathcal{S}(t_3)$.[8]

[8] In Section 8 we discuss the case where the linkability between two events is not possibilistic but probabilistic.

Note that events may basically occur on various layers, the application layer or the network layer, for instance. On the application layer, a law enforcement agency may observe that the same e-mail account was accessed several times. On the network layer, a law enforcement agency may run a honeypot and therefore obtain the exact timing of incoming IP packets which belong to one and the same TCP/IP connection.

6 Setup of Our Study on Intersection Attacks

6.1 Preparation of the AN.ON Client Software

In our study, we quantify the size of an anonymity set that remains after intersection attacks. The main problem with a study of intersection attacks on AN.ON user data is that (due to the very nature of anonymity services) there is no way to link the anonymised sessions of one and the same user. In order to get useful data for our study, additional identifiers were needed to be submitted by users to the AN.ON service.

We adapted the AN.ON client software such that users can decide whether they want to take part in the study. In the adapted software, a random number of 117 Bits has been generated as identifier for those users who take part in the study. The identifier has been transmitted to AN.ON each time the user logs in to the Dresden–Dresden cascade. Thus, sessions of users who voluntarily participated in the study became linkable over the time of the study.

The identifiers have been recorded between 21th of May and 20th of July, 2008. On 21th of May, the adapted client has been released and older clients reacted by requesting the update. Thus, we expect that in the following days, the vast majority of AN.ON users installed the new client and was therefore asked whether to participate in the study or not. In total, we recorded 70,591 replies, 38,738 (54.88%) of which agreed to support the study. The remaining 45.12% of the users continued to use AN.ON without any linkability of their sessions.

6.2 Formal Notation

In the style of the symbol $\mathcal{S}(t)$, which we informally introduced in a previous section, we define the symbol $\mathcal{S}_\cap(T)$ as the AN.ON users which were retained at each of the times $t_1, \ldots, t_n \in T$. This requires the understanding of AN.ON *sessions*. The AN.ON client opens a session when it connects to the anonymity service. The session is closed when the client quits. Thus, a session is always related to a user and can be described by a login and a logout time. The formal definitions of $\mathcal{S}(t)$ and $\mathcal{S}_\cap(T)$ are reflected in Equation (2) and (3).

Let I_u be the set of all user IDs, I_s be the set of all session IDs, and $\mathcal{P}(I_s)$ the power set of all session IDs I_s. Then $X : I_u \rightarrow \mathcal{P}(I_s)$ would be the mapping of user IDs to all related sessions:

$$X(uid) = \left\{ sid \in I_s \;\middle|\; sid \text{ related to } uid \right\}. \tag{1}$$

The login and logout time of a AN.ON session $sid \in I_s$ can be reflected in the two symbols $t_{\text{in}}(sid)$ and $t_{\text{out}}(sid)$. Then $\mathcal{S}(t)$ would be the set of users which have been logged in to AN.ON between the times t and $t + t_{\text{res}}$ where t_{res} is the time resolution (a second or a minute in our study):

$$\mathcal{S}(t) = \{uid \in I_u \mid sid \in X(uid), t_{\text{in}}(sid) < t + t_{\text{res}}, t_{\text{out}}(sid) \geq t\} \qquad (2)$$

With $\mathcal{S}(t)$, we can define $\mathcal{S}_\cap(T)$, the anonymity set after an intersection attack with the times $T = \{t_1, \ldots, t_n\}$. We suppose that all elements in T are pairwise different, that is for $T = \{t_1, \ldots, t_n\}$ holds $|T| = n$:

$$\mathcal{S}_\cap(T) = \bigcap_{t \in T} \mathcal{S}(t) \qquad (3)$$

In our study, we focus on intersections between user sets of *two* points in time only. That is, we explore $\mathcal{S}_\cap(T)$ with the samples T where $|T| = 2$ and the elements of T are chosen by random. This setting can be understood as the case that law enforcement agencies request the set of persons which have been logged in at t_1 and at t_2 as well, or in $T = \{t_1, t_2\}$, respectively.[9]

7 Results of Our Study on Intersection Attacks

Table 1 shows characteristics of distributions of $|\mathcal{S}(t_1)|$, $|\mathcal{S}(t_2)|$, and $|\mathcal{S}_\cap(\{t_1, t_2\})|$ from our study with 5 million samples of two points in time t_1 and t_2 with variations in the time resolution (seconds vs. minutes) and the user data (login/logout vs. activity).[10]

Fig. 3(a) depicts two frequency density diagrams that show immediate results from our study with 5 million samples of two points in time t_1 and t_2. On the horizontal axis, we plot the size of $\mathcal{S}(t_1)$ or $\mathcal{S}_\cap(\{t_1, t_2\}$. On the vertical axis, we see the frequency densities of these set sizes with regard to our samples. The red line marks the frequency densities of set sizes of $\mathcal{S}(t_1)$ (which are nearly the same as for $\mathcal{S}(t_2)$[11]). The blue line mark the frequency densities of set sizes of $\mathcal{S}_\cap(\{t_1, t_2\})$. The parameters and summary measures of the distributions are reported in Table 1. Similar results are shown in Fig. 3(b), 3(c), and 3(d) with variations in the time resolution and the user data (login/logout vs. activity).

Observe that the anonymity set size is greater with a coarser time resolution and, even more significantly, if the adversary has no access to the activity data of AN.ON users, but only to their login/logout behaviour.

We fitted four regression models (using ordinary least squares) to analyse the multivariate relationship between the intersection size and various explanatory variables, cf. Fig. 3(a) and Table 1. The parameter estimates of these models are compiled in Table 2.

---

[9] In practice, law enforcement agencies will rather request who used the IP address of the last mix of a cascade in T than requesting the login state of AN.ON users.

[10] With activity, we refer to channel activity as described in Section 4.

[11] Note that $\mathcal{S}(t_1)$ and $\mathcal{S}(t_2)$ are drawn from the same distribution.

Table 1. Summary statistics of the distributions of $|\mathcal{S}(t_1)|$, $|\mathcal{S}(t_2)|$, and $|\mathcal{S}_\cap(\{t_1, t_2\})|$ over 5 million random draws

	user behaviour	time res.	min	1st quartile	mean	median	3rd quartile	max
$\mathcal{S}(t_1)$	login/out	*sec*	148	529	661	665.6	814	1210
		min	207	534	667	672	821	1220
	activity	*sec*	23	153	202	199.2	245	576
		min	77	181	238	235.9	288	802
$\mathcal{S}(t_2)$	login/out	*sec*	147	529	660	665.5	814	1210
		min	207	534	667	671.9	821	1220
	activity	*sec*	23	153	202	199.2	245	576
		min	77	181	238	235.9	288	802
$\mathcal{S}_\cap(\{t_1, t_2\})$	login/out	*sec*	9	91	120	133.1	159	1118
		min	11	92	121	134.1	161	1125
	activity	*sec*	0	7	11	13.39	17	307
		min	0	10	15	18.42	23	562

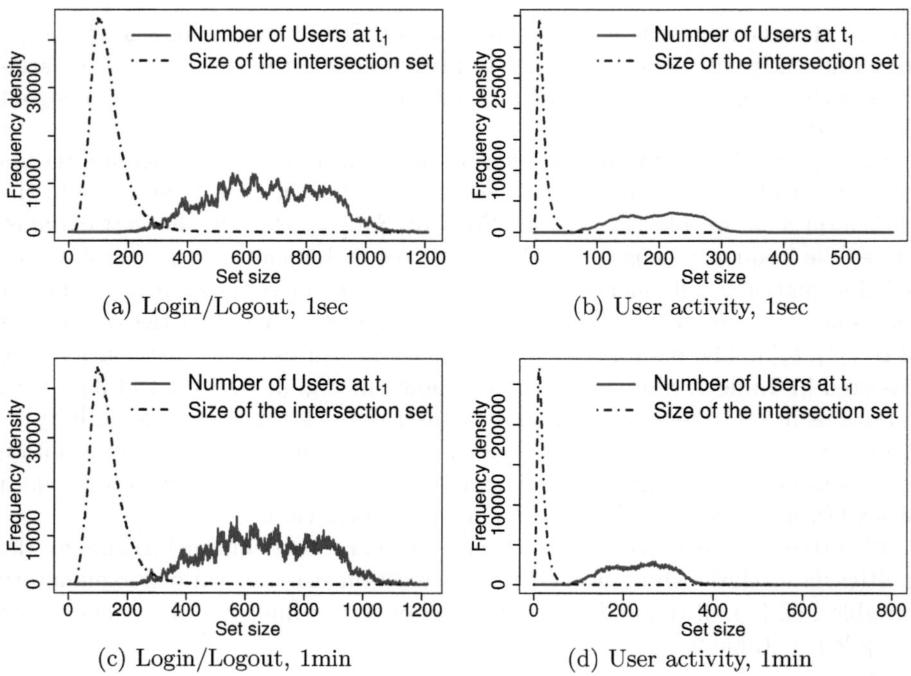

(a) Login/Logout, 1sec

(b) User activity, 1sec

(c) Login/Logout, 1min

(d) User activity, 1min

Fig. 3. Frequency density diagrams of the anonymity set sizes $|\mathcal{S}(t_1)|$ and $|\mathcal{S}_\cap(\{t_1, t_2\})|$

Table 2. Parameters of different linear regression models with dependent variable $\ln\left|\mathcal{S}_\cap(\{t_1,t_2\})\right|$; $N = 5$ million data points; std. errors in brackets; all coefficient significant at 0.001 level

	Model			
	1	2	3	4
Predictors				
intercept	-2.05	-3.13	1.53	1.56
	(0.04)	(0.05)	(0.03)	(0.02)
minimum set size	1.09	1.00	1.00	0.98
$\ln\left(\min\left(\lvert\mathcal{S}(t_1)\rvert, \lvert\mathcal{S}(t_2)\rvert\right)\right)$	(0.01)	(0.01)	(0.00)	(0.00)
maximum set size		0.25		
$\ln\left(\max\left(\lvert\mathcal{S}(t_1)\rvert, \lvert\mathcal{S}(t_2)\rvert\right)\right)$		(0.01)		
time interval			-0.22	-0.22
$\ln\lvert\delta\rvert$			(0.00)	(0.00)
periodicity indicator				0.24
$f_\triangle(\delta)$				(0.00)
Summary				
adjusted R^2	0.48	0.49	0.79	0.82

In Model 1, we try to explain the size of $\mathcal{S}_\cap(\{t_1,t_2\})$ by the minimum size of $\mathcal{S}(t_1)$ and $\mathcal{S}(t_2)$. The results are log transformed to reasonably normalise the residuals. Additionally, in Model 2, we add the maximum size of $\mathcal{S}(t_1)$ and $\mathcal{S}(t_2)$ as a second explanatory variable. We see that the gain of explained variance, cf. adjusted R^2 in Table 2, is small and the coefficient lower – albeit positive and statistically significant. This is what we expect, since the intersection set $\mathcal{S}_\cap(\{t_1,t_2\}) = \mathcal{S}(t_1) \cap \mathcal{S}(t_2)$ is at most as great as the smallest set of $\mathcal{S}(t_1)$ and $\mathcal{S}(t_2)$. As the set size fluctuates heavily over time, the size of the intersection is strongly related to the minimum size of $\mathcal{S}(t_1)$ and $\mathcal{S}(t_2)$.

In all following models, we drop the less-influentical maximum and use solely the minimum set size to control for a varying number of users over time. Model 3 includes the time interval between both events as predictor. The negative sign of the coefficient for term $\ln|\delta|$ indicates that there is an inverse relation between the time interval and the intersection size. That means, smaller time intervals lead to greater intersection sets, since the smaller the time interval between t_1 and t_2, the higher is the likelihood that a user who is logged in at t_1 is still logged in at t_2. The considerable gain in R^2 of 31 percentage points reveals that time between events matters.

In Model 4, we explore the influence of user behaviour on the set size of $\mathcal{S}_\cap(\{t_1,t_2\})$. We expect that the user behaviour follows regular pattern, for instance a periodicity of 24h.[12] This is so because we expect that users pursue similar tasks at similar times of the day. Users who log in to AN.ON during the working hours may regularly use AN.ON in their profession, for instance journal-

[12] It was not possible to explore patterns on a weekly or longer basis, since our study period was too short.

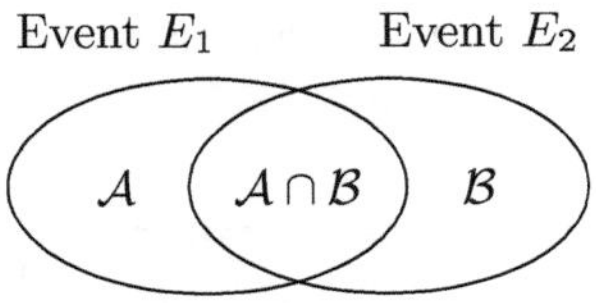

Fig. 4. Terminology for probabilistic intersection attack with $\mathcal{A}$ being the set of users that were logged in when event E_1 occurred and $\mathcal{B}$ being the set of users that were logged in when event E_2 occurred

ists. Those users who use AN.ON for their leisure time activities may regularly log in after the working hours. In order to check the support of our expectation in the sample data, we estimate the coefficient of an indicator variable computed from a periodic triangular function $f_\Delta(\delta)$ which generates an indicator variable that yields a value between 0 and 1, where a value of 0 marks the smallest match with the 24h pattern and a value of 1 denotes the best match.

$$\delta = |t_1 - t_2| \tag{4}$$

$$f_\Delta(\delta) = \left| 1 - \frac{\delta \bmod (24 \cdot 60^2)}{12 \cdot 60^2} \right| \tag{5}$$

The positive coefficient indicates that the sample data in fact shows periodicity, although the additional explanatory power of this simple linear function is rather small (3 percentage points).

8 Probabilistic Intersection Attacks

So far, we have assumed that the law enforcement agency has no uncertainty with respect to the linkability of a set of events. This might be true in some cases (e.g., if the IP packets per TCP/IP connection example above) – but not in general. In the above example of the e-mail account, the login information (username and password) could be shared among a group of persons. Therefore the intersection could lead to false negatives. Consequently, for practical cases it is necessary to consider the uncertainty about the likability of two or more events. This will turn possibilistic intersection attacks into probabilistic ones. Note that previous work in this field (cf. [11,12]) has focused on calculating anonymity sets resulting from intersection attacks using *probabilistic algorithms*, whereas our contribution is to model linkability in a probabilistic sense.

In the following, we formally study the case of two events, E_1 and E_2. Let p be the probability that both events are caused by the same user.[13]

Further, as illustrated in Fig. 4, let $\mathcal{A}$ be the set of suspect senders (i.e., the result of a cross-section attack) at the time of E_1 and $\mathcal{B}$ the set of suspects for

[13] Note that, in this model, there is no uncertainty about the value of p. Of course in an extended model one could also consider that p is not observable and can only estimated with a parametric model.

E_2. The intersection $\mathcal{A} \cap \mathcal{B}$ is the set of senders connected to the anonymity service at the time of both events (not necessarily in one session). We write the cardinality of set $\mathcal{X}$ as $|\mathcal{X}|$ with $\mathcal{X} = \mathcal{A}, \mathcal{B}$.

Problem statement: Given the quantities $|\mathcal{A}|$, $|\mathcal{B}|$, $|\mathcal{A} \cap \mathcal{B}|$ and p (the probability that both events were caused by the same sender, i.e., $p = \Pr(\exists S \in \mathcal{A} \cap \mathcal{B} \mid S \sim E_1 \wedge S \sim E_2)$, where '$\sim$' denotes a causal relationship), what is the probability for individual senders *having caused at least one event*, dependent on which set they belong to. More precisely, we want to calculate

1. $P_{\mathcal{A} \cap \mathcal{B}} = \Pr(S \sim E_1 \vee S \sim E_2 \mid S \in \mathcal{A} \cap \mathcal{B})$, the probability that a specific sender S who has used the anonymity service at the time of both events is responsible for at least one of the events;
2. $P_{\mathcal{A} \setminus \mathcal{B}} = \Pr(S \sim E_1 \vee S \sim E_2 \mid S \in \mathcal{A} \setminus \mathcal{B})$, the probability that a specific sender S who has used the anonymity service at the time of event E_1 *but not* at the time of event E_2 is responsible for at least one of the events; and vice versa,
3. $P_{\mathcal{B} \setminus \mathcal{A}} = \Pr(S \sim E_1 \vee S \sim E_2 \mid S \in \mathcal{B} \setminus \mathcal{A})$, the probability that a specific sender S who has not used the anonymity service at the time of event E_1 *but* at the time of event E_2 is responsible for at least one of the events.

The problem can be solved by evaluating a decision tree (Fig. 5). The root branches distinguish whether both events were actually caused by the same user or not. Hence, the probabilities for the branches are p and $1 - p$. If both events in fact origin from the same sender, then the only possibility is that the actual sender belongs to set $\mathcal{A} \cap \mathcal{B}$. Otherwise, four solutions for the assignment of sets of senders to events are possible, and their probabilities depend on the relative set sizes. Note that members of $\mathcal{A} \cap \mathcal{B}$ may have caused one or both (if $|\mathcal{A} \cap \mathcal{B}| > 1$) events even when both events were caused by different users. We further make the convention that $S_1 = S \in \mathcal{A} \iff S \sim E_1$ and $S_2 = S \in \mathcal{B} \iff S \sim E_2$.

Obviously, probabilities $\pi_1, \ldots, \pi_4$ can be calculated from the number of possibilities in relation to its total per sub-tree. The cardinalities of $\mathcal{A} \setminus \mathcal{B}$ and $\mathcal{B} \setminus \mathcal{A}$

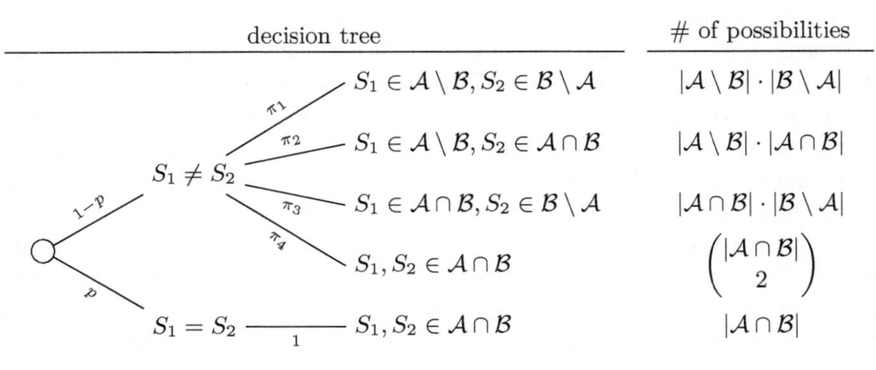

Fig. 5. Decision tree for probabilistic intersection attack with two events

are given implicitly as $|\mathcal{A} \setminus \mathcal{B}| = |\mathcal{A}| - |\mathcal{A} \cap \mathcal{B}|$ and $|\mathcal{B} \setminus \mathcal{A}| = |\mathcal{B}| - |\mathcal{A} \cap \mathcal{B}|$, and $\binom{a}{b}$ denotes the binomial coefficient. The probabilities of interest can be obtained by evaluating the decision tree in Fig. 5. As can be seen in Equation (6)–(8), these probabilities are linear in p.

$$P_{\mathcal{A}\cap\mathcal{B}} = p + (1-p)(\pi_2 + \pi_3 + \pi_4) \tag{6}$$
$$P_{\mathcal{A}\setminus\mathcal{B}} = (1-p)(\pi_1 + \pi_2) \tag{7}$$
$$P_{\mathcal{B}\setminus\mathcal{A}} = (1-p)(\pi_1 + \pi_3) \tag{8}$$

Generalisations of the probabilistic intersection attack to more than two events are up to further research.

9 Conclusions

Due to recent changes in the legislation that now require the retention of identifying information, anonymity services face the challenge to resist a new kind of adversary. Such adversaries can force the anonymity service to collaborate to a certain extent, which is defined by law. The intention of our study is to assess the risk which arises from adversaries that are mounting intersection attacks on retained data of anonymity systems. We have measured the remaining anonymity from real data on user behaviour, which we believe is representative for information that can be requested by a law enforcement agency. The results indicate that hiding in an anonymity set works well as long as adversaries pose single request at distinct points in time without relating several requests to each other. However, the results also show that an adversary who combines the results of different requests, and therefore requests several anonymity sets in order to intersect them, has much more success in narrowing down individuals in the anonymity set. Compared to a single request, the intersection of only two requests reduces the size by far more than 50%. Though this is hardly sufficient for law enforcement agencies that seek to reduce anonymity sets to single persons, the results can be further refined, presumably with similar success, by intersecting more anonymity sets that are known to contain the target person.

Our results show that there is a remarkable difference with regard to the size of the remaining anonymity set between different ways of requesting data. The anonymity sets are larger if the set of those users is requested who were *logged in* in a distinct moment in time. The anonymity sets decrease if only *active* users are requested. Presumably the anonymity sets are even smaller, if the requests do not concern the application layer of the anonymity service, but the underlying network layer. Our study, however, is limited to the application layer.

Even though this discussion may lead to the conclusion that it is necessarily desirable for an adversary or a law enforcement agency to request user sets of active users only, this idea may be misguiding for anonymity systems such as AN.ON: users may send dummy traffic as a countermeasure. The idea behind dummy traffic of users is to make themselves appear active, even though they are actually idle. This can be achieved by regularly sending data packages from the user to the service without any content of interest. It is indeed crucial that besides the user (and, in certain constructions, the anonymity service), nobody is able to distinguish dummy traffic from ordinary traffic. Thus, if users send dummy traffic, a law enforcement agency which is able to obtain the set of all *active* users would not learn more than an agency which is limited such that it can only observe the set of all users that are *logged in*.

Dummy traffic has been discussed with regard to several attack schemes [13,14,15]. In general, it has been found to be a rather weak countermeasure in packet-switched networks. However, due to the specific limitations of the "adversary" defined by the data retention act, a continuous connection to the anonymity service together with weak dummy traffic seems a strikingly good solution. The economical aspects of dummy traffic have been mentioned in literature, but might be of decreasing significance in a world with complete network coverage and flat rates.

Acknowledgements

This paper has benefitted from thoughtful comments by Andreas Pfitzmann.

The research leading to these results has received funding from the European Community's Sixth Framework Programme (FP6/2002–2006) under grant agreement no. 507512 and the Seventh Framework Programme (FP7/2007–2013) under grant agreement no. 216483.

References

1. Claessens, J., Díaz, C., Goemans, C., Dumortier, J., Preneel, B., Vandewalle, J., Dumotier, J.: Revocable anonymous access to the Internet? Internet Research: Electronic Networking Applications and Policy 13(4), 242–258 (2003)
2. Köpsell, S., Wendolsky, R., Federrath, H.: Revocable anonymity. In: Müller, G. (ed.) ETRICS 2006. LNCS, vol. 3995, pp. 206–220. Springer, Heidelberg (2006)
3. Danezis, G., Diaz, C.: A survey of anonymous communication channels. Technical Report MSR-TR-2008-35, Microsoft Research (2008)
4. Bundestag: Gesetz zur Neuregelung der Telekommunikationsüberwachung und anderer verdeckter Ermittlungsmaßnahmen sowie zur Umsetzung der Richtlinie 2006/24/EG vom. 21. Dezember 2007 [Amending act to the German Telecommunications Act]. Bundesgesetzblatt (Teil I, Nr. 70), pp. 3198–3211. ausgegeben zu Bonn (December 2007)
5. Bundestag: Telekommunikationsgesetz vom 22. Juni 2004 (2007) BGBl. I S. 1190, zuletzt geändert durch Artikel 2 des Gesetzes vom 21. Dezember 2007 (BGBl. I S. 3198)
6. Pimenidis, L., Kosta, E.: The impact of the retention of traffic and location data on the internet user. DuD Datenschutz und Datensicherheit 32(2), 92–97 (2008)
7. Pfitzmann, A., Hansen, M.: Anonymity, unlinkability, undetectability, unobservability, pseudonymity, and identity management – A consolidated proposal for terminology (2008), `http://dud.inf.tu-dresden.de/Anon_Terminology.shtml` (Version 0.31e)

8. Díaz, C., Seys, S., Claessens, J., Preneel, B.: Towards measuring anonymity. In: Dingledine, R., Syverson, P.F. (eds.) PET 2002. LNCS, vol. 2482, pp. 54–68. Springer, Heidelberg (2003)
9. Serjantov, A., Danezis, G.: Towards an information theoretic metric for anonymity. In: Dingledine, R., Syverson, P.F. (eds.) PET 2002. LNCS, vol. 2482, pp. 41–53. Springer, Heidelberg (2003)
10. Berthold, O.: Effiziente Realisierung von Dummy Traffic zur Gewährleistung von Unbeobachtbarkeit im Internet [An efficient implementation of dummy traffic to ensure unobservability on the Internet]. Diploma thesis, Technische Universität Dresden, Faculty of Computer Science, Institute for Theoretical Computer Science (1999) (in German)
11. Danezis, G.: Statistical disclosure attacks: Traffic confirmation in open environments. In: Gritzalis, S., di Vimercati, S.D.C., Samarati, P., Katsikas, G. (eds.) Proceedings of Security and Privacy in the Age of Uncertainty (May 2003)
12. Mathewson, N., Dingledine, R.: Practical traffic analysis: Extending and resisting statistical disclosure. In: Martin, D., Serjantov, A. (eds.) PET 2004. LNCS, vol. 3424, pp. 17–34. Springer, Heidelberg (2005)
13. Berthold, O., Langos, H.: Dummy traffic against long term intersection attacks. In: Dingledine, R., Syverson, P.F. (eds.) PET 2002. LNCS, vol. 2482, pp. 110–128. Springer, Heidelberg (2003)
14. Díaz, C., Preneel, B.: Reasoning about the anonymity provided by pool mixes that generate dummy traffic. In: Fridrich, J. (ed.) IH 2004. LNCS, vol. 3200, pp. 309–325. Springer, Heidelberg (2004)
15. Díaz, C., Preneel, B.: Taxonomy of mixes and dummy traffic. In: Proceedings of I-NetSec 2004: 3rd Working Conference on Privacy and Anonymity in Networked and Distributed Systems, Toulouse, France (August 2004)

A Survey on Non-transferable Anonymous Credentials

Sebastian Pape

Databases and Interactive Systems Research Group,
University of Kassel
pape@db.informatik.uni-kassel.de

Abstract. There are at least two principal approaches to prevent users from sharing their anonymous credentials: adding valuable secrets into the system the user does not want to share or embedding biometric access control. This paper seeks to identify possible fields of application and to compare both approaches with respect to the credentials' non-transferability.

The paper shows that both approaches do not ensure the non-transferability of anonymous credentials, but may be applicable in some fields. On the one hand, it might be hard to find valuable secrets to really prevent the sharing of credentials, in particular with close family members. On the other hand, biometric sensors embedded in a smart-card can be circumvented with some effort, especially if access control is unattended. Although the combination of both approaches may prevent more users from sharing their credentials, it suffers from restrictions of both approaches and from the effort needed to put it in place.

However, assuming that anonymous credentials will probably not be used in high-security environments, both approaches might be sufficient to prevent sharing in some applications. If the users already possess personal digital assistants, embedded valuable secrets are a quite cheap solution, even though they raise the system's value. If access control is attended, biometric sensors are reasonably safe and limit the possibility of unintentionally sharing the credentials for free.

1 Introduction

Anonymous credentials introduced by Chaum [1,2] usually consist of cryptographic tokens which allow the user to prove a statement or relationship with an organisation to another person or organisation anonymously. Here anonymous authentication means that the verifier should not gather any information about the user except that the user is authorised. While anonymous credential systems are related to the concept of untraceable or anonymous payments [3] and, hence, credentials can be easily transferred to another person, there are some situations where transferring credentials is undesired. People who have to prove their age to an organisation for the purchase of alcoholic drinks or tobacco or if they want to visit a bar or discotheque, are an example of this scenario. If the organisation is not considered trustworthy by the user, he probably does not want to disclose

V. Matyáš et al. (Eds.): The Future of Identity, IFIP AICT 298, pp. 107–118, 2009.

more information than “I’m 18 or older”. Analogous circumstances apply during online age verification where it is common to show credit card information to prove a certain age. Since the user does not know if the age verification site is trustworthy, he does not want to give this data away. On the other hand, the organisation demands a proof of age of the specific user without involving his relatives or friends who could prove the statement instead. Other examples for utilising anonymous credentials include the proof of a country’s citizenship, driving license or the proof of special abilities, such as academic degrees.

There are two well-known approaches to prevent users from sharing their credentials. One approach to prevent the transfer of credentials is to equate sharing a credential with sharing a valuable secret outside the system [4,5,6] or even all of the user’s secrets inside the system, namely credentials from other issuers [7]. Another possibility of assuring non-transferability of anonymous credentials is to make use of biometric control devices [8]. Of course, it should be guaranteed that these devices do not break the user’s anonymity.

This paper seeks to elaborate on the advantages and disadvantages of both approaches with regard to the non-transferability of credentials. The next section describes anonymous credentials and possible implementations, while Sect. 3 introduces our scenario and attacker model. Section 4 investigates the approaches’ non-transferability and leads to the conclusions in Sect. 5.

2 Anonymous Credentials

The basic idea of anonymous credentials is that users are able to anonymously prove attributes issued by an organisation. As stated above, anonymous authentication means that neither should the verifier learn any information about the user except that the user is authorised nor should he be able to link several authentications of the same user which would allow him to build profiles on authenticating users.

Implementations usually access proofs of knowledge in combination with blind signature [9] and group signature [10] schemes.

“Knowledge” is only one authentication factor [11,12], but it can easily be transformed to “possession” by moving the secret into a smartcard, where we presume it cannot be copied from. More precisely we assume the user is able to use the credential without the credential leaving the card. The smartcard then works as a blackbox for the user and if he does not trust the manufacturer of the card or the issuing organisation, we assume the user carefully observes the communication of the card with the verifier following Chaum’s and Pedersen’s *wallet with observer* architecture [13]. This concept suggests each user has a personal communication device (called *wallet*) with a tamper-resistant chip (called *observer*) either built-in or in the form of a smartcard. Now the user is able to check and prevent the information flow from the organisation to the observer and only has to trust that the observer supports all legitimate operations. The verifying organisation on the other hand only has to trust that the observer is still intact and prevents illegitimate operations (e.g. releasing the secret). To prevent abuse the tamper-resistant chip may be protected by a personal identification number (PIN) resulting in a two-factor-authentication (possession of card and knowledge of the PIN) as already known from today's cash cards.

2.1 Embedded Valuable Secrets

The idea of this approach is to discourage the users from sharing their credentials by equating the sharing of their credential with sharing a valuable secret. The valuable secret can be either a secret from outside the system (called *PKI-assured non-transferability*) [4,5,6] or all secrets and credentials inside the system (called *all-or-nothing non-transferability*) [7]. In [6] each user has a master public key and should be strongly encouraged to keep the corresponding master private key secret. This can be realised for example by registering the public master key at a certification authority as a legal digital signature key which can be used to sign "important legal or financial documents". Lysyanskaya et al. state that it is impossible to share a credential without sharing the master private key.

This way the user's knowledge is made valuable beyond its primary intent and, therefore, it is assumed the user will not share it. Thus, the system's secret is personalised for each user and does not necessarily have to be kept secret from him. This offers two possible implementations: the above concept of embedding the key into a smartcard or delivering a personalised secret to the user. The latter is possible because the user is not technically prevented from sharing his credential. Instead, as aforementioned, it is assumed he does not want to share the additional embedded valuable secret. It is worth mentioning that issuing a credential can be realised by an interactive protocol between issuer and user without revealing the user's credential or valuable secret to the issuer. However, it may be tough for the issuer to verify the secret's accuracy.

2.2 Biometric Access Control

As suggested by Bleumer, the wallet with observer model can be extended by adding a biometric facility to the observer [8,14]. Before starting the proof of knowledge the observer checks the user's biometrics. This could be implemented using a smartcard with embedded fingerprint reader [15] or so called *match-on-card* systems [16] where an external reader delivers the biometrics directly to the card. The advantage of embedding the fingerprint reader into the card to match-on-card systems is that the user's biometrics are not put at risk as has already occurred with PINs of cash cards by manipulated PIN-readers [17]. Contrary to the user's PIN, one may not consider his fingerprints secret, because they cannot be changed and he leaves them anywhere, e.g. at the shop's door. But even if the dealer could get the user's fingerprint at his shop's door, this would require a much larger effort than an automatic acquisition of the user's biometric. Thus, the user's privacy would be invaded by an automatic acquisition of his fingerprints. We therefore assume an implementation with an embedded fingerprint reader in the following.

2.3 Other Approaches

Besides the two well-investigated approaches discussed above one may think of other schemes to prevent users from sharing their credentials. We first need to point out that the biometric access control described in the previous subsection is actually operating against the user. He is not allowed to have his credentials available as pleased to prevent him from passing them around. Thus, it is quite obvious that "traditional access control schemes" such as passwords may not be useful in this case. The most obvious idea for a new approach is to use a combination of the two approaches discussed above. We will take this into account when investigating the approaches' non-transferability in section 4.

In the last years some scientists and technophiles had radio-frequency identification (RFID) chips implanted [18,19]. On the one hand, if the user really trusts all parties involved in the production and implantation of the RFID chip, namely manufacturer and surgeon, this may be an option. On the other hand, the user risks an intrusion into his privacy here. Since the user cannot be sure about the chip's transmission, even if there are some means of control over chip's transmission, the verifier may be able to communicate directly with the chip. Thus, the wallet with observer architecture does not apply here and the user has to trust other parties with all the consequences regarding his privacy. Furthermore, the system's setup seems to be quite complicated and the connection between the user and the chip can simply be broken by another surgeon. Thus, we argue that implanted RFID chips are inappropriate and do not consider them any further in this paper.

2.4 Integral Parts of the Credential System's Security

Before dealing with scenarios and an attacker model in the next section we need to have a look at the integral parts of the credential system's security. These components can be divided into three groups: the security of the basis credential system (G) and the security of the efforts trying to make those credentials non-transferable, either by biometric access control (B) or by embedding a valuable secret (S).

Moreover, the security of non-transferable anonymous credentials depends mostly on the following points:

(G1) The security of the underlying cryptographic functions as stated above, e.g. the used zero-knowledge-proof, blind or group signature schemes.
(G2) The secrecy of the credentials created by the issuer when initialising the smartcard or combining them with an embedded valuable secret.
(B1) The quality of the deployed device's tamperproofness.
(B2) The difficulty of circumventing the biometric sensors.
(S1) The value of the embedded secret.
(S2) The precautions taken by the users in combination with the system's potential to prevent loss, duplication or unauthorised use of credentials.
(S3) The strength of the connection between the anonymous credential and the embedded valuable secret.

2.5 Limiting the Consequences of Abuse

To limit the effect of dishonest users the issuer may want to limit the number of available tokens per time period. Damgård et al. proposed a scheme to allow only one anonymous authentication at a time [20]. Later, Camenisch et al. improved this approach by creating a credential system that lets a user anonymously authenticate at most n times per given time period [21]. The basic idea is that each user has a dispenser which automatically refreshes and creates n tokens every time period. Each token can only be used once and should a token be used twice the verifier is able to revoke the user's anonymity. Camenisch et al. also offer *glitch protection* for basically honest users who only occasionally reuse their tokens for instance if the user's operation system crashes. In this case, he may not know which tokens have already been used and thus mistakenly uses a token twice, even though unused tokens would have been available to him.

Of course the scheme itself does not provide non-transferability of credentials in any way, but in combination with the precautions stated earlier in this section it limits the extent of abuse if the number of available tokens per time period is chosen appropriately.

3 Scenario and Attacker Model

3.1 Scenario

There are at least two cases in which non-transferable anonymous credentials are useful. The first instance tries to prevent infringements by making the user prove a certain attribute, e.g. proof of age, driving licenses, a country's citizenship or special abilities such as academic degrees. These proofs have in common that they realise a kind of access control to enforce laws. People who are of legal age may buy alcohol and tobacco in stores, people who own a driving license may rent cars. In the second case anonymous credentials act as tickets for a given service. Either the service is paid in advance, e.g. weekly or monthly tickets for travelling by train or visiting a pool, or the ticket permits its owner a particular discount, e.g. seniors, student or handicapped ID or the German Railways BahnCard. It may not be obvious at a first glance, but the difference between the two scenarios lies in the injured party if the system is circumvented. The first scenario's aggrieved party is the issuer who wants to enforce a certain law while in the latter scenario the user can obtain a service cheaper or by fraud and, thus, the verifier is, or belongs to, the injured party.

3.2 Attacker Model

There are several parties involved in an anonymous credential system: the issuer, the user and the verifier of the credential. Furthermore, the manufacturer of the software and hardware needs to be trustworthy, especially when using biometric access control and, therefore, tamper-proof devices are needed. Since our main focus lies on the comparison of the strengths and weaknesses of both approaches with respect to the credentials' non-transferability, we make several assumptions to narrow the field of possible attacking parties. First of all, we do not address third party's attacks since – depending on their goal – they will have less power than the involved parties. If a third party wants to gather information about the user, the verifier can be considered more powerful since he already interacts with the user. If we study attacks on the credential system or the credential's non-transferability the user is more powerful since he already has a valid credential. We also assume that anonymous credentials will not be used in high-security environments and that the attacking costs are proportionate to the assessed breach win. Therefore, we adopt a more practical view on the security of the system.

Furthermore, we imply that each party uses only trustworthy hard- and software for its own devices with no backdoors, Trojan horses, etc. We note that the tamper-proof device used for biometric access control is a shared device, since it is operated by the user and either the issuer (first scenario) or the verifier (latter scenario) wants to be sure it executes only trustworthy operations. Due to the fact that the user does not need to trust the tamper-proof device here because we rely on the wallet with observer architecture, it is reasonable to concede the choice of the tamper-proof device to the issuer or the verifier, respectively.

While the verifier has a natural interest to prove the credential in the latter scenario we suppose he shows at least reasonable interest to do so in the first scenario. This assumption is based on the observation that either the verifier, e.g. a police officer, has a certain relationship to the issuer or the verifier is forced to carefully prove the credential by a third party, e.g. the state or an insurance company. Thus, the aim of a dishonest verifier is most likely to gather information about the user and to break his privacy. In addition to transferable anonymous credentials the verifier may want to investigate the user's embedded secret or some of his biometric data. But since we assume the wallet with observer architecture does not leak any biometrics and the embedded secret provides the verifier no additional point of attack, we conclude the verifier is only capable of attacking the underlying credential system even if the embedded secret may provide him a stronger incentive to do so.

We further assume that the issuer generates credentials or initialises the tamper-proof device without leaking any secret information to the user or verifier and, vice versa, that a protocol is used that does not reveal the user's valuable secret [6,7] or biometrics to the issuer.

This leaves us with one possible attacker, the user, and we need to take a closer look at his goals. If the user is seen as an attacker his aim is to trick the authentication either by creating his own credentials or by sharing a valid credential with other persons. As stated above, if the credential can be transferred or the system is broken, it can be easily seen that in most cases either a law is circumvented (first scenario) or the verifier is aggrieved (latter scenario).

4 Attacks on Untransferability

4.1 General Attacks

Before going into detail about the attacks on the specific approaches we discuss a general attack on the wallet with observer architecture which can also be applied if the non-transferability of the credential is provided by an embedded secret. The verifier cannot be sure if the user is in radio contact with a legitimate user (and smartcard) who is willing to accomplish the authentication for him (see Figure 1). A simple but hard to implement countermeasure would be to isolate the user during authentication to prevent him from communicating with others. Another approach, distance-bounding protocols, measures round-trip-times to prevent relay attacks and was proposed by Beth and Desmedt [22] and the first concrete protocol was introduced by Brands and Chaum [23]. Drimer and Murdoch describe an implementation of this defence for smartcards which requires only modest alterations to current hardware and software [24]. Even though the setup is slightly different from [24], since the smartcard in the wallet with observer architecture is not allowed to communicate directly with the verifier to protect the user's privacy, distance-bounding protocols provide an opportunity to prevent or limit relay attacks, if appropriate timing constraints are chosen. Since this attack affects both approaches we do not further elaborate on relay attacks and their countermeasures in this paper.

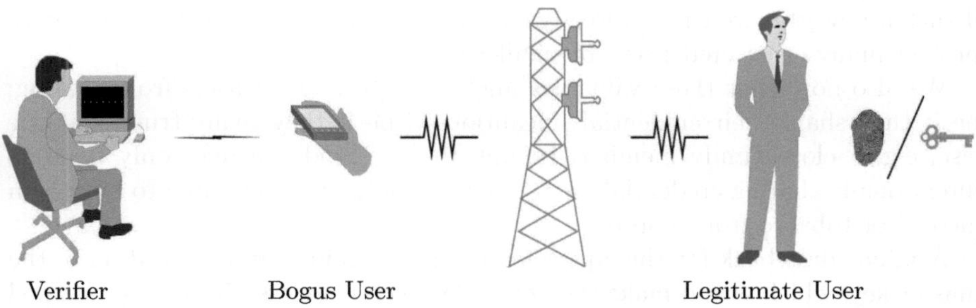

Fig. 1. If they are able to communicate, a bogus and a legitimate user could share a credential

4.2 Attacks on the Specific Approaches

In the previous section we narrowed down the field to one attacker: the user who wants to share or forge credentials. This section aims to compare how biometric access control and embedded valuable secrets fulfil their needs. When taking a closer look at the integral parts of the credential system's security (see section 2.4) it is obvious that both approaches do not differ much as far as the security of the basis credential system (G) is concerned. As we are interested in comparing the provided security we can disregard (G1,2). This reduces our evaluation to approach specific security (B1,2) versus (S1-3).

Biometric Access Control. When evaluating attacks on the approach using biometric access control there are two points of attack, the tamper-proof device and the biometric sensor. Since the biometric sensor is embedded in the device and, therefore, only has probably a moderate security level, it is reasonable to neglect (B1) and consider (B2) the weakest point. Many reports on circumvention of biometric systems include the use of photos with iris codes or facial age verification or forged fingerprints and suggest that unattended biometric access control, e.g. online or automated age verification, is susceptible to fraud while it may be harder but not unfeasible to circumvent attended verification, e.g. at a bar.

This suggests that biometric access control restricts the group of people who are able to share a credential to those who are experts in biometric sensors or tamper-proof devices or at least profit from the experts' work.

Embedded Valuable Secrets. Regarding the security of embedded secrets it is evident that (S2) strongly depends on (S1). Only if the embedded secret has some value to the user, he takes care to protect it. On the other hand, if the system is set up carefully it seems unfeasible to the user to detach the embedded secret from the credentials. We therefore claim that the value of the secret is most important for this approach. To find a reasonably valuable secret is quite a problem. On the one hand, the proposed master secret key in [6] seems capable of preventing most users from sharing. On the other hand, using such a powerful key seems disproportional and dangerous to protect low value credentials. However, if such a powerful credential already exists for other purposes it may be used to protect many other credentials of smaller value.

We also note that these valuables might not prevent all users from sharing; be it they share their credentials incautiously, be it they really trust someone else, e.g. a close family member. Having this in mind, we refer only to users intentionally sharing credentials, e.g. parents sending their children to buy them alcohol or tobacco from a store.

A minor drawback for this approach is the possibility of a revocation of the master key, which would make the embedded secret useless. Since it is assumed that the embedded key is very powerful, and thus valuable, it is inevitable to let the user revoke it. This allows the user to immediately end the validity of a previously shared credential for the cost of needing a reinitialisation of his credentials (the master key and all keys depended on it). Obviously a simple countermeasure is to make the user pay for each reinitialisation as it is already common for example with cash cards or SIM cards. The price of the reinitialisation and the possible savings determine if this is a profitable deal for the user.

Another advantage considering anonymous credentials with embedded values is that they do not necessarily need an extra device. For example, concerning age verification at an online shop, it would be enough to have additional software on the already available computer. But in this case the credential is most likely in a very dangerous environment and can easily be stolen if the computer is compromised. A way to prevent this would be to delegate this task to a smart card. Which of those approaches is the most suitable is mainly a trade-off between the quality of the embedded valuable secret, the required strength of non-transferability, and the economic costs.

Combining Embedded Valuable Secrets and Biometric Access Control. Comparing both approaches we have shown that the decision which approach is most suitable is an estimation between the user's ability to circumvent the biometric sensor versus the value of the embedded secret he might be ready to risk. A combination of both approaches seems to be promising regarding the non-transferability, since a possible attacker has to circumvent the biometric sensors or break the tamper-proof device and, furthermore, the owner of the credentials must be willing to share his secret. Otherwise not only the benefits accumulate but also the restrictions. Users must have usable fingerprints and a valuable secret which they are willing to embed into the system. The combination of the approaches is the most expensive, since each user needs a tamper-proof device with embedded fingerprint reader and the system has to be linked to an already existing "legal digital signature certification authority" which probably will not be free of charge.

5 Conclusion

As the previous section shows, neither biometric access control nor embedded valuable secrets ensure the non-transferability of anonymous credentials. While biometric access control is the more expensive and probably more error-prone solution, it might be hard to find valuable secrets to really prevent the sharing of credentials, especially since the user is able to revoke the sharing at any time.

Table 1 gives an overview on the elaborated attributes of both approaches. The main disadvantage of biometric access control is that it seems feasible to bypass unattended biometric access controls and that the biometric's missing universality might restrict its usage. Otherwise biometric access control limits the possibility of unintentionally sharing the credentials for free and if the biometric measurements are attended it seems applicable. Furthermore, by the use of tamper-proof devices the cloning of credentials gets quite hard and, thus, the issuer can be at least reasonably sure the credential is not cloned.

Embedded valuables in contrast raise the system's value and thus the incentive of stealing them (with the underlying credentials) or breaking the system's architecture. For low value credentials it may be possible to put a certain amount of the user's money at risk if he shares his credential, but naturally this will not prevent all users from sharing. If there already exists a valuable credential, credentials of lower value can be bound to it, but even then the user might decide to share, e.g. with close family members. To avoid unintentional sharing of the credential the user must be very careful or has to additionally use a tamper-proof device to protect his credentials.

Also, the combination of both approaches is not the answer to all drawbacks. While it may prevent more users from sharing it suffers from restrictions of both approaches and from the effort needed to put it in place. Nevertheless, it

Table 1. Attributes of different approaches to ensure non-transferability: biometric access control, embedded valuable secret, a combination of both approaches, and embedded valuable secret with a tamper-proof device

attribute	biometrics	embedded secret
circumvention depends on	(un)attended access control	secret
circumvention by	experts	close family members
tamper-proof device	with biometric reader needed	not needed
universality depends on	biometrics	secret
credential cloning	hard	easy
unintended sharing	unlikely	may occur
system's value	unchanged	raised

attribute	biometrics & embedded secret	embedded secret (TP)
circumvention depends on	(un)attended AC & secret	secret
circumvention by	trusted experts	close family members
tamper-proof device	with biometric reader needed	needed
universality depends on	biometrics & secret	secret
credential cloning	hard	medium
unintended sharing	unlikely	unlikely
system's value	raised	raised

is important to keep in mind that all approaches are not able to assure non-transferability if the user cannot be isolated but is able to communicate with the outside world during authentication. Therefore, all implementations need to take defences against relay attacks into account, e.g. based on distance-bounding protocols.

Acknowledgement

The author is grateful to Lexi Pimenidis for helpful discussions and comments on an earlier version of this work and to the anonymous reviewers for their feedback and suggestions. The author also thanks the participants of the Summer School for their annotations and fruitful discussions.

References

1. Chaum, D.: Security without identification: transaction systems to make big brother obsolete. Communications of the ACM 28, 1030–1044 (1985)
2. Chaum, D., Evertse, J.-H.: A secure and privacy-protecting protocol for transmitting personal information between organizations. In: Odlyzko, A.M. (ed.) CRYPTO 1986. LNCS, vol. 263, pp. 118–167. Springer, Heidelberg (1987)

3. Chaum, D.: Blind Signatures for Untraceable Payments. In: Advances in Cryptology – CRYPTO 1982, pp. 199–203. Springer, Heidelberg (1999)
4. Dwork, C., Lotspiech, J., Naor, M.: Digital Signets: Self-Enforcing Protection of Digital Information. In: Proceedings on Theory of Computing, 28th Ann. ACM Symp. (1997)
5. Goldreich, O., Pfitzmann, B., Rivest, R.L.: Self-Delegation with Controlled Propagation — or — What If You Lose Your Laptop. In: Krawczyk, H. (ed.) CRYPTO 1998. LNCS, vol. 1462, pp. 153–168. Springer, Heidelberg (1998)
6. Lysyanskaya, A., Rivest, R.L., Sahai, A., Wolf, S.: Pseudonym Systems. In: Heys, H.M., Adams, C.M. (eds.) SAC 1999. LNCS, vol. 1758, pp. 184–199. Springer, Heidelberg (2000)
7. Camenisch, J., Lysyanskaya, A.: An Efficient System for Non-transferable Anonymous Credentials with Optional Anonymity Revocation. In: Pfitzmann, B. (ed.) EUROCRYPT 2001. LNCS, vol. 2045, pp. 93–118. Springer, Heidelberg (2001)
8. Bleumer, G.: Biometric yet Privacy Protecting Person Authentication. In: Aucsmith, D. (ed.) IH 1998. LNCS, vol. 1525, pp. 99–110. Springer, Heidelberg (1998)
9. Chaum, D.: Blind signatures for untraceable payments. In: Advances in Cryptology – Crypto 1982, pp. 199–203. Springer, Heidelberg (1983)
10. Chaum, D., van Heyst, E.: Group signatures. In: Davies, D.W. (ed.) EUROCRYPT 1991. LNCS, vol. 547, pp. 257–265. Springer, Heidelberg (1991)
11. FFIEC Press Release: Authentication in an Internet Banking Environment. Techreport, Federal Financial Institutions Examination Council (2005)
12. Brainard, J., Juels, A., Rivest, R., Szydlo, M., Yung, M.: Fourth Factor Authentication: Somebody You Know. In: CCS 2006: Proceedings of the 13th ACM conference on Computer and communications security, pp. 168–178. ACM, New York (2006)
13. Chaum, D., Pedersen, T.P.: Wallet Databases with Observers. In: Brickell, E.F. (ed.) CRYPTO 1992. LNCS, vol. 740, pp. 89–105. Springer, Heidelberg (1993)
14. Impagliazzo, R., More, S.M.: Anonymous Credentials with Biometrically-Enforced Non-Transferability. In: Proceedings of the 2003 ACM Workshop on Privacy in the Electronic Society (WPES 2003), pp. 60–71 (2003)
15. Homepage of Biometric Associates, Inc., http://www.biometricassociates.com
16. Pan, S.B., Gil, Y.H., Moon, D., Chung, Y., Park, C.H.: A Memory-Efficient Fingerprint Verification Algorithm Using a Multi-Resolution Accumulator Array. ETRI Journal 25, 179–186 (2003)
17. Barwise, M., Bachfeld, D.: Attack of the card cloners. IT security news and services at heise Security UK (2007), http://www.heise-online.co.uk/security/features/print/100187
18. Finkenzeller, K.: RFID Handbook: Fundamentals and Applications in Contactless Smart Cards and Identification, 446 pages. John Wiley and Sons, Chichester (2003)
19. Graafstra, A.: RFID Toys: 11 Cool Projects for Home, Office and Entertainment, 336 pages. Wiley, Chichester (2006)
20. Damgård, I., Dupont, K., Pedersen, M.O.: Unclonable Group Identification. In: Vaudenay, S. (ed.) EUROCRYPT 2006. LNCS, vol. 4004, pp. 555–572. Springer, Heidelberg (2006)
21. Camenisch, J., Hohenberger, S., Kohlweiss, M., Lysyanskaya, A., Meyerovich, M.: How to win the clonewars: efficient periodic n-times anonymous authentication. In: CCS 2006: Proceedings of the 13th ACM conference on Computer and communications security, pp. 201–210. ACM, New York (2006)

22. Beth, T., Desmedt, Y.: Identification tokens – or: Solving the chess grandmaster problem. In: Menezes, A., Vanstone, S.A. (eds.) CRYPTO 1990. LNCS, vol. 537, pp. 169–176. Springer, Heidelberg (1991)
23. Brands, S., Chaum, D.: Distance-bounding protocols. In: Helleseth, T. (ed.) EUROCRYPT 1993. LNCS, vol. 765, pp. 344–359. Springer, Heidelberg (1994)
24. Drimer, S., Murdoch, S.J.: Keep your enemies close: distance bounding against smartcard relay attacks. In: SS 2007: Proceedings of 16th USENIX Security Symposium on USENIX Security Symposium, pp. 1–16. USENIX Association (2007)

Security of Wireless Communication*

Dan Cvrček

Brno University of Technology
dancvrcek@gmail.com

Abstract. What are the real security issues of wireless communication and wireless sensor networks in particular? Despite predictions of wireless sensor networks being deployed in many aspects of everyday life, real world deployments are still quite sparse. It seems that monitoring of large civil engineering structures is one of the few applications where wireless sensor networks may give enough value for the necessary investment. The least, several companies managing large civil structures in the UK are keen on investigating the potential of wireless sensor networks.

In the light of this technology, which is built on a new paradigm of dense wireless communication networks, we can see new security challenges never experienced by engineers before. Can we appreciate the difference between wire and wireless communication and also the difference between centralised wireless networks, e.g., WiFi and largely decentralised sensor networks? We show how the shift in the technology introduces new problems that need to be solved to provide secure communication systems. The second part of the paper details particular attacks that work against current implementations of wireless sensor networks and routing, traffic analysis, and cryptography in particular.

1 Introduction

The history of wireless and wired communication intertwines. We have used wireless optical communication systems until the nineteenth century when electricity was discovered and we learnt that it was possible to send sound and signals through a wire. Lengths of communication links increased largely when the voice was replaced with the Morse code. Marconi was behind first practical radios able to send electrical signals over the air at the beginning of the twentieth century. He increased the radio range enough to allow sending messages across the Atlantic ocean.

The wireless communication was cheap but it did not allow to connect two persons willing to speak to each other. The first telephone systems were wired and thanks to the networks built in the early years of telephoning, we still use land-line telephones. The wireless technology is more complicated but it has recently become reliable and cheap to compete with, and possibly replace, wired systems in certain scenarios.

---

* The paper is based on the work carried out with Frank Stajano and Matt Lewis as part of the EPSRC WINES Infrastructures project at the University of Cambridge, UK.

V. Matyáš et al. (Eds.): The Future of Identity, IFIP AICT 298, pp. 119–134, 2009.

Table 1. What is the wire communication about

For Wire	Against Wire
Well defined transmission medium	Cost of the infrastructure
More options for network management	Ownership of links between nodes
Limited interference	Fixed infrastructure
High bandwidth	

What are actually the advantages of wire communication? When you look at Table 1 you may realise that wired communication is more suitable for networks featuring a large number of nodes with many connections. The more the network changes into a sparse graph with long links, the cons gain on the importance. As a matter of fact, we can list specific scenarios, where wireless technology dominates:

- fast-changing topologies – GSM and WiFi;
- sparse network topologies – Microwave links, WiFi;
- short-range communication – Blue-tooth, ZigBee; and
- low-cost, quick network deployment – ZigBee, WiFi.

In any of these scenarios, wireless communication will be the preferred technology and the economic advantage further increases in locations lacking an existing wired, land-line network.

There is one more low-point of wireless communication. It is restricted by regulations of the public frequency spectrum use. There are very few frequency bands available for digital communication systems and they cover frequencies from about 1 to 5 GHz. As a result, the power of transmitters is strictly regulated and the communication distance is limited so that neighbouring transmitters do not interfere with each other.

However, this holds only for "legitimate" networks. Attackers would not feel to be bound by the limitations and not only because they usually stay in one place too shortly to be caught. The transmitting power of adversaries much higher than that of legitimate users is only one of the aspects underlining security challenges for wireless communications.

2 Security Problems

Due to omnidirectional transmission, there are three main security subjects differentiating wireless from the wired communication:

- Authentication / masquerading – robust authentication of the other end of the communication channel;
- Relaying – ensuring that the communication is happening in real time and is not maliciously delayed by a whatever small amount of time; and
- Eavesdropping – ensuring that no one can listen to the communication without being authorised or detected.

2.1 Authentication

Security of any security protocol depends on the assumptions stated for a given system. It is not possible to say whether a protocol is or is not secure until someone defines what is meant by "secure". Everyone knows that the Needham-Schroeder protocol [1] is broken. When one reads the paper, it seems that its authors assumed there are two sets of users, legitimate and attackers, and that the legitimate users were not supposed to attack each other. This is not explicitly stated though and the protocol gets broken only after this assumption is ignored or removed.

We believe that most of you are familiar with the GSM technology. Any communication channel (a connected call) consists of three logical parts: a wireless connection between the caller and a Base Transceiver Station (BTS), a wireless connection between another BTS and a callee, and a back-end wired leg connecting the two BTSes. No one has been really much interested in the security of the middle leg as there is no cryptography deployed and any attack is possible so long as one can get access to the wire. However, a lot of cryptographic research has been carried out for the wireless links.

There are two cryptographic algorithms – A3 and A5 – providing cryptographic assurance that no unauthorised person can eavesdrop on calls or masquerade and initiate or accept calls on someone else's behalf [2,3]. We know today that the algorithms are cryptographically weak but any attack still needs a lot of mathematics and special equipment or software.

It is much less widely known that the GSM protocol suite is also broken because it does not require two-way authentication. The BTS stations do not authenticate themselves. GSM standards only require users (their handsets) to authenticate to a BTS. Is it possible for someone to masquerade as a BTS and accept calls from / to users in their communication range?

This attack does not require breaking any cryptographic protocol but one needs a special equipment that is hard to get by – not even on eBay. One needs a special licence and only mobile phone operators or specialised agencies are able to acquire it. A BTS is also a quite expensive piece of equipment to buy.

This has however changed recently with GSM Femtocells. Vendors of home and small business network routers realised that there may be a demand for devices forwarding GSM phone calls to VoIP systems, e.g., Skype and 3G data connections to a cable broadband connection. It would also solve a problem of weak GSM signal in some buildings. As a result, wireless routers with interfaces for GSM, ADSL and WLAN were introduced with a quite affordable price tag of about twice as much as for WiFi home routers.

Figure 1 shows communication ranges for different types of GSM cells. The range is limited by the antenna used on the cell's base station. A restriction quite easy to overcome. (Attackers usually do not feel to be bound by limits imposed on transmission power by regulators.)

Thanks to the advance in the GSM technology, man in the middle or impersonation attacks are now within reach of attackers with shoestring budgets.

Cell type	Typical cell size	Data rate limitation
Macro	1 – 30 km	Propagation
Micro	200m – 2km	Capacity and propagation
Pico	4 – 200 m	Capacity and propagation
Femto	10 m	Broadband connection and handset

Fig. 1. Types of GSM cells

2.2 Relaying and Eavesdropping

Wireless technology is susceptible to relay attacks when the attacker creates a transparent tunnel between a sender and a recipient. Attacks on communication between RFID cards and readers are typical examples studied in several papers (e.g. [4,5]).

The problem of the RFID technology is that it was designed to remove interventions from users. Any RFID card will start an authentication process whenever it is placed in the proximity of a reader allowing for opening doors or paying for lunch in a canteen without removing the card from a wallet or even pocket.

The security was deemed to be sufficient as the communication range of RFID cards is less than 4 inches and either the card authentication enabled only low value transactions or there have been other security mechanisms in place providing an additional layer of security.

Four inches, is it really the maximum distance? Gerhard Hancke et al. [4] conducted a thorough research of RFID capabilities and studied two scenarios, for a passive and an active attacker.

1. Passive attacker – the attacker is only trying to eavesdrop on messages sent from a card to a reader. This scenario is applicable on situations when cards use a static response for their authentication or when they send sensitive data to readers, e.g., personal information sent by a passport at customs. Authors were able to optimise the antenna and increased the possible distance from an RFID card to the antenna to 4 meters.
2. Active attacker – attacks in this scenario try to increase the distance between a reader and a card by using a stronger electromagnetic field generated by an improved antenna. They were able to increase the communication range to 1.5 meter, while the reader was 15 cm away from the smart-card.

Communication range is quite an interesting topic. John Hering developed a blue-tooth rifle in 2004-5 [6]. The maximum communication range of Bluetooth devices is well below 50 meters, typically 10 meters. John's gun was able to tap bluetooth devices (e.g., perform a passive attack) from over a mile away, during experiments carried out against devices in high office buildings in New York.

Increasing communication range improves attackers' ability to communicate with a card (or other wireless device). They can then use the device as an oracle to authenticate transactions taking place even kilometres away from the card by relaying the card responses via a WiFi or a low-delay wireless connection. RFID standards and implementations introduce maximum delays, but they are very generous in terms of maximum distance available for relay attacks.

3 Wireless Sensor Networks

Wireless sensor networks represent just a small fraction of wireless networks but they abstract some of interesting new concepts in distributed computing and their existing practical implementations re-introduce security challenges of wired communications in a very different environment.

There is an abstraction of sensor motes called smart dust. Smart dust represents tiny motes (just a few square millimeters), powered by a battery or sollar energy, and very cheap to produce. It is also possible, in this abstraction, to deploy tens of thousands of motes in a single network.

There has been published a large body of theoretical research into properties of wireless sensor networks – very large networks of very simple nodes (motes). Such networks were presumed to be deployed in large batches (e.g., by throwing them off a plane) followed by a self-organising phase, automatically and autonomously launched after the physical deployment of the motes. The large quantity of motes brings in practical constraints: it is expensive to "personalise" motes by changing the code or data stored on the motes. It is much easier to mass-produce sensors that are identical even on firmware and configuration level.

A lot of security research has been devoted to key management schemes in this special environment and particularly to key pre-distribution schemes. Key pre-distribution schemes expect any two nodes to establish a shared pairwise (link) key when they happen to be physical neighbours after their deployment. As sensor networks are assumed to form dense graphs, the probability of two randomly selected nodes sharing a common key can be much lower than 100 %. Theoretical models based on this assumption introduce a trade-off between the network connectivity and the memory required to store keys on nodes.

The idea of random key pre-distribution for wireless sensor networks was firstly introduced in [7] as the EG scheme. Here, each node contains a random subset of keys from a large set of keys. Motes perform a key setup phase identifying subsets of shared keys between any two neighbours and these keys are subsequently used to secure communication between the two motes. It is possible to use probability theory to compute ideal sizes of key sets to ensure connectivity of large and dense networks. There are various extensions of this scheme. Authors of [8] introduce a scheme requiring at least q shared keys instead of one. Another approach uses pseudo-random generation, instead of random selection, of key indexes [9].

Pairwise key pre-distribution is another scheme. Any given key is shared by exactly two nodes in a network and a compromise of any mote does not compromise any other mote in the network. As opposed to schemes in the previous paragraph, where capturing of a very small subset of network motes may reveal a majority of keys used in the network.

4 Real Wireless Sensor Networks

The following sections describe practical security issues one encounters when commercial off-the-shelf wireless sensor nodes are to be used. The first thing we have to mention is that the networks are much different from what has been described in the previous section.

There areseveral vendors of general purpose wireless sensor kits, although it seems that academic research is still the main market. Most widely used platform is TinyOS developed as a GNU project. Several commercial products, including Xbow we worked with, are extensions of TinyOS. The presented results are not theoretical results but outcomes of experiments with real implementations of sensor networks.

4.1 Typical Deployment

We experimented with mesh networks built from MICAz motes with mounted sensors designed by civil engineers. These motes run TinyOS system and wireless communication is implemented with IEEE 802.15.4 compliant radio chips. The standard defines maximum link bandwidth to be 250 kbps.

Battery life of motes might provide several years of up-time if the communication was initiated once a day. Current setup introduces communication several times a minute and batteries last for 4-5 weeks. We have built improved nodes with special D and DD size batteries that should last more than a year.

Our mesh networks consist of clusters of 10-30 motes connected to one relaying gateway. These clusters, including the gateway, are independent of each other without any direct connections. The clusters connect via their gateways to a central computer managing the networks and collecting data.

Gateways are Linux boxes (Stargate [10]) with one MICAz mote for a 802.15.4 / ZigBee connection to the mesh network. This mote talks to its gateway via an RS-232 interface. Gateways connect to the central computer using a WiFi router with a GPRS module or an ADSL router (particular technology depends on the physical location and available networks).

5 Attacker Modelling

We tried to model an attacker before we started practical experiments. Practicality of attacks has been re-assessed after experiments to reflect difficulty of attack scenarios. We used two approaches to find out probable attackers. The first approach was to interview owners of large civil structures where we deployed the networks for monitoring to find out what would be the networks' use in a few years time and what they see as major risks. These interviews identified curious hacker interested in the technology as the most likely attacker as the systems are not foreseen to provide any valuable data over short periods of time.

The second approach was to build a simple classification of attackers according to their knowledge and to the access to a sensor network they need to carry out certain attacks. Let us start with different types of access that may be needed for different attacks.

1. Remote access over the Internet – attacker may connect from anywhere and it is very hard to find them, identify them, or prosecute them.
2. Remote access over national/local communication infrastructure – attacker exploits access through infrastructures that are either local (WiFi networks), or with otherwise limited access from a certain area.

3. Physical proximity to system – attacker needs to get very close to the deployed network – distance in the range of tens of meters or less. It allows him to use communication means of motes or perform DoS attacks that require interaction with components of the network.
4. Physical access to single elements of system – attacker is able to physically touch particular motes, gateways of the network. This allows them tampering the device and re-program, replace or remove parts of the device or the device itself. The time and expertise may greatly vary (e.g., connecting to a mote would take a few seconds while reading out a permanent memory may require substantially more time).
5. Physical access to all (or most of) elements of the system – the most expensive scenario requiring attacker to get access to a large number of devices.

One can see that the first three options are achievable even for a low budget attacker. All our networks are connected to the Internet, some of them are even in publicly accessible areas. Physical access to networks deployed in underground systems (London underground in our case) is difficult and a physical proximity can be achieved easily only on a train – i.e. for very short time periods.

The second important issue is power of the attacker. This can be viewed from three different angles: money, knowledge, and personnel. One extreme is formed by an attacker without money, little knowledge and no personal (just him/her) – often called script kiddies. The opposite extreme is someone with unlimited money, detailed knowledge about the system and technologies being used, and of course enough personal to implement desired attack scenarios.

Attack scenarios we want to pursue assume attackers between the least powerful ones and a skillful hacker able to change the code for motes with limited budget that allows buying off-the-shelf products. We will also assume that the attacker can get access to the system as specified in the first three (or four in some cases) options from the list above. The most relevant types of threats are:

1. attacks on wireless communication:
   - eavesdropping communication;
   - analysis of gathered data; and
   - injection of new traffic (or replay attacks).
2. attacks exploiting decentralisation of the network management:
   - data communicated between sensors and sensor-gateway;
   - sources of data;
   - routing algorithms; and
   - how to defeat countermeasures when gateways / sensors check integrity of each other.
3. physical access to a device and subsequent:
   - changes in software/firmware;
   - spread of changes (infection) to other network nodes / gateways; and
   - disabling device.

6 Selective Jamming – Debugging Mode

Jamming is definitely a low-cost attack. We implemented powerful jamming attacks without requiring any special hardware and based only on changes or extensions of available software. Such attacks are highly relevant as they allow for implementations by a relatively high number of potential adversaries.

As we were deploying MICAz motes in our monitoring networks, we chose MICAz (with the CC2420 radio chip) as the basic hardware platform for attack implementations. The motes are easy to buy and all necessary software is available as a freeware on the Internet. Micro-controllers on these motes are quite slow (clocked on less than 8 MHz) and re-implementation of the attack on almost any other platform will be undoubtedly feasible with respect to computational requirements.

Current implementation requires the criteria triggering the attack to be defined in advance. The criteria are in a form of matching conditions for selected bytes of messages and they are compiled into the code.

Once the mote is uploaded with the code and deployed, it keeps listening to the traffic. The mote eavesdrops enough bytes, decides whether the received content satisfies the pre-programmed criteria and if so, it switches the radio to Tx mode and jams the rest of the packet.

The most difficult step was to implement byte by byte listening. CC2420 chip normally receives an entire message (frame), stores it in a buffer, and raises a signal to the micro-controller to download the frame. When the micro-controller needs to transmit a packet, it uploads the whole packet to the internal buffer of the CC2420 and signals back that the content should be transmitted.

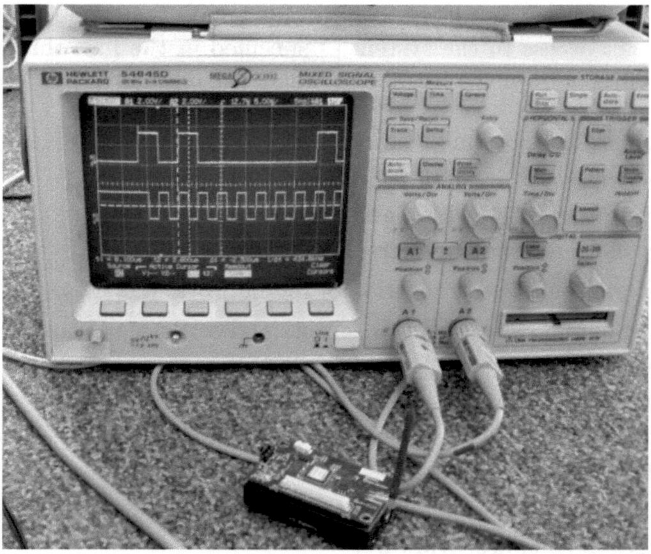

Fig. 2. Start of a frame – clock of the radio chip (top line) and sampled data bits (bottom line)

What we need for the attack to work, is the ability to listen to single bytes of the message and to stop listening at any time. Fortunately CC2420, as all other radio chips we have seen, features a debug mode that should be used for testing basic functionality of the chip. This mode allows single bits to be read by the micro-controller as they are received from the air. It means that we can do exactly what we want. The micro-controller takes care of the synchronisation, reading, and storing the data bits (fig. 2 shows a clock signal and first message bits provided by CC2420).

The application implemented in NesC language (a macro language based on C for TinyOS programming) not only correctly reads / eavesdrops messages, but it is also very code efficient.

6.1 Frame Format

The frame format as used by MICAz motes differs from what was described in [11] as changes were introduced with the switch to the new radio chip.

$$length\ (1B)\ |\ fcf\ (2B)\ |\ dsn\ (1B)\ |\ destpan\ (2B)\ |\ Dest\ (2B)|$$
$$|\ AM\ (1B)\ |\ GrpID\ (1B)\ |\ Data\ (\leq 29B)\ |\ CRC\ (2B)$$

Items *length*, *fcf*, *dsn*, *destpan* are parts of 802.15.4 MAC layer. *fcf* (frame control field) says whether it is a data or some other type of frame. Destination mote address is of just two bytes (*Dest*). *dsn* is an eight bit serial number of the packet (used only to match acknowledge (ACK) frames confirming a frame reception with the original frame). *destpan* is always set to indicate broadcast ($0xFFFF$) to ensure that all motes will listen to all the messages. The remaining items in the depicted frame contain a TinyOS message itself.

TinyOS applications usually compile with multi-hop support. This functionality is based on a special seven bytes long routing header at the beginning of the *Data* field. It contains (*source address* (2B), *original address* (2B), *sequence number* (2B), and *hop count* (1B)). This would be followed by the data generated by the mote with the *original address* ID.

6.2 Jamming

The trigger condition we used was the *original address* to match a certain value. This allows jamming frames from selected motes anywhere in the network because *originaladdress* does not change. We did the first tests on a small network consisting of seven motes around the office. The topology of the network was a simple star as all the motes were able to directly reach the gateway (see Fig. 3).

The visualisation as showed in Fig. 3a) demonstrates immediate disconnection of the jammed node (mote with ID 24) and a short instability of the network topology when the jamming started. The topology has returned to the star shape after a very short time and the jammed node remained disconnected – Fig. 3b).

The second set of tests was based on jamming a mid-range connection (4 – 15 meters) between two motes, with different positions of the jamming mote. Overall

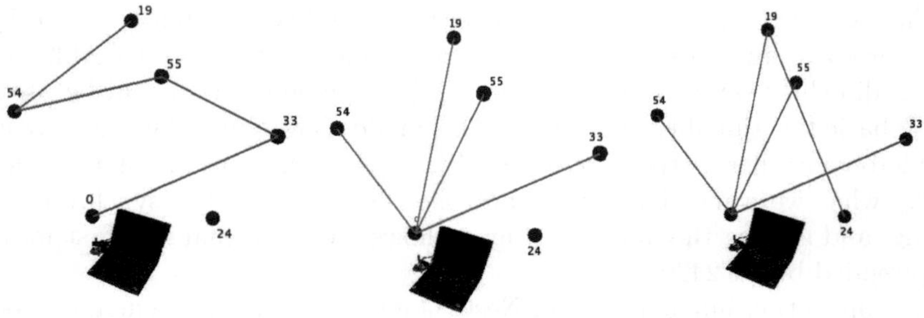

a) jamming started b) stabilised topology c) jamming stopped

Fig. 3. A network during and after jamming of node 24

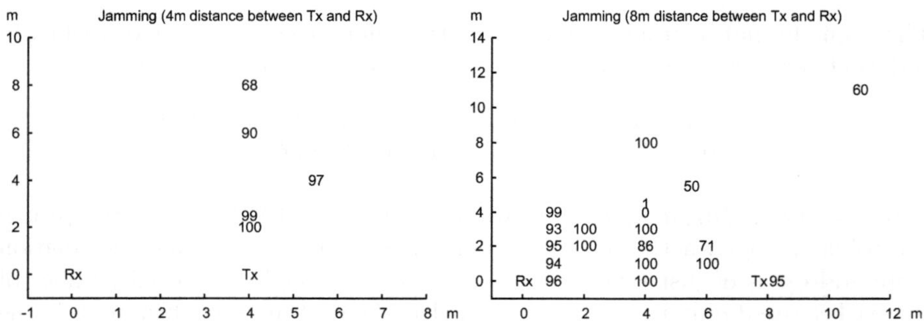

Fig. 4. Success rate of jamming depending on the position of the attacking mote. The Tx and Rx labels are the transmitting and receiving motes. The numbers 0–100 in the graphs denote the percentage of packets that were jammed in particular configurations.

efficiency was usually close to 100%, even for the jammer much further away, and in different directions from the receiver (see Figure 4). However, there were several occasions when the jamming was very ineffective, even in configurations that previously showed high success rates.

Electrical engineers told us that the anomalies are very likely to be caused by signal reflections in the particular environment. It may be therefore plausible to eliminate them with using a couple of jamming motes.

Despite this unpredictability in the test results, we believe that the attack is very powerful, and it constitutes a serious threat. The experiments, we have performed, used jammer with the same antenna and transmission power as were of other transmitters, but these can be easily replaced / increased.

6.3 Defences

We obviously can not eliminate jamming attacks completely. What we can do is to make it harder for adversaries to implement power efficient jamming attacks, and rebalance cost-benefit ratio of the attacks. Wood et al. analyse in

[12] defences against jamming attacks and they propose three basic approaches: changing SFD (start of frame delimiter), shortening frames, and channel hopping. We believe that although the defences may increase complexity of attacks, the efficacy of these three defences varies. The defences also influence reliability of the network communication and incur an increase in the power consumption of the nodes.

Unpredictable SFD. Randomising the start-of-frame (SFD) delimiter seems to be a very promising approach as it makes it very hard for the attacker to detect transmitted frames. Unfortunately, available radio chips allow definition of SFD in such a way that SFD is of zero length or its value is *0x00*. This is the value of the frame preamble preceding SFD that can not be changed. The attacker is thus able to eavesdrop all frames regardless on the value of SFD. Changes in SFD value also imply non-compliance with 802.15.4 standard.

Use of short frames. It assumes that the shorter the frame the more often the attacker has to listen to detect transmissions. The authors achieved this goal by shortening the preamble as much as possible, and with a fragmentation of frames. The former allowed them to decrease the mandatory data overhead to six bytes (four bytes for PHY header and two bytes for frame check sequence – FCS)[1]. They omitted fcf and dsn fields. Particularly missing fcf, however, would make it very cumbersome to process frames – especially discern data, ACK, beacon, and other types of frames.

There is another serious problem related to the use of shorter preambles – reliability of transmissions. We have experienced problems with quality of the signal even in relatively friendly outdoor environments. Any manipulation of frame formats that decreases the length of the frame headers will influence reliability.

Channel hopping. It was suggested as a very powerful defence when combined with the frame fragmentation. It will increase the cost of the hardware as more radios must be used in parallel – there are, however, only sixteen channels available, a fact that limits the increase of the cost for attackers.

A serious problem here may be time synchronisation in larger networks. Neither it is clear whether fragments of frames would be delivered in the correct order. A mechanism re-assembling frames (messages) from fragments sent by different motes and belonging to different frames would be needed.

Authors conclude that the probability of frame delivery went down by 20 % with very small transmission distances and just two motes – avoiding the just mentioned aspects.

It seems that jamming is still a problem worth further research. Attacks, as well as defences, may be strengthened and it is not clear whether higher robustness of networks against jamming attacks must necessarily incur higher energy consumption. Some of the defences could be also moved to higher layers of the protocol stack.

[1] We believe that this overhead would be higher as each PHY frame needs a preamble, SFD, frame length, frame control field, and data sequence number. This would add another three bytes.

You can see that although wireless communication has been with us for a long time, particular technology (frame formats, numbers of available channels, communication speed, and so on) introduces new possibilities for powerful low cost attacks.

7 Stability of Network Topology

Formation of the network topology is quite important for potential attacks on a network. It is hard to imagine an attacker present during the network deployment, but it is much more likely that the attacker will cause fragmentation or complete disconnection of a network by jamming with the goal to initiate re-establishment of the network connections at their chosen time allowing for active attacks.

7.1 Oscillations

We can demonstrate volatility of the topology even for a very small network (composed of motes on an office desk). We have repeatedly analysed traffic information of a small network of three motes (with IDs 2, 3, and 4) and a gateway (ID 0). We have received similar results when analysing the network installed in an anchorage room of the Humber bridge in the Northern England (see Fig. 6).

Remarkable is also the fact that the quality of links, calculated with a rather sophisticated algorithm by every node in the network, remained very high.

Subject	**Parents**
Mote 2	0 for a short while, then repeatedly 3 followed by 0 for briefs
Mote 3	0 and then repeatedly 4 followed by 0 for shorter intervals
Mote 4	0 is assigned as its parent and it remains so

Fig. 5. Topology of a simple network

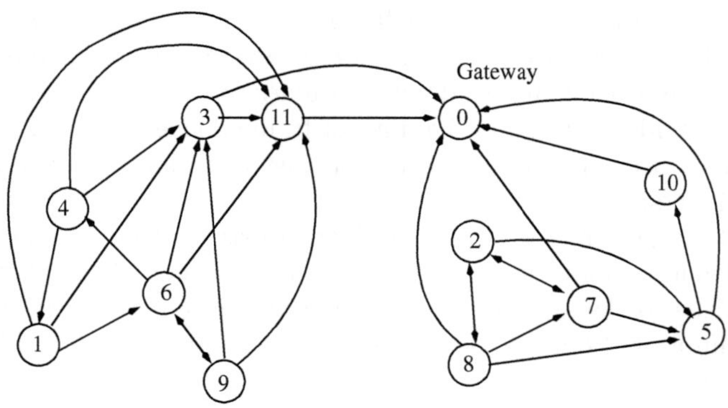

Fig. 6. Graph of all routes appearing in the network deployed on the Humber bridge

7.2 Traffic Analysis

A commercial variant of the MICAz software called XMesh changed addressing of frames. The original version used broadcasting while motes with XMesh address packets to their actual parental motes. Headers with the address cannot be encrypted as they are processed on a very low level of the protocol stack. Use of cryptography would require significant changes in the software and increase processing time and delays required for confirmations of frames delivery.

The attacker can also guess numbers of neighbours from the length of routing packets. Assuming that the attacker is able to jam certain messages, she can easily find the second best neighbour. XMesh will address the second best mote as a parent after six unsuccessful retransmissions of a frame.

It is not sufficient to assume that it is very unlikely for an attacker to be present when a network is being established. Once we start using decentralised, self-forming networks, we allow attackers to bring the networks into a "network state" of their choosing. They can analyse networks and search for the most vulnerable connections even when the communication is encrypted.

8 Attacks on Routing

Indeed, network routing seems to be the most vulnerable part of distributed network infrastructures. There are two main reasons for this. The implementations may be vulnerable to malicious attacks, and routing is a distributed algorithm, difficult to control from one point – the gateway, for example, would not able to detect irregularities in the network topology happening only one hop away.

TinyOS and XMesh use sophisticated algorithms built on the number of undelivered messages to compute quality of communication links and to select the best route to the gateway. Metrics for each direction of communication are treated separately and combined only when a new routing mote is being selected. Messages contain counters allowing for computation of lost messages.

8.1 Forced Selection of Parents

Motes can dynamically change their parental motes according to the numbers of undelivered messages. This feature can be again easily exploited for attacks. One does not even have to jam the communication, just injecting fake messages or replaying old messages with a link quality information would significantly change "quality" of links and the unjammed mote will be selected as a parent.

The parent is always selected according to the link cost computed from the separate numbers of frames lost in each direction. One half of the input information – the number of frames missed by recipients – can be directly forged when transmitted back to the originating mote. The attacker can either lower this estimate, causing the current parental node to be replaced, or improve the estimate for a mote she wants to be selected.

Motes without a route to the gateway are particularly easy to attack and injection of just one message is usually sufficient for the task. Attacks on an already established network are more difficult but there are still two main approaches. The first approach is to jam communication for sufficient amount of time and attack the then disconnected network. The second approach is to lower link quality estimates for all the neighbours except the one we want to become the parent. The latter can be realised by sending spoofed messages to selected motes or by careful jamming of several messages.

It is relatively easy to use selective jamming to change a network topology according to the attacker's objective. It is also notable that this sort of attacks on wireless network is very hard to spot and react upon due to distributed manner of the routing protocol.

8.2 Routing Loops

If the attacker forced a network to create a routing loop, the result would be an enormous increase of the number of messages sent by motes in the loop. What happens is that each message received by any mote in the loop will be forwarded in the loop until it is dropped by one of the motes because its internal buffer of received messages is full or when the message is not acknowledged by any of addressees at some point.

The attack is triggered by injecting a series of messages – one for each mote that is targeted and whose routing table is to be changed and this number does not depend on the length of the resulting loop (see Fig. 7 for simplified attacking code we used with an extended version of Scapy tool).

```
mm=ZigBee()/TOSz(type=0xFA,addr=2)/TOS_MH(src=3,orig=3,seqno=355,
        hops=0x00)/TOS_Route(parent=4,cost=0,nbrs=[TOS_RNbr(ID=3),
        TOS_RNbr(ID=4),TOS_RNbr(ID=2)])
nn=ZigBee()/TOSz(type=0xFA,addr=3)/TOS_MH(src=4,orig=4,...
oo=ZigBee()/TOSz(type=0xFA,addr=4)/TOS_MH(src=2,orig=2,...
mm[ZigBee].length=len(mm[TOS_MH])
nn[ZigBee].length=len(nn[TOS_MH])
oo[ZigBee].length=len(oo[TOS_MH])
...
sends(mm);sends(nn);sends(oo)
```

Fig. 7. Python attacking code targeting motes with IDs 2, 3, and 4. It creates complete messages for all three motes and injects them to the network.

We have measured number of messages passed over in a loop of three motes at around 40 within 0.8 second. It makes it 16 forwarded messages per mote per second. The level of radio utilisation is however derived from 40 because each mote also listens to all the messages in its proximity. It gives radio utilisation of at least 10% in this instance – ignoring waiting time and transmission for ACK frames. The long term average frequency was just below 30 messages per second.

Once established loop usually holds for a relatively long time. This is due to the fact that a loop eventually increases only the number of hops from the gateway, but this number is not used for routing – link quality computations. This was the case in our experiments when the forwarding was occasionally interrupted only by network management ("route update") messages. Frequency of these messages is in real deployments usually very low.

Implications of this attack on the network lifetime are fundamental and the network would die within tens of hours from complete battery exhaustion. The power requirements for the attacker are, on the other side, very modest.

9 Attacks on Cryptographic Boundary

When we reimplemented TinySec, a cryptographic library for MICA2 motes, and started using it, we realised several issues arising from optimisation of cryptographic mechanisms for motes with strong power consumption limitations. We mention only one issue to extend the range of attacks that can be launched against sensor networks.

TinySec encryption and integrity protection is really used only on wireless transmissions. Data that left motes via their RS-232 interface is always decrypted.

This property is very useful for system integration. One can decide to switch the TinySec encryption on or off at any time and the gateway will not see any difference – there is no dependency on the back-end part of the wireless system.

On the other hand, the property introduces a new opportunity for an attacker with physical access to some of the motes and ability to connect to their serial (RS232) interface. The attacker can use a legitimate mote to inject arbitrary messages – the mote functions as a cryptographic oracle encrypting and decrypting over-the-air traffic as needed.

The messages sent to the RS-232 interface are by any mote automatically encrypted and transmitted via the motes wireless interface. From the communication point of view motes function as universal transceivers and all messages delivered to a mote are re-transmitted.

10 Conclusions

We have shown how wireless communication technologies change assumptions on which the current security models are based. As one can never make a system perfectly secure, system decisions are based on security risk and threat analysis. Introduction of wireless communication systems not only introduces new threats but also changes risks of the existing ones. As such, communication systems should be subject of new security analysis and possibly redesigned. However, this happens very rarely.

Wireless sensor networks, as any wireless technology, reintroduce many security threats that have been deemed solved or required a very strong attacker. The technology developments squash prices of devices allowing certain attacks to such an extent that even people driven by pure curiosity in a technology can afford them.

Wireless sensor networks also introduce strong decentralisation of many automatic processes that have been in hands of network or system administrators.

This shift significantly changes attack vectors and again enables potential adversaries with very low budget, and limited non-technical skills, to attack systems with remote technology-based approaches.

These background changes form the biggest challenge for security. It is very easy to forget why a certain attack was not seen as important. It is very hard to re-think security assumptions when these reasons disappear because of a new way of using products or systems, new technologies, tools, price cuts.

The last aspect really worth noticing is how security is dealt with in the development of wireless sensor networks. The take off of sensor networks is very slow and one would expect there is enough space for designing proper security measures. However, our discussions with Xbow, probably the main player in the area, showed that security is not really an interesting issue until the technology starts being deployed commercially.

References

1. Needham, R., Schroeder, M.: Using encryption for authentication in large networks of computers. Communications of the ACM 21(12), 993–999 (1978)
2. Biryukov, A., Shamir, A., Wagner, D.: Real time cryptanalysis of a5/1 on a pc. In: FSE: Fast Software Encryption, pp. 1–18. Springer, Heidelberg (2000)
3. Barkan, E., Biham, E., Keller, N.: Instant ciphertext-only cryptanalysis of gsm encrypted communication. In: Boneh, D. (ed.) CRYPTO 2003. LNCS, vol. 2729, pp. 600–616. Springer, Heidelberg (2003)
4. Hancke, G.P.: Practical attacks on proximity identification systems (short paper). In: IEEE Symposium on Security and Privacy, pp. 328–333. IEEE, Los Alamitos (2006)
5. Hancke, G.P., Kuhn, M.G.: Attacks on time-of-flight distance bounding channels. In: WISEC, pp. 194–202 (2008)
6. Cheung, H.: How to: Building a bluesniper rifle (2005), `http://www.tomsguide.com/us/how-to-bluesniper-pt1,review-408.html`
7. Eschenauer, L., Gligor, V.D.: A key-management scheme for distributed sensor networks. In: CCS 2002, Washington, DC, USA, pp. 41–47 (2002)
8. Chan, H., Perrig, A., Song, D.: Random key predistribution schemes for sensor networks. In: SP 2003, Washington, DC, USA, pp. 197–214 (2003)
9. Pietro, R.D., Mancini, L.V., Mei, A.: Random key-assignment for secure wireless sensor networks. In: 1st ACM Workshop Security of Ad Hoc and Sensor Networks Fairfax, Virginia, pp. 62–71 (2003)
10. Crossbow: Stargate developer's guide (2004)
11. Karlof, C., Sastry, N., Wagner, D.: Tinysec: A link layer security architecture for wireless sensor networks. In: Proc. 2nd SenSys., pp. 162–175 (2004)
12. Wood, A.D., Stankovic, J.A., Zhou, G.: Deejam: Defeating energy-efficient jamming in ieee 802.15.4-based wireless networks. In: Proc. 4th IEEE SECON, pp. 60–69. IEEE, Los Alamitos (2007)

Enhancing Multilateral Security in and by Reputation Systems

Sandra Steinbrecher

Technische Universität Dresden, Fakultät Informatik, D-01062 Dresden, Germany
steinbrecher@acm.org

Abstract. With the increasing possibilities for interaction between Internet users exceeding pure communication, in multilateral security the research question arises to rethink and extend classical security requirements. Reputation systems are a possible solution to assist new security requirements. But naturally also reputation systems have to be designed in a multilateral secure way. In this paper we discuss both multilateral security by and in reputation systems. An overview on the possibilities how such systems could be realised is given.

1 Introduction

The Internet offers its users numerous possibilities to interact with each other. Interactions cover various fields of interest for many people, e.g. trades via marketplaces like eBay[1] or online games like Second Life[2].

For interactions security requirements and trust issues are important. An interaction partner first wants to know what to expect from others and then wants to trust in the fulfilment of his expectations. Usually only users who fulfil these expectations are seen as trustworthy in the future. Social scientists and theoretical economists model the problem whether two interaction partners should place trust in each other as a so-called trust game [4,9].

On the Internet users often only interact once with each other. To help new interaction partners to estimate the others' behaviour reputation systems have been designed and established to collect the experiences former interaction partners made [20]. A very-popular example of a reputation system is implemented by eBay. As marketplace eBay offers its members the possibility to sell and buy arbitrary objects. The exchange of object and money usually is done by bank transfer and conventional mail. Many of these exchanges are successful, but unfortunately some are not. For this reason a reputation system collects the experiences sellers and buyers make. After every exchange they may give comments or/and marks to each other that are added to the members' public reputations (usually together with the annotator and the exchange considered as context information).

[1] http://www.ebay.com/ (last visited Jan. 09).

[2] http://www.secondlife.com/ (last visited Jan. 09).

V. Matyáš et al. (Eds.): The Future of Identity, IFIP AICT 298, pp. 135–150, 2009.

Currently the vision arises to establish stand-alone reputation systems that collect information from various interactions and in various contexts and also to make reputation information in different systems interoperable [13]. For the latter there is already an OASIS group[3] established.

For the collection of large reputation profiles for Internet users privacy becomes an important issue. Reputation systems often collect information about who interacted with whom in which context. Such information should be protected by means of technical data protection to ensure users' right of informational self-determination [16].

Privacy-enhancing user-controlled identity management [8,7] like PRIME[4] assists users platform-independent in controlling their personal data in various applications and selecting pseudonyms appropriately depending on their wish for pseudonymity and unlinkability of actions.

Reputation needs not be linked to real name but can be assigned to a pseudonym as well. But the interoperability of a reputation system with a user-controlled privacy-enhancing identity management needs a privacy-respecting design of reputation systems while keeping the level of trust provided by the use of reputations.

In section 2 we give an overview of the security requirements a reputation system should resp. can help to fulfil for interactions. Based on this analysis in section 3 we explain how reputation systems can be realised in a multilateral secure way themselves. Especially we give a categorisation of building blocks able to fulfill the security requirements in reputation systems. Finally in section 4 we describe an example for an implementation of a system following the concept of multilateral security by and in reputation systems.

2 Multilateral Security by Reputation Systems

When interacting with others users necessarily have several security requirements. Interactions between interaction partners usually consist of several actions depending on each other. On the Internet these actions are usually transmitted as distinct messages. For a single message security requirements of its sender and recipient(s) are well studied. But the dependency of several messages and the meaning of the messages as actions introduces new security requirements as we will outline in this section.

2.1 Security Requirements for Communication

For pure communication security requirements have been studied in [25]. One should differentiate between the content of the communication and the circumstances under which it is made. Clearly, the sender and the recipient are

[3] `http://www.oasis-open.org/committees/tc_home.php?wg_abbrev=orms` (last visited Jan. 09).

[4] Privacy and Identity Management for Europe (`http://www.prime-project.eu/` (last visited Jan. 09)), funded by the European Union in the 6. Framework Program, 2004-2008.

circumstances of the communication, however there might be further circumstances senders and recipients want to protect, e.g., the time of communication or the location they are in when communicating with each other. Based on this, security requirements are structured as in Table 1.

Table 1. Security requirements for communication [25]

threats \ protection of	content	circumstances
unauthorised access to information	confidentiality hiding	anonymity unobservability
unauthorised modification of information	integrity	accountability
unauthorised impairment of functionality	availability	reachability legal enforceability

The requirements are defined as follows:

- *Confidentiality* ensures the confidentiality of user data when they are transferred.
- *Hiding* ensures the confidentiality of the transfer of confidential user data.
- *Anonymity* ensures that a user can use a resource or service without disclosing his identity.
- *Unobservability* ensures that a user can use a resource or service without others being able to observe that the resource or service is being used.
- *Integrity* ensures that modifications of communicated content (including the senders name, if one is provided) are detected by the recipient(s).
- *Accountability* ensures that sender and recipients of information cannot successfully deny having sent or received the information.
- *Availability* ensures that communicated messages are available when the user wants to use them.
- *Reachability* ensures that a peer entity (user, machine, etc.) either can or cannot be contacted depending on user interests.
- *Legal enforceability* ensures that a user can be held liable to fulfill his legal responsibilities within a reasonable period of time.

2.2 Fulfilment of Semantic Security Requirements

Interaction partners necessarily have security requirements in common concerning the content of the message transferred. These requirements can be fulfilled by technical measures only to the extent the interaction partners cooperate and behave as expected. This means, interaction partners typically have an expectation regarding the behaviour of the interaction partners that these might fulfil or not. Fulfilment of expectation might be defined implicitly (e.g., behaviour follows social norms) or even explicitly (e.g., on the basis of a contractual agreement). In an interaction system this means:

- Technical confidentiality might become useless for a user if interaction partners redistribute the content of confidential messages.
- Technical integrity might become useless if the one who wrote an message with integrity gives a false or useless statement by the message.
- Technical availability of an interaction system might become useless for a user if none is willing to interact.

For this reason the security requirements regarding the content of the message have to be reformulated in comparison to [25] as already outlined similarly in [1]:

- *Confidentiality* does not only address the confidentiality of data transferred in an action, but also *discretion* of the interaction partner regarding the data he received and may forward to third parties.
- *Integrity* does not only address that modifications of communicated content (including the senders name if one is provided) are detected by the recipient(s), but also that the recipient is able to decide on the *bona fides* of the action performed by the message, i.e. that he is able to decide on it.
- *Availability* does not only address that resources are available when the user wants to use them, but also the *willingness* of others to interact.

By these definitions security requirements have an explicit part addressing the technical system and an implicit part addressing the semantic fulfilment of the requirement by the (possible) interaction partner(s). It is difficult to judge on the implicit part of security requirements in an objective way. Willingness usually can be judged on in an objective way because it is easy to see whether users participate in interactions or not. Bona fides usually are subjective. Breakage of discretion often might not become known directly.

Although numerous cryptographic primitives and building blocks help to fulfil requirements of interactions on the explicit technical level, interaction partners still have numerous possibilities for misbehaviour regarding the implicit requirements. Legal enforceability helps to ensure an interaction partner behaving as agreed beforehand. But many interactions between individuals might be more informal, or it might be too expensive to enforce liability.

Reputation systems have been established to collect experiences about users' behaviour in interactions and thereby they collect the fulfilment of implicit forms of security requirements. Currently reputation systems (e.g., the one eBay uses) are mainly used to collect information about users' bona fides but also information on users' willingness and discretion could be collected.

2.3 Linkability of Actions and Resulting Security Requirements

An interaction usually consists of numerous individual but correlated actions. Correlating actions lead to new security requirements:

The *unlinkability* of two or more items of interest (e.g., of actions) from the attackers perspective means that within the system (comprising these and possibly other items), the attacker cannot sufficiently distinguish whether these items of interest are related or not [15].

The linkability of actions transmitted by messages has an effect on the security requirements formulated for single messages. Particularly in terms of anonymity, the linkability of actions can reveal identities. In the case of pseudonyms, it is at least possible to link actions performed under the same pseudonym. This is exactly what pseudonyms are used for. With respect to security requirements and as security requirement itself, *pseudonymity* can have various flavors, e.g., the unlinkability of actions performed under different pseudonyms, and the unlinkability of the pseudonym to the holder (i.e., holder anonymity) with the possible exception of specific pre-defined conditions to reveal information about the holder [15].

Further, the *absolute linkability* of actions could have positive effects on fulfilling integrity and availability requirements and, therefore, could be desirable [25]. In particular, it allows additional security requirements to be applied to a set of actions or messages: *Authorisability* of a pseudonym ensures that a pseudonym can be authorised to perform a certain action after it has authenticated itself with another action.

2.4 Multilateral Security

In interactions often security requirements are contradicting. Here multilateral security means providing security for all parties involved, requiring each party to only minimally trust in the honesty of others [19]:

- Each party has its particular security requirements.
- Each party can formulate its security requirements.
- Conflicts between security requirements can be recognised and compromises negotiated.
- Each party can enforce its security requirements within the agreed compromise.

2.5 Identity Management

Identity management systems (IMS) both try to help users to manage the various digital identities and the corresponding user accounts they establish with Internet applications and/or help application providers to manage the users registered with them. Depending on the application and the situational context a user is in, he decides which user account to create or to use. Many applications require users to declare at least some (often reliable, e.g., by external authentication) personal data when creating a user account. However, users often want to stay as anonymous as possible as long as it is not necessary to disclose data to get certain services. The use of a user account and the often corresponding consecutive disclosure of personal data (beginning with just surfing through shops to order certain products) have to be supported by IMS which assist the user in the explicit (and hopefully also implicit) disclosure of personal data.

This requires privacy-enhancing IMS (PE-IMS) to support and integrate techniques of multilateral security in order to achieve especially the following two of the security requirements outlined above [6]:

- *Pseudonymity controlled by the user* consists of two aspects: Unlinkability of a user account to its holder (called holder anonymity): Other parties do not know, which holder the user account is linked to. Unlinkability of user accounts: Other parties do not know, whether or not different user accounts are of the same user.
- *Accountability of a user controlled by others:* A pseudonym can be authenticated in a secure way and, based on this, be authorised to use specific services. When necessary (e.g., in the sense of legal enforceability), the holder of the pseudonym can be held liable for actions performed under this pseudonym.

3 Multilateral Security in Reputation Systems

A reputation network is a social network that links entities (possibly pseudonymously) to each other and allows them to interact and exchange information with each other. On the one hand entities within the reputation network can learn possible interaction partners' reputation from former interaction partners or other entities within the network who observed the possible interaction partner. In social sciences this is called the **learning mechanism** of the reputation network [2]. On the other hand entities within the reputation network may control others in the reputation network by spreading information about the entities' former interactions. In social sciences this is called the **control mechanism** of the reputation network [2].

Both entities and interactions within the reputation network can be reputation objects. Entities and non-completed interactions are *dynamic reputation objects* while completed interactions are *static reputation objects.* Reputation systems assist reputation networks technically. We assume that they collect explicit reputation only about members who agreed on collecting it because according to [3] opinions about a natural person can be seen as personal data the respective person's right on informational self-determination should be applied to. For this reason a reputation system has to assist explicit membership actions regarding a reputation network resp. system. A person must be able to apply for membership under a certain pseudonym in a reputation network and also must be able to terminate his membership.

For interactions within the reputation network we assume different interaction systems to be in place (e.g., simple e-mail, file sharing, community systems).

To implement both learning and control mechanism of the reputation network a reputation system has to offer the following actions to the members:

- **Learning mechanism through evaluation of reputation:** All members that influence the reputation of an object by their ratings, additional trusted third parties, the reputation object itself and possible future interaction partners might evaluate a reputation's object following specific rules that are fixed by the designer of the reputation system. Every evaluator might receive a different reputation of the reputation object.

The selection of ratings used for the evaluation depends on both the information flow of ratings in the reputation network and the trust structure on the reputation network, i.e. how evaluators trust in ratings from other members. Those who rate need to be trusted in giving a correct rating which is in line with their view on a specific interaction.
- **Control mechanism through rating:** There are two types of members who can make use of the control mechanism, the interaction partner in the form of interaction-derived reputation and possible observers in form of observed reputation [17]. The system provides authorised raters with a rating function that allows them to map reputation objects to ratings. The reputation system updates the reputation of the reputation object from the ratings received.

After the creation of reputation it has to be stored somewhere. Reputation might be stored

- *centralised* at reputation servers designated for this purpose.
- *locally* at the device of the user whose pseudonym received the reputation
- *distributed* at the devices of other users.

The reputation selection for evaluation can be:

- *global:* This means the information flow within the reputation network is complete and every evaluator gets the same reputation of a reputation object.
- *individual:* This means an evaluator only gets a partial view on the reputation available.

In [24] a simpler categorisation in four classes is made that merges the aspects of storage and data flow but we found it advisable to separate these aspects.

As outlined above there are five components of a reputation system:

- **rating algorithm** of a rater,
- **reputation algorithm** for reputation update,
- **propagation of reputation and ratings** for reputation selection,
- **storage of ratings and reputation**, and
- **evaluation of a reputation object's reputation** by the reputation evaluator.

To find design options for these components one has to consider several security requirements.

The rating and update of reputation has to follow specific rules fixed by the system designer. These rules usually depend on the application scenario and have to fulfil sociological and economic requirements. We abstract here from the concrete functions to allow a universal design interoperable with various IMS and various application scenarios. An overview over possible functions is for example given in [17]. For an economic introduction we refer to [10].

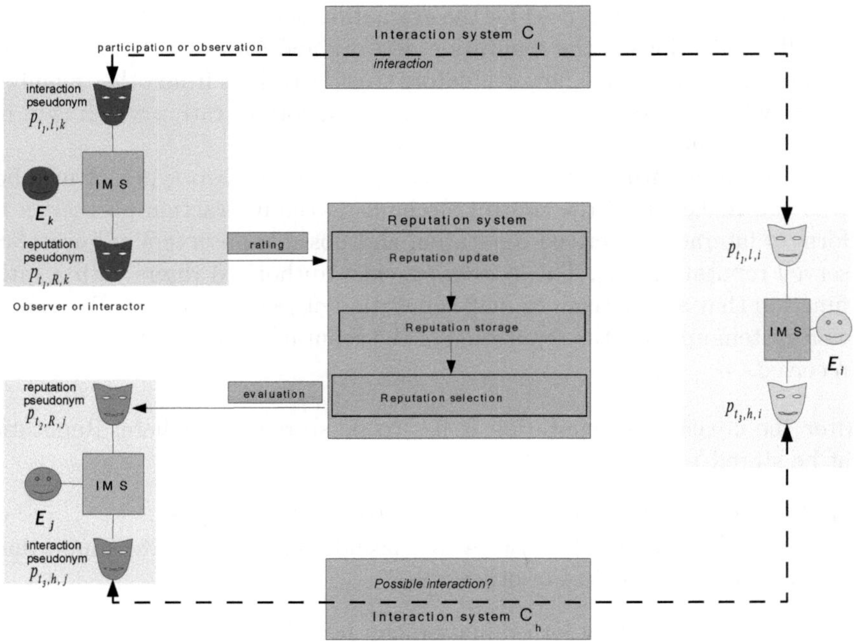

Fig. 1. System design

The model of a reputation system interoperable with an interaction system and a PE-IMS to enable multilateral security for the user is illustrated in Figure 1.

When a reputation system interoperates with an PE-IMS it is possible and intended that entities have several partial identities (pIDs) which cannot be linked, neither by other entities using the systems nor by the underlying system (as long as the entity does not permit this). Therefore an entity uses at least different unlinkable pseudonyms for every system he interacts in resp. with.

If there would exist only one reputation per entity, all pIDs of this entity would have the same reputation. This would ease the linking of the pIDs of one entity because of the same reputation value. Thus, having separated reputations per pID and not only one per entity is a fundamental condition for a reputation system in the context of identity management.

The use of pIDs brings forward the problem that a malicious entity may rate himself a lot of times using new self created pID for every rating in order to improve his own reputation. This kind of attack is also known as Sybil attack [12]. If the reputation system is not defined carefully it would be easy for such an attacker to improve the own reputation unwarranted. This can be limited/prevented by entrance fees or the use of once-in-a-lifetime credentials as suggested in [14].

3.1 Multilateral Security

Beneath the security requirements for communication based on the functional requirements of the learning and control mechanism of the reputation network new security requirements for reputation systems can be identified:

- *Bona fides of ratings and reputation:* If it would be possible for all members of a reputation network to observe an interaction and if all of them would give the interaction the same rating this rating would have *objective bona fides*. But most ratings depend on subjective estimation of the interaction partners or observers at a certain point in time. As a special action a rating has *subjective bona fides* for an observer if it corresponds to his expectation of the interaction. Accordingly a reputation has subjective bona fides if it is created by bona fides from ratings done by bona fides.
- *Fairness of the underlying game-theoretic trust game:* A reputation system is fair if every authorised entity has the same possibilities for rating an interaction partner. The authorisability in the reputation system has to follow the control mechanism of the reputation network. Only entities that gave a leap of faith to interaction partners should be able to rate them.
- *Completeness of reputation:* Members of a reputation network expect to receive as much information as possible from interactions performed in the reputation network. This needs the willingness of authorised interaction partners to rate each other and the willingness of all members to distribute reputation in the reputation network.
- *Persistence of reputation objects:* To help the control mechanism to be employed longevity resp. persistence [20] of members as reputation objects has to be realised resp. the binding of reputation to them. This can be done pseudonymously.
- *Absolute linkability of a user's membership in a reputation network:* To prevent a user from leaving a reputation network with a bad reputation and re-entering it with a neutral reputation membership actions of the same user in the same context have to be absolutely linkable.

By actions in the reputation network no other requirements on interactions should be affected. This needs unlinkability of actions and pseudonyms of the same user in different interaction systems and the reputation network as well as providing anonymity to him.

The following building blocks are able to reach a compromise between the users' wish for completeness of reputation and the unlinkability and anonymity of his actions in the sense of multilateral security:

Parallel usage of pseudonyms: *Unlinkability of a user's actions in different contexts* can be reached by context-specific pseudonyms [23]. This enables users to collect reputation in different contexts separately. Hopefully this should also increase the *objective bona fides of reputation* because users usually behave different in different contexts and also have different expectations in different contexts.

Convertible credentials between interaction and reputation system: The rater's actions in interaction system and reputation system can be unlinkable. This needs a Third Party to be in place that issues a convertible credential [5] to an interaction pseudonym that the respective user can convert to his reputation pseudonym and that allows him to give a rating to an interaction partner specified in the credential. This enables *fairness of the interaction's trust game*. Both *pseudonyms are unlinkable* to each other for everyone but himself. Certainly he can only be *anonymous* in the set of other users who might be allowed to give a rating to the same pseudonym.

Pseudonym change with reputation transfer: If members want to limit the pseudonymous profile that can be built for them based on the interactions they were involved in they have to change their pseudonym from time to time in the form that the old pseudonym gets invalid and a new one with the same reputation gets valid. The same reputation is needed to ensure *persistence of reputation objects* and *completeness of reputation.* According to [22,23] this can be realised by convertible credentials. A pseudonym change with reputation transfer only makes sense if there are enough other users with the same reputation who also change their pseudonyms. These users form the anonymity set for the pseudonym change.

Limitation of the rating and reputation set: The size of the anonymity set possible for a pseudonym change depends also on the reputation set and the visibility of raters and ratings in a user's reputation. Both reputation and rating set should be chosen small enough to enable sufficiently large anonymity sets.

4 System

To show how the building blocks can be composed to a multilateral secure reputation system in a multilateral secure environment we implemented a system design as outlined in [18]. We decided to use a centralised implementation of an interaction system as test bed for interactions between users. In a centralised system interactions between members take place via a central server where they are stored and globally available. Thereby a virtual community [21] is created. To become a member of the community a user has to register with the community server by declaring a pseudonym for use within the community. We chose the web forum software phpBB[5] for our implementation.

The reputation system we implemented uses global reputations that are stored at the users' device to give him control over personal data including his reputation. Our design is independent from concrete rating and reputation algorithms.

We assume all communication to be secured by encryption to reach confidentiality of all ratings and actions performed. All actions and ratings have to be secured by digital signatures given under a pseudonym for integrity reasons. By the use of an identity provider accountability of the pseudonym can be given.

[5] `http://www.phpbb.com/` (last visited Jan. 09).

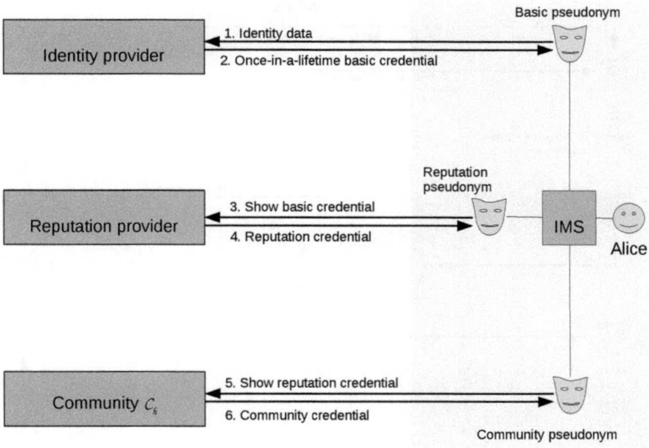

Fig. 2. Registration process enabling unlinkability of a user and his pseudonyms

For the identity management a user Alice registers a basic pseudonym with an identity provider by declaration of her identity data (step 1 in Fig. 2). After verifying the data the identity provider issues a basic credential (step 2 in Fig. 2).

When Alice wants to register in a reputation network within a certain context she sends the reputation provider her basic credential (step 3 in Fig. 2). This guarantees no user is able to build up reputation under multiple pseudonyms within the same context and every user can be identified in the case of misbehaviour. The reputation provider creates a reputation pseudonym based on the basic pseudonym and sends it back to Alice (step 4 in Fig. 2).

The reputation credential contains the pseudonym and its initial reputation. The credential is a pseudonymous convertible credential the user can convert to another pseudonym within the reputation network whenever he wants to reach unlinkability of actions. The credential also contains an attribute for the context, a number of attributes for the number of last ratings to be stored and an attribute for the expiration date.

After the conversion of the reputation credential to a community pseudonym Alice can register this pseudonym with a community $\mathcal{C}_h$ by showing the converted credential (step 5 in Fig. 2). Thereby she agrees that she will collect reputation for her interactions in the community with the reputation network she registered with. Based on this she gets a community credential to her community pseudonym and becomes a member of the community (step 6 in Fig. 2).

By the use of these distinct pseudonyms, unlinkability of the actions performed under these pseudonyms is given initially. The only exception are Alice's reputation pseudonym and community pseudonym because Bob wants to assure that he actually gave the rating to the pseudonym he interacted with.

4.1 Design

In the following we outline the design of our reputation system.

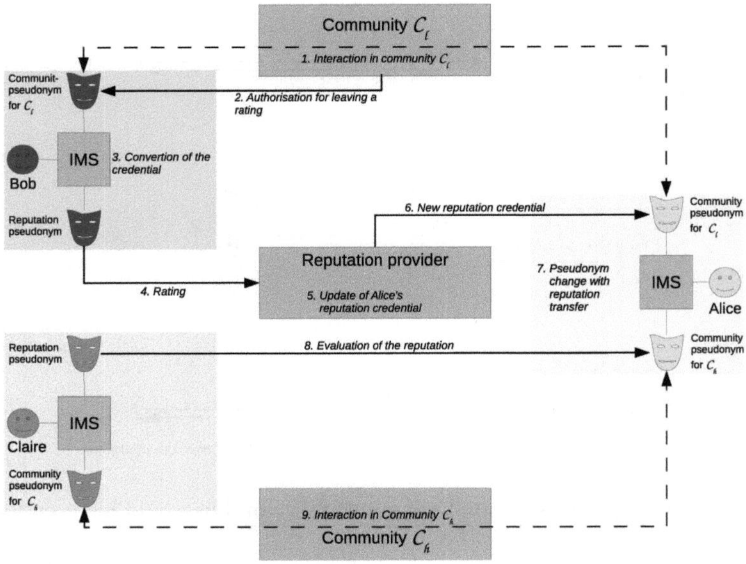

Fig. 3. System design

After an interaction (step 1 in Fig. 3) between pseudonyms of Alice and Bob Bob receives a convertible credential from the community that states that an interaction has been finished and Bob is allowed to rate Alice's pseudonym (step 2 in Fig. 3). Bob is able to convert this credential from his community pseudonym to his reputation pseudonym (step 3 in Fig. 3).

For the rating (step 3 in Fig. 3) Bob sends this credential, Alice's pseudonym and the actual rating he wants to give to Alice to the reputation provider who tests its validity and stores the rating until the update of Alice's reputation.

After a fixed number $k \geq 1$ of ratings have been given to Alice's pseudonym its reputation has to be updated by the reputation provider (step 5 in Fig. 3). We do not fix $k = 1$ here because according to the game-theoretical analysis in [11] it might make sense economically not to update a reputation after every rating but only after $k > 1$ ratings. This also increases Alice's unlinkability.

For the update Alice has to send her reputation credential to the reputation system. This might be either initiated by Alice or by the reputation provider. The attribute containing the reputation has to be updated in the reputation credential and the new rating has to be added as attribute to resp. substitute of one of the existing expired rating attributes. The reputation provider does not need to know the reputation value. Only the relationship between the old and the new credential must be guaranteed by the reputation provider. Therefore in principal the calculation is possible on encrypted values if the reputation computation algorithm is homomorphic regarding the encryption.

The reputation computation algorithm can be chosen arbitrarily by paying attention to the fact that users are recognisable by their reputation even if they use convertible credentials to reach unlinkability of their actions. For this reason the sets of possible reputations and ratings have to be small enough to reach large enough anonymity sets. Details about this idea are outlined in [23].

For the update the reputation provider sends the new reputation credential to Alice (step 6 in Fig. 3). The old reputation credential would still be valid if it did not contain the attribute for the expiration date.

To increase the unlinkability between different interactions of a user, the change of pseudonyms with reputation transfer is possible as suggested in [23] (step 7 in Fig. 3). This is realised by pseudonymous convertible credentials that allow a user to maintain his reputation but use a new pseudonym without trusting the reputation provider.

A pseudonym change only makes sense when a large number of users with the same attributes (here the same reputation if no other attributes are known) changes their pseudonym at the same time to guarantee an appropriate anonymity set. For this reason the sets of possible rating and reputation values are limited.

If Alice wants to change her pseudonym while a rating has been left at the reputation provider for her credential, it cannot be guaranteed that the mapping between the new pseudonym and the rating could be made. Therefore the reputation provider has to authorise the pseudonym change indirectly by issuing credentials with new expiration dates. By this he helps to collect an anonymity set of users willing to change their pseudonyms.

Before deciding on an interaction with a member of the community $\mathcal{C}_h$ Claire can evaluate pseudonymously its reputation after the member send her the reputation credential (step 8 in Fig. 3).

To augment the availability of the reputation a storage at the reputation server or the community server should be possible with the chance for the user to appoint authorisation to other members of the community to see the reputation.

Alice can always leave the community or reputation network. If she then has a reputation less than the initial reputation her identity should be revealed to all identity providers cooperating with the respective reputation provider and community system. They will ban Alice for further registration to guarantee that she does not get any new basic pseudonyms she could use for a new registration in the reputation network or a community. This implements the once-in-a-lifetime-credentials introduced in [14].

4.2 Implementation

phpBB. The software phpBB was originally developed as software for forums. Therefore text-based interactions can be carried out with the help of phpBB. The framework has a centralised architecture that must be installed on a web server using PHP as script language. It supports various database schemes (MySQL, etc.). The user uses the system only with the help of a web-based interface. The basic phpBB implementation allows users to register with the community, to start and answer a thread. For a reputation system like ours where users should be rated based on interactions it is crucial that a mechanism exists, which proves that the interaction has actually happened and was finalised. Such a mechanism provides the MOD "Geocator's Feedback Ratings MOD"[6]. Besides it includes a whole reputation system in an eBay-like style we do not make use of.

Reputation system. The credentials and the required functions for handling them were implemented using the idemix-Framework[7], which is written in Java.

The reputation system is independent from the community server but can be called over links integrated in the phpBB framework. These links lead to PHP-based websites, offering different functions of the reputation system.

The websites request the users to fill in the necessary specifications like the reputation credential or the rating value. If the inputs are valid after checking by the reputation system, the PHP-scripts call a Java program implementing the respective reputation functions. The programs are either dealing on the credentials (e.g. the update function) or on one of the databases also implemented by the idemix framework (e.g. the rating function, where the rating remains in the database till the reputation object updates his reputation credential). Also the published reputation is in one of these databases. Functions to remove one's reputation and to search for other members' reputation are also existent.

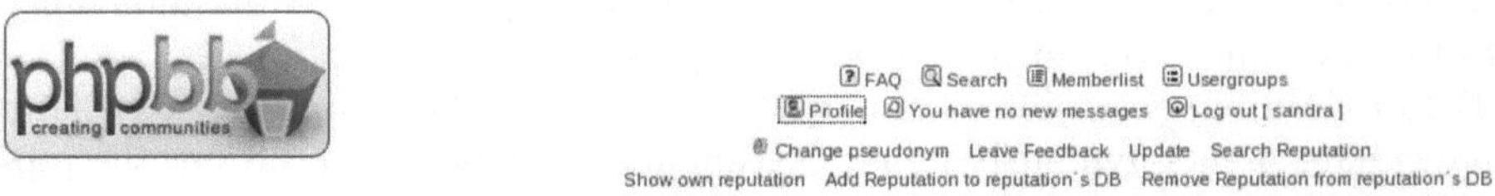

Fig. 4. Extended interface of phpBB

The prototype does not use PRIME yet but uses the authentication methods of phpBB. Therefore the registration process takes place simultaneously in the phpBB community and the reputation system. The phpBB community could be used as usual, but the member can call the reputation functions within the phpBB interface that have been extended for this reason as illustrated in Fig. 4.

Pseudonym change. The pseudonym change is implemented in an Java-program which can be executed on the user's system without knowledge of the reputation provider, the community or other members.

5 Conclusion

The basis and preconditions to design reputation systems in a multilateral secure way were introduced. This concept becomes more and more important with the growing number of applications which need reputation systems.

[6] `http://www.phpbb.com/community/viewtopic.php?f=16&t=381862` (last visited Jan. 09).

[7] `http://www.zurich.ibm.com/security/idemix/` (last visited Jan. 09).

Our current research concentrates on different forms of interactions systems and the interoperability arising between them. Here our focus lies on authentication methods using a PE-IMS like PRIME.

For the future is planned to develop distributed alternatives to the central reputation providers. This will hopefully allow for individual reputation additionally to the global reputation in our current system design.

6 Thanks and Disclaimer

I would like to thank Vacláv (Vashek) Matyáš and Simone Fischer-Hübner for their invitation to write this paper for the FIDIS summerschool proceedings. The research described in section 4 was partially done with Franziska Pingel whom I want to thank for this. I also thank Marc van Lieshout for his helpful review of this paper.

The research leading to the results presented in this paper has received funding from the European Communitys Sixth and Seventh Framework Programme (FP6/2002-2006 resp. FP7/2007-2013) for the projects FIDIS, PRIME and PrimeLife. The information in this document is provided as is, and no guarantee or warranty is given that the information is fit for any particular purpose. The consortium members shall have no liability for damages of any kind including without limitation direct, special, indirect, or consequential damages that may result from the use of these materials subject to any liability which is mandatory due to applicable law.

References

1. Borcea-Pfitzmann, K., Hansen, M., Liesebach, K., Pfitzmann, A., Steinbrecher, S.: Managing one's identities in organisational and social settings. DuD, Datenschutz und Datensicherheit 31(9), 671–675 (2007)
2. Buskens, V., Raub, W.: Embedded trust: Control and learning. In: Lawler, E., Thye, S. (eds.) Group Cohesion, Trust, and Solidarity. Advances in Group Processes, vol. 19, pp. 167–202 (2001)
3. Bygrave, L.: Data Protection Law, Approaching Its Rationale, Logic and Limits. Kluwer Law International, The Hague (2002)
4. Camerer, C., Weigelt, K.: Experimental tests of a sequential equilibrium reputation model. Econometrica 56, 1–36 (1988)
5. Chaum, D.: Showing credentials without identification. Signatures transferred between unconditionally unlinkable pseudonyms. In: Pichler, F. (ed.) EUROCRYPT 1985. LNCS, vol. 219, pp. 241–244. Springer, Heidelberg (1986)
6. Clauß, S., Kesdogan, D., Kölsch, T., Pimenidis, L., Schiffner, S., Steinbrecher, S.: Privacy enhancing identity management: Protection against re-identification and profiling. In: Goto, A. (ed.) DIM 2005, Proceedings of the 2005 ACM Workshop on Digital Identity Management, Fairfax, Virgina, USA, November 2005, pp. 84–93. ACM, New York (2005)
7. Clauß, S., Köhntopp, M.: Identity management and its support of multilateral security. Computer Networks 37(2), 205–219 (2001)
8. Clauß, S., Pfitzmann, A., Hansen, M., Van Herreweghen, E.: Privacy-enhancing identity management. The IPTS Report 67, 8–16 (2002)

9. Dasgupta, P.: Trust as a commodity. In: Gambetta, D. (ed.) Trust: Making and Breaking Cooperative Relations, pp. 49–72. Department of Sociology, University Oxford (2000)
10. Dellarocas, C.: The digitization of word-of-mouth: Promise and challenges of online feedback mechanisms. Management Science, 1407–1424 (October 2003)
11. Dellarocas, C.: Research note – how often should reputation mechanisms update a trader's reputation profile? Information Systems Research 17(3), 271–285 (2006)
12. Douceur, J.R.: The sybil attack. In: Druschel, P., Kaashoek, M.F., Rowstron, A. (eds.) IPTPS 2002. LNCS, vol. 2429, pp. 251–260. Springer, Heidelberg (2002)
13. ENISA. Position paper. reputation-based systems: a security analysis (2007), http://www.enisa.europa.eu/doc/pdf/deliverables/enisa_pp_reputation_based_system.pdf (letzter Abruf 09.02.08)
14. Friedman, E., Resnick, P.: The social cost of cheap pseudonyms. Journal of Economics and Management Strategy 10, 173–199 (1999)
15. Hansen, M., Pfitzmann, A.: Anonymity, unobservability, and pseudonymity - a proposal for terminology. Version 0.8 in: Federrath, H. (ed.) Designing Privacy Enhancing Technologies. LNCS, vol. 2009, pp. 1–9. Springer, Heidelberg (2001); Version 0.30 in: Balzer, R., Kpsell, S., Lazarek, H. (Hg.) Fachterminologie Datenschutz und Datensicherheit Deutsch - Russisch - Englisch; FGI - Forschungsgesellschaft Informatik, Technische Universitt Wien, Wien, February 2008, pp. 111-144 (2008); Version 0.31, http://dud.inf.tu-resden.de/literatur/Anon_Terminology_v0.31.pdf (2007)
16. Mahler, T., Olsen, T.: Reputation systems and data protection law. In: eAdoption and the Knowledge Economy: Issues, Applications, Case Studies, pp. 180–187. IOS Press, Amsterdam (2004)
17. Mui, L.: Computational Models of Trust and Reputation: Agents, Evolutionary Games, and Social Networks. Ph.D Thesis, Massachusetts Institute of Technology (2003)
18. Pingel, F., Steinbrecher, S.: Multilateral secure cross-community reputation systems. In: Furnell, S.M., Katsikas, S.K., Lioy, A. (eds.) TrustBus 2008. LNCS, vol. 5185, pp. 69–78. Springer, Heidelberg (2008)
19. Rannenberg, K., Pfitzmann, A., Müller, G.: IT security and multilateral security. In: Mller, G., Rannenberg, K. (eds.) Multilateral Security in Communications, Mnchen. Technology, Infrastructure, Economy, vol. 3, pp. 21–29. Addison-Wesley, Reading (1999)
20. Resnick, P., Kuwabara, K., Zeckhauser, R., Friedman, E.: Reputation systems. Communications of the ACM 43(12), 45–48 (2000)
21. Rheingold, H.: The Virtual Community: Homesteading on the Electronic Frontier. Perseus Books (1993)
22. Steinbrecher, S.: Balancing privacy and trust in electronic marketplaces. In: Katsikas, S.K., López, J., Pernul, G. (eds.) TrustBus 2004. LNCS, vol. 3184, pp. 70–79. Springer, Heidelberg (2004)
23. Steinbrecher, S.: Design options for privacy-respecting reputation systems within centralised internet communities. In: Proceedings of IFIP Sec 2006, 21st IFIP International Information Security Conference: Security and Privacy in Dynamic Environments (May 2006)
24. Voss, M.: Privacy preserving online reputation systems. In: International Information Security Workshops, pp. 245–260. Kluwer, Dordrecht (2004)
25. Wolf, G., Pfitzmann, A.: Properties of protection goals and their integration into a user interface. Computer Networks 32(6), 685–699 (2000)

An Overview of Electronic Passport Security Features

Zdeněk Říha

Faculty of Informatics, Masaryk University, Botanická 68A, 602 00 Brno, Czech Republic
zriha@fi.muni.cz

Abstract. Electronic passports include contactless chip which stores personal data of the passport holder, information about the passport and the issuing institution. In its simplest form an electronic passport contains just a collection of read-only files, more advanced variants can include sophisticated cryptographic mechanisms protecting security of the document and / or privacy of the passport holder. This paper describes security features of electronic passports and discusses their efficiency.

Keywords: Electronic passport, basic access control, passive authentication, active authentication, extended access control.

1 Introduction

A passport is a government issued identification document proving that the holder is a citizen of a particular country; belongs under its protection and is authorized to enter foreign countries. Passports must be resistant to counterfeiting, but the time available for passing through passport control is only limited. Machine readable travel documents have the potential to speed up the process of passing through the passport control. The ICAO (International Civil Aviation Organization – a UN organization responsible for civil aviation and international travel) already standardized the storage of some passport data in two machine processible lines already in the 1980s. This zone (Machine Readable Zone – MRZ) contains basic data about the passport and its holder (name, surname, date of birth, date of expiry etc.) and it is printed in a standardized font so that it is machine readable (by optical character recognition – OCR) and can be processed by computer systems.

As the amount of data stored in the MRZ is only very small (88 characters) and the only "security" factor is the check digit, new ways of storing data for automated processing were investigated. The 6th version of the ICAO Document 9303 describing travel documents uses the technology of contactless smartcards, symmetric and asymmetric cryptography and biometrics. The new passports equipped with chips and antennas (allowing contactless communication) are called electronic passports.

Although the electronic part of the passport remains optional at the worldwide level, the USA have asked all its Visa Waiver Program partners to introduce electronic passports and the European Union agreed on mandatory introduction of electronic passports in EU member states (to be exact, this regulation is not mandatory for the UK and Ireland and three non-EU countries – Norway, Switzerland and Iceland – do participate).

V. Matyáš et al. (Eds.): The Future of Identity, IFIP AICT 298, pp. 151–159, 2009.

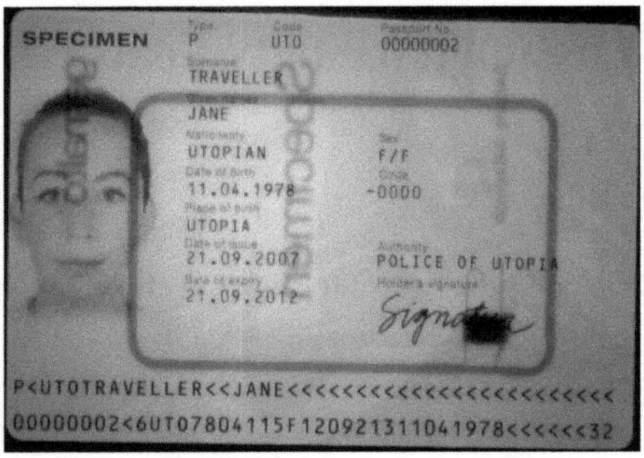

Fig. 1. Chip and antenna integrated in the polycarbonate data page

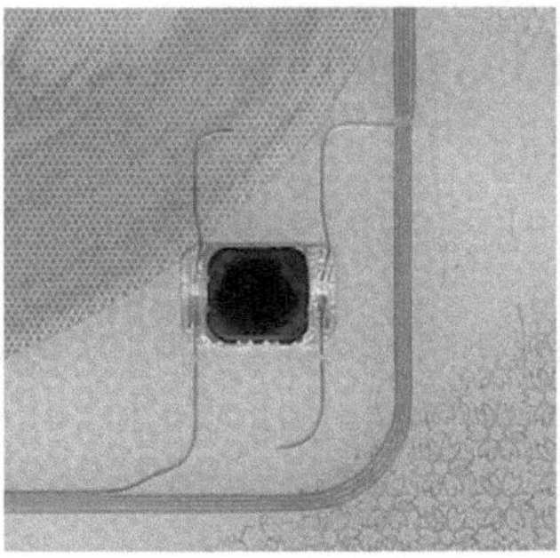

Fig. 2. Chip and antenna in UK passports

Table 1. Data groups which can be stored in electronic passports

Data group	**Stored data**
DG1	**Machine readable zone (MRZ)**
DG2	**Biometric data: face**
DG3	Biometric data: fingerprints
DG4	Biometric data: iris
DG5	Picture of the holder as printed in the passport
DG6	Reserved for future use
DG7	Signature of the holder as printed in the passport
DG8	Encoded security features – data features
DG9	Encoded security features – structure features
DG10	Encoded security features – substance features
DG11	Additional personal details (address, phone)
DG12	Additional document details (issue date, issued by)
DG13	Optional data (anything)
DG14	Data for securing secondary biometrics (EAC)
DG15	Active Authentication public key info
DG16	Next of kin

The chip and the antenna are integrated into the cover of the booklet or another page of the passport. The chip and antenna are typically not directly visible and can be only seen using a strong light (see Figure 1). An exception is the UK passport where the chip and antenna is laminated in one of the pages and can be directly seen (see Figure 2). An electronic passport can be easily recognized by the logo on the front page. The communication is contactless and complies with the ISO 14443 standard (both variants – A and B – are allowed). Technology based on ISO 14443 is designed to communicate over a distance of 0-10 cm and supports also relatively complex cryptographic chips and permanent memory of kilobytes or megabytes.

Higher communication layer is based on the classical smart card protocol ISO 7816-4 (i.e., commands like SELECT AID, SELECT FILE and READ BINARY are used).

The data in electronic passports are stored as elementary files in a single folder (dedicated file). Up to 16 data files named as DG1 to DG16 (DG for Data Group) can hold the data. See Table 1 for the overview of the content of the data groups.

Two additional files with metadata are also present. The file EF.COM contains a list of available data groups (and the information about versions used) and the file EF.SOD contains the digital signature of the data. The files EF.COM, EF.SOD, DG1 and DG2 are mandatory for all electronic passports. The data group DG3 will be mandatory in the EU countries after 28th June 2009 (and will be protected by an additional mechanism). All other data groups are optional.

2 Data Integrity (Passive Authentication)

Data integrity of the stored information is protected by a digital signature stored in the EF.SOD file. The file uses the SignedData structure of the CMS (Cryptographic Message Syntax) standard. The PKI hierarchy has a single level. Each country establishes its own CSCA (Country Signing Certification Authority[1]), which certifies bodies responsible for issuing the passports (e.g., the state printers, embassies etc.). These bodies are called Document Signers. Data in the passport are then signed by one of these Document Signers.

To verify signatures, the CSCA certificates of the issuing country must be available and their integrity must be guaranteed. Countries should use diplomatic exchange of the CSCA certificates, but experience shows that it is not simple in reality.

The certificate of the Document Signer is either directly stored in the passport (in the certificate part of the SignedData structure – and this is mandatory in the EU) or must be obtained from other sources (the issuing country, the ICAO public key directory –PKD, etc.). To verify whether a document signer's key was not revoked the CRL must be checked. CRLs must be regularly obtained from the ICAO PKD or by other means (some countries publish their CRLs on web or LDAP servers).

The data which is being signed is a special structure containing hashes of all present data groups in the passport. Integrity of each file can be verified separately (i.e., first the digital signature in EF.SOD is verified and then integrity of each file is checked by verifying its hash against the hash stored in the EF.SOD file).

It is not surprising that a digital signature alone cannot prevent identical copies from being made of the passport content (including the EF.SOD file with digital signature) – so-called cloning. As such, the inspection of the classical security features (security printing, watermarks, holograms, etc.) still makes sense, but the correspondence between the printed data and the data stored on the chip should also be verified.

3 Active Authentication (AA)

Cloning of passports can be prevented by using a combination of cryptographic techniques and reasonable tamper resistance. In such a case a passport-specific

[1] For more information on Public Key Infrastructure see for example the FIDIS document D3.2 http://www.fidis.net/resources/deliverables/hightechid/

asymmetric key pair is stored in the chip. Whereas the public key is freely readable (stored in DG15 and its hash is digitally signed), the private key is not readable from the chip and its presence can be only verified using a challenge-response algorithm (based on ISO 9796-2). This protocol is called the active authentication (AA) and it is an optional security feature of electronic passports Also for EU countries AA is an optional feature and indeed not all the countries implement it (e.g., Germany, Greece, Italy and France do not implement AA).

The aim of the active authentication is to verify whether the chip in the passport is authentic. The inspection system generates an 8-byte random challenge asks the chip to authenticate itself using it. The chip generates its own random string and cryptographically hashes both parts together. The chip's random string and the hash of both parts are then signed by the chip's private key. The result is sent back to the inspection system, which verifies the digital signature. If the digital signature is correct the chip is considered to be authentic. The result of the AA only makes sense if the passive authentication has succeeded. Possible attacks might try to exploit weaknesses in the tamper resistance of the chip or can be based on the analysis of side-channels. If you have a genuine passport at your disposition you might also be able to produce a "copy" that talks back to the genuine passport when the active authentication needs to be performed. For a more detailed description of such a proxy (also called relay) attack see e.g. [2, 4].

There is an interesting privacy attack against an AA passport. If the challenge sent to the chip is not completely random, but rather specifically structured (for example encoding place and time), the inspection systems can store the challenge and the signature as a proof that the passport in question was at the given place at the given moment. In reality, such a proof would have to face the fact that the passport signs any arbitrary challenge at any place and the evidence value is therefore very limited. Even so some countries (e.g. Germany) decided not to implement the active authentication in their passports because of this privacy threat.

4 Basic Access Control (BAC)

Basic access control is a mechanism that prevents reading of the passport data before the authentication of the inspection system (i.e., prevents so-called skimming). The authentication keys are derived from data printed in the machine-readable zone of the data page. The document number, the birth date of the holder and the passport expiration date are used. All these items are printed in the second line of the machine readable zone and are protected with a check digit (the optical character recognition is error prone; hence the choice of data fields with check digits). During the authentication, session keys are established and further communication is secured using Secure Messaging, protecting the data transfer from eavesdropping.

BAC is based on a standard mutual authentication technique, which is considered secure as long as the keys are kept secret. In the case of electronic passports the keys are not secret in the classical sense as they are derivable from the data printed in the passport, but even so can prevent the random remote reading. Unfortunately the data used to derive the key do not necessarily have much entropy. Although the theoretical maximum is 58 bits and in case of alphanumerical document numbers even 74 bits, real values are significantly lower. Let us discuss the particular entries in more detail [3, 9]:

- Holder's birth date: one year has 365 or 366 days, theoretical maximum is 100 years, i.e., around 36524 days total (15.16 bits of entropy). The holder's age can be realistically estimated with a precision of 10 years (3652 days, 11.83 bits entropy), often even more accurately.
- Day of expiry: maximal validity of passports is 10 years (therefore approximately 3652 days, 11.83 bits entropy). Passports of children can have a shorter validity (typically 5 years).
- Document number: 9 characters are dedicated for the document number. Shorter document numbers must be padded with padding (<) characters and longer document numbers must be truncated. Document numbers consisting of digits only (and the padding character <) allow for the total number of 11^9 combinations (31.13 bits of entropy); if numbers can be alphanumerical then the maximum number is 379 of combinations (thus 46.88 bits of entropy). These values can be accomplished only when the passport number is truly random. And that is often not the case. Many countries assign sequential numbers to their passports. In such cases passport numbers and expiry date (and date of issue) are not independent.
- Every entry is followed by the check digit. The algorithm is publicly known and the check digit does not introduce any new information.

To estimate the (total) entropy, we might sum the entropies of entries listed above. But that is correct only when the individual entries are independent. Often the date of expiry and passport number is not independent. Then the total entropy does not reach the sum of individual items. For example in the case of sequential document numbers and a country issuing 1 million passports uniformly over the year and in the case of a detailed knowledge of the document numbers issued on particular days the entropy of the document number can decrease to about 12 bits. Total entropy then decreases from 58 respectively 74 bits to approximately 32 bits. The brute-force key search can be then mounted against a significantly smaller number of possible keys [10].

Intended communication range of devices compliant with ISO 14443 is 0-10cm. This does not necessary mean that eavesdropping on longer ranges is not possible, but an attacker has to cope with a low signal-to-noise ratio problem. Whereas the signal from the inspection system (reader) is detectable at longer distances, eavesdropping of the data sent from the chip becomes more difficult with distance. For discussions about the possible ranges for skimming and eavesdropping see e.g. [5, 7]. The eavesdropped authentication data can be used to mount an off-line key search attack, where the low entropy of the static key can be used to reduce the key space for brute-forcing the key.

An on-line attack against the chip can search the key space in the same way, but a single verification of the authentication data is significantly slower – we must communicate with the chip first and then we have to compute the MAC (Message Authentication Code) key and MAC code as well. A single verification then takes approximately 20 milliseconds for standard contactless readers and the attack is about 10 000x slower than an off-line attack.

It is necessary to realize that BAC does not restrict access to anybody who is able to read the machine readable zone. If you leave your passport at a hotel reception desk, BAC will not protect your data. On the other hand, there is no additional information stored in chip than printed in the passport (in EU this is even a legal requirement; except for the fingerprints, of course).

There are also other issues related to contactless communication technology where BAC cannot help. First of all it is possible to remotely detect the presence of passive contactless chips. Second even before the BAC it is possible to communicate with the chip (e.g., to start the BAC). Anti-collision algorithms need unique chip IDs to address the chips. These chip IDs are typically randomly generated each time the chip is powered, but some chips of type A use fixed chip IDs, which makes their tracking very simple. Similarly some error codes may leak information about the chip manufacturer and/or model, which might also increase the chances of guessing the issuing state [8].

5 Extended Access Control (EAC)

EU passports will store fingerprints (in DG3) at the latest after 28th June 2009. Germany was the first European country storing fingerprints in their passports introducing their passports of the "second generation" already on 1st November 2007. Fingerprints in EU passports have to be stored as images in the WSQ format (lossy compression optimized for images of fingerprints). As fingerprints are considered to be more sensitive data than facial images (their recognition capabilities are much better), reading of DG3 will be protected by an additional mechanism. This mechanism is called the Extended Access Control and was developed by the German Federal Office for Information Security [1]. At the time of writing this paper (November 2008) EAC was not an international (ICAO) standard. The European EAC is based on asymmetric cryptography and is a combination of Terminal authentication and Chip Authentication protocols.

5.1 Terminal Authentication

The aim of the terminal authentication (TA) is to restrict reading of sensitive biometric data (fingerprints, possibly also iris images) to authorized persons, e.g. border guards. Each country establishes a CV (Country Verifying) certification authority that decides which other countries will have the access to sensitive biometric data in their passports. A certificate of this authority is stored in passports issued by that country and it forms the starting trust point (root certificate) for the access control. Other countries wishing to access sensitive biometric data (in their own passports or in passports of other countries), must establish a DV (Document Verifier) certification authority. This authority will obtain the certificate from all countries willing to grant access to sensitive biometric data in passports they are issuing. The DVCA will then issue the certificates to end-point entities actually accessing the biometric data – the inspection systems (IS). See fig. 3.

Let's illustrate the process on an example. Each passport stores a CVCA certificate of the issuing country (e.g., Austria). If an inspection system (e.g., a Belgian one) needs to convince the passport that it is authorized to access sensitive biometric data, it must provide the DV certificate (the Belgian one in our case) signed by the issuing CVCA (Austria) and its own IS certificate (for that particular IS) signed by the DV

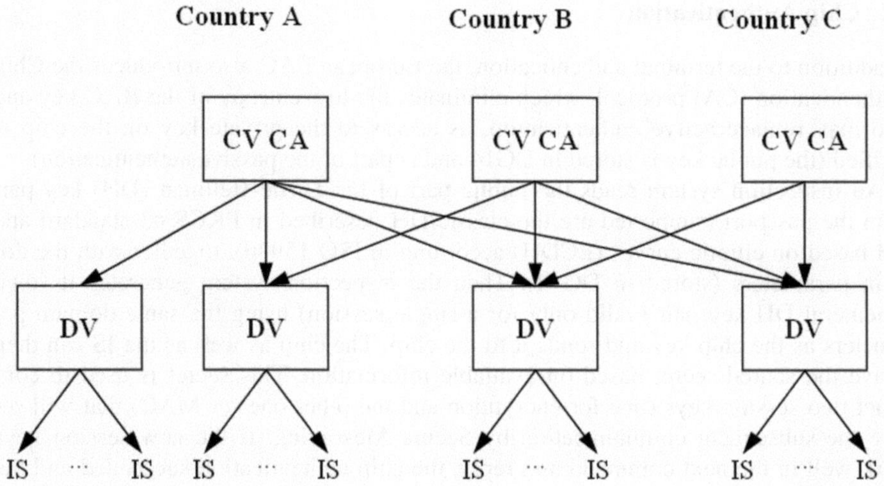

Fig. 3. A simplified view of an EAC PKI hierarchy

certification authority (i.e., Belgian in this case). After the passport verifies the whole certification chain it has to check whether the inspection system can access the corresponding private key. That is performed using a challenge-response protocol. If the authentication succeeds, the inspection system can access sensitive biometric data (i.e. read the DG3 and/or DG4 files).

The above mentioned process can be slightly more complicated as the CVCA certificates are updated from time to time (by link certificates) and the bridging link certificates have to be provided (and verified by the passport) at first.

Once the chain verification succeeds, the passport obtains the public key of the IS and its access rights. Only two access rights are specified at the moment, these are reading access to DG3 (fingerprints) and to DG4 (iris image).

As the computational power of electronic passports is limited, simplified certificates (card verifiable (CV) certificates) are used instead of common X.509 certificates. An interesting point is the verification of certificate validity. As the chip has no internal clock, the only available time-related information is the certificate issue date. If the chip successfully verifies the validity of a given certificate issued on a particular day, then it knows that this date has already passed (or is today) and can update its own internal time estimate (if the value is newer than the one already stored). It is clear that if a CVCA or DVCA issues (either by a mistake, intentionally or as a result of an attack) a certificate with the issue date in a distant future, the passport will then be rejecting valid certificates and will become practically unusable. For that reason, only the CVCA (link certificates), DV and domestic IS certificates are used to update the internal date estimate.

Short validity of certificates helps recovery from situations when an inspection system is stolen or is compromised. Naturally only those passports that are often read with the advanced inspection procedure (i.e. certificates are sent, validated and the date estimate in the passport is updated) are protected from unauthorized reading by inspection systems with expired certificates.

5.2 Chip Authentication

In addition to the terminal authentication, the European EAC also introduces the Chip Authentication (CA) protocol, which eliminates the low entropy of the BAC key and also may replace active authentication, as access to the private key on the chip is verified (the public key is stored in DG14 and is part of the passive authentication).

An inspection system reads the public part of the Diffie-Hellman (DH) key pair from the passport (supported are the classic DH described in PKCS #3 standard and DH based on elliptic curves (ECDH) according to ISO 15946), together with the domain parameters (stored in DG14). Then the inspection system generates its own ephemeral DH key pair (valid only for a single session) using the same domain parameters as the chip key and sends it to the chip. The chip as well as the IS can then derive the shared secret based on available information. This secret is used to construct two session keys (one for encryption and the other one for MAC) that will secure the subsequent communication by Secure Messaging. If the new session keys work well in the next command and reply, the chip authentication succeeded and the chip can be considered authentic.

Although chip authentication replaces active authentication, the chip can support both to allow verification of the chip authenticity at inspection systems that are not EAC-specific and only recognize international ICAO standards.

It is assumed that the protected biometric data will be initially accessible only among the EU member states. There have already been some speculations about involvement of countries like United States of America, Canada and Australia in the European extended access control system. Looking at the PKI structure of the EAC it becomes clear that is up to each member state to decide what other countries will have the access to data in the member state's passports.

6 Conclusions

The passive authentication securing authenticity of the data stored in electronic passports is a clear security benefit of the electronic part of the passport. But it can only be effective if the Country Signing CA certificates are available at all inspection systems (including relevant CRLs). How to achieve that in practice is still an open question.

While the BAC can prevent basic skimming, low entropy of the authentication key constitutes its major weakness. Efforts to include the optional data field from the machine-readable zone in the key computation (i.e., to increase the entropy) were rejected by ICAO in order not to break interoperability with existing systems. The only way to improve the strength of BAC is to use random alphanumeric document numbers. Some countries have already changed their numbering policy in order to make the attacks against BAC more difficult (e.g. Germany since Nov 2007 [11]). If you are worried that an attacker could communicate with your passport without your knowledge and either try to break the BAC or at least guess some information about the chip, just store your passport in a shielding cover which is widely available.

Active authentication preventing passport cloning is implemented by a surprisingly small number of countries. Cloning can also be prevented by chip authentication, which is a part of the EAC and will be implemented in the second generation EU passport. EAC is also able to protect fingerprints and iris images stored in DG3/4 from unauthorized reading. The key management behind it is, however, not trivial – especially from the organizational point of view. And although the DV and IS certificates will have short validity to limit the use of stolen inspection systems, this will only be effective for passports of frequent travelers.

References

1. BSI: Advanced Security Mechanisms for Machine Readable Travel Documents – Extended Access Control (EAC), Version 1.11, TR-03110
2. Hlaváč, M., Rosa, T.: A Note on the Relay Attacks on e-passports? The Case of Czech e-passports. Tech. report 2007/244, Int'l Assoc. for Cryptologic Research (2007), http://eprint.iacr.org/2007/244.pdf
3. Hoepman, J.-H., Hubbers, E., Jacobs, B., Oostdijk, M., Schreur, R.W.: Crossing Borders: Security and Privacy Issues of the European e-Passport. In: Yoshiura, H., Sakurai, K., Rannenberg, K., Murayama, Y., Kawamura, S.-i. (eds.) IWSEC 2006. LNCS, vol. 4266, pp. 152–167. Springer, Heidelberg (2006), http://www.cs.ru.nl/~jhh/publications/passport.pdf
4. ICAO, Document 9303, Edition 6 Part 1, Part 2 and Part 3
5. Kirschenbaum, I., Wool, A.: How to Build a Low-Cost, Extended-Range RFID Skimmer, http://www.eng.tau.ac.il/~yash/kw-usenix06/index.html
6. Kosta, E., Meints, M., Hansen, M., Gasson, M.: An analysis of security and privacy issues relating to RFID enabled ePassports. In: IFIPSEC 2007 International Federation for Information Processing, May 2007. New approaches for Security, Privacy and Trust in Complex Environments, vol. 232, pp. 467–472 (2007)
7. Kügler, D., Naumann, I.: Sicherheitsmechanismen für kontaktlose Chips im deutschen Reisepass. Ein Überblick über Sicherheitsmerkmale, Risiken und Gegenmaßnahmen. Datenschutz und Datensicherheit (March 2007), http://www.bsi.de/fachthem/epass/dud_03_2007_kuegler_naumann.pdf
8. Richter, H., Mostowski, W., Poll, E.: Fingerprinting Passports. In: NLUUG 2008 Spring Conference on Security, pp. 21–30 (2008), http://www.cs.ru.nl/~erikpoll/papers/nluug.pdf
9. Říha, Z.: Bezpečnost elektronických pasů, část I. Crypto-World 10/2006, http://www.crypto-world.info
10. Witteman, M.: Attacks on Digital Passports, WhatTheHack Conference, http://wiki.whatthehack.org/images/2/28/WTH-slides-Attacks-on-Digital-Passports-Marc-Witteman.pdf
11. Wikipedia: German entry for 'Reisepass', http://de.wikipedia.org/wiki/Reisepass

Location Privacy Issues in Wireless Sensor Networks

Jiří Kůr and Andriy Stetsko

Faculty of Informatics
Masaryk University
{xkur,xstetsko}@fi.muni.cz

Abstract. We discuss location privacy issues in wireless sensor networks. We consider sensor nodes with more responsible roles and the need to protect locations of such nodes. Available countermeasures against various types of traffic analysis attacks are examined and their problems are identified. We do not propose new traffic analysis resistance technique. Instead, we draw attention to blanks in current situation and identify several open questions, which should be answered in order to ensure location privacy of nodes.

1 Introduction

A wireless sensor network (WSN) is a heterogenous network composed of a large number of tiny low-cost devices, denoted as nodes, and a few general-purpose computing devices referred to as base stations. A general purpose of the WSN is to monitor some physical phenomenons (e.g. temperature, barometric pressure, light) inside an area of deployment.

Nodes are equipped with a communication unit (e.g., radio transceiver), processing unit, battery and sensor(s). General nodes are constrained in processing power and energy, whereas base stations (also called sinks) have laptop capabilities and unlimited energy resources. The base stations act as gateways between the WSN and other networks (e.g., Internet).

There is a wide variety of applications for WSNs [1], ranging from military applications (e.g., battlefield surveillance) through environmental (e.g., forest fire detection) to health applications (e.g., patient health monitoring). However, security of the WSNs has to be examined prior to their massive deployment.

In this paper we consider large WSNs with thousands of nodes, which have static geographical locations. We primarily aim to defend nodes with additional responsibilities (e.g., base stations) against traffic analysis which helps to reveal the locations. We do not propose new solutions for the problem, but we recapitulate and analyse the state-of-the-art countermeasures. Furthermore, we put down design considerations which have to be taken into account while designing new traffic decorrelation techniques. This paper is a starting point for the future research in this area and identifies several open questions.

V. Matyáš et al. (Eds.): The Future of Identity, IFIP AICT 298, pp. 160–169, 2009.

2 Identity and Location Privacy in WSN

In the context of WSNs we propose to use the following definition of node identity [8][1]: "An identity is any subset of attributes, which sufficiently identifies the node within any set of nodes. So, usually there is no such thing as 'the identity', but several of them". So far, we have identified several attributes, which can constitute an identity in itself or in combination with other ones:

- *Unique ID.* An application dependent identifier. An artificial identity used for the purposes of a particular application. It is typically represented by a bitstring. This identity can be abused not only on the particular application level, but also on other levels, for example, for tracking messages.
- *Global network address.* Typical identity in conventional networks. This identity can be forged by the adversary to attack, for example, routing algorithm, e.g. Sybil attack. However, global addressing scheme is not always implemented in WSNs due to resource limitations.
- *Local network address.* Local network address is not unique within the whole network and therefore it cannot in itself constitute the identity. However, it is unique within a neighborhood and thus can be used in combination with other attributes.
- *Sensed data.* Sensed data are often used to address nodes. For example, base station requests data from the nodes, which experience temperature above specified value. This data-centric approach substitutes classic network addressing schemes. Thus, sensed data can be considered as an attribute of node's identity. By these data, an adversary can identify a particular node or at least significantly reduce an anonymity set. For example, she can be interested in the location of nodes, which have experienced specific temperature during last hour. So, in this case the specific temperature represents a node identity.
- *Geographic location.* Geographic location of sensed data is very important (e.g. forest fire detection). We consider this location as an attribute, which comprise a special case of identity. We call this *location identity.* Protecting the location identity means ensuring a location privacy.

In order to ensure node location privacy the following requirements should be fulfilled [10]: (a) no one knows the exact location of the node, except itself; (b) other nodes, typically intermediate nodes on route, have no information about their distance, i.e. the number of hops, from that node.

Together with a node identity we can also define its *role.* The role is an expected behavior (i.e., sequence of actions) in a given context[8][2]. There is a number of roles in WSNs (e.g., a "base station" role, a "cluster head" role or

[1] In the original definition a term "person" is used instead of "node".

[2] "In sociology, a "role" or "social role" is a set of connected actions, as conceptualized by actors in a social situation (i.e., situation-dependent identity attributes). It is mostly defined as an expected behavior (i.e., sequences of actions) in a given individual social context."[8].

"sensing node" role). Some of them involve more responsibilities and hence nodes in such roles are more tempting for an adversary than other ones (e.g., a base station, a cluster head). In the rest of the paper, we call these nodes *important nodes.*

In order to protect the important node we should provide an unlinkability of the node's identity and its role. For example, if an adversary links a node's location identity to the "base station" role, she can either isolate the node (base station) or physically destroy it and hence ruin the whole network. Therefore, we primarily aim to ensure the location privacy of the important nodes.

3 Traffic Analysis

Traffic analysis attacks help to reveal communication patterns, which allow an adversary to deduce a location of important nodes and then to compromise or to destroy them. Three classes of the traffic analysis attack are identified in WSNs: the rate monitoring attack, the time correlation attack and the content analysis attack.

In the rate monitoring attack, an adversary observes nodes sending packet rate and moves closer to the node, which has the highest sending packet rate. In the time correlation attack, an adversary monitors a correlation in sending times between a node and its neighbors. The adversary tries to detect which node forwards the current packet and traces the path directly to a base station. In the content analysis attack, an adversary tries to obtain a valuable information (e.g., a base station location) from packet headers and payloads.

In [3] the authors employ two metrics to evaluate effectiveness of proposed mechanisms against the rate monitoring attack. First, an entropy metric measures a randomness of network traffic. Second, a heuristic-based algorithm combines a hill-climbing search algorithm with a random restart mechanism. In this algorithm, an adversary starts at some location and monitors network traffic within his/her range. The adversary moves to the node with the highest sending rate. In case he/she reaches a local sending rate maximum he/she selects another location at random and repeats this algorithm. This algorithm is based on the rate monitoring analysis and can be used by an adversary to locate a base station.

4 State-of-the-Art

Many solutions that provide location privacy and anonymity have been proposed for MANETs [6,9,10]. However, these schemes are not suitable for highly resource-constrained WSNs where the predominant traffic pattern is many-to-one.

Only a few satisfying solutions have been proposed for WSNs. Encryption techniques can be used to hide a destination address, a packet type and a packet payload. However, the end-to-end encryption does not solve a problem with a packet appearance, which remains the same along the path. In order to make it harder for an attacker to trace packets to a base station, a hop-by-hop re-encryption scheme should be used. However, this technique introduces extra delays in forwarding packets. In [2] the authors propose a mechanism which defends against the rate monitoring attack. The packet to send is repeatedly transmitted by a child node until the packet is accepted by a parent node. If the child node has no packet to send it injects a dummy packet. This mechanism ensures a uniform sending rate across the entire network but significantly decreases the lifetime of WSN. In order to defend against the time correlation attack, the authors of [5] propose to add random delays to packet retransmission at each forwarding node. Tolerance against base station isolation might be increased by usage of several base stations [2]. In this approach a node sends packets to the different base stations.

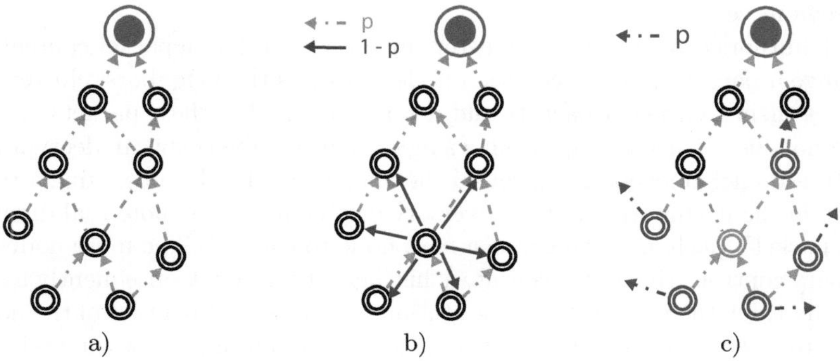

Fig. 1. Multi-parent routing schemes

More advanced techniques are presented in [4]. The rate monitoring attack can be partially prevented by a multiple parent routing scheme since traffic spreads along multiple paths. Each node has multiple parent nodes, which route packets to a base station, see Fig.1 a). In order to forward a packet, a node randomly selects one of its parent nodes. This scheme can be extended by a controlled random walk. A node forwards a packet to one of its parent nodes with probability p. With probability $1 - p$ the node forwards the packet to one of its neighbors – this does not eliminate the fact that the node selects a parent node, see Fig.1 b). This technique introduces delivery time delays, which are proportional to extra hops used for forwarding the packets. This technique is still vulnerable to the time correlation attack. Therefore, the authors propose a new technique called the multi-parent routing scheme with fractal propagation. When a node hears that a neighbor forwards a packet to a base station, the node generates a fake packet with probability p and forwards it to one of its neighbors, see Fig.1 c). The main problem with this technique is that it generates a large amount of traffic near a base station. This can be solved by a differential fractal propagation technique. When a node forwards packets more frequently it sets a lower probability for creating new fake packets. In order to make traffic analysis more difficult, the authors propose to generate artificial areas (called hot-spots) of high communication activity.

In order to minimize the damage of nodes compromise, the authors propose to use a directional pairwise identification mechanism [4], such that each node uses a different identification for communication with its child nodes and parent nodes. That means that a compromised child node does not know a parent node identification used to send data. This idea is extended in [7]. A base station is responsible for routing process and it assigns incoming and outgoing labels to nodes in both uplink and downlink directions. Each node only forwards packets with labels which match either its downlink or uplink label.

5 Suggested Improvements

In this section we try to identify shortcomings of some techniques presented in the previous section.

In [4] authors propose to use a cluster key both to protect a packet content and to change a packet appearance. Each node possesses the neighbors' cluster keys and uses them to decrypt packets and determine whether these packets are fake or original ones. Thus, by capturing a single node, an adversary can decrypt traffic within its neighborhood and reveal the neighbors' IDs. By observing a traffic pattern in the neighborhood, the adversary may estimate the potential direction of the packet's path and determine a next node to capture. The more nodes the adversary controls, the more accurate is his/her estimation. Consequently he/she can easily track the packets to a base station by subsequent capture of the nodes.

We propose to use double encryption to mitigate an impact of the node capture. First, the packet is encrypted by a pairwise key, then an information whether the packet is fake or original is concatenated and finally the result is encrypted with the cluster key. This reduces area compromised by a single captured node from the node's neighborhood to the node itself. By capturing a node, the adversary can still distinguish fake packets from original ones in the whole neighborhood, but he/she can completely decrypt only packets passing right through the captured node instead of packets passing through its neighbors. Thus, an adversary has to capture significantly larger number of nodes in order to trace packets to a base station. We assume that the amount of original packets passing through the nodes is large enough to prevent simple time correlation attacks and a decryption is needed to link two distinct packets.

We have also encountered a problem with the differential fractal propagation scheme, which had been proposed in [4]. In order to prevent a creation of a large amount of traffic near a base station, authors propose a mechanisms, which ensures that nodes with higher sending rate (nodes closer to a base station) generate fake packets with lower probabilities. This rule applies to the nodes with a sending rate higher than some threshold h. Thus, there is an area around the base station, in which these probabilities indicate a distance of the node to the base station. Therefore, by capturing the nodes from this area an adversary can easily find out whether he/she moves closer to the base station or not. The size of the area depends on the threshold value h. The area has to be large enough to prevent a creation of a significant amount of traffic near the base station. On the other hand the larger the area is the higher is a probability that the adversary captures a node within this area. Hence, the area size should be small enough to prevent an adversary from capturing a node within the area.

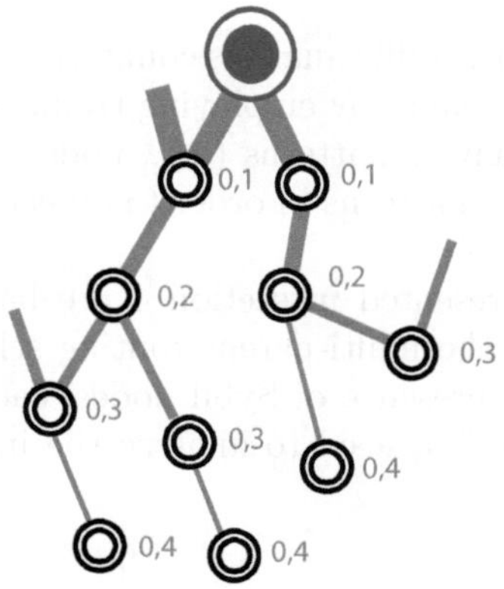

Fig. 2. Differential fractal propagation scheme

There is a question whether it is possible to find a solution that would satisfy both requirements. Obviously, we can find the tradeoff that would minimize the probability of capturing a node within the area while still keeping the amount of traffic near base station at reasonably low level. While being an optimal tradeoff, the size of area can be still too large to apply this technique in practice.

6 Open Questions

In this section we want to introduce several open questions, which we have encountered during the study of identity and location privacy issues in WSNs.

6.1 Attacker Model

Some authors assume an attacker model with a global eavesdropper, which monitors all possible communication links between all nodes all the time. We think that this model is not adequate for the most WSN applications and we should assume an adversary, which observes only a limited part (but variable for different applications) of the network. Someone might argue that the global eavesdropper model is stronger and hence by taking into account this model we gain a better security in WSN. It is not necessary true. In order to defend against a stronger attacker we design a stronger countermeasures, which typically consume more energy resources and hence decrease a WSN lifetime.

The global eavesdropper model is a passive attacker model. However, WSNs are not physically protected and it is necessary to assume an active attacker, which in addition to the traffic analysis attack can launch a variety of other attacks (e.g., attacks on network layer). However, authors of countermeasure techniques described in the section 4 do not consider the presence of internal attacks. In some cases it turns into an increase of damage done by these internal attacks. For example, in the sinkhole attack, where an adversary tries to attract all traffic destined to the base station, the traffic analysis countermeasures presented in the section 4 create useless traffic and waste network energy resources. By performing the sinkhole attack, the adversary can drain batteries of the nodes in its neighborhood.

Also it might happen that traffic analysis countermeasures hinder in detection of malicious nodes. On one hand, by employing traffic analysis countermeasures we want to hide some behavior patterns (e.g., nodes sending rates). On other hand we want to keep these patterns in order to detect attacks such as selective forwarding attack.

The countermeasures presented in section 4 are based on the multi-parent routing scheme. However, the multi-parent routing scheme has not to be necessary multi-parent in the presence of Sybil nodes, each of which owns several identities. Therefore, there is a need to analyze the influence of the attack on the proposed techniques.

6.2 Location Privacy of Other Important Nodes

A base station is often considered as the only important node, whose location privacy has to be protected. However, WSNs might include other important nodes, for example cluster heads or nodes, which run intrusion detection system (IDS). There is a need to search for new sources of information, which might reveal a location of these nodes. There are two types of IDS: cooperative and non-cooperative. The cooperative IDSs may have either peer-to-peer or hierarchical architecture. In both architectures, IDS nodes share a detection state information, which might be used to deduce their location. Since there is no sense to employ an IDS without a response system, we assume that a detection of an attack is always followed by actions, which try either to stop or prevent the attack. Therefore, an adversary can capture a node and generate internal attacks in order to force the IDS to react and provide the adversary with traffic, which is sufficient to locate IDS nodes. Some attacks might be detected locally (e.g., blackhole attack) but others require a cooperation from IDS nodes (e.g., wormhole attack). This fact can be exploited by an adversary to force IDS nodes to cooperate and hence produce additional traffic.

In some scenarios a base station is involved in the response system. It might flood a WSN with certain actions, which should be taken by nodes in order to stop or prevent an attack. We are not aware of decorrelation techniques or attacks, which take into account a traffic broadcasted by a base station. This might provide an adversary with new possibilities to reveal a base station location.

A proper IDS placement strategy has to be chosen in order to minimize energy consumption and maximize an IDS effectiveness. For example, as a criteria of effectiveness we may choose a number of IDS nodes, a volume of analyzed traffic and accuracy of detection. It is more "effective" to deploy IDSs in traffic concentration points. Hence, by performing the rate monitoring attack an adversary can find out a location of IDS nodes. In general, taking into account the placement strategy an adversary can significantly reduce a set of nodes, which may run an IDS and hence significantly increase a probability to locate these nodes. We are not aware of placement strategies, which take into account a location privacy issue. It means that an adversary might find a large subset of IDS nodes and compromise them in order to subvert detection results. Obviously, the traffic analysis countermeasures can be applied in this case. However, they can be more resource consuming than a design, which counts with the location privacy issue from the beginning. Therefore, we think that a location privacy should be considered as one of parameters of IDS placement strategy effectiveness.

The problem with the placement strategy holds also for base stations. In most cases, when designing a placement strategy, efficiency is the only design consideration and its actual meaning is dependent on a particular application. Sometimes we need a low latency, whereas in other case we prefer a strong energy awareness. Anyway, the location privacy needs are neglected. Suppose the adversary knows the area of deployment and the placement strategy. In that case he/she can focus his/her attention only to the particular places, where the probability of the base station being placed is the highest.

6.3 A WSN Model

The strength of proposed decorrelation techniques has to depend on a variety of input parameters. As long as these parameter are not taken into account, the decorrelation technique either underestimates or overestimates some threats. The underestimating of threats may lead to an easy compromise of the whole network and their overestimating may lead to a wastage of energy due to excessive prevention, detection or reaction mechanisms, which in turn significantly decrease a total WSN lifetime. We think that used WSN models are too simplified and techniques proposed under these models can be employed only under very limited circumstances. Ideally, the required strength of decorrelation technique should change gradually according to the changes of input parameters. In this section we present some parameters, which we think have to be taken into account while designing traffic analysis countermeasures.

There is a need to consider a presence of several base stations since they can share responsibility and mitigate network traffic patterns. Authors propose sophisticated decorrelation mechanisms assuming a presence of only one base station. We believe, that in some cases it would be more profitable to use several base stations instead of the decorrelation technique at all. Both situations are extremes and will be realistic only under very limited circumstances. The more realistic case is when there are several base stations and a decorrelation technique is employed. In order to ensure a wider application range of decorrelation technique, its strength should change according to the number of available base stations. Intuitively, the higher number of base station is, the more mitigated traffic patterns are and hence the less complex decorrelation technique we need. There is a need to find a trade-off between a number of base-station and a complexity of decorrelation technique used.

Different WSN applications require different sending data rates. These data rates may be so small that it takes much more time to perform traffic analysis and locate a base station than a total lifetime of a WSN, which does not employ any decorrelation technique. So, the strength of decorrelation technique depends on the sending data rate parameter and should vary for different WSN applications with different sending rates.

A number of nodes and their density also have an impact on the required strength of decorrelation technique. We can imagine a WSN network, where a number of nodes is not high and the deployed area is relatively small for adversary to find out a location of base station(s). In that case there is no sense to employ any decorrelation technique at all. In the section 4 there are discussed decorrelation techniques, which are based on the multi-parent routing scheme. However, the density of the nodes might be so low that no multi-parent routes will exist. In that case the decorrelation techniques also will not be profitable at all. We conclude, that a number of nodes and their density should be also taken into account when designing traffic analysis countermeasures.

There is a need to deeply analyze relations between different parameters and to propose an adequate WSN model. The more precise model we make, the more effective solution we will be able to obtain. We are aware of the fact that very precise model might not lead to any solution at all as we will not be able to solve the problem under this model. However, we believe that currently available models are too simplified and are not adequate enough.

7 Summary

We examined identity issues in WSNs and showed the need to ensure a location privacy of important nodes, especially base stations. State-of-the-art traffic analysis techniques and countermeasures against them were briefly described. We tried to identify shortcomings and blanks of the presented countermeasures. We also outlined problems of hiding a location identity of the important nodes. It comes out, that this area is not adequately examined yet and new mechanisms have to be designed. We identified several open questions, which, we hope, will encourage interesting discussions. We think that a field of identity and location privacy in the WSNs has a great potential for the future research.

References

1. Akyildiz, I.F., Su, W., Sankarasubramaniam, Y., Cayirci, E.: Wireless sensor networks: a survey. Computer Networks 38(4), 393–422 (2002)
2. Deng, J., Han, R., Mishra, S.: Intrusion tolerance and anti-traffic analysis strategies for wireless sensor networks. In: DSN 2004: Proceedings of the 2004 International Conference on Dependable Systems and Networks, Washington, DC, USA, p. 637. IEEE Computer Society, Los Alamitos (2004)
3. Deng, J., Han, R., Mishra, S.: Countermeasures against traffic analysis attacks in wireless sensor networks. In: SECURECOMM 2005: Proceedings of the First International Conference on Security and Privacy for Emerging Areas in Communications Networks, Washington, DC, USA, pp. 113–126. IEEE Computer Society, Los Alamitos (2005)
4. Deng, J., Han, R., Mishra, S.: Decorrelating wireless sensor network traffic to inhibit traffic analysis attacks. Pervasive and Mobile Computing 2(2), 159–186 (2006)
5. Hong, X., Wang, P., Kong, J., Zheng, Q., Liu, J.: Effective probabilistic approach protecting sensor traffic. In: Military Communications Conference, vol. 1 (2005)

6. Kong, J., Hong, X.: Anodr: anonymous on demand routing with untraceable routes for mobile ad-hoc networks. In: MobiHoc 2003: Proceedings of the 4th ACM international symposium on Mobile ad hoc networking & computing, pp. 291–302. ACM, New York (2003)
7. Nezhad, A.A., Makrakis, D., Miri, A.: Destination Controlled Anonymous Routing in Resource Constrained Multihop Wireless Sensor Networks. In: Wireless Sensor and Actor Networks, December 2007. IFIP International Federation for Information Processing, vol. 248, pp. 83–94. Springer, Boston (2007)
8. Pfitzmann, A., Hansen, M.: Anonymity, unlinkability, undetectability, unobservability, pseudonymity, and identity management - a consolidated proposal for terminology (February 2008)
9. Seys, S., Preneel, B.: Arm: Anonymous routing protocol for mobile ad hoc networks. In: AINA 2006: Proceedings of the 20th International Conference on Advanced Information Networking and Applications, Washington, DC, USA, vol. 2, pp. 133–137. IEEE Computer Society, Los Alamitos (2006)
10. Zhu, B., Wan, Z., Kankanhalli, M.S., Bao, F., Deng, R.H.: Anonymous secure routing in mobile ad-hoc networks. In: LCN 2004: Proceedings of the 29th Annual IEEE International Conference on Local Computer Networks, Washington, DC, USA, pp. 102–108. IEEE Computer Society, Los Alamitos (2004)

Design and Analysis of a Practical E-Voting Protocol

Marián Novotný

Institute of Computer Science, Pavol Jozef Šafárik University,
Jesenná 5, 041 54 Košice, Slovakia
marian.novotny@upjs.sk

Abstract. In this paper we design an e-voting protocol for an academic voting system which should be independent from other university applications. We briefly discuss security requirements for e-voting schemes focusing on our proposed scheme. We design a receipt-free e-voting protocol which requires neither anonymous channel nor other physical assumptions. We give a short survey on formal analysis of e-voting protocols. Using the applied pi-calculus we model and analyze some security properties of the proposed scheme.

1 Introduction

Voting is one of the most important and fundamental institutions of democratic society. The process of informatisation brings the possibility of cheaper and more comfortable alternative to classical voting – voting through the Internet. The increase of the *turnout* using e-voting is generally disputable [9], but we believe that it can be achieved in the domain of academic field, because of young and more computer proficient participants.

On the other hand it is desirable to protect the *privacy* of voters and shield them from the possibility of *frauds*. Design and analysis of e-voting protocols have become a challenge in cryptography and security research field. Since design of cryptographic protocols is notoriously error-prone, it is necessary to prove security properties using *formal methods*.

There are many schemes [14,15] which realize different kinds of demands for e-voting. They use various cryptographic primitives [14] such as *blind signature [6], bit commitment, homomorphic encryption, mixnets, zero-knowledge proofs, deniable encryption* [5] etc. We may distinguish three main kinds of protocols in literature according to the mechanism for providing the privacy of voters: blind signature schemes [8,12], homomorphic encryption schemes [14,15] and schemes based on mixing the votes [14]. A good survey on e-voting schemes can be found in [14,15].

This paper is organized as follows. The next section describes the academic voting system and security requirements and phases of e-voting schemes. The section following next introduces the proposed e-voting scheme. In section 4 we give a short survey on formal analysis of e-voting protocols and analyze our proposed scheme. The last section presents our conclusions and suggestions for the future work.

V. Matyáš et al. (Eds.): The Future of Identity, IFIP AICT 298, pp. 170–183, 2009.

2 Academic Voting System

Nowadays academic institutions are using various applications such as university information system, video-conference, portal of virtual collaboration etc. The evolution of these systems and corresponding demands for them requires to implement modules for providing various private voting services, e. g., *election to academic boards*, *balloting of commissions*, *anonymous questionnaires* about lectures, teachers or *anonymous psychological questionnaires* etc.

Our aim is to design and implement an *academic voting system*, which should be independent from other university applications. These will be extended by a *module for managing of voting*, such as creating and defining voting with obligatory properties as the type of voting, the list of eligible voters and candidates, in the case of questionnaires the questions and possible answers, the start and the deadline for the vote-casting etc. We assume a pre-established *Public Key Infrastructure* with registered conceivable voters with relevant *certificates* of public keys. Each certificate must contain a part, which uniquely identifies various potential voters such as students, teachers, foreign visitors etc.

The act of vote-casting or filling questionnaire will be accomplished by using a *Java Web Start* application in order to have a program without installation which can use a keystore of voter's keys and secrets on his device. The source code of the client-side software will be signed by the trusted registration authority and verified by the user and the *Java Virtual Machine* during loading the application. This way we assume that the client-side will be trusted.

In the beginning of realization of the academic voting system we do not assume *qualified* certificates. It will be sufficient to obtain a certificate by the e-voting client where a user creates a pair – a private key with corresponding public key. By using the client application the user authenticates and authorizes himself in a university application and sends the public key together with the proof of knowledge of the corresponding private key. The university application then issues the certificate of the public key for him.

Security Requirements and Phases of e-Voting Schemes. There exist several possible types of voting [14]. According to the requirements for the academic voting system we need to implement *yes/no, 1-L, 1-L-K* and special *"write-in"* [14] for questionnaires.

The stages of voting can be seen on Fig. 1. After creating and defining voting, the process of voting consists of six stages in general. We focus mainly on the phases of *registration*, *vote-casting*, *tallying* and *verification*, which are realized by the e-voting protocol.

A voting scheme is expected to satisfy certain security requirements, which are summarized and compared in [15]. In the following we enumerate and briefly describe these properties which are relevant for the academic voting system.

- *Eligibility.* Only valid voters who meet certain pre-determined criteria are eligible to vote.
- *Privacy.* In a secret ballot, a vote must not identify a voter and any traceability between the voter and his vote must be removed.

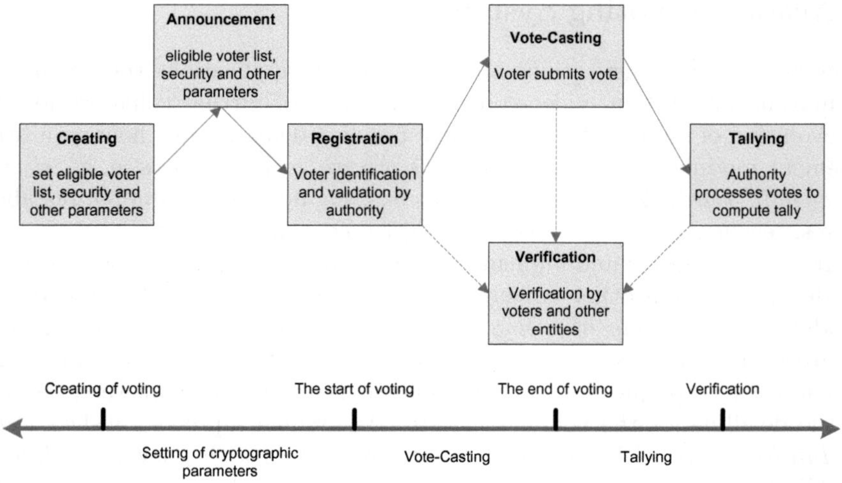

Fig. 1. The stages of a voting scheme

- *Verifiability.* A voter should be able to verify whether his vote was correctly recorded and accounted in the final vote tally. We distinguish between *individual* and *universal* verifiability. In the latter case not only the voter but anyone can verify that all valid votes were included and the tally process was *accurate.*
- *Dispute-freeness.* A voting scheme must provide a mechanism to resolve all disputes at any stage.
- *Accuracy.* A voting scheme must be error-free. Votes of invalid voters should not be counted in the *final tally.*
- *Fairness.* No one should be able to compute a *partial tally* as the election progresses.
- *Robustness.* A scheme has to be robust against active or passive attacks and faults as well.
- *Receipt-freeness.* A voter should not be able to provide a receipt with which he may be able to prove his vote to any other entity.
- *Practicality.* A voting scheme should not have assumptions and requirements that may be difficult to implement for a real application.

3 The Proposed Scheme

In the protocol we assume neither anonymous nor other physical assumptions such as *untappable channel* [14]. On the other hand our scheme requires a pre-established public key infrastructure. In this way each eligible voter has a valid certificate of a public key according to the private key for signing.

We use three servers – two *registration* and one *tally* as sketched in Fig. 2. Each registration server has a list of eligible voters for certain voting. We doubled registration servers, because we consider *blind signature* schemes to be problematic due to the possibility of creating votes of abstain voters by the registration server. The problem can be caused if a voter has been registered and then *abstains.* In this case the single registration server knows registered voters and is able to create a "fake" vote which substitutes a vote of the abstain voter in the final tally. We would like to avoid this problem by using two registration servers for controlling themselves. Machines on which the registration servers will be running should be mounted on different places under the control of different authorities. Moreover they serve in the protocol also as a simple *decryption mixnet* for providing anonymity of the communication in the vote-casting phase.

First we introduce a basic scheme which does not provide the receipt-freeness property. Next we will extend it by using trapdoor bit commitment combined with deniable encryption in order to provide the receipt-freeness property. In the description of the scheme we use the following notations. For a participant X we denote his public key for encryption (signing) Pk_X^E (Pk_X^S) and the corresponding private key Sk_X^E (Sk_X^S). Encryption of a message m under the public key Pk_X^E is denoted as $E_{Pk_X^E}(m)$ and signing the message m by the participant X using his private key Sk_X^S as $S_{Sk_X^S}(m)$.

The Scheme Based on Blind Signature. For ensuring the privacy property, i. e., removing any traceability between a voter and his vote we use a blind signature scheme. The concept of the blind signature was introduced by D. Chaum in [6]. This kind of signature solves the problem when a *requester* R wants to sign a message m from an *authority* A without revealing any information about m. The content of the message m for the signer A with the public key Pk_A^S is *blinded* by the requester using the function $Bl(m, r, Pk_A^S)$ with a random parameter r. The signer A signs the blinded message as $S_{Sk_A^S}(Bl(m, r, Pk_A^S))$ and sends it to the requester. The requester retrieves the desired signature using the *unblind* function $Unbl(S_{Sk_A^S}(Bl(m, r, Pk_A^S)), r, Pk_A^S) = S_{Sk_A^S}(m)$.

Registration phase. First a voter V_i obtains public keys of all servers and a public parameter of the tally server for the voting g_T^t. The private parameter t of the tally server can be shared by many authorities such as members of a voting committee and $g_T \in \mathbb{G}$ is a generator of a cyclic group $\mathbb{G}$ on which we can map the set of asymmetric keys for the encryption of a vote. We assume that for the group $\mathbb{G}$ is the *CDH problem* [11] hard. This way we would like to ensure the scheme to be more robust in the sense of the fairness property.

The voter V_i chooses his vote $vote_i$, then he randomly chooses v_i and computes the asymmetric key $K_i = (g_T^t)^{v_i}$ for the decryption with the corresponding key K_i^{-1} for the encryption of the vote. For all public key encryptions including the encryption of the vote we use an *IND-CCA* [11] probabilistic encryption scheme and for hashing a hash function H which fulfills appropriate security requirements for hash functions [11].

The voter V_i prepares his *ballot* $b_i = E_{K_i^{-1}}(vote_i), g_T^{v_i}$ and computes its hash value $h_{i_1} = H(b_i)$. Then he blinds this hash value as $bl_{i_1} = Bl_{Pk_{RS_1}^S}(h_{i_1}, r_{i_1})$ by a random parameter r_{i_1}. The voter registers in RS_1 server and signs the hash value of his ballot by RS_1 server in the following messages:

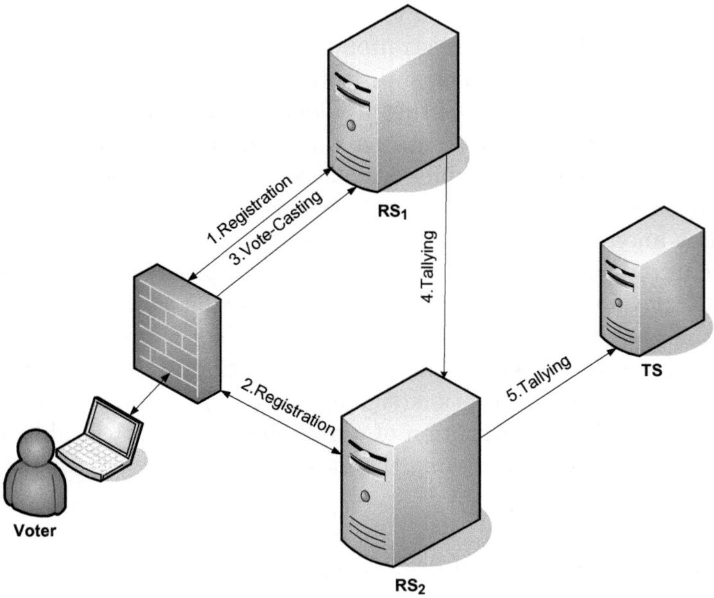

Fig. 2. The servers and the communication in the protocol

1. $V_i \longrightarrow RS_1 \; E_{Pk^E_{RS_1}}(V_i, S_{Sk^S_V}(ID_{voting}, V_i, bl_{i_1}))$
2. $RS_1 \longrightarrow V_i \; S_{Sk^S_{RS_1}}(bl_{i_1})$

After receiving and encrypting the first message the registration server RS_1 examines whether the voter V_i is on the voter's list for the voting ID_{voting} and checks the signature. If the check succeeds, it signs the blinded message bl_{i_1} and sends it back to the voter in the second message. The voter unblinds this message using the random parameter r_{i_1} and obtains the signature of the hash value of his ballot: $S_{Sk^S_{RS_1}}(h_{i_1})$.

The voter V_i after successful registration in RS_2 server will obtain a "token" for the vote-casting phase. First the voter prepares the message $m_{i_2} = E_{Pk^E_{RS_2}}(E_{Pk^E_{TS}}(b_i, S_{Sk^S_{RS_1}}(h_{i_1})))$ and computes its hash value as $h_{i_2} = H(m_{i_2})$. Then he blinds it by a random parameter r_{i_2} thus has $bl_{i_2} = Bl_{Pk^S_{RS_2}}(h_{i_2}, r_{i_2})$. The voter registers in RS_2 server in the following messages:

1. $V_i \longrightarrow RS_2 \; E_{Pk^E_{RS_2}}(V_i, S_{Sk^S_V}(ID_{voting}, bl_{i_2}, V_i))$
2. $RS_2 \longrightarrow V_i \; S_{Sk^S_{RS_2}}(bl_{i_2})$

After receiving and encrypting the first message the registration server RS_2 examines whether the voter V_i is on the voter's list for the voting ID_{voting} and checks the signature. If the check succeeds, it signs the blinded message bl_{i_2} and sends it back in the second message. The voter unblinds this message using the random parameter r_{i_2} and obtains $S_{Sk^S_{RS_2}}(h_{i_2})$ which is the "token" for the vote-casting phase.

Vote-casting phase. After the above mentioned registration the voter V_i can abstain or take part in the voting by sending the following message until the deadline of the voting:

$$V_i \longrightarrow RS_1\ E_{Pk^E_{RS_1}}(m_{i_2}, S_{Sk^S_{RS_2}}(h_{i_2}))$$

The registration server RS_1 decrypts the received message, then it examines the validity of the signature of RS_2 server on the hash value of the message m_{i_2} and finally it stores it in its local database together with the signature $S_{Sk^S_{RS_2}}(h_{i_2})$.

Tallying phase. After the deadline of the voting, the registration server RS_1 sends *lexicographically ordered* messages m_{i_2} of all participated voters V_i with corresponding signatures $S_{Sk^S_{RS_2}}(h_{i_2})$ to the registration server RS_2. It also publishes the list of signatures in order to avoid possible disputes. The server RS_2 examines the validity of its signature for each message. If the check succeeds, then it decrypts each message m_{i_2} and sends them lexicographically ordered to the tally server TS with its signature of the hash value of the complete list. Furthermore it publishes the list of signatures of messages which were sent by it.

1. $RS_1 \longrightarrow RS_2\ m_{i_2}, S_{Sk^S_{RS_2}}(h_{i_2})$
2. $RS_2 \longrightarrow TS\ E_{Pk^E_{TS}}(b_i, S_{Sk^S_{RS_1}}(h_{i_1}))$

The tally server TS checks the signature of the RS_2 server on the incoming list and then decrypts each message from the list and checks the signature of the RS_1 server on each ballot b_i. It obtains the shared secret t from shareholders and then for each ballot b_i it computes the key $K_i = (g_T^{v_i})^t$ for the decryption of the vote. After decrypting it publishes t and the list $S_{Sk^S_{RS_1}}(h_{i_1}), (E_{K_i^{-1}}(vote_i), g_T^{v_i}), vote_i$.

3.1 Informal Analysis of the Protocol

In this part we provide informal arguments about the security properties of the proposed basic scheme. In section 4 we will define a formal model of the protocol and specify and prove some security properties using the applied pi-calculus.

The protocol should provide the fairness property under the assumption that all servers and shareholders of the parameter t do not cooperate in order to know the partial tally. The ballot is encrypted three times under the public keys of all servers. The servers can decrypt the message cooperatively in the vote-casting phase and obtain the ballot. But for acquiring the vote from the ballot it is required to know the secret parameter t which can be shared by many authorities such as members of voting committee etc.

The privacy property is ensured by the blind signature scheme. During the registration in the RS_1 server, the trace between a voter and his ballot is removed. The voter obtains the "token" for the vote-casting phase during the registration in the RS_2 server. In the vote-casting phase it is possible to deduce the communication link between the sender of the message and the vote by cooperation of all servers. At this stage three serves serve as a small decryption mixnet. The message from the voter in the vote-casting phase is waiting for processing in the

RS_1 server until the deadline of the voting. Hiding the communication link can be achieved by a single honest server, which does not cooperate with others.

The voter is authenticated in the registration servers using his signatures of messages during registration. If he registers in the RS_1 server and does not register in the RS_2 server, he is not able to send his vote in the vote-casting phase. If he registers in RS_2 and not in RS_1 and he sends the message in the vote-casting phase, the message is not correct and cannot be counted in the final tally. If the voter has been registered in both servers, he can abstain from voting if he does not send the message in the vote-casting phase. For creating a "fake" vote of an abstain voter it is necessary that two registration servers cooperate. If the voter correctly registers in both servers and sends the message in the vote-casting phase and his vote is not published in the final tally, he can look at the published lists of registration servers and find the problem. If it is necessary he can resend his message with the "token" to the server RS_1.

3.2 A Receipt-Free Version of the Scheme

Instead of the ballot b_i from the above mentioned basic scheme we redefine the ballot and denote it as b_i^{RF} in the receipt-free version scheme in order to send the *bit commitment* of a vote and deniable encryption of the parameter for *opening* the commitment. In this way the tally server can open the bit commitment in one way only, but the voter can fake a coercer about his vote by faking the parameter for opening the commitment. To ensure that the scheme is more robust in the sense of the fairness property it is sufficient to encrypt just the bit commitment under the key K_i^{-1} defined above.

Trapdoor Bit Commitment. We use the trapdoor bit commitment scheme from the paper [13]. Several parameters p, q, g are generated and published by the voting system, where p, q are primes, $q|p-1$, $g \in \mathbb{Z}_p^\star$ and $q = order(g)$. The voter V_i has own secret α_i and computes $G_i = g^{\alpha_i} \bmod p$. We define the bit commitment $BC(vote_i, r_i) = g^{vote_i} G_i^{r_i} \bmod p$ where $vote_i$ is the vote of the voter V_i and r_i is a random parameter. The voter is able to open the bit commitment as an arbitrary vote $vote^{c}$[1] by using his secret α_i and from the equation $vote_i + \alpha_i r_i = vote^c + \alpha_i r_i^c \bmod q$ he can compute r_i^c such that $BC(vote_i, r_i) = BC(vote^c, r_i^c)$.

We assume that the list of candidates (possible votes) is not very large and the tally server for each candidate c can compute and store g^{vote^c}. In this way it is sufficient for opening to send $BC(vote_i, r_i), r_i, G_i$. The tally server computes $G_i^{r_i} = g^{\alpha . r_i} \bmod p$, then the inverse $(G_i^{r_i})^{-1} \bmod p$. The value of g^{vote_i} computes as $g^{vote_i} = BC(vote_i, r_i).(G_i^{r_i})^{-1} = g^{vote_i}.G_i^{r_i}.(G_i^{r_i})^{-1} \bmod p$ and in order to find the vote $vote_i$ compares g^{vote_i} with pre-computed values of $g^{vote^c} \bmod p$ for each candidate c.

Deniable Encryption. We use a public key sender deniable encryption $DE_{Pk_X^{DE}}(m, l)$ of a message m under a public key Pk_X^{DE} with an random

[1] We denote parameters which depends on a candidate c with the superscript c.

parameter l. The public key sender deniable encryption scheme should fulfill the following requirements [5]: only receiver possesses the decryption key and the scheme should be *semantically secure*; with overwhelming probability the value decrypted by the receiver contains no flipped bits; the sender should have an efficient *faking algorithm* ϕ such that for a given ciphertext s, which is encryption of the message m with the random factor l ($s = DE(m, l)$) and a faking message m_f, he can compute $l' = \phi(s, m, l, m_f)$, such that $s = DE(m_f, l')$.

The Receipt-Free Version of the Protocol. The voter V_i in the receipt-free version similar to the basic scheme of the protocol randomly chooses v_i and computes the asymmetric key $K_i = (g_T^t)^{v_i}$ for the decryption with corresponding key K_i^{-1} for the encryption of the bit commitment. He prepares the ballot $b_i^{RF} = (E_{K_i^{-1}}(BC(vote_i, r_i)), g_T^{v_i}, G_i, DE_{Pk_{TS}^{DE}}(r_i, l_i))$. For each candidate c he computes r_i^c using his secret α_i and the equation $vote_i + \alpha_i r_i = vote^c + \alpha_i r_i^c \mod q$. This way the voter can open the bit commitment $BC(vote_i, r_i)$ as the vote of the arbitrary candidate c using computed appropriate value of r_i^c. For each parameter r_i^c the voter is able to compute using the faking algorithm ϕ in the deniable encryption scheme the value $l_i^c = \phi(DE_{Pk_{TS}^{DE}}(r_i, l_i), r_i, l_i, r_i^c)$. In the time of coercion he can show the suitable l_i^c such that $DE_{Pk_{TS}^{DE}}(r_i^c, l_i^c) = DE_{Pk_{TS}^{DE}}(r_i, l_i)$ and $BC(vote_i, r_i) = BC(vote^c, r_i^c)$ for each candidate c. In this way the voter is able to fake the coercer about his vote.

The tally server TS in the tallying phase checks the signature of the RS_1 server on the hash value of the ballot b_i^{RF}. It obtains from shareholders the shared secret t. For each ballot it computes the key $K_i = (g_T^{v_i})^t$ for decryption of $E_{K_i^{-1}}(BC(vote_i, r_i))$ and obtains the bit commitment $BC(vote_i, r_i)$. Then it decrypts deniable encrypted r_i and opens the bit commitment as mentioned above.

On the other hand it is required that the voter or anyone else can verify correctness of the final tally. This way we use the *zero-knowledge proof* from the paper [12]. TS server publishes the list of bit commitments $bc_i = BC(vote_i, r_i)$ with relevant signatures of the RS_1 server. It also publishes the list of votes $vote'_i$ in random order using the *random permutation* π such that $vote'_i = vote_{\pi(i)}$. More precisely the tally server TS *divides* all votes into disjoint groups so that each group contains at least one candidate if possible. For each group it publishes the list of bit commitments $bc_1, \ldots, bc_k$ and the list of votes $vote'_1, \ldots, vote'_k$. Using the non-interactive version of the zero-knowledge proof [12] it proves that it knows the permutation π and the random parameters r_i for opening the bit commitments, such that $bc_i = BC(vote_i, r_i)$, $vote'_i = vote_{\pi(i)}$ without revealing π, r_i. The description how to calculate the proof can be found in [12].

Unfortunately the known public key sender deniable encryption schemes rapidly *lengthen* a message. For our purposes we need to encrypt the parameter r_i for opening the bit commitment. We can use a simple trick in which we generate random short keys SK_i^c for symmetric encryption of each parameter r_i^c of each candidate c. We use the public key deniable encryption only for the "right" key SK_i for encryption of the parameter r_i which is used for opening the vote $vote_i$. The tally server decrypts deniable encrypted symmetric key SK_i and try to decrypt all encrypted parameters. By using some redundancy for example some bit pattern it can distinguish the "right" parameter r_i and correctly open the bit commitment as $vote_i$. On the other hand, in the time of coercion the voter can show the suitable symmetric key SK_i^c for decrypting $E_{SK_i^c}(r_c)$ and opening the bit commitment as the candidate c.

4 Formal Analysis of the Proposed Scheme

In this section we briefly describe formal modeling of security protocols by the applied pi-calculus and give a short survey on formal analysis of e-voting protocols. Next we will model our proposed scheme and analyze some security properties.

4.1 The Applied pi-Calculus

The *applied pi-calculus* is a language for describing concurrent processes and their interactions. It is based on the *pi-calculus*, but is intended to be less pure and therefore more convenient to use. The applied pi-calculus is similar to the *spi-calculus* [2]. The key difference between them is in the way of handling of cryptographic primitives. The spi-calculus has a fixed set of cryptographic primitives, while the applied pi-calculus allows us to define less usual primitives by means of an *equational theory* on terms.

We briefly describe the *syntax* and the *operational semantics* of the applied pi-calculus from the paper [1]. *Terms* are defined by means of a *signature* Σ, which is a set of function symbols with arities. The set of terms is built from *names*, *variables* and *function symbols* from Σ applied to other terms. Terms and function symbols are sorted and function symbol application must respect sort and arities. Terms are equipped with an equational theory E, i.e., an equivalence relation on terms that is closed under *substitution* of terms for variables and under application of term *contexts* (terms with a *hole* [1]).

Plain processes are defined as follows. The null process $\mathbf{0}$ does nothing; $\nu n.P$ generates a fresh name n and then behaves as P; $if\ M = N\ then\ P\ else\ Q$ behaves as P if $E \vdash M = N$ and as Q otherwise; $a(x).P$ receives a message N from channel a and then behaves as $P\{N/x\}$; $\overline{a}\langle N\rangle$.P outputs the message N on channel a and then behaves as P; $P|Q$ executes P and Q in parallel; $!P$ generates an unbounded number of copies of P. Active substitutions generalize the *let* construction. The process $\nu x.(\{N/x\})$ corresponds exactly to $let\ x = N$ $in\ P$. Moreover we use *let* with the pattern matching of tuples and denote it as $let\ (= x, y) = M$. For successful substitution M must be a tuple and the first part of M must be equal in the equational theory with the value of a variable x.

As for the pi-calculus, the operational semantics of the applied-pi calculus is defined in terms of *structural equivalence* and *internal reduction*. Structural equivalence captures rearrangements of parallel compositions and restrictions and the equational rewriting of the terms in a process. Internal reduction defines the semantics of process synchronization and conditionals. *Observational equivalence* captures the equivalence of processes with respect to their dynamic behavior. Two processes are observational equivalent if no context can distinguish them. The formal definitions of these relations can be found in [1].

4.2 Formal Analysis of an e-Voting Protocol

E-voting protocols use unusual cryptographic primitives such as the blind signature, the trapdoor bit commitment etc. For formal modeling of these protocols it is necessary to model properties of these primitives. In this way the applied pi-calculus allows us to express unusual primitives as equations in the equational theory on terms and therefore is appropriate for modeling this kind of protocols.

Seminal work on analysis of e-voting protocols was done by Delaune, Kremer, Ryan in [10]. Authors of this paper modeled and analyzed FOO-scheme [8] using the applied pi-calculus. They formulated the fairness property as an *reachability* property in the sense that the vote of particular voter is not leaked to an attacker before publishing the final tally. They expressed the eligibility property as an reachability property in the sense that an attacker cannot trick system into accepting his vote. They used the ProVerif tool [4] for an automatic analysis of these properties. Privacy property was expressed as an observational equivalence of two processes which differ in two voters which swapped their votes. This property was proved manually by shoving that two processes are *labeled-bisimilar* [1].

In the paper [7] authors defined the receipt-freeness property as an observational equivalence. Roughly speaking, the protocol following this definition satisfies the receipt-freeness property if there exists a cheater process and the coercer cannot tell the difference between a situation in which the cheater process cooperates with him in order to cast the vote c and one in which the cheater pretend to cooperate with him, but casts the vote a. For defining the *coercion-resistance* property authors of [7] defined the *adaptive simulation* relation. They also showed that in the sense of their definitions the coercion-resistance implies the receipt-freeness and this implies the privacy property. Unfortunately these specifications of security properties cannot be proved automatically by using the ProVerif tool.

In the recent paper [3] Backes et al. presented a general technique for modeling remote e-voting protocols in the applied pi-calculus and automatical verification of their security properties. They formalized three fundamental properties of electronic voting protocols: *inalterability* (votes are not modified), *eligibility* (only eligible voters can vote), and *nonreusability* (every voter can vote only once). This formalization of these properties is by means of correspondence assertions. The main idea is to impose a causality relation among certain protocol events in execution traces. Such formulated properties can be analyzed automatically using ProVerif. The authors also formulated the coercion-resistance and the receipt-freeness properties using observational equivalences. This property can be verified automatically by ProVerif for *biprocesses* [3]. But it still requires non-negligible human effort to transform process specification into biprocesses.

Equational Theory of the Proposed Scheme. In the following we describe the formal model of the receipt-free version of the scheme. The equational theory on terms in the formal model is built from the function symbols and equations from Table 1.

Table 1. Function symbols with arities and corresponding equations

Function	Meaning	Equations
$H/1$	hash function	
$pk/1$	public key according to private key	
$g/0, exp/2$	group exponentiation	$exp(exp(g,a),b) = exp(exp(g,b),a)$
$idvoter/1, getpk/1$	identification of the voter	$getpk(idvoter(k)) = k$
$PE/3, PD/2$	probabilistic encryption (decryption)	$PD(y, PE(pk(y), x, r)) = x$
$DE/3, DD/2$	deniable encryption (decryption)	$DD(y, DE(pk(y), x, r)) = x$
$TBC/3, OTBC/2$	trapdoor bit commitment	$OTBC(TBC(m, r, s), r) = m$
$S/2, checkS/3$	signature and its checking	$checkS(S(m, sk), pk(sk), m) = true$
$getm/2$	getting message from signature	$getm(S(m, sk), pk(sk)) = m$
$bl/3, unbl/3$	blinding (unblinding)	$unbl(pk(sk), S(bl(pk(sk), m, b), sk), b) = S(m, sk)$

Modeling and Analysis of the Protocol. For the communication between processes we use a public channel c, which is under the complete control of an attacker. We assume that all voters are honest and eligible for voting. The process *voter* uniquely generates his private key, then he computes his *id* which binds his public key and registers this *id* in the process *manager* using the private channel p^m_{voter}. The *manager* sends the *id* of the legitimate voter to the exactly one copy of processes of registration servers RS^S_1, RS^S_2 using their private channels $p^m_{RS_1}, p^m_{RS_2}$. They can obtain from the received *id* the public key of the eligible voter for checking his signature in the registration phase. The *manager* also sends the *id* of the eligible voter to the public channel c. The process *voter* chooses his vote non-deterministically by using the process *vchoser* and the private channel p_{vote}. The possible votes v_a, v_b, v_c are free names which are known to the attacker. The process *voter* generates all random parameters including v for computing the asymmetric key $K = exp(g^t, v)$ for the decryption of the bit commitment and then it follows the instructions of the scheme as defined in the previous section. Two kinds of processes are running on each registration server: the first for registration (RS^S_1, RS^S_2) and the later for mixing (RS^M_1, RS^M_2). The whole process *voting* consists of creating the private keys of servers and the secret parameter t, publishing corresponding public keys and the public parameter g^t to the public channel c and parallel composition of unbounded copies of all defined processes.

We formulate the eligibly property as an causality relation among protocol events in execution traces of the protocol. We added to the specification of the process TS the event $ENDVOTE(X, Y)$ after accepting of a vote X in a ballot Y. Into the process voter we added the event $BEGINVOTE(X, Y, Z)$ for marking the event of starting of voting of a voter Z, which is intended to vote X in a ballot Y. Using the ProVerif tool we proved reachability of the event $ENDVOTE(X, Y)$ and also we proved the assertions $ENDVOTE(X, Y) \Rightarrow BEGINVOTE(X, Y, Z)$ for unbounded number of copies of processes in the formal model of the protocol from Table 2. This assertion means that for all execution traces it holds that an occurrence of the event $ENDVOTE(X, Y)$ implies that an event in which an honest voter Z begun the vote-casting the vote X in the ballot Y has occurred in the particular trace before.

Table 2. The formal model of the protocol in the applied pi-calculus

$$vchooser \triangleq \overline{p_{vote}}\langle v_a\rangle \mid \overline{p_{vote}}\langle v_b\rangle \mid \overline{p_{vote}}\langle v_c\rangle$$

$$manager \triangleq p^m_{voter}(id)\ .\ \overline{p^m_{RS_1}}\langle id\rangle\ .\ \overline{p^m_{RS_2}}\langle id\rangle\ .\ \overline{c}\langle id\rangle$$

$$\begin{aligned} RS_1^S \triangleq\ & p^m_{RS_1}(id)\ .\ c(m_1)\ .\ \mathbf{let}\ (=id, m_2) = PD(Sk^E_{RS_1}, m_1)\ \mathbf{in} \\ & \mathbf{let}\ Pk_V = getpk(id)\ \mathbf{in}\ \mathbf{let}\ (=id, m_3) = getm(m_2, Pk_V)\ \mathbf{in} \\ & \mathbf{if}\ checkS(m_2, Pk_V, (id, m_3)) = true\ \mathbf{then}\ \overline{c}\langle S(m_3, Sk^S_{RS_1})\rangle \end{aligned}$$

$$\begin{aligned} RS_2^S \triangleq\ & p^m_{RS_2}(id)\ .\ c(m_1)\ .\ \mathbf{let}\ (=id, m_2) = PD(Sk^E_{RS_2}, m_1)\ \mathbf{in} \\ & \mathbf{let}\ Pk_V = getpk(id)\ \mathbf{in}\ \mathbf{let}\ (m_3, =id) = getm(m_2, Pk_V)\ \mathbf{in} \\ & \mathbf{if}\ checkS(m_2, Pk_V, (m_3, id)) = true\ \mathbf{then}\ \overline{c}\langle S(m_3, Sk^S_{RS_2})\rangle \end{aligned}$$

$$\begin{aligned} voter \triangleq\ & \nu Sk^S_V\ .\ \mathbf{let}\ id = idvoter(pk(Sk^S_V))\ \mathbf{in}\ \overline{p^m_{voter}}\langle id\rangle\ .\ p_{vote}(vote)\ . \\ & \nu v\ .\ \nu\alpha\ .\ \nu r_{tbc}\ .\ \nu r_{DE}\ .\ \nu r_{bl1}\ .\ \nu r_{bl2}\ .\ \nu r_1\ .\ \nu r_2\ .\ \nu r_3\ .\ \nu r_4\ .\ \nu r_5\ .\ \nu r_6\ . \\ & \mathbf{let}\ K = exp(g^t, v)\ \mathbf{in}\ \mathbf{let}\ g^v = exp(g, v)\ \mathbf{in} \\ & \mathbf{let}\ b = (PE(pk(K), TBC(vote, r_{tbc}, \alpha), r_1), g^v, DE(Pk^{DE}_{TS}, r_{tbc}, r_{DE}))\ \mathbf{in} \\ & \mathbf{let}\ h_1 = H(b)\ \mathbf{in}\ \mathbf{let}\ bl_1 = bl(Pk^S_{RS_1}, h_1, r_{bl1})\ \mathbf{in} \\ & \overline{c}\langle PE(Pk^E_{RS_1}, (id, S((id, bl_1), Sk^S_V)), r_2)\rangle\ .\ c(m_1)\ . \\ & \mathbf{let}\ b^S = unbl(Pk^S_{RS_1}, m_1, r_{bl1})\ \mathbf{in}\ \mathbf{if}\ checkS(b^S, Pk^S_{RS_1}, h_1) = true\ \mathbf{then} \\ & \mathbf{let}\ m_2 = PE(Pk^E_{RS_2}, PE(Pk^E_{TS}, (b, b^S), r_3), r_4)\ \mathbf{in}\ \mathbf{let}\ h_2 = H(m_2)\ \mathbf{in} \\ & \mathbf{let}\ bl_2 = bl(Pk^S_{RS_2}, h_2, r_{bl2})\ \mathbf{in}\ \overline{c}\langle PE(Pk^E_{RS_2}, (id, S((bl_2, id), Sk^S_V)), r_5)\rangle\ .\ c(m_3)\ . \\ & \mathbf{let}\ m_2^S = unbl(Pk^S_{RS_2}, m_3, r_{bl2})\ \mathbf{in}\ \mathbf{if}\ checkS(m_2^S, Pk^S_{RS_2}, h_2) = true\ \mathbf{then} \\ & \overline{c}\langle PE(Pk^E_{RS_1}, (m_2, m_2^S), r_6)\rangle \end{aligned}$$

$$\begin{aligned} RS_1^M \triangleq\ & c(m)\ .\ \mathbf{let}\ (m_1, m_2) = PD(Sk^E_{RS_1}, m)\ \mathbf{in} \\ & \mathbf{if}\ checkS(m_2, Pk^S_{RS_2}, H(m_1)) = true\ \mathbf{then}\ \overline{c}\langle (m_1, m_2)\rangle \end{aligned}$$

$$\begin{aligned} RS_2^M \triangleq\ & c((m_1, m_2))\ .\ \mathbf{if}\ checkS(m_2, Pk^S_{RS_2}, H(m_1)) = true\ \mathbf{then} \\ & \mathbf{let}\ m_3 = PD(Sk^E_{RS_2}, m_1)\ \mathbf{in}\ \overline{c}\langle m_3\rangle \end{aligned}$$

$$\begin{aligned} TS \triangleq\ & c(m)\ .\ \mathbf{let}\ ((m_1, m_2, m_3), m_4) = PD(Sk^E_{TS}, m)\ \mathbf{in} \\ & \mathbf{if}\ checkS(m_4, Pk^S_{RS_1}, H((m_1, m_2, m_3))) = true\ \mathbf{then}\ \mathbf{let}\ r = DD(Sk^{DE}_{TS}, m_3)\ \mathbf{in} \\ & \mathbf{let}\ K = exp(m_2, t)\ \mathbf{in}\ \mathbf{let}\ bc = PD(K, m_1)\ \mathbf{in}\ \mathbf{let}\ vote = OTBC(bc, r)\ \mathbf{in} \end{aligned}$$

$$\begin{aligned} Voting \triangleq\ & \nu Sk^E_{TS}\ .\ \nu Sk^{DE}_{TS}\ .\ \nu Sk^E_{RS_1}\ .\ \nu Sk^S_{RS_1}\ .\ \nu Sk^E_{RS_2}\ .\ \nu Sk^S_{RS_2}\ .\ \nu t\ . \\ & \mathbf{let}\ (Pk^E_{TS}, Pk^{DE}_{TS}, Pk^E_{RS_1}, Pk^S_{RS_1}, Pk^E_{RS_2}, Pk^S_{RS_2}, g^t) = \\ & (pk(Sk^E_{TS}), pk(Sk^{DE}_{TS}), pk(Sk^E_{RS_1}), pk(Sk^S_{RS_1}), pk(Sk^E_{RS_2}), pk(Sk^S_{RS_2}), exp(g, t))\ \mathbf{in} \\ & \overline{c}\langle (Pk^E_{TS}, Pk^{DE}_{TS}, Pk^E_{RS_1}, Pk^S_{RS_1}, Pk^E_{RS_2}, Pk^S_{RS_2}, g^t)\rangle\ . \\ & !voter \mid !vchooser \mid !manager \mid !RS_1^S \mid !RS_2^S \mid !RS_1^M \mid !RS_2^M \mid !TS \end{aligned}$$

In order to maintain simplicity we do not distinguish between phases of the protocol. But this possibility is supported by ProVerif tool. In this way we can divide processes into phases and simply formulate the fairness property as an secrecy property of leaking the ballot and the vote before the tallying phase.

5 Conclusions

In our work we designed the concept of the academic voting system, which is independent from university applications. For this system we proposed the receipt-free e-voting scheme which requires neither anonymous channel nor other physical assumptions and is based on the blind signature. This scheme was primarily designed for the academic voting system, but can be implemented for other e-voting applications as well.

In contrast to other blind signature schemes we originally doubled registration servers thus avoiding problems with a corrupted registration server. Moreover we use registration servers in the vote-casting phase for providing anonymity of the communication. This way we improved the FOO-scheme [8] and we do not need to assume an anonymous channel. In the receipt-free version we originally combined the trapdoor bit commitment with deniable encryption. This way we improved the Okamoto scheme [13], which requires an untappable channel for sending the parameter for opening the bit commitment and moreover we save one message for sending it.

For better understanding of the requirements of the protocol we defined the formal model of the scheme using the applied pi-calculus and specified and analyzed some security properties using ProVerif tool. In the future work we would like to prove privacy-type properties of the proposed scheme. After this analysis we are planning to design and implement the academic voting system which will provide the universal interface for other university applications and enable them to use voting services without the need to implement individual voting systems.

References

1. Abadi, M., Fournet, C.: Mobile values, new names, and secure communication. In: Proceedings of the 28th ACM SIGPLAN-SIGACT Symposium on Principles of Programming Languages. ACM, New York (2001)
2. Abadi, M., Gordon, A.D.: A calculus for cryptographic protocols: the spi calculus. In: Proceedings of the 4th ACM Conference on Computer and Communications Security. ACM, New York (1997)
3. Backes, M., Hritcu, C., Maffei, M.: Automated Verification of Remote Electronic Voting Protocols in the Applied Pi-calculus. In: Proceedings of 21st IEEE Computer Security Foundations Symposium (2008)
4. Blanchet, B.: An Efficient Cryptographic Protocol Verifier Based on Prolog Rules. In: 14th IEEE Computer Security Foundations Workshop. IEEE Computer Society, Los Alamitos (2001)
5. Canetti, R., Dwork, C., Naor, M., Ostrovsky, R.: Deniable Encryption. In: Kaliski Jr., B.S. (ed.) CRYPTO 1997. LNCS, vol. 1294, pp. 90–104. Springer, Heidelberg (1997)
6. Chaum, D.: Blind signatures for untraceable payments. In: Advances in Cryptology - Crypto. Springer, Heidelberg (1983)
7. Delaune, S., Kremer, S., Ryan, M.D.: Coercion-resistance and receipt-freeness in electronic voting. In: Proc. 19th IEEE Computer Security Foundations Workshop. IEEE Computer Society Press, Los Alamitos (2006)
8. Fujioka, A., Okamoto, T., Ohta, K.: A Practical Secret Voting Scheme for Large Scale Elections. In: Zheng, Y., Seberry, J. (eds.) AUSCRYPT 1992. LNCS, vol. 718. Springer, Heidelberg (1993)
9. Kersting, N., Baldersheim, H. (eds.): Electronic Voting and Democracy A Comparative Analysis. Palgrave Macmillan, Hampshire (2004)

10. Kremer, S., Ryan, M.D.: Analysis of an Electronic Voting Protocol in the Applied Pi Calculus. In: Sagiv, M. (ed.) ESOP 2005. LNCS, vol. 3444, pp. 186–200. Springer, Heidelberg (2005)
11. Mao, W.: Modern Cryptography: Theory and Practice. Prentice Hall Professional Technical Reference, Englewood Cliffs (2003)
12. Okamoto, T.: An electronic voting scheme. In: IFIP World Conference on IT Tools. Chapman & Hall, Boca Raton (1996)
13. Okamoto, T.: Receipt-Free Electronic Voting Schemes for Large Scale Elections. In: Christianson, B., Lomas, M. (eds.) Security Protocols 1997. LNCS, vol. 1361. Springer, Heidelberg (1998)
14. Rjaskova, Z.: Electronic voting schemes. Master's thesis. Comenius University (2002)
15. Sampigethaya, R., Poovendran, R.: A Framework and Taxonomy for Comparison of Electronic Voting Schemes. Elsevier Computers & Security 25 (2006)

Comparing Identity Management Frameworks in a Business Context

Jaap-Henk Hoepman, Rieks Joosten, and Johanneke Siljee

TNO, The Netherlands
jaap-henk.hoepman@tno.nl, rieks.joosten@tno.nl,
johanneke.siljee@tno.nl

Abstract. Several frameworks for identity management exist, each of them with its own distinguishing features. These frameworks are complex however, and their features not easily understood. This makes it hard for businesses to understand the intricacies, and difficult to select and deploy one. This paper develops business selection criteria and applies them to four popular identity management frameworks. The resulting score card (1) helps businesses to select and deploy an identity management system, and (2) provides valuable feedback to developers of identity management systems on the criteria that they should take into account when designing and implementing an identity management system that is useful for specific businesses.

1 Introduction

Businesses that provide a meaningful IT service require that only users with proper privileges, e.g. because of a subscription, can access this service. To check these privileges, the application providing the service must establish and verify the user's identity. Traditionally, applications handle this by themselves, meaning that many user registrations exist, each with its own ways of user authentication. While this is not user-friendly (users need to remember many passwords for example), it is also not efficient for the business as they cannot tell whether the same customer uses multiple services (which makes him a more interesting customer). Similar considerations apply when considering users that are in fact employees of a business, who need access to different sets of documents and business applications.

Identity management systems separate the act of identifying and authenticating the user from the act of providing a service to a user. This is attractive for large enterprises as it bears the promise of easier, more centralized management of users and their access rights. For users it promises to provide a uniform service access experience, without the need to enter usernames and passwords again and again.

Apart from the data needed to identify and authenticate users, services store additional information about their users in so-called user profiles. Most of that data is the same for many different services. By delegating (some of) the administration and storage of that data to the identity management system, that data is more easily kept up to date, and does not have to be entered by the user for every new service that he accesses.

V. Matyáš et al. (Eds.): The Future of Identity, IFIP AICT 298, pp. 184–196, 2009.

Several frameworks for identity management exist: OpenID [13], Shibboleth [16], Liberty [10] and the Identity Metasystem [8], [9] (also referred to as CardSpace), to name but a few. While each of these systems has its own distinguishing features, at a high abstraction level they have several things in common, as shown in Figure 1. This figure shows that each framework incorporates:

- a technical component called a user agent[1] (UA), e.g. a web browser, that is operated by a person that wishes to access a service,
- a technical component called identity provider (IdP[2]), for instance a computer application or web service, that identifies and authenticates the person (user) that operates the UA and provides identity data, and
- a technical component called service provider (SP), again a computer application or web service, that offers the service the aforementioned person is interested in. As SPs rely on IdPs for user authentication, SPs are also called Relying Parties (RPs).

To accommodate communication between these components, identity frameworks (a) use common 'languages' (e.g. XML, SAML) for exchanging messages, (b) use common protocols (such as HTTP, SOAP and others) for exchanging messages between two individual components and (c) define the protocol(s) that govern the sequence in which components talk to one another and the types of data exchanged.

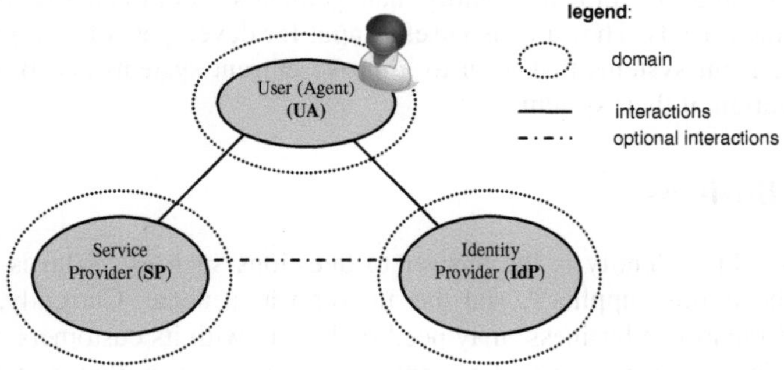

Fig. 1. Typical Identity Management architecture

As technical components cannot be held accountable, we introduce the notion of 'domain' to represent a legal entity (a business or individual person), that is responsible (and accountable) for the activities thereof. As bearing responsibility is associated with risk, businesses manage this by defining measures and policies for a domain. Identity systems in a domain must then implement such measures and follow the policies (for identity related risks). For example, a business in the Netherlands may trust banks and the Dutch government to provide identity data, but it may not trust telecom operators or a foreign government to do the same. It may state that data be

---

[1] Individual identity management systems may have slightly different terminology, e.g. 'user' for 'user agent'.

[2] We write IdP instead of the also used abbreviation IP, which is already used for Internet Protocol.

digitally signed according to some Digital Signature Act, etc. Its identity management system must ensure this. As the risks that businesses face can be quite diverse, policies will differ from business to business, and identity management frameworks are challenged to provide a good match for that.

The fact that the merits and drawbacks of identity systems are to be judged by technical as well as business criteria, makes it all complex, hard to oversee, and difficult to make decisions about. In this paper we discuss how identity management can be applied in business contexts, thus giving a helping hand to future decision makers seeking to deploy one or more identity management components in their businesses.

Our contribution in this paper is the following. We describe the business context in which identity management systems need to operate and discuss the main business concerns that originate from that. These concerns are translated into business requirements against which we score the aforementioned four popular identity management frameworks. Running an identity management platform raises its own issues. We also discuss these operational requirements and score the four frameworks against those. To complete the picture, we also score the same four frameworks against the widely accepted 7 Laws of Identity [4], that are mostly user-centered (adding an 8th Law of Location Independence, as the final necessary user-centred requirement that was lacking in the former seven laws). This extends the work of Maler and Reed [12], and complements the comparison of identity management systems on the associated costs and organisational issues of Royer [15]. Our results are a useful tool helping organisations seeking to deploy an identity management system to choose the system that best suits their needs. They are also useful input for developers of next generation identity management systems that wish to improve current systems and broaden the range of application of their systems.

2 Identity Business

Traditionally (in IT), Identity is the answer to questions such as: 'Who is this customer?' or 'Who is this supplier?', and the answer was a name. Currently, Identity includes all information a business[3] may need in dealing with its customers, suppliers etc. For example, if a business needs to send letters to an entity, then name and address will be part of its Identity. Note that as the business continuously improves its processes, its need for information changes over time, Identities change as well. For example, when email became available, Identities came to include one or more email addresses. Thus:

The Identity of a person or organisation, from the perspective of a given business, consists of all data (information) that this business needs or has at that particular point in time for dealing with that specific person or organisation[4].

This is not to say that businesses can gather, use, or provide identity data to others as they like. Laws and regulations, such as various EU Directives and domestic

[3] In this article, governmental organizations are also considered to run a business, with individual people as well as organizations playing the roles of customers, suppliers, etc.

[4] A person or organization thus has as many Identities as there are businesses that have information about them.

legislation that constrain the processing of personal data and the (free) movement thereof, must be complied with. Additional constraints may originate from e.g. supplier contracts that may impose restrictions with respect to the purpose for which the data may be used.

Businesses (and individuals alike) should have comprehensive policies for gathering, using and providing data. Such policies may state which individuals or organizations are trusted to obtain identity data from, or to provide such data to, or for what purposes certain identity data may be used. There may also be rules that govern the trustworthiness (integrity) of personal information, e.g. an email address can be decided to be trustworthy only after a response has been received to a message sent thereto.

Also, businesses and individuals may have concerns with respect to the possible consequences of correlating identity data over time. An individual may not want a web-shop to know what it has bought in earlier sessions, or he may not want the government to supply their address information to arbitrary businesses. If any organisation could freely collect identity data from other businesses, and aggregate and sell it to whoever pays for it, then this could for example facilitate identity theft. However, if identity data cannot be passed along, then people and businesses need to fill in the same information over and over again.

The identity business thus consists of specifying business objectives and policies regarding the processing of identity data and the exchange thereof, as well as managing them and realizing/enforcing them. Identity systems should accommodate not only for differences in identity data (types) and the way they are exchanged, but also for the management and realization of business goals and policies.

To be able to assess whether identity systems truly accommodate business goals and policies, we developed a set of business requirements. These requirements and the assessment of a number of currently popular identity systems can be found in section 3.

Note however that while business policies have impact on how identity management systems should operate, the converse is true as well: capabilities of identity systems may inhibit or enable businesses. An example of inhibition is identity systems that are susceptible to phishing attacks should not be used for commercial services as attackers could then use that service using someone else's account. An example of business enablement is given by identity systems that guarantee that identity data is only released to an SP with the user's consent, so that a business can act as an IdP for all identity related data that it has. An even further reaching idea is that of Identity Oracles; in which IdPs provide higher level information derived from personal data, as in "this person is at least 21 years old" [3].

3 Comparing Four Identity Management Frameworks

In this section we provide a set of requirements for identity systems that are useful for an organisation to assess which identity system to deploy.

3.1 Approach

By looking at current identity management systems and related work we derived a set of requirements. Part of the requirements are the widely accepted [1] 7 Laws of Identity [4], which is a set guidelines, aiming explaining the successes and failures of identity management systems from a user-centric perspective. In our opinion one important law is missing from this set, namely the requirement that a user should be able to access a SP using an identity management system not only from his PC, but also from a computer at a cybercafé in Hong Kong, for example. We call this the 8th Law of Location Independence [17]. This essentially means that the identity management system should not rely on any persistent data stored locally at the user's machine.

Dhamija and Dusseault [5] raise seven flaws of current identity management systems that need to be resolved before identity management systems will be adopted. Although these flaws can be translated into requirements as well, it is not useful to include them in our comparison as none of the current identity management systems fulfil them. An approach a bit similar to ours is presented in [12], where three popular federated identity protocols are profiled: the Security Assertion Markup Language (SAML), the OpenID specification, and the InfoCard specification underlying Microsoft's Windows Cardspace.

Furthermore, we add a set of requirements addressing business concerns, e.g. dealing with operationalisation of such systems, policy management, privacy concerns and known vulnerabilities. These requirements are derived from the discussion in the second section on Identity Business.

The total set of requirements, presented in the next section, is used to compare the four currently popular user-centric identity systems: OpenID 2.0, Shibboleth and Liberty (both based on SAML), and CardSpace 1.0.

3.2 Identity Management System Requirements

The first set of requirements are user-related, the first of which are the 7 Laws of Identity for which an underpinning is given in [4]:

1. **User Control and Consent** (LI1)**:** The solution only reveals identity data with the user's consent.
2. **Minimal Disclosure for a Constrained Use** (LI2)**:** The solution discloses no more than the necessary identifying information.
3. **Justifiable Parties** (LI3)**:** The design ensures that disclosure of identifying information is limited to parties that have a necessary and justifiable place in a given identity relationship).
4. **Directed Identity** (LI4)**:** The solution supports both "omnidirectional" identifiers for use by public entities and "unidirectional" identifiers for use by private entities, thus facilitating discovery while preventing unnecessary release of correlation handles.
5. **Pluralism of Operators and Technologies** (LI5)**:** The solution channels and enables the interworking of multiple identity technologies run by multiple identity providers.
6. **Human Integration** (LI6)**:** The solution defines the human user to be a component of the distributed system, integrated through unambiguous human-machine communications mechanisms offering protection against identity attacks.
7. **Consistent User Experience across Contexts** (LI7)**:** The solution provides a simple consistent experience while enabling separation of contexts through multiple operators and technologies.

However, another requirement dealing with mobility is crucial for widespread acceptance of identity management:

8. **Location Independence** (LI8)**:** The solution does not restrict users in access to their identity system to one location, such as one personal computer that holds specific data.

Then, from the discussion in section 2, we derive business-centred requirements for the SP and IdP. First, there are technical requirements that allow for technical implementation and usage:

9. **Use of standards:** The solution makes use of existing, well known and broadly used standards.
10. **Openness:** The solution itself should be freely usable, i.e. no patent fees or licenses required.
11. **Availability of (open) components:** The solution should consist of existing components that are usable in a wide variety of environments (Windows, UNIX, Linux, MAC, etc.) and preferably have an open source implementation for better evaluation of the correctness and security.
12. **Technical Interoperability:** The solution can interoperate (technically) with the other solutions.

Then, there are also operational requirements that relate to the business of running an SP and/or IdP:

13. **Pseudonymous and anonymous use:** The solution should provide means for users to use pseudonyms for identification, and/or remain completely anonymous towards SPs. This allows the system to be used in a more diverse set of usage scenarios (improving the business case by including the users that want or need to be anonymous) and potentially limits liability issues.
14. **Attribute semantics:** the solution should guarantee and/or provide means to unambiguously define the semantics of identity attributes.
15. **Validity and up-to-dateness:** The solution provides guarantees with respect to the validity of identity data, and the up-to-dateness thereof.
16. **Ease of local policy management:** The solution provides means to easily configure identity policies (i.e. without having to recompile code or create (virtual) connections/adapters), in the event of regulatory changes, changes in business relationships, security incidents and so on.
17. **Business Case:** The solution should provide every party (domain) with a valid business case.
18. **Governance support:** The solution provides suitable means by which to achieve demonstrable compliance with (identity) legislation, policies.

3.3 Comparison

Currently, there are four popular user-centric identity systems: OpenID 2.0, Shibboleth and Liberty (both based on SAML), and CardSpace 1.0. We compare these four identity systems against the requirements.

In Table 1 the fulfilment of each identity system with respect all requirements is given. The scores in the table have the following meaning:

++	full support/compliance
+	reasonable support/compliance, but not to the full extent
+/-	support/compliance is subject to debate
-	some support/compliance, but only very little
--	no support/compliance

Table 1. Requirement fulfilment of OpenID, Shibboleth, Liberty, and Identity Metasystem

	1. User control and consent		2. Minimal disclosure	
OpenID 2.0	+	Users control which identity provider (IdP) they trust, what attributes the IdP may store, and which relying parties (RP) access which IdP in each session. Users do not control the actual identity data transferred in a session. Susceptible to phishing attacks, which is a violation of the first law	+	OpenID Attribute Exchange 1.0 supports attribute exchange; however, minimal disclosure is not enforced, but decided by the RP.
Shibboleth	-	See Liberty	+	Use of temporary handles ensures that users cannot be traced; SP can retrieve identity from the IdP later if allowed
Liberty	-	Federation of identity attributes without user consent is default after user gives permission for the first time. Also susceptible to phishing attacks, which violates this law.	+	Uses pseudonyms and thereby limits disclosure of identity information
CardSpace (Identity Metasystem)	+	Users control which identity provider (IP) they trust, what attributes the IP may store, and which relying parties (RP) access which IP in each session. Also, users can see which identity data is transferred in a session and decide not to, if necessary.	+	While the user controls the data to be transferred, it does not control the actually provided information per se, i.e. more (detailed) information than strictly necessary could be asked for and provided. 'Personal identifiers' can be used that prevent RPs to link identity data to similar data of other RPs.

Table 1. (*continued*)

		3. Justifiable parties		4. Directed identity		5. Pluralism of operators, techniques
OpenID 2.0	+/-	OpenID is designed as a fully decentralized mechanism. Since RP and IdP (optionally) create an association, they know that the user is associated with the other and which information is shared. OpenID defines 'realms', i.e. RP-servers that may share the identity information. The IdP should inform the user what the realm is (which is outside the scope of OpenID).	+	OpenID supports the use of multiple identities (pseudonyms) and leaves it up to the user to what end each identifier is used.	+	OpenID is an open, extensible standard, based on HTTP, and allows for multiple IdPs that each can provide attributes, but each needs to be "OpenID-enabled".
Shibboleth	+/-	No mechanisms in place to enforce this; on the other hand, unknown parties are not part of the federation and will not obtain any useful information	+	Both are supported (see Liberty)	+	Uses SAML, but all parties must conform to the standard
Liberty	+/-	The circle of trust is a logical context for the business partners involved; untrusted parties cannot be part of it. Other than that IdP and SP decide whether a new relationship is necessary and justifiable.	+	Pseudonyms are Liberty's uni-directional handles; cookies can be used as omnidirectional identifiers.	+	Is open source, integrates SAML, and allows for multiple (Liberty-enabled) attribute providers.
CardSpace (Identity Metasystem)	++	The Identity Metasystem is designed such that RPs can be visually recognized by users (as opposed e.g. to having to interpret certificate attributes). The same holds for recognizing IPs. Also, there are some provisions that assist users to recognize RPs that it has used before.	+	Uses Private Personal IDs to create pseudonyms that are unidirectional for each individual RP. Claims may also contain omnidirectional handles.	+	Is an open design, supporting Kerberos tickets, SAML tokens, X509 etc., and is extendable. Each needs to be "Identity Metasystem" enabled.

Table 1. (*continued*)

	6. Human integration		7. Consistent user experience		8. Location independence	
OpenID 2.0	-/--	OpenID does not provide protection against phishing attacks or any other common security problems that stem from the human-machine communication. Also, users are required to use a URL or XRI as identifier, of which only part can be chosen by the user himself.	+/-	User experience is consistent, but not simple for average users, as they need to check e.g. IdP certifications	++	Users can enter their identifiers any place, any time.
Shibboleth	-	Not part of the specification	+/-	User experience is consistent. Separation of contexts unclear	++	See Liberty
Liberty	-	No protection against phishing attacks or any other common security problems that stem from the human-machine communication.	+/-	User experience is consistent. Separation of contexts is unclear.	++	Interaction with SPs and IdPs are not dependent on the user's location.
CardSpace (Identity Metasystem)	+	Specifies interactions tailored for humans (using visual clues - see also Law 3). The Identity Selector runs in a separate desktop to resist spyware/malware attacks. It also resists phishing attacks. However, Identity Metasystem does not provide facilities that allow users to use their identities at other locations.	+	The user experience is consistent and user-friendly. Separation of contexts is supported. Interoperability has been demonstrated[5].	-	Currently, users can only export their InfoCards as XML files, transfer them to another device and import them there in the local Identity Selector.

[5] See http://osis.idcommons.net/wiki/I3:Overall_Results for (results of) interoperability events that have taken place or are going to take place.

Table 1. (*continued*)

13. Pseudonymous and anonymous use		12. Technical interoperability	11. Availability of (open) components		10. Openness		9. Use of standards		
+	Pseudonyms: yes ('user-supplied identifier'); no protection against colluding SPs. Anonymous use: no	Technical interoperability is to be evaluated on a product comparison basis, which is too detailed for this article. However, significant effort is being made to test implementations of frameworks against one another, for example the OSIS Interops [14]	+	Various implementations can be downloaded from the Internet, for Windows as well as Linux	++	The standards are open , and various implementations include sources, tutorials, help, etc.	++	HTTP, HTML, SHA, HMAC authentication, DH-key agreement, URI, XRI, Yadis, and more.	**OpenID 2.0**
+	See: Liberty		+	Open source, platform independent	++	Open standards, open source implementations available	+	SAML, HTTP	**Shibboleth**
+	Anonymous handle sent to SP. No built in support for pseudonyms		+	Multiple open source projects exist (e.g. Open Liberty, Lasso, Cahill)	++	Open standards, open source implementations available	++	SAML 2.0, SOAP, HTTP	**Liberty**
+	Pseudonyms: yes (through PPIDs, which also protect against colluding SPs) Anonymous use: no		+	Example code (C#, PHP) downloadable from Microsoft. See also the Bandit project, Higgins, etc.	++	Open source (see Microsoft's Open Specification Promise (OSP) http://www.microsoft.com/interop/osp/default.mspx.	++	WS-* (Security, MEX, Policy, Trust, etc.), SAML, Kerberos, X509v3, etc.	**CardSpace (Identity Metasystem)**

Table 1. (*continued*)

		14. Attribute semantics		15. Validity and currency		16. Ease of local policy management		17. Business Case
OpenID 2.0	+/-	Through OpenID Service Extension Attribute types are managed centrally. Semantics not always unambiguous.	+	Validity: attributes may be signed by IdP Timeliness: time-stamp is available in the response nonce	-	out of scope for OpenID	+/-	OpenID is primarily useful for simple, non-security critical, IdM applications.
Shibboleth	+	see: Liberty	+	see: Liberty	+	SPs and IdP can update the Circle of Trust using the corresponding metadata.xml file.	+	See: Liberty; but easier management.
Liberty	+	Attributes are encoded in SAML tokens: use XML namespaces to define semantics	+	SAML tokens are time stamped. SP decides how long to accept/keep	+/-	Depends on Liberty-enabled implementation	+/-	Primarily useful for federating IdPs and SPs of already federated domains.
CardSpace (Identity Metasystem)	+	Attributes can be defined by anyone, and use XML namespace to define semantics.	+	Validity: depends on IdP; IdP assertions are signed Timeliness: Tokens are time stamped, and can be (near to) real time.	++	SPs control the attribute types they request and the IdPs they trust to provide them. IdPs control whether or not identity data is to be audited, and if so, which SPs are entitled. Users see all requested and provided data pass, and may abort the protocol at any point.	+	SP can ask as much or as little as it likes; IdP can provide all data it has User is in control Suitable for a wide range of usage scenarios.

Table 1. (*continued*)

	OpenID 2.0		Shibboleth		Liberty		CardSpace (Identity Metasystem)	
18. Governance support	While UA can be authenticated, the User cannot (due to phishing vulnerability). SP can change identity data. Any support must be build around OpenID	-	Not enforced by standard	+/-	Not enforced yet, work in progress through Id Governance Framework [7]	+/-	Data used in CardSpace carries signatures of data providers and provides proof of consent of user	+

4 Conclusions and Recommendations

In this paper we have investigated the requirements on an identity management system from three different perspectives: User, Technical, and Business. We have formulated a set of important requirements from each of these perspectives, and have scored four existing, popular identity management systems against these requirements. The results show that each have their advantages and shortcomings, which can be summarised as follows:

- OpenID is highly location independent, and gives the user a lot of control, but scores badly with respect to the more business-oriented requirements.
- Shibboleth and Liberty are very similar, technologically wise. Within the limits of a browser-only (and hence location independent) IdM framework, they achieve a good overall score on most of the requirements.
- OpenID, Shibboleth and Liberty are susceptible to phishing and similar attacks. This is a common drawback of browser-only IdM frameworks.
- CardSpace fulfils many of the listed requirements. Currently, its major drawback is the fact that it is not location independent because Infocards are locally stored on the PC. This is a drawback of all IdM systems that rely on extra software beyond the browser.

For businesses seeking to deploy an identity management solution, we recommend that they first select the requirements most important to their business, and use the scorecard to select the solution that scores best on those requirements. This helps businesses taking balanced decisions.

References

1. Bhargav-Spantzel, A., Camenisch, J., Gross, T., Sommer, D.: User Centricity: A Taxonomy and Open Issues. Journal of Computer Security 15(5) (2007)
2. Blakley, B.: Identity and Community in Human Society. In: Catalyst Conference 2006, June 15 (2006), http://podcast.burtongroup.com/ip//2006/06/identity_and_co.html
3. Blakley, B.: Ceci n'est pas un Bob, December 7 (2006), http://notabob.blogspot.com/2006/07/meta-identity-system.html
4. Cameron, K.: The Laws of Identity, May 21 (2005), http://www.identityblog.com/stories/2005/05/13/TheLawsOfIdentity.pdf
5. Dhamija, R., Dusseault, L.: The Seven Flaws of Identity Management: Usability and Security Challenges. IEEE Security & Privacy 6(2), 24–29 (2008)
6. Information Card Foundation, http://www.informationcard.net/
7. Liberty Alliance Project, An Overview of the Id Governance Framework, Version: 1.0 (2007)
8. Daemen, T., Rubinstein, I. (eds.): The Identity Metasystem: Towards a Privacy-Compliant Solution to the Challenges of Digital Identity, Microsoft white paper (October 2006), http://identityblog.com/wp-content/resources/Identity_Metasystem_EU_Privacy.pdf
9. Cameron, K., Jones, M.B.: Design Rationale behind the Identity Metasystem Architecture, http://www.identityblog.com/wp-content/resources/design_rationale.pdf
10. Liberty Alliance Project, http://www.projectliberty.org
11. Landau, S., Hodges, J.: A Brief Introduction to Liberty, February 13 (2003), http://research.sun.com/liberty_intro/
12. Maler, E., Reed, D.: The Venn of Identity: Options and Issues in Federated Identity Management. IEEE Security & Privacy 6(2), 16–23 (2008)
13. OpenID specifications, http://openid.net/developers/specs/
14. Open Source Identity Systems, http://osis.idcommons.net/
15. Royer, D.: Assessing the Value of Enterprise Identity Management (EIdM) - Towards a Generic Evaluation Approach. In: Proc. 3rd Int. Conf. on Availability, Reliability and Security (ARES 2008), Barcelona, Spain, pp. 779–786 (2008)
16. The Shibboleth project, http://shibboleth.internet2.edu/
17. Siljee, J., Hoepman, J.-H.: Issues in Identity Management, Usability, Security and Privacy, TNO Whitepaper (2008) (to appear)

Security Policy Satisfiability and Failure Resilience in Workflows

Meghna Lowalekar, Ritesh Kumar Tiwari, and Kamalakar Karlapalem

Center for Data Engineering,
International Institute of Information Technology,
Hyderabad, India - 500032
meghnal@students.iiit.ac.in, ritesh@research.iiit.ac.in, kamal@iiit.ac.in

Abstract. *Security policy satisfiability* and *high failure resilience* (i.e. survivability) are desirable properties of every system. Security issues and failure resilience are usually treated in stand alone mode and not in synergy. In this paper, we bridge this gap for workflows. We propose techniques which ensure that user-task assignment is both secure and failure resilient and present frameworks that meet different criteria of *security policy*, *security constraints*, and *failure resilience*.

1 Introduction

A user is capable of doing certain tasks in an organizational workflow. But from the security perspective, all the information and resources cannot be made accessible to every user as allowing such uncontrolled access gives unbounded privileges to the user, thereby increasing the chances of attack and subsequent damage. Hence an access control mechanism based on *user capability* that satisfies the *security policy* and *constraints* is needed for assigning users to tasks and their subsequent enactment during runtime. *Failure resilience* (survivability) is a pivotal issue in any organization. Current state of art focuses mainly on fault tolerance at the resource level. It is evident that users can also fail (or be unavailable). Hence there is a need to focus on user level failure resilience for ensuring overall system survivability. For achieving high failure resilience at the user level, a user should have the capability to do a large number of tasks, which results in providing each user with access to a lot of information, thereby increasing the chances of knowledge attacks.

Consider the tendering process which involves many tasks such as advertisement of the requirement for goods or services, preparation of tender documents, registration of suppliers, response to tenders (filling of quotations), evaluation of responses to tenders and finally awarding the contract to a supplier. The process of tender management (including tasks involved and why they are performed) is a company property and should be preserved. In case of large tenders the process of responding to tenders also involves many steps and many users. The response should be submitted by due date even if some users who are involved in response preparation/processing are absent. A user should not get the complete knowledge about the tendering process as this can lead to knowledge attack. Therefore, it is important to achieve security along with failure resilience (tendering process is deadline driven and should be completed even if some users are not

V. Matyáš et al. (Eds.): The Future of Identity, IFIP AICT 298, pp. 197–210, 2009.

present). Similarly in case of defense procedures where tasks are very critical and delay due to absence of any user is not allowed the problem of achieving high failure resilience along with security is important.

1.1 Related Work

Hung et al. [1] present the security features of workflow systems. They discussed the trade off between security and failure resilience. They have proposed a greedy algorithm that determines task assignments that would achieve high failure resilience and low security risk factor. In [1], access control policies and separation of duty constraints are not considered.

Li et al. [2] introduced the concept of resilience policies in access control. Resilient policies ensure that access is properly enabled so that a critical task can be completed even in the absence of some users. Their work mainly focuses on checking the satisfiability of a resilience policy in an access control state. They have shown the complexity of the problem. They also described methods to determine whether a resilient policy is consistent with the separation of duty policies.

Wang et al. [3] studied the resiliency problem in workflow systems. They described that the resiliency in workflow systems differs from resilience policies. In a workflow system, due to the existence of authorization constraints, there is a possibility that even if a set of users together have the permission to perform all steps of the workflow, they can not complete the task. They defined three levels of resiliency: *static*, *decremental* and *dynamic*. The work mainly focuses on checking whether a workflow model is resilient or not i.e whether a workflow can be completed in the absence of some users.

1.2 Contributions and Organization of Paper

In this paper, we focus on operational failure resilience and access control in a user-based system. Ideally, we want a user-task assignment which is both failure resilient and secure (i.e. it satisfies the organizational security policy and associated constraints and also does not provide a user access to a lot of information). To achieve this goal, we use the following two approaches which are described in section 3.

i. Generating *all possible* user-task assignments which satisfy security policy and constraints (refer section 3.1).
ii. Formulating the problem using *Quadratic Programming*(refer section 3.2).

Our work focuses on finding user-task assignments satisfying policy and separation of duty constraints such that the workflow is *min* $\mathcal{K}$ failure resilient i.e workflow can be completed even if $\mathcal{K}$ users fail.

The paper is organized as follows. In section 2, we describe the preliminaries and calculation of failure resilience. In section 3, we explain the approaches for computation of user-task assignments. In sections 4 we present results and in section 5, we conclude with future work.

2 Preliminaries

A workflow can be defined as a set of tasks ($\mathbb{T}$) coordinated by a set of events ($\mathbb{E}$) whose successful execution results in the completion of an instance of the activity. The sequence of tasks in a workflow can have:

i. *Sequential constraints* ($T_i \prec T_j$): Execution of task T_i should be completed before T_j starts executing.
ii. *Temporal constraints*: Temporal constraints can be further classified as *activation time constraints* and *execution time constraints*. Activation time constraints (i.e. $\{T_i\}^{activated_{[p,\,q)}}$) denotes that task T_i can be activated by an authorized user only within time period $[p,q)$. Execution time constraints (i.e. $\{T_i\}^{exec_p}$) denote that task T_i can be executed by an authorized user for atmost p time units after the invocation.

Workflow tasks can be treated as a combination of automated and manual processes which are represented (and controlled) by users. In most of the practical workflows, user-task assignment is static due to specialized users that can do specific tasks or due to initial work assignment to users. The approaches proposed in this paper, to achieve failure resilience with access control are applicable for scenarios where Task-Based Authorization Control [4] is used for enforcing access control on users.

Table 1. Notations Used

$U_1, U_2, \ldots, U_n$	: Users
$T_1, T_2, \ldots, T_n$	: Tasks
pol	: Policy
$C_1, C_2, \ldots, C_n$	: Constraints
cap	: Capability
FR_{T_i}	: Failure resilience of task T_i
$FR_{activity}$	: Failure resilience of activity
$exec(T_i)$	: Set of users having capability to execute task T_i
$assigned(T_i)$	: Set of users assigned to task T_i

2.1 User-Task Assignment

Let *capability of a user* (cap: $U \xrightarrow{cap} \{T\}$) denote the set of tasks that the user is capable of doing. Similarly, *executability of a task* $\left[exec(T_k)\right]$ denotes the set of users that possess the capability to execute *task* T_k. Using the capability sets of users, we can compute the executability set corresponding to every task of the workflow.

A user might possess the capabilities to perform all tasks of a workflow but the organization security policy can prevent it from performing some. Thus, if a user possesses the capability of performing a task, it does not necessarily imply that it is assigned to the task. But if a user does not possess the capability, then it *can not* be assigned to the task. The organization security policy forces restrictions on the capability sets of users and hence the executability set of a task. Separation of duty constraints further reduce this set. If $\left[assigned(T_k)\right]$ denotes the set of users that are assigned to task T_k after satisfying security policy and constraints, then $assigned(T_k) \subseteq exec(T_k)$. Out of all the users that are assigned to tasks, one user per task is chosen for executing the task.

Security policy defines which users are authorized to execute tasks based on organization security requirements. The term *policy* used in this paper encapsulates the notion of both *confidentiality* and *integrity policy* associated with access control. *Security constraints* place additional (*activation* and/or *privilege level*) restrictions on users and tasks that satisfy the security policy.

Security constraints enforced on users can be classified [5] into:

i. *Temporal* constraints,
ii. *Separation of duty* (*Static*[1]/ *Dynamic*/ *Operational*[2]/ *Object Based*) constraints, and
iii. *Location* constraints.

There are two types of scenarios considered in the paper, which are as follows:

1. *Purely static* - All user task assignments are fixed before the execution of workflow. Users are assigned to tasks considering all the constraints and this assignment does not change at runtime. Failure resilience has a fixed value.
2. *Purely dynamic*- Before the execution of workflow users are assigned to tasks considering all the constraints but assignment can change at runtime to get more failure resilience. Failure resilience changes dynamically but has a lower bound.

In static scenario, for all the tasks of a workflow, the set $assigned(T_k)$ can be computed using any of the approaches described in section 3. In case of dynamic scenario quadratic programming approach (section3.2) can be used. Section 3.2 also shows how to apply quadratic programming to change the assignments at runtime.

In the next part, we show the computation of failure resilience for a workflow activity. The definitions and formulae hold for purely static scenario. For purely dynamic scenario these constitutes the lower bound of failure resilience. This is because, in dynamic scenario assignment is changed to get more failure resilience, therefore, we will get the failure resilience which we were getting in static case.

2.2 Failure Resilience of Task and Activity

Failure resilience of a task denotes the maximum number of user failures a task can handle. Similarly, failure resilience of an activity is the maximum number of user failures in the presence of which activity execution can continue uninterrupted. The activity will fail when any of its constituent task can not be completed successfully. Therefore, failure resilience of activity depends on the failure resilience of its constituent tasks.

Definition 1. *Failure Resilience of a task is one less than the number of users that are assigned to the task* $\left(i.e.\ \mathrm{FR}_{T_i} = (|assigned(T_i)| - 1)\right)$.

Lemma 1. *Given an assignment of n users to t tasks, the workflow activity is guaranteed to execute as long as the number of failed users* $\leq min_{\forall_i}(FR_{T_i})$.

[1] If two tasks T_1 and T_2 are in SSoD and if $(U_i, T_1) \in$ *user task assignment* $\Rightarrow (U_i, T_2) \notin$ *user task assignment*.

[2] If $\{T_1, T_2, \ldots T_n\}$ is set of critical tasks in a workflow, then as per operational SoD, any user U_i cannot execute all critical tasks in any instance of workflow.

Proof. For the successful execution of an activity, all its constituent tasks should be completed successfully. The activity will fail if all users in any of the constituent tasks of the activity fail. In the *worst case*, the activity will fail when the number of users that fail is $\lceil min_{\forall i}(|assigned(T_i)|) \rceil$. Therefore, an activity is guaranteed a successful completion when the number of users that fail is $\leq \lceil min_{\forall i}(|assigned(T_i)|) - 1 \rceil$.

Definition 2. *Failure resilience of an activity is the minimum of failure resilience of its constituent tasks i.e* $\mathrm{FR}_{activity} = min_{\forall i}(FR_{T_i})$

Corollary 1. *Given an assignment of n users to t tasks and the number of failed users* $> min_{\forall_i}(FR_{T_i})$*, the activity can still continue; but there exists at least one specific combination of* $min_{\forall_i}(FR_{T_i})$ *users whose failure will fail both a task and the activity.*

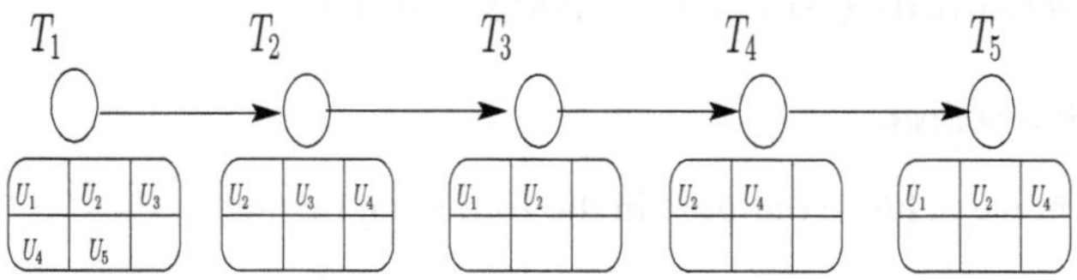

Fig. 1. Workflow activity consisting of five tasks

Example 1. Figure 1 shows five tasks and users assigned to each of them. As tasks T_3 and T_4 have the minimum number of users, in the worst case, an activity will fail when either of the user sets (U_1,U_2) or (U_2,U_4) fails. However, if user set (U_1,U_3,U_4) fails, even then the activity will be successfully completed. Therefore, it will not always be the case that when $\lceil min_{\forall i}(|assigned(T_i)|) \rceil$ users fail, then activity fails too.

Note that we have not considered sequence constraints in doing failure resilient user-task assignment. Failure resilience is independent of simple task precedence. Constrained precedence can be handled by incorporating them as SoD constraints (refer Proposition 1).

Relationship between Task Precedence and Failure Resilience. Consider a simplistic workflow consisting of three tasks T_1, T_2, T_3. Let T_1 and T_2 have a precedence relationship ($T_1 \prec T_2$) while T_3 does not have any precedence relationship ($(T_1,T_2) \nprec T_3$). Precedence relationships between the tasks can be of two types:

i *Simple precedence*: ($T_1 \prec T_2$) implies that the execution of T_1 precedes T_2, but users in the set $\{assigned(T_1)\}$ will have no dependency relationships with those in $\{assigned(T_2)\}$ at runtime.

ii *Constrained precedence*: ($T_1 \prec^{\mathbb{C}} T_2$) implies that the execution of T_1 precedes T_2 and if $\mathbb{C}$ is a separation of duty constraint, then all users in the set $\{exec(T_1)\}$ will have a dependency relationship with those in $\{exec(T_2)\}$. For example, if user $U_1 \in \{exec(T_1), exec(T_2)\}$ and if it executes T_1, then it cannot execute T_2 in that workflow instance. But as the set $\forall k\{assigned(T_k)\}$ is calculated after taking all security constraints into account (refer section 3), users in $\{assigned(T_1)\}$ will have no dependency relationship with users in $\{assigned(T_2)\}$.

Proposition 1. ***Precedence relationships do not have any implication on failure resilience.***

Reason. Consider the above example. As the set $\{assigned(T_1)\}$ has no dependency relationship with $\{assigned(T_2)\}$ and $\{assigned(T_3)\}$, the number of users who can execute T_i (i.e. $|assigned(T_i)|$) in any workflow instance will not depend on task precedence. Hence, task precedence is not a determinant of the failure resilience of the workflow activity.

In this section, we have computed failure resilience for workflows assuming we know the user-task assignment. In the next section, we show how to assign tasks to users to achieve failure resilience.

3 Failure Resilient User-Task Assignments

3.1 Exhaustive Search

In this approach, we achieve our goal in the following manner:

i. Based on user capability, we derive/identify all the tasks an user can possibly perform (without considering the security policy and constraints).
ii. Applying *security policy* restrictions and *separation of duty* constraints, we identify the combinations of user-task assignments that are not allowed in a *secure* state of the system.

   The permitted user task assignments satisfying security policy and constraints can be derived as:

   $\{User\ Task\ Assignment\}_{Step_i} \backslash \{User\ Task\ Assignment\}_{Step_{ii}} =$
   $\{Permitted\ user\ task\ assignment\}$
iii. From the *permitted user task assignment* set, we select the user-task assignments that have *min* $\mathcal{K}$ failure resilience (definition 3).

The diagrammatic representation of the system model for this approach is shown in Figure 2. (a) represents the possible user-task assignments considering only the capabilities of users. The assignments that violate the security policy are removed from (a) to obtain (b). (c) gives the different possible combinations of user-task assignments derived from (b) that satisfy security constraints. (d) is derived from (c) to obtain the desired level of failure resilience. The steps that the model follows (Figure 2) to achieve security and failure resilience are described below.

Step (a): Initially, all users are assigned to tasks that they are capable of doing. Therefore, the outcome of executing step *(a)* in Figure 2 will be the set $\left[\forall k\ \{exec(T_k)\}\right]$.

Step (b): The executability set of a task after applying the security policy (pol) will be a subset of the executability set before applying the security policy. Therefore, $\left[\forall_k\left(\text{exec}(T_k)^{pol} \subseteq \text{exec}(T_k)\right)\right]$ is what we get after executing step *(b)* of Figure 2.

Step (c): Security constraints on users are specified as *rules* in the *rule base* (refer Figure 3). $(T_1)_{U_i} \Rightarrow \neg(T_2)_{U_i}$ represents static SSOD of user U_i over tasks T_1 *and*T_2.

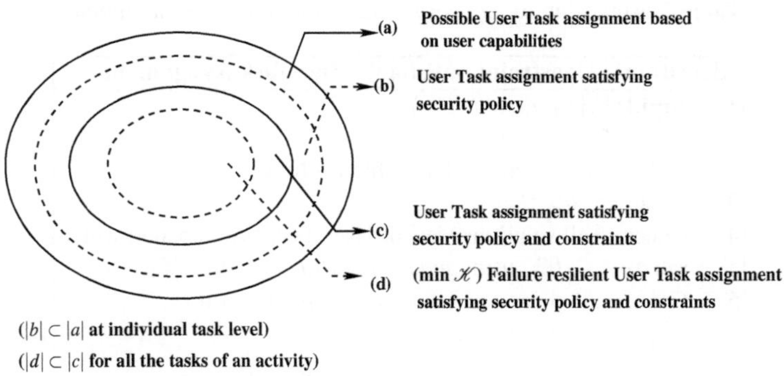

Fig. 2. Stepwise user task assignment

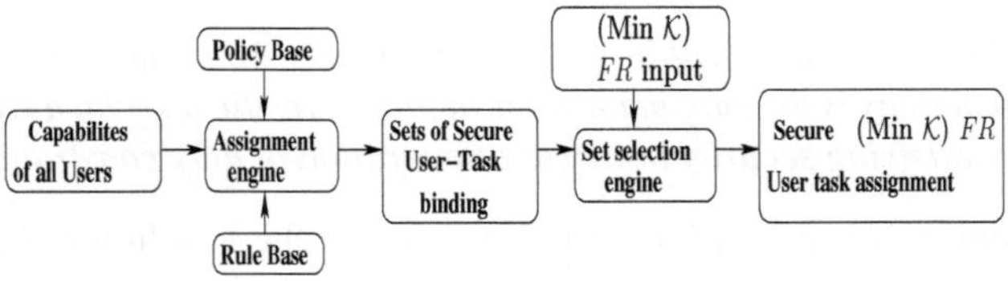

Fig. 3. Conceptual model of proposed system

If there are n security constraints $\mathbb{C} = \{C_1, C_2, \ldots, C_n\}$, then all of them (i.e. $C_1 \wedge C_2 \wedge \ldots \wedge C_n$) need to be satisfied for secure user-task binding. The literals in $C_1, C_2 \ldots$ are all of the form $(T_i)_{U_j}$. We convert $\mathbb{C}$ into *Conjunctive Normal Form* (CNF) and then find all the solutions that satisfy $\mathbb{C}$ using the *modified DPLL algorithm* [6]. Each solution is represented in the form $S_i = \forall_k (U')^i_{T_k}$ where S_i is the ith solution and $(U')^i_{T_k}$ represents the set of users which *cannot perform* task T_k in the ith solution. We need user-task bindings which satisfy both security policy and constraints. Therefore, $(U')^i_{T_k}$ should be removed from $exec(T_k)^{pol}$. For the ith solution, $\left[(exec(T_k)^{pol+\mathbb{C}})^i = exec(T_k)^{pol} - (U')^i_{T_k}\right]$ is the set of users which can be assigned to task T_k. The outcome of step 6 of *Algorithm1* is the solution for step (c) of Figure 2. The time taken by this approach largely depends on this step.

Step (d): From the previous step, we have all possible sets of user-task assignment that satisfy both the security policy and constraints. All these sets give a different secure user-task assignment. But it is desirable to have failure resilience along with security. Here we introduce the notion of *min* $\mathcal{K}$ failure resilience.

Definition 3. *min* $\mathcal{K}$ *failure resilience: For achieving min* $\mathcal{K}$ *FR for an activity, there should exist a set of user-task assignments in the activity for which* $FR_{activity} \geq \mathcal{K}$.

If $\mathcal{K}$ is greater than maximum achievable failure resilience then solution can not be computed.

Table 2. Algorithm for *constraint satisfiable* User-Task assignment

Algorithm1: Constraint Satisfiable User-Task Assignment($\mathbb{C}$)	
1.	**Input:** [i.] $\forall_k(exec(T_k)^{pol})$ [ii.] Constraints $\mathbb{C}$
2.	$\forall_i(C_i \in \mathbb{C})$, generate CNF of literals for C_i
3.	Generate $\wedge_{(\forall i)}(C_i)$
4.	Generate all solutions (sets of User-Task assignments) which satisfy $\wedge_{(\forall i)}(C_i)$ using *modified DPLL* algorithm [6].
5.	Convert all generated solutions ($\forall_i(S_i)$) in form $\forall_i\left[S_i = \forall_k(U')^i_{T_k}\right]$ where $(U')^i_{T_k}$ = Set of users that cannot do T_k in i^{th} solution.
6.	$\forall_i, \forall_k\left[(exec(T_k)^{pol+\mathbb{C}})^i = exec(T_k)^{pol} - (U')^i_{T_k}\right]$

Definition 4. *Maximum achievable failure resilience: Maximum achievable failure resilience of an activity is the maximum value of failure resilience which can be achieved for the activity satisfying security policy and separation of duty constraints.*

If $\mathcal{K} <$ *Maximum achievable failure resilience* and for the ith solution ($FR^i_{activity} \geq \mathcal{K}$), then $\forall_k(exec(T_k)^{pol+\mathbb{C}})^i$ will give the *min* $\mathcal{K}$ failure resilient user task assignment corresponding to that solution. There can be more than one solution which have $FR_{activity}$ $\geq \mathcal{K}$; in that case first we look for the solution with minimum average number of tasks per user. If the average number of task per user is same for two solutions, then the solution with minimum variance of number of tasks an user is doing is chosen (as it minimizes the knowledge gained by users). If the chosen solution is the pth solution then $\forall_k(exec(T_k)^{pol+\mathbb{C}})^p$ is the set which constitutes step (*d*) of Figure 2 and also the set $\forall_k$ *assigned*(T_k), that is,

$$\forall_k\, assigned(T_k) = \forall_k(exec(T_k)^{pol+\mathbb{C}})^p$$

3.2 Quadratic Programming Approach

The problem of achieving *min*$\mathcal{K}$ failure resilience while satisfying the security policy and constraints is formulated in the form of a 0-1 quadratic programming problem. Let $T = \{T_1, T_2, ...T_n\}$ be a set of n tasks and $U = \{U_1, U_2, ..., U_m\}$ be a set of m users which will be assigned to the tasks. $X_{ij}(i = 1,2,...,n; j = 1,2,...,m)$ is used to denote assignment of user j to task i. X_{ij} is 1 if user j is assigned to task i, and is 0 otherwise.

	U_1	U_2	...	U_m
T_1	X_{11}	X_{12}	...	X_{1m}
T_2	X_{21}	X_{22}	...	X_{2m}
...	...	...	...	...
T_n	X_{n1}	X_{n2}	...	X_{nm}

We need to assign users to tasks by taking into account the *capabilities* of users, *security policy* and *Separation of duty constraints*. As described in section 2, if a user does not possess the capability to perform a task, then it can not be assigned to that task. Therefore, X_{ij} is set to 0 if U_j is not capable of performing task T_i i.e. $T_i \notin cap(U_j)$. If U_j can not be assigned to T_i as per the security policy, then also X_{ij} is set to 0. We want to achieve min $\mathcal{K}$ failure resilience while satisfying separation of duty constraints. The separation of duty constraints are expressed in the form of inequality constraints.

If T_1, T_2 are in static SoD then T_1 *and* T_2 both can not be assigned to user U_i simultaneously. Therefore, X_{1i} and X_{2i} both can not be 1 at the same time i.e.

$$X_{1i} + X_{2i} \leq 1 \tag{1}$$

Similarly, if a set of p tasks $T_1, T_2, ..., T_p$ is in static SoD, then no two of them can be assigned simultaneously to user U_i, that is,

$$X_{1i} + X_{2i} + ... + X_{pi} \leq 1$$

For operational SoD, if T_1, T_2 are critical tasks for user U_i, then U_i can not execute both T_1 *and* T_2 at runtime, hence X_{1i} and X_{2i} can not be 1 at the same time, that is,

$$X_{1i} + X_{2i} \leq 1 \tag{2}$$

Similarly, if there is a set of q critical tasks $T_1, T_2, ..., T_q$, all of which can not be done by user U_i simultaneously then at least one of $(X_{ji}) < j = 1, 2, .., u >$ should be 0, that is,

$$X_{1i} + X_{2i} + ... + X_{qi} \leq q - 1$$

To achieve min $\mathcal{K}$ failure resilience each task should be assigned to at least $\mathcal{K}$ users. Therefore,

$$\forall_i \sum_{j=0}^{m} X_{ij} \geq \mathcal{K} + 1 \tag{3}$$

Knowledge gained by a user by executing the workflow is the weighted sum of knowledge gained in doing its constituent tasks. Let w_i $1 \leq i \leq n$ denote the weight corresponding to each task (T_i $1 \leq i \leq n$) of a workflow then total knowledge gained by user U_j is:

$$\sum_{i=1}^{n} w_i * X_{ij}$$

If v_j $1 \leq j \leq m$ denote the weight of a user (U_j $1 \leq j \leq m$) (a user with higher weight should be more knowledgeable then user with lower weight). Therefore, in order to minimize the risk, any user should not have more knowledge in proportion to its weight. Therefore we should minimize the weighted standard deviation and hence weighted variance. Weighted average of knowledge gained by user

$$weightedavg = (\sum_{j=1}^{m} v_j * \sum_{i=1}^{n} w_i * X_{ij}) / \sum_{j=1}^{m} v_j$$

Variance, which is the objective function of *QPP* and is to be *minimized*, is given by

$$variance = (\sum_{j=1}^{m} v_j * \left[(\sum_{i=1}^{n} X_{ij}) - weightedavg \right]^2) / \sum_{j=1}^{m} v_j \tag{4}$$

The weights are subjective in nature and there is no known scientific standard which can measure the knowledge of a task of an activity and the knowledge gained a user by performing the activity. For simplicity we have assumed, all tasks and users are of equal weight and hence $\forall_{i=1,2,..,n}\, w_i = 1 \; and \; \forall_{j=1,2..,m}\, v_j = 1$

Therefore, this is a 0-1 quadratic programming problem(QPP) with linear constraints ((1, 2 and 3) and convex quadratic objective function(4), which can be solved using any of the available MIQP (mixed integer quadratic programming) solver.
After computing the values of $\forall_{i,j} X_{ij}$,if X_{ij}=1 then, user U_j is assigned to task T_i i.e, $assigned(T_i) = \forall j|_{X_{ij} \neq 0} U_j$. If $\mathcal{K} > Maximum\ achievable\ failure\ resilience$ then solution with Maximum Achievable failure resilience is obtained.(refer Algorithm 2).

The users in the set $assigned(T_k)$ will be given privileges to perform the task T_k. The assignment of privileges to users is either *static* (at activation time) or *dynamic* (at runtime). In case of static assignment of privileges, all privileges are given to the users at the very beginning and are retained forever. In case of dynamic assignment of privileges, privileges are given just before the task is to be executed. The privileges are revoked after the task has executed.

Table 3. Algorithm for *user-task assignment* using QPP

Algorithm2: User-Task assignment with QPP
$\mathcal{K}$ is expected failure resilience.
Form QPP with constraints 1 or 2 and 3 with objective function(4)
Solve QPP with MIQP solver
while *solution* is not *feasible*
modify constraint 3 replace $\mathcal{K}$ by $\mathcal{K}-1(\mathcal{K}=\mathcal{K}-1)$
Solve modified QPP with MIQP solver
Solution is obtained with Failure resilience $\mathcal{K}$.

Change of Assignment in Dynamic Scenario. In case of dynamic scenario we get the initial user-task assignment by solving the QPP. On failure of a user, this assignment can be modified at runtime to get more failure resilience. Consider the workflow in figure fig4,

There are four tasks T_1, T_2, T_3 *and* T_4. Suppose there are five users U_1, U_2, U_3, U_4 *and* U_5. All users can do all the tasks of the workflow as per security policy. Let us say $(T_1, T_2), (T_2, T_3)$ *and* (T_3, T_4) are sets of mutually exclusive tasks, so no user can do two tasks in a set simultaneously. Also, let us assume that we need a failure resilience of 2.

In this case, the initial QPP is:

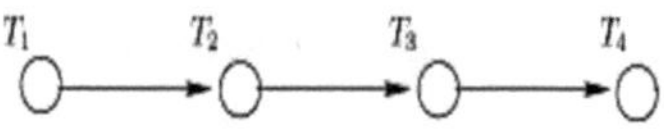

Fig. 4. Example workflow

minimize

$$variance = (\sum_{j=1}^{5} [\sum_{i=1}^{4} X_{ij} - avg]^2)/5$$

where

$$avg = (\sum_{j=1}^{5}\sum_{i=1}^{4} X_{ij})/5$$

subject to constraints

SoD constraints

$X_{11}+X_{21} \leq 1; X_{12}+X_{22} \leq 1; X_{13}+X_{23} \leq 1; X_{14}+X_{24} \leq 1; X_{15}+X_{25} \leq 1$
$X_{21}+X_{31} \leq 1; X_{22}+X_{32} \leq 1; X_{23}+X_{33} \leq 1; X_{24}+X_{34} \leq 1; X_{25}+X_{35} \leq 1$
$X_{31}+X_{41} \leq 1; X_{32}+X_{42} \leq 1; X_{33}+X_{43} \leq 1; X_{34}+X_{44} \leq 1; X_{35}+X_{45} \leq 1$

Failure resilience constraints

$X_{11}+X_{12}+X_{13}+X_{14}+X_{15} \geq 2; X_{21}+X_{22}+X_{23}+X_{24}+X_{25} \geq 2$
$X_{31}+X_{32}+X_{33}+X_{34}+X_{35} \geq 2; X_{41}+X_{42}+X_{43}+X_{44}+X_{45} \geq 2$

The solution to this *QPP* is:

$assigned(T_1) = (U_5, U_3); assigned(T_2) = (U_1, U_4); assigned(T_3) = (U_3, U_2)$
$assigned(T_4) = (U_4, U_1)$

This is the user-task assignment in case we take static user-task assignment and is the initial assignment for the dynamic case. Now suppose user U_5 has executed task T_1 and user U_1 has executed task T_2. If user U_3 fails at this stage, then in static scenario user U_2 executes T_3, assignment remains fixed and failure resilience at this stage is 1. On the other hand, in case of dynamic scenario, a new *QPP* is formed as given below. The objective function remains the same as we still want to minimize the knowledge gain. The constraints which were there still hold on as tasks are still mutually exclusive. There will be some new constraints which are as follows:

$\forall_i X_{i3} = 0$ % As user U_3 failed
$X_{15} = 1; X_{21} = 1$ % As U_5 *and* U_1 executed T_1 *and* T_2 respectively, so this assignment can not be changed.

On solving the new *QPP* we get the assignment as:

$assigned(T_1) = (U_5, U_4); assigned(T_2) = (U_1, U_2); assigned(T_3) = (U_4, U_5)$
$assigned(T_4) = (U_1, U_2)$

Now U_4 executes T_3 and we can get a failure resilience of 2 even after the failure of a user.

As shown in the example we can get a high failure resilience by changing the assignment at runtime. To change the assignment at runtime, we use iterative quadratic programming approach. We form a new *QPP* at each failure by introducing the constraints arose due to failure of a user and also because of execution of tasks preceding the task at which failure occurs(shown in the example).

The problem with the iterative quadratic programming approach is that the time taken to solve *QPP* at runtime increases the time of execution of workflow. But, since the number of unknown variables reduces in each iteration, it takes less time to solve resulting *QPP*.

4 Results

We carried out our experiments on a 2.8 GHz processor with 512 MB of RAM. The two approaches described in the paper are both NP hard but there are commercial tools available for solving quadratic programming problems which can compute the solution really fast. For solving MIQP, we used ILOG OPL-CPLEX Analyst Studio [7] which provide the fastest possible execution times.

Test cases [8] are randomly generated. Table 5 shows the time taken by exhaustive search approach and the quadratic programming approach. In *time* column for exhaustive search approach, if the solution can not be generated within 1000 seconds then a '-' is kept. In *time* column for quadratic programming approach the value *before/* indicates the time taken to compute a feasible solution and value */after* indicates the time taken to compute the optimal solution. If optimal solution is not computed within 60 seconds then a '-' is put. The ILOG CPLEX [9] finds a good feasible solution early but it takes time to prove that solution is optimal. A good feasible solution is one which satisfies all the constraints and the value of objective function for this solution is very close[3] to optimal value (minimum value of variance).

Table 4. Results: Failure resilience for some examples [8]

Instance Name	*No. of users*	*No. of tasks*	*Total Const-raints*[4]	SoD Const-raints	max achievable FR	Avg no. of tasks per user	min no.of tasks assigned to a user	max.no of tasks assigned to a user
50_5_2_1.*mod*	5	50	332	240	1	20	19	21
10_10_5_1.*mod*	10	10	61	35	4	5	5	5
15_10_5_1.*mod*	10	15	103	63	4	7.5	7	8
20_15_6_2.*mod*	15	20	239	162	5	8	8	8
30_15_6_3.*mod*	15	30	407	292	5	12	12	12
20_20_9_1.*mod*	20	20	340	238	8	9	9	9
10_30_14_1.*mod*	30	10	259	188	13	4.67	3	5
2_40_22_3.*mod*	40	2	60	46	21	1.1	0	2
10_40_17_1.*mod*	40	10	416	323	16	4.25	4	5
2_50_22_2.*mod*	50	2	125	106	21	0.88	0	2
5_50_22_5.*mod*	50	5	261	207	21	2.2	1	3

Table 4 shows the maximum achievable failure resilience for some of the instances available at [8]. The maximum achievable failure resilience of an activity does not depend on number of users, tasks and constraints. For same number of users, tasks and

[3] The difference between the optimal value and the good value is less than 1%. As all the security constraints are satisfied and *min* $\mathcal{K}$ failure resilience constraint is also satisfied, the solution is secure and failure resilient. The 1% difference affects the knowledge gained by each user. The optimal solution can always be computed but time required will be more. Thus, there is a trade off between the knowledge gained by the users and time taken to compute the assignment.

[4] In case of quadratic programming approach total constraints include failure resilience constraints in addition to SoD constraints. Also the X_{ij} values which need to be initialized to 0 are initialized using the inequality $X_{ij} \leq 0$ (All X_{ij} are integers and are either 0 or 1).

Table 5. Results: Comparison of time taken by the two approaches

No. of users	*No. of tasks*	*Total Constraints*	SoD Constraints	Time(in sec) (Quadratic Programming)	Time (in sec) (Exhaustive Search)
2	2	2	0	1.11/1.11	1
2	2	3	0	0.84/0.84	1
5	5	8	1	0.75/1.53	1.2
5	5	11	2	0.8/1.11	1.4
10	10	54	21	0.51/–	639
10	10	57	26	0.53/–	850
20	20	314	215	2.9/–	–
20	20	329	228	4.0/–	–

constraints maximum achievable failure resilience will be different as it depends on policy and type of constraints. Table 4 also contains average number of tasks, minimum number of tasks and maximum number of tasks assigned to a user. The results (in table 5) show that a feasible solution can always be computed in a small duration using quadratic programming approach. However if more than one feasible solution is generated(whenever a better solution, i.e close to optimal, is generated), then the time for that new solution is recorded. Therefore, the time in the results is the time taken to generate the optimal solution (if optimal solution is not possible within the maximum time limits(60 sec) then closest to optimal solution is considered).

It is evident from the results that formulating the problem as a quadratic programming problem is a better approach as it gives solutions quickly and also does not generate redundant solutions. As time taken is less, the approach is practically applicable in dynamic environments.

5 Conclusion

Many of day to day activities are modeled using workflows. A workflow is a set of tasks which can be executed by a set of users. The users which can execute many of the sensitive and critical tasks of an activity/workflow can be software or humans. Failure to accomplish these critical tasks may lead to delay in activity execution and potential loss to the organization. On the other hand, allowing users to execute multiple critical tasks will lead to potential security attacks through these users (insider attacks). There needs to be a balance between failure resilience constraints and user-task assignments. We have developed two approaches namely *Exhaustive search* and *Quadratic Programming approach* for assigning users to tasks. We have shown that quadratic programming approach is not only efficient but also gives quality results.

The main focus of this work is to provide failure resilience while satisfying security policy and constraints. These concerns are addressed in this paper. We have considered *static* and *decremental* resilience in this paper but plan to incorporate *dynamic* resilience [3] in future. We have considered task based access control, therefore, we are finding resilient user-task assignment. We are working on extending the current framework for role based access control environments [10] where failure resilient user-role assignment need to be identified.

References

1. Hung, P.C.K., Karlapalem, K., GrayIII, J.W.: A Study of Least Privilege in CapBasED-AMS. In: International Conference on Cooperative Information Systems, pp. 208–217 (1998)
2. Li, N., Tripunitara, M.V., Wang, Q.: Resiliency policies in access control. In: ACM Conference on Computer and Communications Security, pp. 113–123 (2006)
3. Wang, Q., Li, N.: Satisfiability and resiliency in workflow systems. In: Biskup, J., López, J. (eds.) ESORICS 2007. LNCS, vol. 4734, pp. 90–105. Springer, Heidelberg (2007)
4. Thomas, R.K., Sandhu, R.S.: Task-Based Authorization Controls (TBAC): A Family of Models for Active and Enterprise-Oriented Authorization Management. In: Eleventh International Conference on Database Security, pp. 166–181 (1997)
5. Solworth, J.A.: Approvability. In: ASIACCS 2006: ACM Symposium on Information, computer and communications security, pp. 231–242 (2006)
6. Jin, H., Han, H., Somenzi, F.: Efficient Conflict Analysis for Finding All Satisfying Assignments of a Boolean Circuit. In: Halbwachs, N., Zuck, L.D. (eds.) TACAS 2005. LNCS, vol. 3440, pp. 287–300. Springer, Heidelberg (2005)
7. `http://www.ilog.com/products/oplstudio/`
8. `http://students.iiit.ac.in/~meghnal/inputs/`
9. `http://eaton.math.rpi.edu/cplex90html/pdf/usrcplex.pdf`
10. Sandhu, R.S., Coyne, E.J., Feinstein, H.L., Youman, C.E.: Role-Based Access Control Models. IEEE Computer 29(2), 38–47 (1996)
11. Tan, K., Crampton, J., Gunter, C.A.: The consistency of task-based authorization constraints in workflow systems. In: CSFW, p. 155 (2004)
12. Helsinger, A., Kleinmann, K., Brinn, M.: Framework to Control Emergent Survivability of Multi Agent Systems. In: AAMAS, pp. 28–35 (2004)
13. Navarro, G., Borrell, J., Ortega-Ruiz, J.A., Robles, S.: Access control with safe role assignment for mobile agents. In: AAMAS, pp. 1235–1236 (2005)
14. Kern, A., Walhorn, C.: Rule support for role-based access control. In: ACM symposium on Access control models and technologies, pp. 130–138 (2005)
15. Crampton, J.: A reference monitor for workflow systems with constrained task execution. In: SACMAT, pp. 38–47 (2005)

User Control Problems and Taking User Empowerment Further

Rowena Rodrigues

School of Law, University of Edinburgh
R.E.Rodrigues@sms.ed.ac.uk

Abstract. User control in identity management is beset with a number of problems, as outlined in this paper. It is argued that akin to traditional contexts, greater user control will result in greater user liability, which is demonstrated with the help of digital and non-digital examples. In this context, there is a critical need for greater user empowerment. This could be achieved in two ways– first, facilitating user awareness of identity management technologies, their scope and effects and second, through the implementation of proposed control-liability notices.

Keywords: User control, limitations of identity management systems, user liability, user empowerment, control-liability notice.

1 Introduction

User control in identity management refers to the power of the user[1] to determine and direct how one's digital identity, its attributes, relationships are created, constructed, maintained and decommissioned. It is a key factor of identity management; particularly in the user centric forms of identity management, which moot that individuals must be placed in greater control over their identities, attributes and identity relationships [1]. It is also hailed as one of the elements that determines the success or failure of an identity management system [2].

The user control approach to identity management is fraught with a number of problems. This paper examines such problems from the user's perspective. But the greatest challenge will potentially be the increase in user responsibility and liability, and in this light this problem is explored further. In this light it is suggested that users need to be empowered through greater awareness (public and private) and the implementation of control-liability notices.

2 The Problems of Control

2.1 Control – A Terminological Misnomer?

Technologists and identity providers' talk in terms of designing and providing solutions that help users control their identity. The use of the terminology of control is very

[1] In the context of this paper, the "user" refers to human beings.

V. Matyáš et al. (Eds.): The Future of Identity, IFIP AICT 298, pp. 211–225, 2009.

confusing at times. Different identity management technologists and providers conceptualise and implement identity management differently e.g. Sun Microsystems refers to identity management as its ability to help users "manage, audit, protect, share and store identity data" [3], the OpenID framework works more in terms of eliminating "the need for multiple usernames across different websites, simplifying your online experience" [4], Higgins speaks of enabling users and applications to integrate identity, profile, and relationship information across multiple data sources and protocols" [5].

Users, as individuals, expect different things from identity management systems in different contexts – organization of identities in some contexts, privacy or security in other contexts or a combination of all, in different measures. For instance, from a particular system they may require a high level of privacy with minimal data security [6], and from another simply a high level of data security. But, users and identity management providers do not always sing from the same hymn sheet. The difficulty arises when users fail to understand that different identity management systems offer varying levels and varieties of identity management since identity management is still by and large not a seamless experience across domains. Users may carry their expectations across domains, which may or may not adhere to common rules. Not all identity players play by the same rule and identity management systems are not restricted to local application (due to their global nature) whereas notions of control, privacy and security are.[2]

2.2 Control Not Primary Goal for Users

Controlling their digital identity is not per se, a primary goal for users. Using the Internet to network socially, seek information, make purchases, conduct banking transactions, and make travel arrangements, however may be. Managing one's identity on different websites or databases that hold personal data, profiles or other forms of identity is often less important than earning a living, writing up a thesis or caring for a sick family member. These are social facts that are often ignored in the user control debate.

The behaviour of users on social networking sites shows how users despite being given the technical possibility of protecting their profiles or personal information either do not bother to enforce stricter privacy settings or are sufficiently lax in their attitude towards taking steps in that direction [7].

Then again, control is a continuous and dynamic process. Users do not want to become constant vigilantes or puppeteers of their identity [8]. Nor can they effectively play this part indeterminately. Users are individuals with other and varied life contexts and any identity management solution must fit smoothly into these milieus and not disrupt them. Individuals simply will not adopt identity management solution enabling better user control if this is not the case.

2.3 Control Is Limited in Scope and Nature

Control is not and cannot be absolute. It is limited in nature and scope by various factors. Control, in terms of identity management, may not equate to effective identity security as opposed to what is repeatedly being told and sold to the users. Control

[2] Notions of identity control, privacy and security are still by and large culturally and jurisdictionally diverse, even taking into account the current state of technological globalisation.

may eliminate some risks, but the larger security issues still remain. The user of an identity management system is like the owner of a gun (indicative of identity). The gun owner keeps his gun in a combination safe (denoting an identity management system) – the combination of which is known to him and also to his wife, who he trusts. While this ensures that his children and other unauthorized people do not get hold of the gun and use it destructively or to his disadvantage, there is nothing to prevent his wife (who has access to the gun) from removing it from the safe and in a betrayal of trust using it for a violent or illegal purpose. A wife is well placed to compromise her husband's identity because she has intimate knowledge of his personal data or physical and behavioural identity.[3] Then again, a burglar could also break into the safe and steal the gun. An identity management system could, in similar manner, be internally or externally compromised.[4]

The ability to control may also be limited by factors such as whether one has the authority, power or means to control. One may not be able to control identity aspects or attributes one has not created or which are within the command of another and may be in that entity's interests not to relinquish control over. When identities are assigned or derived, control and ownership may lie elsewhere, and even if some form of limited control is possible, it may prove practically impossible, inconvenient or problematic. A simple example is one's identity or profile on a database. The identity or profile on the database may *relate* to me, but may not per se *belong* to me.

There may be a property interest in one's identity and its attributes and manifestations but one may be forced, coerced, inveigled or simply have to relinquish control for a number of reasons.[5] For instance, Google was ordered [9] to hand over to Viacom all data from the Logging database concerning each time a YouTube video had been viewed on the YouTube website or through embedding on a third-party website (including more importantly user names and IP addresses).[6] Users had no say or choice in the matter of this use of their personal information.

2.4 Ease, Convenience and Affordability

Another problem at the ergonomic level of identity management is that users will often resort to the "easy-quick-cheap" solution – a widely accepted view. It has been determined that if there is a trade off between risk and convenience, users "will take the easy option" [10]. For example, some digital users do not upgrade their anti-virus software because they find the process too complicated or get complacent. In the case of identity management systems, users may reject a high security system if they find that it is difficult to use or does not provide the desired level of interoperability or flexibility. Then again, they may resort to a convenient and easily accessible solution e.g. a fake anti-virus program they were directed to on the Internet [11].

[3] Or for instance, A's friend could create a fake profile for A with A's personal information that s/he is privy to. See Applause Store Productions Limited, Matthew Firsht v Grant Raphael, [2008] EWHC 1781 (QB); An identity management system might be similarly compromised by insider threats.

[4] E.g. through phishing, destruction and modification of data by malicious bots etc.

[5] E.g. employee digital identities or government/public authority created digital identities.

[6] This may have been implied in the Terms of Service, but it does not necessarily mean this would please users or that they would not feel a violation of their rights.

Affordability of solutions is also a factor that comes into play in securing and protecting identity. Users are often reluctant to invest money into security unless it is life threatening or visibly fraught with very serious consequences, e.g. many people now invest in shredders after becoming aware of how personal information is being used to facilitate fraud [12].

2.5 The "Human" Factor

The most important factor in user control of identity is "the human factor." Users are individuals, groups, companies (made up of people). Users have different attributes – some users are more technology savvy, others less.[7] Some are young, some are old. Some are disclosure paranoid while others are disclosure prone. Erasmus, so eloquently stated that being human meant living in folly, erring, and being deceived [13]. This also applies excellently to the digital domain. Digital users are human beings who sometimes live in digital folly, make digital errors and get defrauded. They may forget email passwords and bank accounts. Users also may have vulnerabilities e.g. very young users, users with disabilities, users who need help to access the Internet or other digital technologies, or persons with mental impairments.[8]

Humans do not fully understand the intricacies and complexities of security (they do know what they want from security) and become expert at it through experience. Some may argue this is a naive assumption as people are generally adept at ensuring high security for that which they value. But, this assumes that people understand or are aware that there is a security problem (i.e. an identity threat or compromise, phishing attacks) and are empowered to act or deal with the problem. This also implies that when people weigh up an identity management system's security they make a correct risk assessment in terms of how their digital identities will be treated and how secure they are.[9] This may often be more in terms of what they "perceive," than what actually "is."

2.6 The Illusion and Impossibility of Control and Security

Users' over-reliance on technological measures and identity management systems might leave them more vulnerable through perpetuating illusions of control. What they see or get, may not be equivalent to what they think they are getting. If identity management systems are only effective in giving users a semblance of control, this is not going to be successful in helping users control their identity.

Use of identity management systems may lull users into a false sense of security. Risk and trust issues may remain unaddressed. For example, some identity management

---

[7] In a survey carried out in the United Kingdom, it was found that 56% of users found the Internet to be complex and 35% found it frustrating to work with. See W Dutton & E Helsper, "The Internet in Britain 2007," OxIS Oxford Internet Surveys, University of Oxford, 2007.

[8] We must also take into account individuals who chose not to lead technologically oriented lifestyles.

[9] A risk assessment is dependant on a number of factors and presupposes effective forseeability of value of data and possible harms. A view supported by L Edwards & G Howells, "Anonymity, Consumers and the Internet: Where everyone knows you're a dog," in Digital Anonymity and the Law, C Nicoll et al (eds.), Chapter 10, p 207-248 at 242, (2003).

systems are vulnerable to phishing attacks and an attacker could capture a person's credentials or "sniff" out where the person's logs in [14]. Also, the user needs to "trust" the identity provider.

Security in identity management is a big challenge in itself [15]. Technologists constantly grapple with fixing bugs, while code-breakers and hackers continue to wreck havoc with the systems they design. There can never be 100% security, [16] although an optimal level of security can be sought to be achieved. There are intrinsic challenges in controlling security breaches and unauthorised access to identities and identifiable information [17]. Machines can be compromised by key loggers, trojans, viruses, malware and spyware.

2.7 The Merging of Actors; The Fusing of the Worlds

Technologies have brought about the merging of actors (state and private)[10] in a fusion of worlds (digital and offline). This is not a problem except for the fact that individuals often need to separate aspects of their identities according to contexts and purposes. User control is not only about controlling how private companies deal with one's digital identity but also about protecting one's identity from other individuals who are active participants in the identity stakes. With the merging of private and state interests in identity management and regulation both online and offline, user control takes on new dimensions.

Certain traditional forms of user control no longer remain singly effective. It is for this reason one can question whether technology (or for that matter norms or market)[11] by itself will be able to sufficiently support the user control his/her identity interests. And perhaps, it does make sense not to casually dismiss the part that perhaps the law could play in such a case.[12]

2.8 The Problematic "Privacy" Dimension

Identity management systems embody privacy and data protection norms as a primary means of protecting and enabling users' greater identity control. Identity and privacy have been deeply meshed, but there are some challenges to this approach, as explained below:

2.8.1 The Philosophy, Expectations and Implementations of Privacy Vary

Privacy arguably is as much a cultural concept (it is generally recognised as a western philosophical concept) as it is a legal one [18]. It has been interpreted differently in different countries and assumes different connotations for different people [19]. The expectations of people of privacy are as different as is the enforcement of the law on

[10] The merging of private actors happens on a constant basis – e.g. Yahoo and Flickr in 2005, Google and YouTube in 2006, LiveJournal and SUP in 2007.

[11] As postulated by L Lessig in Code and Other Laws of Cyberspace, New York, Basic Books, (1999).

[12] We acknowledge the call for a right to identity to protect individuals' identity. See P De Hert, "A right to identity to face the Internet of things," Ethics and Human Rights in the Information Society, 13-14 September 2007, Strasbourg, http://portal.unseco.org/ci/en/files/25857/12021328273de_Hert-Paul.pdf/de%2BHert-Paul.pdf (2008).

privacy. In countries like India, where sharing of information is a common age-old and modern practice, informational privacy is virtually non-existent and the right to privacy developed through its judicial reading into the constitutional right to life.[13] There are fundamental differences between the philosophy of privacy of the United States and the European Union [20]. De Boni and Prigmore reported that in relation to the Internet, "current approaches to privacy are culturally biased, reflecting only one of a number of possible standpoints" [21].

2.8.2 Privacy's Out of Favour

While many people have come to value privacy as a fundamental right,[14] governments do not seem to like privacy.[15] A review of privacy rankings by Privacy International illustrates this very clearly [22]. Brazil, China, India, Japan, Russia, South Africa and the USA were amongst the worst for privacy enforcement. Also considered worst in regards to communication interception were China, Greece, India, Italy, Russia, United Kingdom and the USA amongst others. One EU law report goes so far as to state, "governments are even promoting privacy-invasive tools in fields such as e-government."[16] There is extensive documentation and evidence of pervasive surveillance even among privacy oriented societies like the UK.[17] Justifications range from national security interests, to public order, public health and law enforcement [23].

There is a common argument made that one cannot have privacy if one wants security. States use the national security clause to do away with aspects of what is private and such that is shielded as private. This is because of the widespread belief and fact that criminals (and terrorists) shield themselves and their actions in cloaks of secrecy and anonymity. Thus, we can see that enforcing strict privacy standards through technological means can pose a problem and conflict with the general public interest.

2.8.3 Consent and (Informed) Choice – Still Knotty Issues

Privacy (and data protection) balances on two important elements: consent and choice (read informed consent and choice). Most identity management solutions are premised on this. Both consent and choice have been rather problematic in the data protection domain. An examination of the implementation and working of other choice based mechanisms like P3P will show that these have not worked optimally in protecting the interests of the users. This may be because systems are often designed with a "smart user" (a powerful or expert computer user) [24] in mind. But users often are not "smart," "sophisticated" or even "reasonable" enough to enable them make the "right"

[13] Article 21, Constitution of India.

[14] Article 12 of the Universal Declaration of Human Rights, Article 17 International Covenant on Civil and Political Rights, See EU Charter of Fundamental Rights of the European Union - Article 7 and 8.

[15] Some writers make the case for limits on privacy – see A Etzioni, The Limits of Privacy, Basic Books, (2000) and D Brin, The Transparent Society, Basic Books, (1999).

[16] Main outcomes of the technical workshop on Privacy-Enhancing Technologies, 4 July 2003 http://ec.europa.eu/justice_home/fsj/privacy/docs/lawreport/pet/200304-pet-outcome_en.pdf; see also L Cranor, "The Role of Privacy Enhancing Technologies, in Considering Consumer Privacy: A Resource for Policymakers and Practitioners, P Bruening (ed.), Center for Democracy and Technology, (March 2003).

[17] See the UK ICO's Surveillance Society Report 2006 and its May 2007 follow up at www.ico.gov.uk

or "necessary" choices. [25] They may not even have a choice in some cases e.g. if they wish to avail of a service they may have to consent or be deprived of the service. Often, they are not given a free choice (e.g. restriction on cross domain migration of avatars) or may be forced to make a choice to avail of a service they crucially depend upon. Other similar restrictions on behaviour may negate choice and action.

The "consent" aspect is a challenge too. Sherwin states, "…no one is sure just what consent is" [26]. Westen in similar vein stresses that when consent as a legal term has different meanings depending on the thing that is being consented to and the consequences of its non-existence [27].

From the above, we can infer that privacy laden user control approaches to identity management are inherently problematic given that privacy is coloured with cultural differences, there is strong state resistance to individual control and informed consent and choice, while widely deployed, remain complicated in practice.

2.9 Increase in User Liability

The problems with control are not only those inherent in its nature. There are also consequences that arise from control. Already most identity based service providers like Yahoo,[18] LiveJournal,[19] and Google[20] contractually provide that users are responsible for their actions and omissions.

The legal field is rich testing ground for the hypothesis that greater control results in greater liability, for example - command responsibility, parental responsibility, employer liability etc. In these cases, a right to control implies a duty to control and the responsibility for any consequent liability. A basic principle in law is that if one has a legal right of control and one ought to be in control, liability can be imposed whether or not the person concerned was in actual control [28].

Here are some further examples that reinforce the claim that the greater the user control, the greater the responsibility and liability.

2.9.1 E-Commerce

Perhaps the most germane example to illustrate how increased user control leads to increased user liability is the deployment of Chip and PIN cards in the UK.[21] The implementation of Chip and PIN[22] cards has meant that while users of such cards have gained extra security against misuse of their cards, they have acquired a corresponding responsibility and a duty to act with reasonable care towards safeguarding the cards and the PINs. Users have to take care of their cards, keep their PIN separate from the card, memorise their PIN, not write it down, not give it to anyone else, change it from time to time, not keep the card and PIN in one place, shield their entry of the PIN onto any PIN pad from shoulder surfers or security web cameras etc.

---

[18] See Yahoo! Terms of Service at http://uk.docs.yahoo.com/info/terms.html, specifically Terms Nos. 5 & 6.

[19] Live Journal Terms of Service at http://www.livejournal.com/legal/tos.bml, see terms IV, XIV and XVI.

[20] See Google Terms of Service, http://www.google.com/accounts/TOS?hl=en, Terms 5, 6 and 8.

[21] A Chip and PIN card means "a chip card that uses PIN as the preferred method of Cardholder verification at the point-of-sale (not only at ATMs)," http://www.chipandpin.co.uk/

[22] Personal Identification Number.

2.9.2 Data Protection Law

Data protection law imposes obligations and liabilities for all those who fall within the scope of the definition of "data controllers."[23] Directive 95/46/EC [29] prescribes the responsibilities and mandates for data controllers. A data controller must process personal data fairly and in compliance with the principles as enshrined in law, e.g. data must be processed fairly, lawfully, for a limited purpose. Individuals, it has been suggested, can be brought within the ambit of data protection legislation within certain limitations [30]. The *Bodil Lindqvist* judgment supports this principle [31]. In this case, a catechist in Sweden who had set up Internet pages permitting parishioners to obtain information from web pages containing information like people's full names, telephone numbers, hobbies, medical conditions, was held to have processed personal data within the meaning of the Article 3(1) of Directive 95/46/EC. This judgment thus shows that if an individual has control over identifying information (i.e. personal data); they incur a responsibility to act in accordance with established law and become accordingly liable for their actions or omissions. Users of identity management systems must then be similarly responsible, amongst other things, for the accuracy of their data, for maintaining the confidentiality of their accounts and passwords, notification of any breaches, security of their computer systems or they could cause themselves harm by becoming vulnerable to the effects of doing otherwise, as identity management companies would be inclined to shrug off any liability on the grounds that the user had not complied with reasonable expected practices, most of which are already embodied in most prevailing Terms of Service.

2.9.3 Intellectual Property Law

There are also intellectual property law cases that illustrate how control results in liability. For e.g. in *MGM v Grokster* [32], a case relating to whether distributors of P2P file sharing software[24] could be held liable for copyright infringement by users, it was held that the respondents "could not be held liable under a vicarious infringement theory because they did not monitor or control the software's use, had no agreed-upon right or current ability to supervise its use, and had no independent duty to police infringement" [33]. Grokster and StreamCast did not "operate and design" an integrated service of monitoring and control, they were decentralised and it was more of the users responsibility. But, the fact that it was the user who was "in control" in the P2P system of file sharing was certainly a contributory factor that led to widespread suits against individual file sharers by the music industry [34].

In another case, a lawsuit was filed by a leading business news organization against an investment group (and its employees) for unspecified damages for copyright infringement and violation of computer fraud and abuse law [35]. It is alleged

---

[23] Defined in Article 2(d) of Directive 95/46/EC as "'controller' shall mean the natural or legal person, public authority, agency or any other body which alone or jointly with others determines the purposes and means of the processing of personal data; where the purposes and means of processing are determined by national or Community laws or regulations, the controller or the specific criteria for his nomination may be designated by national or Community law.

[24] Peer to peer (or P2P) file sharing enables "users to share files online through an informal network of computers running the same software," http://www.onguardonline.gov/topics/p2p-security.aspx

that a single account set up by one of the investment group's employee was used by multiple persons on its US and non US-based network servers, other than the account holder to access articles on the news site. If this action succeeds, a clear liability will arise particularly for companies that permit or do not monitor how employees use their login ids.

2.9.4 Property Law

If we analyse the relationship between a landlord and his tenant there are some interesting observations to be made to support our user-control and liability hypothesis. A tenant is liable for his or her activities in the place of occupation after he or she is put in control of the premises. Conditions of lease or rental agreement make this very clear. There are also regulations that support this premise.

An identity management company/provider is like a landlord. Users are akin to tenants. When they use the services of identity providers they enter into a contractual relationship with the company and a legally binding relationship comes about much like that of the landlord and tenant.[25] There is one significant difference however. While a tenant is generally aware of his rights and responsibilities (either by virtue of tenancy agreements and terms becoming streamlined, commonplace or because tenants are aware of the dangers of entering into such relationship without reviewing terms that may go against them), the same may not be true of users who use the services of identity management companies or providers. Hitting the "I accept" button of terms of service without reading the full terms and conditions that are binding has become bit of a standard practice amongst users of Internet based services.

The tenant as occupier of the premises may also have other responsibilities – e.g. shielding other people on the property from any harm that is foreseeable,[26] or even making sure that he or she does not take any unreasonable measures to stop people venturing into the property or premises and must even take steps to warn of any harm that might be caused by erecting signs etc.[36] Users are similarly being provided with the means to erect digital fences for their identity and this means that they will have to ensure that they do make use of these means as a consequent duty has now become attached to them. This will mean that they will have to take due care and be responsible for what happens within the boundaries of their digital identity fence or any effects caused thereby.[27]

2.9.5 Tort Law

Since the relationship of the identity management systems and users has been compared to that of a car manufacturer and car driver by a certain section of the identity management industry [37], it is relevant to examine this relationship further in the light of its legal implications.

A car manufacturer designs the car. A prospective driver buys the car. The driver may have bought the car because it was popular, of a particular model, gave good mileage, was recommended or for any other reason. The driver uses the car to get from one destination to another.

---

[25] What this analogy mostly relates to are cases where identity providers provide users with identity that users may be in possession and use of but ultimately do not have ownership rights to.

[26] See the UK Occupier's Liability Act 1984.

[27] E.g. as explained in 2.9.2.

The driver controls the car. He starts it and keeps it going at whatever pace is required. He uses the steering wheel, the gears, and the brakes in the process. There are certain norms and rules that the car driver must respect while driving the car. He must ensure that he wears a seat belt (for his own safety), drive at a safe speed, show respect to other users, ensure that the car is in working order. He is expected to be reasonable, prudent and careful. The law imposes a duty on the car driver – a duty of caution and care and if he fails to exercise that caution and care, the driver will be responsible for any consequences that result and will be held liable.

Similarly, the user of an identity management system will be expected to use the identity management system appropriately, adhere to its norms, and understand its limitations. But just as there are good, average and bad drivers, the same is the case for users of identity management systems. Just like drivers, users of identity management systems may be inexperienced, alcoholic, drugged, distracted, drowsy, fatigued or simply reckless in their digital behaviour.

A driver is also required to maintain the car. However, in a case there is a mechanical defect in the car and the driver was unaware of the same, he may have a defence in law to any prosecution that arises [38]. Similarly, if there are circumstances beyond the control of the driver that lead him to lose control of the car, the driver may also successfully plead a defence e.g. nails on the road, stormy weather [39]. Thus, while there may be mitigating circumstances to allow a driver to escape liability, if it can be successfully proved that s/he had control over the car and/or knowingly broke the rules s/he will be made accountable for their actions.

The above examples show how liability follows control or is the flip side of control. In the long run, as identity management systems give more and more control to the user, the user will also acquire greater liability for actions or omissions in regard to the use of such systems.[28] Therefore, there is a pressing need to empower users, the biggest stakeholders in the identity management stakes.

3 Empowering Users

There are two key factors in effective control, which also extend in application to the digital realm: awareness and action. This section focuses primarily on the awareness aspect, which as currently being implemented leaves much to be desired.

3.1 User Awareness

Only if the user is aware of how control in identity management system truly works, its true scope, limits and the associated the obligations and liabilities, will user control be truly effective. Raising awareness has been a key focus of the data protection regime, and a number of steps have been and are undertaken in this light: e.g. establishment of a Data Protection Day, national data protection authorities undertake

[28] In this light see Recommendation 7 in R Anderson, R Böhme, R Clayton & T Moore, "Security, Economics and the Internal Market," http://www.enisa.europa.eu/doc/pdf/report_sec_econ_&_int_mark_20080131.pdf (2008).

publicity exercises. But does awareness work or is it optimally working? Apparently not [40]. Even the Council of Europe website acknowledges that, "it is a well-known fact that European citizens are generally unfamiliar with data protection issues and unaware of their rights in this respect" [41].

Awareness is the condition of "being aware" or "conscious,"[29] a relative state of understanding or knowing (fully, reasonably or partially), which may or may not form the basis of rational action. There is a pressing need for increasing responsible public and private awareness of identity management systems be it through public information, education, media broadcasts etc. The results of the many excellent research studies into identity management systems, their scope, limitations and advantages need to be simplified and disseminated to wider audiences – something the academic community must take charge of, to do away with current limited approaches which are largely subject to different biases.

3.2 Proposal for a Control-Liability Notice[30]

There is a pressing need for identity management companies to assert and inform users of what levels of control a particular identity management system offers and what its remits and limitations are and also make clear that the use of identity management systems will leave them open to greater responsibility and liability. This must be done in an explicit, clear and concise manner, unlike long-winded privacy policies or Terms of Service that people hardly ever read[31] or do not read in entirety. There is a vital need to simmer complexities into simplicity.

The Article 29 Data Protection Working Party set up under Article 29 of Directive 95/46/EC proposed a layered approach to data protection notices: *short, condensed and full* [42]. This may be a good place to start. The UK Information Commissioner's Office has given guidance over what an effective data protection "notice" should constitute and this could be adapted and used as a template for a "control-liability" notice. A draft format is outlined in Figure 1.

This notice[32] could be placed prominently and must be aimed at general users not shrouded in legal terminology and aimed at legal experts. Such notices could have an embedded code that makes them quickly readable and acceptable line by line before users can proceed to the actual use of the application.

[29] See the Oxford English Dictionary. Aware has also been defined as meaning: watchful, vigilant, cautious, on one's guard, informed, cognizant, conscious, sensible.

[30] At this stage, this is a working proposal, a full analysis is out with the limited scope of this paper.

[31] The general view is that Privacy policies and Terms of Service are quite complicated and shrouded in legal jargon and not at all aimed effectively at users, rather in attempting to meet the legal requirement they have failed on this ground. See A McDonald & L Cranor, "The Cost of Reading Privacy Policies," The 36th Research Conference on Communication, Information, and Internet Policy, 26-28 September 2008; V Arlington & I Pollach, "What's wrong with online privacy policies?" Communications of the ACM, Vol. 50, Issue 9, pp 103-108, at 107, (September 2007) and G Milne and M Culnan, "Strategies for Reducing Online Privacy Risks: Why Consumers Read (or Don't Read) Online Privacy Notices" J. Interactive Marketing, 18, 3, pp. 15–29, (Summer 2004).

[32] We acknowledge the limitations and challenges of notices in putting forth this proposal.

CONTROL-LIABILITY NOTICE

[Name of Identity Management System]

Statement of Onus of Control

[state who is in control-whether it is the user or the provider & who makes the decisions]

Statement of Nature of Control

[what users have control over & what they do not have control over]

Rights and Obligations of Users

[short, clear and concise statement/local language based]

Statement of Liability

[user actions/omissions that would incur liability & nature of such liability]

Fig. 1. Control-Liability Notice

4 Conclusion

The user control approach to identity management is not to be disregarded despite the problems it is challenged with. It is a positive approach, but it also has limitations and effects that cannot be pushed to one side in a holistic treatment of the identity management debate. The terminological confusion, the limitations of identity control, privacy and security, the human factors, the fusion of the non-digital and digital worlds and merging of actors must be taken into account.

The most important effect of all is how greater user control in identity management may result in greater user liability. This is why users need all the more to be empowered through awareness of what identity management systems can and cannot do for them and what they themselves will become responsible for. At the moment, this is not very clear to users. The role of academics in responsible dissemination of research information to the general public about identity technologies and systems is the need of the hour. A possible way forward is the control-liability notice, which could be a starting point for further research in the area. Such a notice will enable greater consciousness and make things clear not just for individual users but also for the organisations that implement it.

Acknowledgements

The author wishes to thank all the reviewers who contributed to the shaping of this paper with their valuable comments, suggestions and feedback.

References

1. Bhargav-Spantzely, A., Camenisch, J., Gross, T., Sommer, D.: User centricity: A Taxonomy and Open Issues. In: DIM 2006, Proceedings of the Second ACM Workshop on Digital Identity Management, pp. 1–10 (2006)
2. Cameron, K.: The Seven Laws of Identity, December 5 (2005), `http://www.identityblog.com/stories/2005/05/13/TheLawsOfIdentity.pdf`

3. Sun Microsystems, Identity Management Solutions: Overview, http://www.sun.com/software/products/identity/ (As at January 5, 2009)
4. OpenID.Net, What is OpenID, http://openid.net/what/ (As at January 5, 2009)
5. Higgins: Open Source Identity Framework, The Eclipse Foundation, http://www.eclipse.org/higgins/index.php (As at January 5, 2009)
6. Hansen, M.: Marrying Transparency Tools with User-controlled Identity Management," The Future of Identity in the Information Society. In: Fischer-Hubner, S., Duquenoy, P., Zucatto, A., Martucci, L. (eds.) Proceedings of the 3rd IFIP WG 9.2, 9.6/11.6, 11.7/FIDIS International Summer School, Karlstad, Sweden, August 2007, pp. 199–222. Springer, Heidelberg (2008)
7. Edwards, L., Brown, I.: Data Control and Social Networking: Irreconcilable Ideas? In: Matwyshyn, A. (ed.) Harboring Data: Information Security, Law and the Corporation. Stanford University Press (2009), http://ssrn.com/abstract=1148732
8. Dhamija, R., Dusseault, L.: The Seven Flaws of Identity Management: Usability and Security Challenges. IEEE Security & Privacy 6(2), 24–29 (2008), http://ieeexplore.ieee.org/iel5/8013/4489835/04489846.pdf?isnumber=4489835&prod=JNL&arnumber=4489846&arnumber=4489846&arSt=24&ared=29&arAuthor=Dhamija%2C+R.%3B+Dusseault%2C+L; Gotterbarn, D.: Informatics and Professional Responsibility. Science and Engineering Ethics 7.2, 221–230 (2001)
9. Viacom International Inc., v YouTube Inc., YouTube LLC and Google Inc., Case 1:07-cv-02103-LLS, March 13 (2007), http://docs.justia.com/cases/federal/district-courts/new-york/nysdce/1:2007cv02103/302164/1/
10. British Telecommunications plc, Comprehensive Identity Management: Balancing Cost, Risk and Convenience in Identity Management , White Paper, p 7 (2007), http://www.btglobalservices.com/business/global/en/docs/whitepapers/22872_Identity_Mgmt_wp_en.pdf
11. National Computing Centre, Beware fake anti-virus programs, Industry News (Winter 2008), http://www.nccmembership.co.uk/pooled/articles/BF_WEBART/view.asp?Q=BF_WEBART_308688
12. Acquisti, A., Grossklags, J.: Privacy and Rationality in Decision Making. IEEE Security & Privacy 3(1), 26–33 (2005)
13. Erasmus, D.: The Praise of Folly, 1514
14. Laurie, B.: OpenID: Phishing Heaven, p. 187, January 19 (2007), http://www.links.org/?; Leyden, J.: How Poor Crypto Housekeeping Left OpenID Open to Abuse, The Register, August 13 (2008)
15. Schneier, B.: Secrets and Lies: Digital Security in a Networked World, p. xi (2000)
16. Eap, T., Hatala, M., Gašević, D.: Enabling User Control with Personal Identity Management. In: 2007 IEEE International Conference on Services Computing, SCC 2007, pp. 60–67 (2007)
17. Joinson, A., Paine, C.: Self-disclosure, privacy and the Internet. In: Joinson, A., et al. (eds.) The Oxford Handbook of Internet Psychology, ch. 16, pp. 237–252 at 248–249. Oxford University Press, Oxford
18. Lyon, D.: Surveillance Studies: An Overview. Polity, Malden (2007)
19. Post, R.: Three Concepts of Privacy. 89 George. L J., 2087 (2001)

20. Heisenberg, D., Fandel, M.-H.: Projecting EU Regimes Abroad: The EU Data Protection Directive as Global Standard. Paper presented at the Annual Meeting of the American Political Science Association, Boston Marriott Copley Place, Sheraton Boston & Hynes Convention Center, Boston, Massachusetts, August 28 (2002), http://www.allacademic.com/meta/p65517_index.html
21. De Boni, M., Prigmore, M.: Cultural Aspects of Internet Privacy. In: Proceedings of the UKAIS Conference, Leeds (2002), http://www.leedsmet.ac.uk/ies/comp/staff/deboni/papers/Cultural_Aspects_of_Internet_Privacy.pdf; Ruiz, B.: Privacy in Telecommunications: A European and an American Approach, p 40. Martinus Nijhoff Publishers (1997)
22. Privacy International, The 2007 International Privacy Ranking, December 28 (2007), http://www.privacyinternational.org/article.shtml?cmd%5B347%5D=x-347-559597
23. UK House of Commons Home Affairs Committee, A Surveillance Society? Fifth Report of Session 2007-2008, Volume I, Report, together with formal minutes, published on June 8, 2008 by authority of the House of Commons London, The Stationery Office Limited, http://www.publications.parliament.uk/pa/cm200708/cmselect/cmhaff/58/58i.pdf
24. Wu, T.: Application-Centered Internet Analysis. 85 Va. L. Rev. 1163, 1203–1204 (1999); see also Goldsmith, J., Wu, T.: Who Controls the Internet? Illusions of a Borderless World, p.123 (2006)
25. Ohm, P.: The Myth Of The Superuser: Fear, Risk, And Harm Online, U. of Colorado Law Legal Studies Research Paper, No. 07-14, http://Ssrn.Com/Abstract=967372
26. Sherwin, E.: Infelicitous Sex. Legal Theory 2, 209–231 at p 229 (1996)
27. Westen, P.: Introduction at p 307, and Chapter 8. The Confusions of Consent, 309–336 in The Logic of Consent: The Diversity and Deceptiveness of Consent as a Defense to Criminal Conduct (2004)
28. Samson v Aitchison [1912] AC 844; 82 LJPC 1; 107 LT 106; 28 TLR 559
29. Directive 95/46/EC of the European Parliament and of the Council of 24 October 1995 on the protection of individuals with regard to the processing of personal data and on the free movement of such data
30. Grey, T., et al.: US and EU Authorities Review Privacy Threats on Social Networking Sites: Part 2. ITLT 16 5 (7) (May 1, 2008); Wong, R.: Social Networking: Anybody is a Data Controller!, Working Paper, Revised Version (October 2008), http://ssrn.com/abstract=1271668
31. European Court of Human Rights, Judgment of 6 November 2003, Case C-101/01
32. Metro-Goldwyn-Mayer Studios Inc. v Grokster, Ltd. (04-480) 545 U.S. 913 (2005) 380 F.3d 1154
33. Metro-Goldwyn-Mayer Studios Inc. v Grokster, Ltd., as above
34. EFF, RIAA v. The People: Four Years Later (August 2007), http://w2.eff.org/IP/P2P/riaa_at_four.pdf; Reuters, 459 European P2P users sued, October 7 (2004), http://www.afterdawn.com/news/archive/5675.cfm; J Borland, RIAA sues 261 file swappers, CNET News.com, September 8 (2003), http://news.com.com/2100-1023_3-5072564.html; Engel, J.: Music Industry Targets CMU, The Saginaw News, April 16 (2007) (quoting the RIAA as filing 18,000 lawsuits)
35. The Financial Times Limited v The Blackstone Group LP et al., US District Court Southern District of New York, Case Number 1:2009cv00783, Filed on January 28 (2009)
36. Poppleton v Trustees of the Portsmouth Youth Activities Committee [2008] EWCA Civ 646

37. Cameron, K.: The Seven Laws of Identity, Version 2, August 18 (2008), http://www.identityblog.com/?p=1007
38. R v Spurge [1961] 2 All ER 688
39. Burns v Bidder [1996] 3 All ER 29
40. Privacy Awareness Not Backed up by Behaviour, Survey Finds. Out-Law News, August 13 (2008), http://www.out-law.com/page-9345
41. Council Of Europe, http://www.coe.int/t/e/legal_affairs/legal_co-operation/data_protection/Data_Protection_Day_default.asp
42. Opinion on More Harmonised Information Provisions, WP 100, November 25 (2004), http://ec.europa.eu/justice_home/fsj/privacy/docs/wpdocs/2004/wp100_en.pdf and Appendices: http://ec.europa.eu/justice_home/fsj/privacy/docs/wpdocs/2004/wp100a_en.pdf

Privacy Awareness: A Means to Solve the Privacy Paradox?

Stefanie Pötzsch

Technische Universität Dresden*
Faculty of Computer Science
D-01062 Dresden, Germany
stefanie.poetzsch@tu-dresden.de

Abstract. People are limited in their resources, i.e. they have limited memory capabilities, cannot pay attention to too many things at the same time, and forget much information after a while; computers do not suffer from these limitations. Thus, revealing personal data in electronic communication environments and being completely unaware of the impact of privacy might cause a lot of privacy issues later. Even if people are privacy aware in general, the so-called privacy paradox shows that they do not behave according to their stated attitudes. This paper discusses explanations for the existing dichotomy between the intentions of people towards disclosure of personal data and their behaviour. We present requirements on tools for privacy-awareness support in order to counteract the privacy paradox.

Keywords: Privacy, Privacy Awareness, Privacy Paradox.

1 Introduction

The protection of privacy is an important issue in modern information society. The release of personal information in electronic communication environments may cause severe privacy issues in the future, if people are completely unaware of their privacy. Secondary uses of data promote these problems further [22]. Even if people have a theoretical interest in keeping their privacy when acting on the Internet and do not want everybody to know their personal data and private information, studying their real online communication often shows a different behaviour. This seems to be a paradox.

In this paper we present an approach for how the privacy paradox can be addressed. Therefore options for supporting awareness of privacy by technical means are discussed and requirements on these tools are outlined.

The structure of the paper is as follows. In Section 2, we briefly summarise two understandings of privacy which are relevant in the scope of interactive applications on the Internet, and based on that definitions we introduce our concept of privacy awareness. In Section 3 we present studies about the attitudes of people towards

* The research leading to these results has received funding from the European Community's Seventh Framework Programme (FP7/2007-2013) under grant agreement no. 216483.

V. Matyáš et al. (Eds.): The Future of Identity, IFIP AICT 298, pp. 226–236, 2009.

privacy and their actual behaviour and we discuss potential reasons for the dichotomy between both. Objectives and requirements for technical tools to support privacy awareness are outlined in Section 4. We conclude the paper in Section 5 and indicate directions for further research.

2 Privacy Awareness of People

The term privacy awareness is not well established in the literature. Hence, as a starting point, we present interpretations of privacy, which are taken into consideration for this work. After the concept of awareness is introduced, we give a definition of privacy awareness.

2.1 Privacy

Various meanings and dimensions of privacy have been discussed in literature (e.g. [3, 7, 15, 16]). Instead of going into detail on all these concepts, only two viewpoints are presented here, which are most important when discussing privacy awareness for interactive applications such as e-Commerce scenarios or Web communities. The two viewpoints are the privacy of personal sphere and the privacy of personal data.

- **Privacy of personal sphere**
  Samuel Warren and Louis Brandeis published the influential paper "The Right to Privacy" in 1890 and defined privacy as "the right to be let alone" [23]. In this regard, privacy is understood as solitude and non-intrusion. It refers to (a) the secrecy of an individual's own thoughts, properties and actions and (b) the amount of data about others which flows towards the individual and possibly interrupt him/her [5]. In everyday life, this kind of privacy is respected due to well-established social norms. People are easily able to understand whether they are in an open-plan office with several colleagues around or if they are in a mountain shelter with nothing other than green grass and stones surrounding them. In the first case it is obvious that documents, which lie on a table, may be noticed - intentionally or unintentionally - by others and that colleagues at any time may interrupt the work of the individual.
- **Privacy of personal data**
  Another view on privacy, often applied by computer scientists and labelled as information privacy, refers to "the right to select what personal information about me is known to what people" [24]. This definition stresses the aspect of control over information about the individual, his/her conversations and his/her actions. The disclosure of personal data is bound to the recipient and to the usage and, in contrast to the concept of solitude, actively determined by the individual as owner of the data. To be able to select which data to disclose to whom, does not only comprise options to keep data confidential but also options to disclose data to selected receivers, e.g. through the availability of communication means.

Comparing these interpretations, it is to say that the first one considers especially social aspects of privacy, whereas the second definition is more focussed on the data and therefore technical-oriented. Both views need to be taken into account when solutions that support privacy of individuals in technically mediated interactions with each other should be designed.

2.2 Privacy Awareness

Awareness is based on an individual's attention, perception and cognition of physical as well as non-physical objects. The state of being aware of something fades away as soon as there is no longer any stimulus present. Information from the environment or from other people constitutes such stimuli. Since the focus of this paper lies on privacy in the context of interactive scenarios between customers and service providers as well as collaborative use cases, where arbitrary entities interact with each other, the privacy awareness of people will be discussed.

Taking into account the two views on privacy presented above, privacy awareness of an individual encompasses the attention, perception and cognition of:

- *whether* others receive or have received personal information about him/her, his/her presence and activities,
- *which* personal information others receive or have received in detail,
- *how* these pieces of information are or may be *processed* and *used*, and
- *what amount* of information about the presence and activities of others might reach and/or interrupt the individual.

There are two main parameters for content and representation of information that serves as a stimulus for privacy awareness: the individual and the application. On the one hand, privacy-awareness information are of general nature, i.e., independent from individual preferences and independent from a particular application. On the other hand, privacy-awareness information are geared personally to an individual or to a specific application. These different dimensions of privacy-awareness information can be found in Table 1 and are described below.

- **User-independent vs. User-specific privacy-awareness information**
  Means to build up and enhance privacy awareness can be identical for each user of a system or be tailored to group-specific or even to individual requirements and needs. Whereas privacy disclaimers on Websites can be seen as an example of general, user-independent privacy-awareness hints, the evaluation of individual privacy preferences can serve as a basis for more individualised and user-specific features of privacy-awareness support.
- **Application-independent vs. Application-specific privacy-awareness information**
  A broad spectrum of possibilities exists for raising the awareness of people for privacy issues and sensitising them towards their own personal privacy – in terms of personal sphere as well as in terms of personal data. On the one end of the spectrum privacy-awareness information is of general nature, i.e., independent from any special use case. On the other end, information regarding privacy is tailored towards a specific application.

  Talks, privacy campaigns or tutorials, e.g. the PRIME General Public Tutorial [18], are various means of providing application-independent privacy-awareness information. In such cases, the wish of people to be informed is necessarily required. They actively need to access the tutorial, attend the talk or read the campaign and afterwards apply their gained application-independent privacy awareness in concrete use cases, when they act within specific applications. Additionally, the application might have its own features for privacy awareness integrated and thus provide information which fits well in the current situation and privacy issues that may arise within the specific application. Obviously, intermediate levels and combinations between application-independent and application-specific information for privacy awareness exist and are necessary to support privacy awareness of people comprehensively.

Table 1. Dimensions of Privacy-Awareness Information

	User-independent	User-specific
Application-independent	*Talks, Campaigns, Tutorials*	*Individual advice from a Privacy Commissioner*
Application-specific	*Privacy Disclaimers on Websites*	*Feedback from Website's policy evaluation (e.g. Privacy Bird)*

3 The Privacy Paradox

Privacy awareness enables people to make informed decisions and should lead to less unintentional privacy-invasive behaviour. Consequently, it can be assumed that people who are conscious about privacy issues and state the intention to protect their personal data and their personal sphere, i.e., who can be considered privacy-aware, will act according to their statements if the have the choice between different options for action. However, several studies show a contradictory finding and are outlined in the next section. We discuss reasons for the observed phenomenon considering an economic approach to explain the behaviour first and the misconception of recipients of information second.

3.1 Studies about Intentions and Behaviour

An online shopping experiment compared self-reported privacy preferences of people with their actual self-disclosing behaviour and found out that a majority of the test participants – regardless of their previously stated privacy attitudes – disclosed a large amount of personal information [21]. Similar results are shown in another study about intentions and behaviours of people towards privacy [17]. The participants provided significantly more personal data than they claimed beforehand. Within this study the researchers also tested whether the perception of risks is more salient and has a negative influence on the stated intentions of people when they are asked in general, whereas this is not the case in real situations when they decide to disclose data. This hypothesis was supported by the results of the study. A further study was conducted in order to test the ratio between people's value for personalisation and their concern for privacy [6]. A core finding from this research indicates that the value of personalisation is nearly two times more influential in the actual decision to use personalisation services and therefore to disclose personal data than the concern for privacy. This result shows that, even if people may be privacy-aware in general, they need to be at least two times more aware of privacy than of the benefits which they can gain from personalisation in order to make a balanced decision about whether personal data to disclose and which.

The contradiction between attitudes towards privacy and actual behaviour, identified in all of the cited studies, is called the *privacy paradox* [17]. It would be of further interest to investigate the existence of this phenomenon in Web communities. First results of Acquisti and Gross [1] in this field indicate that a share of privacy-concerned people simply does not join in online social networks, which is not surprising. However, privacy-concerned people who are members of an online social network, share nearly the same amount of personal data (e.g. birth date, sexual orientation or personal address) as other members of the network. This indicates the existence of the privacy paradox in online social networking applications.

3.2 Balancing Values

When searching for explanations for the privacy paradox, the appreciation of values seems to play an important role.

The balancing of benefits and costs can be described by a utility function [4]:

$$U(X) = \text{Benefit} - \text{Cost} \tag{1}$$

On the one hand, there are several benefits resulting from the disclosure of personal information in specific situations. On the other hand, people have their attitudes and evaluation of privacy, which can be seen as costs of disclosure. Table 2 presents arguments for both perspectives. This occurs first in eCommerce situations as an example of a traditional customer-service provider orientated approach and, second, in Web communities which illustrate interactions among arbitrary individuals.

Table 2. Benefits and Costs for Disclosure of Personal Data

	Benefits	Costs
eCommerce	– Convenience – Automated processes – Price premiums – Selected information	– Price discrimination – Marketing spam – Identity theft
Web Communities	– Social exchange – Relationships – Collaborations – Reputation	– Identity theft – Marketing spam – Stalking, Kidnapping – Negative reputation in other contexts

If people are asked in general about privacy, and not in a specific situation, many of them are to some extent privacy-aware, as the cited studies show. However in real situations the concrete value of privacy (*costs*) is hard to estimate and is no longer salient to people. The quantity of possible price premiums or the "universe of new friends" (*benefits*) is primarily advertised; it is just a few clicks and disclosure of a few personal data items away. It is assumed that the privacy awareness of people in such situations is low, since there is a lack of stimuli at the moment of attention. The previously summarised studies support this hypothesis for eCommerce scenarios. With regard to the handling of personal data of members in social networks, this seems to be valid for Web community scenarios, too [10, 1], although the type of benefits and costs differ slightly. Web communities offer primarily social contacts, easy ways to find new friends, business cooperation, and so on. Since profiles of Community members are accessible for a lot of people on the Internet, identity theft in these cases is possible without great efforts. The risks of becoming a victim of crimes, which are based on personal information, or getting bad reputation in other contexts are costs of the disclosure of personal data which are discussed in the media from time to time. However, such issues do not appear to be salient to people in special situations when they interact within a Web community.

3.3 Misconception of Recipients

People are less concerned about their privacy if they have established relationships with other entities who are the perceived recipients [19]. This causes additional privacy issues especially in Web communities, when members simply do not realise or "forget" that they potentially share personal information not only with some friends or a small group of forum members, but with a quiet mass of all Internet users who may have access to the social network or read their postings about their private life on public bulletin boards.

For conducting a study on "social phishing", researchers have used freely accessible profile data from a social network [12]. After completion, the researchers explained the experiment on a Website and provided a public forum for anonymous discussion among the groups of victims and their friends. From this feedback it can be learnt that many of the subjects simply did not understand how information about them and their relationships were obtained. They believed that data on the social network is not public and is only accessible to their friends. However, it was not clear to them that anyone on the Web had access to their profiles and can snoop around in personal information. This fact illustrates the privacy paradox in terms of Web communities, since people obviously do not want everybody to have access to their private data. However, they publish this information on online social networks and do not realise that they provide their names, hobbies, phone numbers, addresses etc. not only to their friends, but to a broad public on the Internet.

4 Tools to Support Privacy Awareness

In principle, there exist two options to encounter the privacy paradox: either the behaviour of people would have to be adapted with their attitudes or vice versa. In order to enhance privacy, the first option should be pursued, i.e., people should be "reminded" about their intentions to protect privacy during interactions. Therefore tools and features need to be designed and developed that increase privacy awareness in specific software applications.

4.1 Objectives of Tools to Support Privacy Awareness

Privacy awareness is important for people in order to make informed decisions about the disclosure of data and to control the amount of possible interruptions during their work. Whereas the data disclosure refers to information privacy as defined previously, the consideration of possible interruptions caused by other parties is related to the notion of privacy as personal sphere.

It is usually incumbent on the users of applications not to forget their values of privacy whereas the scaling pan with the benefits for disclosure of personal data is advertised by providers of services and appears obvious in software applications. Tools for privacy-awareness support should help to increase available privacy-relevant information in order to balance the scale.

In Web communities, for instance, tools for privacy-awareness support can remind individuals about the mass of "quiet users" who are involved in the community only in a passive manner or about the providers of social networks who also have access to data from the profiles such as e-mail addresses, telephone numbers or special interests. To restrict access to contact data helps to keep these personal data items confidential as well as to protect the personal sphere. In this way, no unwanted offers will reach the individual by e-mail, phone or letter.

Further, especially in Web communities people are not only responsible for their own privacy protection. When thinking about relationship-based access control (friends-of-my-friends) to personal profiles or possibilities of putting photos and videos of others online maybe without their consent, privacy awareness of people should encompass the privacy of persons related to them, e.g. their friends or other persons on the photos and in the videos, as well.

Tools for privacy-awareness support would surely not cover all of those issues, but they aim to prevent uninformed and unintended privacy violations.

4.2 Requirements on Tools to Support Privacy Awareness

For the design of tools that support privacy awareness, a number of requirements emerge and should be considered. In the following section, these requirements are pointed out and explained. Ambivalences, which ensue from the demand for a high flexibility of tools, user-control and freedom of choice for the individual on the one hand and strict definition of rules for implementation on the other hand, are discussed.

- **Measure privacy attitude of people**
  In order to "remind" people about their privacy attitude in specific situations, their general attitude have to be known by the support tool. There are two ways to capture the privacy preferences of people: (a) ask them directly or (b) gather preferences from observation of actual behaviour. The latter option has at least two problems. First, monitoring of the behaviour might be privacy-invasive itself and, second, the privacy paradox describes the gap between attitude towards privacy and behaviour. Hence, drawing conclusions from monitored behaviour would simply not help. Asking people directly means in fact to let them customise their tool for privacy-awareness support. The challenge here is to motivate people to configure and to change preferences, particularly since usually people rarely customise their preferences but rather use default settings [14, 10]. Cognitive science refers to this phenomenon as the "status quo bias".

- **No invasion to privacy itself**
  As discussed previously in this paper, privacy means not only minimal disclosure of data to the public, but also minimal interruptions. Thus, the tool for privacy-awareness support should not interrupt its user all time and be annoying to him/her.
- **Understandable for target group**
  The choice of words and descriptions need to be understandable for ordinary people, not only for computer specialists. It is not sufficient to rely on expert opinions about what may be useful to display and how to inform people. As pointed out by Adams and Sasse, it is important to identify and consider the perception, understanding and needs of the target group for designing usable applications [2]. The majority of people is not an expert and their level of technical knowledge differs.
- **Consider cognitive boundaries**
  The concept of "bounded rationality", which is well known in cognitive science, signifies the limited ability of individuals to acquire, process, and remember information [20]. That is, even if people would theoretically have all privacy-relevant information available, they will not be able to use all the information for making a rational decision, however they apply a simplified mental model. When designing tools to support privacy awareness this needs to be considered and opportunities have to be researched how to present data to people in a way that they are able to handle it cognitively.
- **Tailored to the specifics of situations**
  Tools to support privacy awareness should influence people's behaviour in concrete situations and therefore need to be user-specific and application-specific. Presentation of information should depend on the current context, i.e., the task, kind of information, recipients, usage, etc. This means either a rule set of all possible contexts has to be defined beforehand by the system's designers or users need to configure their personal sets of contexts, which means making an additional effort for them.
- **Offer support, no assumption of responsibility**
  Tools need to be designed in such a way that they offer support to people. The tools should not convey the impression that they fully protect the privacy of the users according to their preferences or that there is no longer any need for people to be aware of privacy and to take care for themselves.
- **Performance**
  It is essential that tools or features for privacy-awareness support do not decrease performance of the primary application to a perceptible extent, since people will not accept long delays. This is documented for usage of Web sites [9], anonymisation services [13], and it is assumed to be true for privacy-awareness support as a secondary feature as well.

4.3 Opportunities and Limitations of Technical Solutions

Privacy awareness can be supported by several technical tools and mechanisms. Evaluation of privacy metrics or individual privacy preferences and policies are already used as basis for provision of user-specific privacy-awareness features. Privacy Bird [8], for instance, evaluates the matching between the stated privacy preferences of people and Website policies. The tool provides warning signals in case of conflict and thus raises awareness of the user. Indeed, the evaluation process is of what is stated about access to and usage of personal data by the provider of the Website and not how the data really is processed. However, even if actual information processing is considered, the reliability of such tools always depends on the calculations in the background and can only capture technical processing of personal data within the application. For Web communities, not all the information that others would notice and probably store on their own systems individually is ascertainable by metrics and policies. Individuals may find multiple ways of copying information, even if such methods were not technically foreseen, e.g. if a photo sharing community does not offer the option to download photos from others, this does not mean that members cannot take a screenshot of a portrait. In this case, it cannot be guaranteed that a photo cannot be copied, and the individual cannot even be informed if someone makes a copy. The owner of the photo might get a hint of the possibility that another Internet user can make a copy of the photo before putting it online. However, such warnings carry the risk of not being particularly helpful in increasing privacy awareness in that specific situation; rather they can lead either to ignorance or paranoia. Both should be avoided of course.

5 Conclusions and Future Work

In this paper an introduction to privacy awareness is given. Several studies, mainly from the field of eCommerce, are examined and show the existence of the privacy paradox, i.e., a discrepancy between the stated attitudes of people and their actual behaviour regarding handling of personal data. This also seems to be valid for Web communities where there additionally is a gap caused by the difference between the intended groups of recipients of information and those people who actually can access these data legitimately.

To solve the privacy paradox no solely technical solutions are needed to "protect" people from their own behaviour. People can make informed decisions when not only the benefits of disclosing personal data are pointed out to them, but when they are also reminded about their intentions towards privacy and the existence of possible data recipients. We argue that solutions should also consider cognitive and behavioural aspects by supporting the privacy awareness of people in all online situations. Further, the objective of informed decisions will be facilitated if people are not only aware of the fact that they are going to disclose personal data, but also about the potential consequences. Recent research about transparency enhancing tools (TETs) aims to investigate technical options for providing such information about facts and consequences of disclosure of personal data [11].

The implications of enhanced privacy awareness among Web community members on development of relationships, group awareness and collaborations will be the topic of further research on cognitive and behavioural aspects of privacy and privacy awareness.

Acknowledgements

Many thanks to Stefan Berthold, Rainer Böhme, Hans Hedbom, and Andreas Pfitzmann in particular and my colleagues from TU Dresden in general for inspiration and suggestions to improve this work. I also would like to thank the participants of the IFIP/FIDIS Summer School 2008 for helpful discussions and especially Diane Whitehouse for her comments and improvements of the language.

References

1. Acquisti, A., Gross, R.: Imagined communities: Awareness, information sharing, and privacy on the Facebook. In: Danezis, G., Golle, P. (eds.) PET 2006. LNCS, vol. 4258, pp. 36–58. Springer, Heidelberg (2006)
2. Adams, A., Sasse, M.A.: Privacy in multimedia communications: Protecting users, not just data. In: Blandford, A., Vanderdonkt, J. (eds.) People and Computers XV - Interaction without frontiers. Joint Proceedings of HCI 2001, pp. 49–64 (2001)
3. Altman, I.: Privacy: A conceptual analysis. Environment and Behavior 8(1), 7–29 (1976)
4. Awad, N.F., Krishnan, M.S.: The Personalization Privacy Paradox: An Empirical Evaluation of Information Transparency and the Willingness to be Profiled Online for Personalization. MIS Quarterly 30(1), 13–28 (2006)
5. Birnholtz, J.P., Gutwin, C., Hawkey, K.: Privacy in the open: how attention mediates awareness and privacy in open-plan offices. In: Proceedings of the 2007 international ACM Conference on Supporting Group Work. GROUP 2007, Sanibel Island, Florida, USA, November 04 - 07, pp. 51–60. ACM, New York (2007)
6. Chellappa, R.K., Sin, R.G.: Personalization versus Privacy: An Empirical Examination of the Online Consumer's Dilemma. Inf. Technol. and Management 6(2-3), 181–202 (2005)
7. Clarke, R.: Introduction to Dataveillance and Information Privacy, and Definitions and Terms. Latest revs. (August 7, 2006), `http://www.anu.edu.au/people/Roger.Clarke/DV/Intro.html` (last access 2008-07-29)
8. Cranor, L.F., Arjula, M., Guduru, P.: Use of a P3P user agent by early adopters. In: Proceedings of the 2002 ACM Workshop on Privacy in the Electronic Society. WPES 2002, Washington, DC, November 21, pp. 1–10. ACM, New York (2002)
9. Galletta, D.F., Henry, R., McCoy, S., Polak, P.: Web Site Delays: How Tolerant Are Users? Journal of the Association for Information Systems 5(1), 1–28 (2004)
10. Gross, R., Acquisti, A., Heinz, H.J.: Information revelation and privacy in online social networks. In: Proceedings of the 2005 ACM Workshop on Privacy in the Electronic Society. WPES 2005, Alexandria, VA, USA, November 2005, pp. 71–80. ACM, New York (2005)
11. Hedbom, H.: A Survey on Transparency Tools for Enhancing Privacy. In: Matyáš, V., et al. (eds.) The Future of Identity in the Information Society. IFIP AICT, vol. 298, pp. 67–82. Springer, Heidelberg (2009)
12. Jagatic, T.N., Johnson, N.A., Jakobsson, M., Menczer, F.: Social phishing. Communications of the ACM 50(10), 94–100 (2007)
13. Köpsell, S.: Low Latency Anonymous Communication - How long are users willing to wait? In: Müller, G. (ed.) ETRICS 2006. LNCS, vol. 3995, pp. 221–237. Springer, Heidelberg (2006)
14. Mackay, W.E.: Triggers and barriers to customizing software. In: Proceedings of the SIGCHI Conference on Human Factors in Computing Systems: Reaching Through Technology. CHI 1991, New Orleans, Louisiana, United States, April 27 - May 02, pp. 153–160. ACM, New York (1991)
15. Manny, C.H.: European and American privacy: Commerce, rights, and justice. Computer Law and Security Report 19(1), 4–10 (2003)
16. Newell, P.B.: Perspectives on privacy. Journal of Environmental Psychology 15(2), 87–104 (1995)
17. Norberg, P.A., Horne, D.R., Horne, D.A.: The Privacy Paradox: Personal Information Disclosure Intentions versus Behaviors. Journal of Consumer Affairs 41(1), 100–126 (2007)

18. PRIME General Public Tutorial v2, https://www.prime-project.eu/tutorials/gpto (last access 2008-05-15)
19. Sheehan, K.B., Hoy, M.G.: Dimensions of privacy concern among online consumers. Journal of Public Policy & Marketing 19(1), 62–72 (2000)
20. Simon, H.A.: Models of bounded rationality. MIT Press, Cambridge (1982)
21. Spiekermann, S., Grossklags, J., Berendt, B.: E-privacy in 2nd generation E-commerce: privacy preferences versus actual behavior. In: Proceedings of the 3rd ACM Conference on Electronic Commerce. EC 2001, Tampa, Florida, USA, October 14 - 17, pp. 38–47. ACM, New York (2001)
22. Varian, H.R.: Economic aspects of personal privacy. In: Privacy and Self-Regulation in the Information Age, National Telecommunications and Information Administration (1996)
23. Warren, S., Brandeis, L.: The right to privacy. Harvard Law Review 4, 193–220 (1890)
24. Westin, A.F.: Privacy and Freedom. Atheneum, New York (1967)

Testing Privacy Awareness

Mike Bergmann

Technische Universität Dresden, Germany

Abstract. In web-based business processes the disclosure of personal data by the user is an essential part and mandatory for the processes. Privacy policies help to inform the user about his/her rights and to protect the user's privacy. In this paper we present a test to empirically measure how the user's privacy awareness changes by presenting specific elements of the privacy policy in close proximity to the required data items. We compare an experimental group using an enhanced interface to a control group using a conventional interface regarding their capability to recall the agreed privacy-related facts. A concrete online survey has been performed. The major results are presented.

1 Introduction

Privacy has received particular attention in the media and the Internet in the last few years. Classical desktop applications were transferred into the context of the Internet and enable sharing documents over large distances. New web services were created serving various user demands and introducing a complete new application landscape. The major resource of all these services are data and in many cases user data. European legislation acknowledged the situation by defining regulations regarding user rights and privacy protection [7]. Each web site which processes user data has to present a privacy policy to declare the main facts about its data processing. There also exists a technical solution to communicate the essential facts of the privacy policy in a machine readable form [22]. However, usually the user does not read these statements. First, the texts contain lots of legal statements that are difficult to understand [2]. Second, the companies use the privacy policy to rephrase painful facts in vague and sweet words [21]. So the current legislation is rather protecting the interests of companies than the interests of the users.

The need to present privacy policies in a more effective way is obvious. Thereto the presentation should accompany the original business processes, should present the main facts regarding user data and user privacy and should not monopolize the user's attention. In [20] we proposed a solution to solve this Gordian Knot in a user-friendly manner. This paper aims to validate the proposed approach by comparing the resulting privacy awareness to the ordinary presentation approach.

In Section 2 we start with an overview about the related work on this topic. We sketch roughly the major parts of the interfaces, we have to test, while Section 3 then lists the current configuration of our experiment, discusses special aspects

V. Matyáš et al. (Eds.): The Future of Identity, IFIP AICT 298, pp. 237–253, 2009.

of the experiment and presents the statistical methods to analyze the results of the experiment. Finally we close our paper with an outlook to further interesting topics.

2 Related Work

In this section, we elaborate the term *privacy*, some legal and technical factors of it, the term *privacy awareness* and discuss some of the existing approaches to present privacy policy in a privacy-enhancing manner. Furthermore we give a short overview about existing privacy surveys.

2.1 Privacy

There exist various privacy definitions, starting with Warren and Brandeis in 1890 [23], a more popular and general definition by Westin in 1967 [24] and for instance a definition by Fischer-Hübner [13]. According to the latter, we focus on a special branch of privacy, namely *informational privacy* as the *right of informational self-determination*. Based on these facts, we define:

> **Privacy** in the context of this paper means the right of self-determination regarding data disclosure, i.e., each user should be able to control *how much* personal information he is *willing* to give *to whom* and for *what purpose*.

This includes the following components: data minimization, purpose binding, data transfer statement, minimal data retention and informed consent (cp. also [7,9,3]). The European legislation acknowledged the increased importance of user's privacy protection and the necessity of secure and privacy-friendly data processing by issuing legal foundations, namely the Data Protection Directive 95/46/EC [7]. The directive defined that the purpose of data processing and the data processor itself are mandatory to state in the privacy policy.

The P3P specification [22] goes one step ahead and defines various privacy-related attributes, which are machine readable, to allow automatic evaluation of privacy policies. Based on the P3P specification, Cranor et al. developed a new approach for configuring and presenting P3P preferences [8]. Their approach visualizes the degree of the correspondence of the user's privacy preferences with the privacy policy of the web service. However the proposed approach has some drawbacks. The user's privacy concerns are strongly related to the communication partner [9]. So we miss the possibility to define dedicated privacy preferences with respect to the communication partner for the user. Besides, the visualization of a missing P3P policy[1] as less critical as a mismatch of a certain preference, we count as not appropriate for enhancing the user's privacy.

Until now in conventional data-submission forms, the corresponding privacy policy is missing. Often it is accessible via a separate link referring to the privacy

[1] What in fact means that the service could do anything with the personal data.

policy. This implies additional actions for the user to get informed about the circumstances of the data disclosure. Sometimes additional marks are set to separate mandatory respectively optional data (see Figure 1). In [5] an approach is sketched to present privacy policies as a mapping of user defined privacy preferences and to emphasize the non-matching details. It allows the definition of privacy preferences per communication partner and takes the main privacy facts *data minimization, purpose binding and informed consent* into account. We also follow the suggestions to design user interfaces, proposed in the PRIME project [19].

The corresponding graphical presentation of our enhanced interface is shown in Figure 2. Using the icon in the right upper corner allows to access the full privacy policy. We include data transfer and retention statement into the presentation as we consider it as important to enhance the end user's privacy (regarding the privacy definition above). However these additional statements are not required by the EU directive 95/46/EC [7].

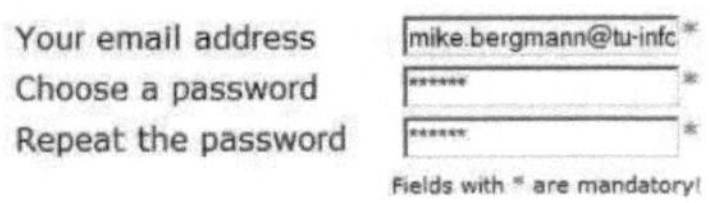

Fig. 1. Conventional interface for online forms

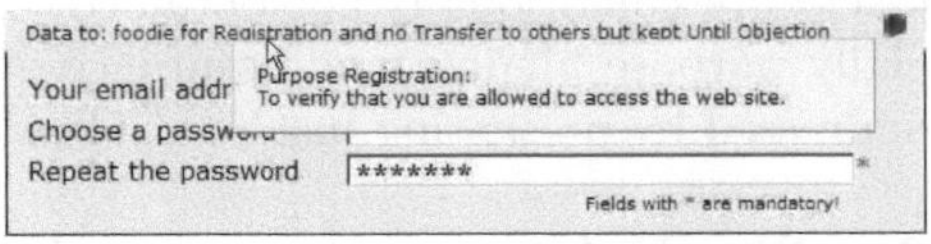

Fig. 2. Enhanced interface – information about the privacy policy nearby the data to disclose

According to our privacy definition, we simplify the meaning of privacy awareness for the testing and define it as:

> **Privacy Awareness** in our context is seen as the user's ability to reflect the communication partner's privacy policy statements regarding purpose binding, transfer assertion and retention period applied for a certain data disclosure.

We mention the obligation of the service provider to make the user aware of the privacy policy in Section 2.1. Usually it is taken into account by offering an omnipresent always available link to the privacy policy. However earlier and recent user tests documented that the ordinary web user neither reads nor understands the complex legal texts and has a blind spot regarding secondary information (like advertisement, banners etc.) [4,6]. We have to make sure that we counter this by using appropriate visualization technologies. A simple text-based, not intercepting approach to present privacy policies seems to be better [11].

2.2 Privacy Surveys

Privacy studies have a long history. In the late 1960s, Alan Westin started to conduct privacy surveys [25]. He did fundamental research in creating various general and specific indices regarding privacy. He partitioned the population into three classes, the so called *fundamentalists, pragmatists* and *unconcerned users* [26]. A description of these surveys is given in [18]. However reliable details about these surveys are not available.

Gideon et al. [15] tested the influence of information regarding the corresponding privacy policy available nearby the search results on web users' purchase decisions. They found that the simple existence of a privacy policy does not influence the purchase decisions. But the presence of a clear indicator about privacy-related facts influenced the purchase decision. A so-called privacy-bird symbol, a graphical metaphor visualizing the degree of the matching of the privacy policy with the users' privacy preferences, was displayed nearby the search result. Depending on the concrete matching details, a red, yellow or green bird was shown [8]. These results are supported by further surveys [12,10]. However the studies do not evaluate the privacy awareness of the user. It is not verified whether the user really is aware of the privacy issue or is just afraid of the red signs. Informed consent in the sense of really informing the user about the disclosure conditions is not obtained. The privacy-policy representation, especially purpose binding and assurance evaluation (see also [1]) are insufficiently addressed by presenting just red/yellow/green indicators.

3 The Privacy Awareness Test

In this section, we motivate our approach to test the privacy awareness of the user. We describe the methodology, the global settings and the potential participants of the experiment. We continue by explaining the single experimental steps *Preparation, Application Scenario, Post Processing and Debriefing* in detail. The expected results based on concrete indices and statistical features are listed and discussed.

3.1 Motivation

One of the questions the test should answer is: "Does the user really perceive the privacy policy statements, presented in a superficial manner such that we could achieve an increased privacy awareness?" (see Figure 2). We need two different groups, the *Control Group* G_{NoPet} using the conventional web forms for data disclosure and the *Experimental Group* G_{Pet} using our enhanced interface presenting the details regarding the privacy policy.

In this context, a sub-question will be how the perception of the privacy policy differs among the various user classes. Our hypothesis is that privacy fundamentalists and pragmatists appreciate the enhanced presentation form, while the unconcerned users still ignore it.

By saying this we have to check, how the proposed approach increases the privacy awareness, in particular how it influences the user's knowledge about privacy-related facts. As measurable privacy-related facts about privacy, we see e.g. the following[2]:

[2] cp. [7,24,13].

- Contact Partner - Various surveys have shown that the most prominent decision factor is the communication partner itself [9]. For well-known and established partners, web users are less concerned about their privacy.
- Purpose Binding - The requested data is bound to a dedicated purpose. Many users have expressed concerns about potential abuse of their personal data [14]. A clear purpose statement helps the user to understand what the requested personal data is used for, e.g., that the disclosed email address is for order confirmation only.
- Data Transfer Statements - Users are very concerned that their data is transferred to other recipients without permissions. An example is the anxiety about the abuse of email addresses to send them spam [21,14].

3.2 The Design of the Test

a) Preface: There are different methods to answer the questions, mentioned above. In a supervised setting we could just monitor (e.g., eye tracking) the test subjects during the usage of the proposed interfaces and interview them afterwards about their understanding of the interface elements. However, this interview approach is applicable only for a limited set of participants. Besides we think this test approach does not cover the usual user behaviour in the context of the Web2.0. Because of the these limitations, an interview will not deliver representative results. A more valuable approach would be a simulation of a real Web2.0 scenario with community components deployed as an online experiment, accessible for a much broader audience. An appropriate questionnaire before and after the simulation should gather the desired facts and should replace the conventional observation and interview.

b) Requirements: Existing online communities are a promising environment to recruit participants for the experiment. They do have appropriate knowledge about business processes in the Internet and they are used to disclose personal data for various purposes. Besides, they are the main target group for our enhanced interface.

Because of the online experience of the prospective participants we have to deal with some top-level requirements regarding the plausibility and authenticity of the experimental scenario. We have to take existing applications as a model paragon. The awareness of the test participants about the fact that it is "just an experiment" should be lowered by simulating real Internet business processes and using the corresponding terminology and presentation styles. We have to simulate the email-confirmation mechanism and we have to place advertisements into the web sites of our online application. We will use a similar color schema like Google (www.google.com) uses to get close to a realistic and well known Web service application.

c) Focus of the experiment: Due to the characteristics of online media, we are able to attract people from all over the world and with various social and educational backgrounds. Our experiment should gather these properties in a first step. These properties will help us to recruit representative test participants to achieve representative results. We will elaborate the concrete difference between the groups of unconcerned participants, pragmatists and fundamentalists. In detail we will collect demographic facts about the test participants and capture the ability of the participants to express concrete facts about the preferences of the privacy policy of a dedicated Web service. Besides, tracking the click stream of the participants enables us to answer the question whether web users do read the privacy policies in general and what are the differences between the privacy fundamentalists, pragmatists and privacy unconcerned users in particular.

d) Methodology: For our test we combine the classical survey method with an experimental part. The survey frames the experiment, aims to collect the participants' demographic preferences, the knowledge about online business processes, common privacy concerns, and will collect our relevant feature set. The questionnaire is construed as a differential cross-sectional survey questionnaire to determine the relationship between privacy concerns and privacy-related behaviour in general and between presentation and perception of privacy-related interface elements among the different privacy-concerned groups in particular. In the pre-questionnaire we use the common Likert scaling [17]. It offers equidistant and well elaborated scaling. We do not allow neutral values to force the participant to make a dedicated yes/no decision. However we allow the refusal to a dedicated question at all.

To gather the experimental results in the post-questionnaire we use a direct scaling, listing concrete options as answers with a dedicated "not sure" option. The selection of "not sure" marks the answer as not countable for the calculation of the result. This avoids the so-called "water down" effect because of valueless data records.

Based on the questionnaire before the simulation, we select a representative sample of all participants. We use common statistical measures to apply the selection. The participants are invited using various international online-sources like mailing lists of online communities, business networks, professional survey and marketing portals.

To design the questionnaire and the experimental part, we perform pre-tests and interviews with potential participants. The found problems and issues were documented and fixed before putting the survey online.

3.3 The Configuration of the Test

The test is performed in three steps. At step one, we are querying items to classify the participants. As a second step, we present a typical online application. The third step aims to gather knowledge of the user about the privacy policy assigned to the disclosure process, respectively to the disclosed data items. This step is accompanied by a debriefing section where the participant is informed that no personal data at all have been transmitted. Questions about whether the data disclosed by the user were true or faked conclude the test. A cookie-based mechanism avoids that normal users perform the test twice. However we acknowledge that experienced users may overcome this protection mechanism.

Table 1. Pre-questions to gather statistics and privacy concerns

Test	Question	T/F[3]	Valid Answer
stat	Please specify your age.		18-24; 25-34; ... 55-64; 65 and older
	Please specify your gender.		Male/female
	Please state your country/region.		list of countries to select
	I use the Internet for e-shopping ...		weekly or more often, monthly, rarely, never
	I spend most of my spare time using the Internet.		Strongly agree, ... strongly disagree
	I speak English very well.		
	I don't need help when I am using a computer.		
pc	I always change my browser settings to protect information about myself.	T	Strongly agree, ... strongly disagree
	It makes sense to use different email addresses for different situations.	T	
	The probability of personal data (like credit card number, email address, online account information) misuse on the Internet is very high.	T	
	Consumers have lost all control over how personal information is collected and used by companies.	T	
	Most businesses handle the personal information they collect about consumers in a proper and confidential way.	F	
	Existing laws and organizational practices provide a reasonable level of protection for consumer privacy today.	F	
sn	Customer feedback is valuable to make decisions about products and services.		Strongly agree, ... strongly disagree
	When choosing a restaurant, I take suggestions from my personal circle into account (family, friends, colleagues).		
	Only unsatisfied customers are posting feedback about products and services on the Internet.		

[3] T=True, the scale is direct; F=False, the scale is inverted.

We posted messages to distribute our invitation for the survey in international and social networks (www.xing.com, www.linkedin.com) and at mailing lists of online research communities (Association of Internet Researchers, German Society for Online Research, University of Maryland, web2list.com, www.i-worker.de, genpsylab-wexlist.unizh.ch, etc.).

Step 1: Preparation. The preparation step aims to motivate the test participants and to collect statistical facts about the participants with regard to demography (e.g., male/female, nationality etc.) and privacy concerns. We collect common statistical features like gender, age, nationality, general Internet skills etc. Besides, we ask questions about general privacy concerns to be able later on to cluster our participants regarding their expressed privacy concerns. This step is introduced with some moderation and the offer to participate in a draw for some material stimulation of the participants. The preparation is concluded by a short explanations of the next steps and a suggestion to print this text to have it available as a handbook for the web application.

We avoid any mentioning of the word *experiment* and *privacy* to not bias the user before performing the test. We add special *social networking* questions (see the *sn* rows in Table 1) to make the user believe we survey about Web2.0 topics. We will enlighten the user after the application scenario in the debriefing section.

Step 2: Application Scenario. As a typical online application we present a "Foodie" web service. This service pretends to collect user recommendations about restaurants, including evaluation of food quality and price level. Therefore the participant has to perform some data disclosure, namely to register to the service submitting an email address and to assess a restaurant (details below). The privacy policy is available at any time.

To answer the question raised at the beginning of this chapter, we separate the participants randomly into two groups. The first groups is presented with the ordinary interfaces, the second group is presented with our enhanced interface (see Figure 1, 2).

Registration: We require a valid email address as user name for the purpose "registration" and a password. To increase the plausibility, we promise to send a confirmation email with an activation link. Various other data that are not really necessary for the transaction are requested. We ask for surname and city. The specified purpose is "personalization".

We apply a privacy policy according to the European Data Protection Directive 95/46/EC [7]. The privacy policy states that the data is not sent to any partner by default, that the data was requested to offer personalization, to provide validity check for the service provider and that the data is stored until objection by the participant (see Figure 3 - "Foodie" Privacy Policy).

Optional: A check box "use this email for product information and special offers" is presented for marketing purpose. The checkbox is selected by default. A separate page with the privacy policy for that purpose is accessible via a "privacy policy" link. The page contains information about the possible usage of the email address for possibly sending suitable special offers and news.

FOODIE PRIVACY POLICY(fragment): Foodie will not share with, sell or transfer any data or personal information provided to us through usage of the Service to any third party without prior and explicit consent.
The requested personal data (email address, first name) is used to allow you to create an account at Foodie. The email address will be necessary for authentication and to contact you for product announcements and marketing information. We use your personal data to personalize our Services.
All content uploaded to the Service is your own private property. Foodie will not read, change, destroy or forward the contents of your account, unless entitled to do so by this Agreement or forced to do so by law, regulation or any extraordinary circumstance.
By making content public on your profile you give an explicit consent to show the information chosen to the audience specified for statistical purpose. Your first name and city of origin stored in your own account profile is visible to other users by default.
Foodie retains the right to temporarily or permanently discontinue any specific features at its own discretion. Foodie has no obligation to keep the uploaded data. Foodie stores your personal data until you object.
...

Fig. 3. "Foodie" Privacy Policy

Table 2. The Post-Questionnaire

Var	Question	Valid Answer
F_A	The email address was requested for the following purpose(s):	Registration, personalization, marketing, statistics, not sure[4]
F_a	I accepted the following usage of the email address for the following purpose(s):	
F_D	The additional personal data (name, city) were requested for:	
F_d	I accepted the following purpose(s) for additional data usage:	
F_R	Did the "Foodie" web services promise to delete your personal data if you send a deletion request?	yes, no, not sure
F_T	Does the "Foodie" web services transfer your email address to restaurants for special offers?	
F_C	Did the "Foodie" web services request your personal data via a secure https connection?	

Input: To add a restaurant evaluation/assessment, the user has to create a new restaurant entry. The user is requested to fill out four data fields describing the restaurant (name, place, kind of, price category) and may add a free descriptive text including tags. The data entered here are public. A privacy policy informs the user about this fact. The data is not sent to the restaurant itself. For statistical purposes, the first name and city of the participant are displayed nearby

[4] Multiple choices allowed or "not sure".

It was just a simulation!
Sorry for being devious, but we had to make you believe it's real. Actually, the 'Foodie' service was just a simulation. We did not transfer any personal data like your name, email etc. As we promised in our privacy policy, no personal data at all was disclosed. The application just generated a pseudonymized data record only to allow further research on the survey results, but without your concrete personal data.

Please answer our last questions about the data items themselves, which you putatively disclosed to the 'Foodie' service. Please tell us honestly...

Fig. 4. Debriefing

the restaurant assessment entry. This quite unusual purpose helps us to avoid that the user guesses the questioned purposes in the post-question section.

Step 3: The post-questionnaire and debriefing part will be presented after the successful finish of the application scenario.

Post questionnaire: To answer the survey questions we raised at the beginning of Section 3, we have to find out whether or not the participant can recall the statements about the privacy policy, he/she agreed on during the test. Therefore, we ask about the stated purpose for disclosing the data item 'email' and additionally 'name' and 'city' for the restaurant-assessment entry. The corresponding questions are listed in Table 2. Depending on the participant's knowledge about the correct purposes we calculate a privacy awareness index (see Section 3.4).

Debriefing: The closing part of the experiment is introduced by a short debriefing as follows in Figure 4. It may happen that the respondents are feeling cheated at this point. By offering the chance to win a valuable technical gadget, we try to compensate this feeling.

Table 3. Debriefing

Var	Question	Valid Answer
T_D	Was the "data item"[5] correct?	yes, no, not sure
T_{R1}	Did you believe the 'Foodie' website was real?	
T_{R2}	Did you answer the questionnaire seriously?	
F_S	I need more privacy-related information about usage of my data during disclosure.	Strongly agree, ... strongly disagree
F_E	I wish to see an easier-to-understand presentation of privacy related information about usage of my data during disclosure.	

The test was scheduled to be performed within a two months period. We planned to have at least 50 participants in each of the two groups, successfully passed the test, with valid test results and acknowledged that they passed the test seriously

[5] There are three separate questions. Valid values for "data item" are email, first name, city.

(see the question F_{R2} in Table 3). Participants, who cancelled the test before answering the post questionnaire are not counted.

3.4 Expected Results

Hypothesis: Even if the test participants do not read the privacy policy, the participants who received the enhanced interface do know the answers better than the control group with the ordinary interface.

Privacy Concerns Index (px): Based on the results of the pre-tests, we classify the two groups (experimental group and control group) each into the classes of privacy *Fundamentalists, Pragmatists* and *Unconcerned* similar to Westin's approach [26]. The participants are clustered by using the pc index (px). It is calculated as the sum of the six privacy-related answers (see Table 1, pre-questions, part 'pc').

The "strongly agree" answer gets assigned the value 4, the "strongly disagree" answer gets the value 1 assigned. In case of inverse meaning (see the true/false column in Table 1) we invert the assignment.

To assign the participants to the corresponding classes, we use the quartiles of the value of px. The first quartile represents the privacy-unconcerned participants. The following two quartiles represent the privacy pragmatists. The fourth quartile represents the privacy fundamentalists. This approach differs from the approach Westin used for classification. However, due to the huge differences in the sample size and setting, in the method the survey was performed, etc., a direct comparison seems not useful.

Privacy Awareness Index (ax): For the first four post-test questions F_A,F_a, F_D and F_d multiple answers are allowed (see Table 2). The answer F_A is correct, if only the checkboxes for purpose "registration" and "marketing" are checked. For each correctly checked respectively not checked checkbox, F_A is increased by 1, so $0 \leq F_A \leq 4$.

To avoid that the participant guesses the answer, we introduced the purpose "statistics". The answer F_D is correct if the checkboxes for purposes "statistics" and "personalization" are checked, all others should remain unchecked. For each correct checkbox, we increase F_D by 1, so $0 \leq F_D \leq 4$.

The correct value for answer F_a depends on the status of the checkbox allowing the usage of the email address for "marketing" purpose. If this purpose was allowed, then the test participant should check the corresponding checkbox, so $0 \leq F_a \leq 4$. In this work, we ignore this answer.

The correct value for answer F_d depends on the status of the checkbox allowing the usage of the first name and the city for statistical purpose. It follows the same schema as for F_a. In this work, we ignore this answer.

For the results F_R, F_C, F_T we have only one correct answer. If the answer is correct, the corresponding value is 1. In case the value is not correct we assign -1, so allowed values for these variables are ± 1.

To take into account participants just exercising the test for scientific reason or curiosity we offer the option to invalidate the own data record by answering "no" to the question T_{R2} (see Table 3). So we are able to lave out these data records.

The coefficients F_S and F_E are representing the information requirements of the test participant. In the current experiment we ignore these answers. In the future we could use these answers to evaluate the overall result in more detail.

As an indication of privacy awareness, we use the sum $ax = F_D + F_R$. These answers allow to conclude whether the participant read respectively perceived the purpose "statistics" and the statement about the possibility to object the data disclosure afterwards. Higher values for ax represent a more correct response. Summarizing the two value ranges of F_D and F_R the awareness index ax has the value range of $-1 \leq ax \leq 5$.

The results F_A, F_C and F_T are control variables. Assuming an influence of the enhanced interface the results F_A and F_C should be similar in both groups because the answers are not depending on the enhanced interface. The answer for F_T should underline the trend, found in ax. Corresponding to our *hypothesis* we expect a higher percentage of correct answers (a higher index ax) in the group with the enhanced interface, especially in the sub-groups of the "pragmatists" and "unconcerned". We will list the results per group.

3.5 Statistics

Equidistance: The answers of the test participants have to be distributed equidistant, so instead of naming all values like *Strongly agree, agree, disagree, strongly disagree* we only offer the names for the edge values *Strongly agree, . . . , strongly disagree.* A neutral value is missing so the test participants have to vote in a clear direction. This forces them to make clear statements about their position.

Participants classification: To classify the participants with regard to their privacy concerns we suggest to use the corresponding quartiles of the privacy concerns index. In [26] Westin proposed a different algorithm to separate survey participants into privacy fundamentalists, pragmatists and unconcerned participants. However the algorithm seems to be arbitrary with regards to the quantitative distribution. To improve this and to be more objective, we propose the separation using the quartiles of the privacy concerns index px.

Stochastic independence of the results: To prove that the data collected for ax are stochastically independent, we use Pearson's chi-square test.

4 Results and Outlook

In this section, we summarize the main results of the survey. We will assess the instrument and discuss further ideas and research questions extending or reusing the developed instrument.

4.1 Common Results Regarding Participation and Classification

The survey was announced to a broad audience in various online forums. Therefore we got many participants. Counting the participants using the start button to start the survey, we got 618 participants. An overview about the participants

Table 4. Overview about the survey participants

Participants	G_{NoPet}	G_{Pet}	Sum
Overall	not available		618 (100%)
Completed the pre-questionnaire	not available		496 (80.3%)
Entered the registration form	217 (35.1%)	214 (34.6%)	431 (69.7%)
Filled out the registration form	86 (13.9%)	86 (13.9%)	172 (27.8%)
Completed the survey	78 (12.6%)	78 (12.6%)	156 (25.2%)

Table 5. Participants classification regarding the privacy concerns index *px*

Class	Unconcerned		Pragmatists		Fundamentalists	
Range of *px*	12 – 17		18 – 20		21 – 24	
Overall participants	28 (17.9%)		75 (48.1%)		53 (34.0%)	
Participants per group	G_{Pet}	G_{NoPet}	G_{Pet}	G_{NoPet}	G_{Pet}	G_{NoPet}
	11 (7.1%)	17 (10.9%)	40 (25.6%)	35 (22.4%)	27 (17.3%)	26 (16.7%)

for the experimental group G_{Pet} and control group G_{NoPet} at different stages of the survey is given in Table 4. There was no statistical selection performed towards a more representative data sample regarding demographical or social parameters like age, gender, education etc.

The classification of the participants similar to Alan Westin's classification [26] is shown in Table 5. We applied the classification schema as described in Section 3.4. In the following we take into account only these participants completing the survey successfully. As the corresponding criterion, we use the state of the checkbox T_{R2} (see Table 3). Following this criterion, 156 participants completed the survey. For these participants we got *px* in the range of $12 \leq px \leq 24$. Using quartiles usually gets four equally distributed sets. Due to the discrete character of *px* we had to adopt this quartile approach. We first separated our participants in four equal parts of 39 participants per part according to the quartiles. Then we looked for the transition of *px* to the next lower value. This point we took as the class limit. So we got as a first part of the participants a class of 28 unconcerned participants. The parts two and three we count as pragmatists (75). Participants belonging to the fourth part are counted as fundamentalists (53). Inside these classes, we show how the participants are distributed regarding assignment to the experimental group and control group. We got the classification, shown in Table 5.

Summary. In our sample about 18% of the participants were counted as *Unconcerned* regarding privacy. About 48% of our participants were *Pragmatists* regarding privacy. About 34% we count as *Fundamentalist.* This does not ideally represent the separation into quartiles as proposed at the beginning, because the fourth class is much bigger than the first. However this may be plausible due to the omnipresent news about data leakage and data misuse in the media, the raised importance of data protection on the Internet in the last years and the need and requirement to use the Internet for daily business and private activities. This could be subject of further research.

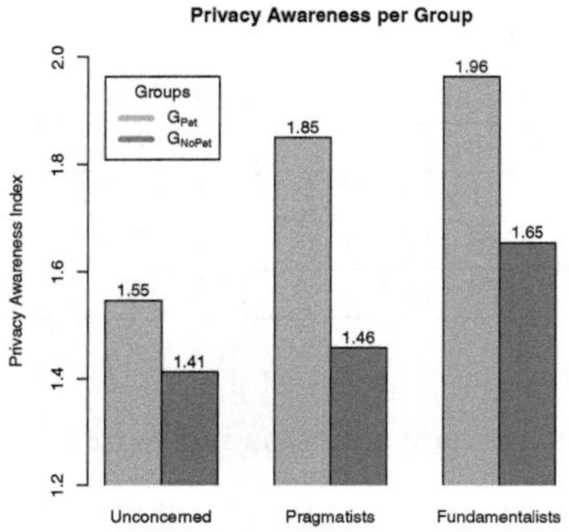

Fig. 5. Contrasting experimental and control group regarding mean ax

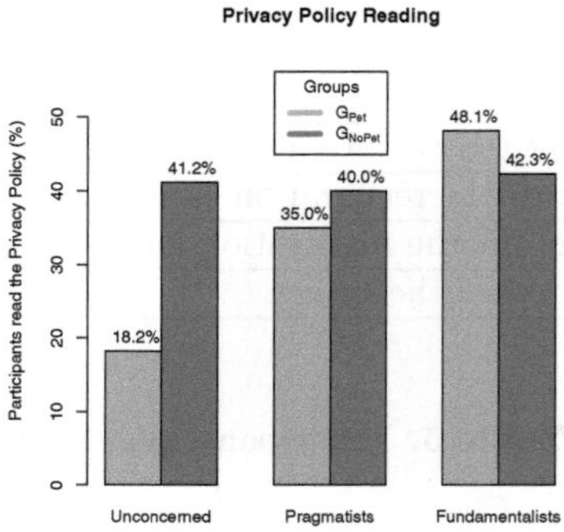

Fig. 6. Contrasting experimental and control group regarding policy reading

4.2 Results Regarding Our Hypothesis

In Section 3.4 we postulated our hypothesis. We assumed that participants belonging to our experimental group G_{Pet} do have a higher privacy awareness than the participants of the control group G_{NoPet}. This is indeed the case. Figure 5 shows the mean value for ax per group and class[6]. Figure 5 shows that in general the ability of the participants of the experimental group G_{Pet} to reflect the main preferences regarding the privacy policy, stated by the service provider, is higher. The significance of this outcome we prove with Pearson's chi-square test. The results are stochastically independent with the probability of approximately 0.995%. This fulfills our requirements formulated in Section 3.5.

Conclusion. We have shown that the proposed approach for presenting information related to the privacy policy of a certain transaction does significantly help the user to perceive the essential privacy preferences, like purpose of data usage. The effect was observed for all classes, but with most success for pragmatists. Our hypothesis was confirmed. The effect is even excelling our expectations because the increase of ax was also observed for the class of fundamentalists. Initially we expected that the fundamentalists read and perceive the preferences of the privacy policy anyway. The increase of ax may be due to the mismatch between stated vs. observed behaviour [16]. So we may conclude that the usage of enhanced interface pays off for all classes of web users.

4.3 Further Interesting Results

Besides we may have a look at the question "Does the Internet user read the privacy policy?" (see Section 3.1). Based on the 156 valid data records, we may state that in general there is no correspondence of stating privacy concerns and acting privacy-concerned, respectively privacy-aware, as shown in Figure 6. The

[6] For details regarding calculation of ax see Section 3.4.

frequency for reading the privacy policy in the control group is nearly uniformly distributed. So even fundamentalists do not read the privacy policy more often than the unconcerned in the control group. This corresponds to the findings of Jensen et al. [16].

However in the experimental group it looks different. Except the fundamentalists all other participants of the experimental group G_{Pet} did read the privacy policy less often. This may be due to the fact that in general, the presence of the privacy-related information satisfied the desires regarding privacy information of the participants belonging to the classes of unconcerned and pragmatists. For the fundamentalists it increased the policy-reading frequency. This may be due to the fact that the presence of the privacy-related information 'remembers the user to have a look at the privacy policy'. Due to the thin result set, the findings however are not very reliable and have to be validated.

A further topic of interest could be how the validity of the submitted data varies through the different classes of web users. However we did not elaborate this relationship. This is definitely a topic of further research. As a hypothesis we may state that we expect more valid results within the well-informed group using the enhanced interface.

4.4 Outlook

The results of this survey are promising and may contain further interesting facts. Using direct and indirect survey outputs, we could elaborate the following questions:

- Is there a difference between the Personal Data Validity Index (vx) within the different privacy concerned user groups? To estimate the validity of the answers given by the test participants, we introduced post-test questions after the debriefing of the users (see Section 3.3). The index may show whether the enhanced interface increases the quality of the disclosed data or not. It could also be taken as an implicit measure of the applied privacy protection of the participants. If the participant disclosed incorrect data (e.g. a wrong city, a misspelled name etc.) we may assume more privacy awareness. It could also be taken as a measurement to assess how users vary their privacy protection requirements based on available privacy policy information.
- What part of participants disabled java script and/or cookie functionality? Are these participants related to the fundamentalists? This may be a measure for the consistency of stated and observed behaviour.
- Is there a difference in the percentage of participants who do not continue to complete the tests between the different user groups?
- Is there any difference between different demographic and ethnic groups (e.g. between young/old, male/female people)?

Acknowledgement

Thanks to our colleagues for the helpful comments. Special thanks to the team of the Technische Universität Dresden, namely Andreas Pfitzmann, Rainer Böhme,

Stefanie Pötzsch, Sandra Steinbrecher, Sebastian Clauß, Stefan Köpsell, Stefan Berthold and Wiltrud Kuhlisch, to the Karlstad University team, namely Simone Fischer-Hübner, Maria Lindström, John-Sören Pettersson and Erik Wästlund, and to Diane Whitehouse.

The research leading to the results presented in this paper has received funding from the European Community's Sixth and Seventh Framework Programme (FP6/2002-2006 resp. FP7/2007-2013) for the projects FIDIS, PRIME and PrimeLife. The information in this document is provided "as is" and no guarantee or warranty is given that the information is fit for any particular purpose. The PrimeLife consortium members shall have no liability for damages of any kind including without limitation direct, special, indirect, or consequential damages that may result from the use of these materials subject to any liability which is mandatory due to applicable law.

References

1. Andersson, C., Camenisch, J., Crane, S., Fischer-Hübner, S., Leenes, R., Pearson, S., Pettersson, J.S., Sommer, D.: Trust in PRIME. In: Proceedings of the 5th IEEE Int. Symposium on Signal Processing and IT, Athens, Greece, December 18-21 (2005)
2. Antón, A.I., Earp, J.B., Bolchini, D., He, Q., Jensen, C., Stufflebeam, W.: The lack of clarity in financial privacy policies and the need for standardization. In: IEEE Security and Privacy, March 2004, vol. 2, pp. 36–45 (2004)
3. Antón, A.I., Earp, J.B., Vail, M.W., Jain, N., Gheen, C., Frink, J.M.: An Analysis of Web Site Privacy Policy Evolution in the Presence of HIPAA, `http://www4.ncsu.edu/~njain/publications/hipaa_7_24_submit.pdf`
4. Benway, J.P.: Banner Blindness: The Irony of Attention Grabbing on the World Wide Web. In: Proceedings of the Human Factors and Ergonomics Society 42nd Annual Meeting. Rice University Research, Houston (1998)
5. Bergmann, M.: Generic Predefined Privacy Preferences for Online Applications. In: Hübner, S.F., Duquenoy, P., Zuccato, A., Martucci, L. (eds.) The Future of Identity in the Information Society: Proceedings of the Third IFIP WG 9.2, 9.6/11.6, 11.7/FIDIS International Summer School, International Summerschool Karlstad, Sweden, August 4-10, 2007. Springer, Boston (2008)
6. Burke, M., Hornof, A., Nilsen, E., Gorman, N.: High-cost banner blindness: Ads increase perceived workload, hinder visual search, and are forgotten. In: ACM Transactions on Computer-Human Interaction (TOCHI), December 12, 2005. Rice University Research, Houston (2005)
7. Council of Europe. Data Protection Directive 1995/46/EC of the European Parliament and of the Council of 24 October 1995 on the protection of individuals with regard to the processing of personal data and on the free movement of such data. Official Journal L No. 281, 23.11.1995 (1995)
8. Cranor, L.: P3P: Making privacy policies more useful. IEEE Security and Privacy, pp. 50–55 (2003)
9. Cranor, L., Reagle, J., Ackerman, M.: Beyond Concern: Understanding Net Users Attitudes About Online Privacy. AT&T Labs-Research Technical Report, TR 99.4.3 (April 1999), `http://citeseer.ist.psu.edu/cranor99beyond.html`
10. Cranor, L.F.: What do they "indicate?": Evaluating Security and Privacy Indicators. Interactions XIII(3), 45–57 (2006)

11. Diaper, D., Waelend, P.: World Wide Web working whilst ignoring graphics: good news for web page designers. Interacting With Computers 13 (December 2000)
12. Egelman, S., Tsai, J., Cranor, L., Acquisti, A.: Studying the Impact of Privacy Information on Online Purchase Decisions. In: Workshop on Privacy and HCI: Methodologies for Studying Privacy Issues at CHI 2006 (2006), `http://cups.cs.cmu.edu/pubs/chi06.pdf`
13. Fischer-Hübner, S.: IT-Security and Privacy, vol. 1958, p. 35. Springer, Heidelberg (2001)
14. Fox, S., Rainie, L., Lenhart, J.H.A., Spooner, T., Carter, C.: Trust and Privacy Online: Why Americans want to rewrite the Rules. In: The Pew Internet & American Life Project, August 20 (2000), `http://www.pewinternet.org/pdfs/PIP_Trust_Privacy_Report.pdf` (last visited November 11, 2008)
15. Gideon, J., Cranor, L., Egelman, S., Acquisti, A.: Power Strips, Prophylactics, and Privacy, Oh My! In: ACM International Conference Proceeding Series, Proceedings of the second symposium on Usable privacy and security, Pittsburgh, Pennsylvania, vol. 149, pp. 133–144 (2006), `http://portal.acm.org/citation.cfm?id=1143120.1143137` ISBN:1-59593-448-0
16. Jensen, C., Potts, C., Jensen, C.: Privacy practices of Internet users: Self-report versus observed behavior. International Journal of Human-Computer Studies 63, 203–227 (2005)
17. Kallmann, A.: Skalierung in der empirischen Forschung. München (1979)
18. Kumaraguru, P., Cranor, L.: Privacy Indexes: A Survey of Westin's Studies. ISRI Technical Report, CMU-ISRI-05-138, Carnegie Mellon University (December 2005)
19. Pettersson., J.S. (ed.): HCI Guidelines, PRIME Deliverable D6.1.f. PRIME Deliverable (version 1, February 2008), `https://www.prime-project.eu/prime_products/reports/arch/`
20. Pettersson, J.S., Fischer-Hübner, S., Danielsson, N., Nilsson, J., Bergmann, M., Clauß, S., Kriegelstein, T., Krasemann, H.: Making PRIME Usable. In: Symposium on Usable Privacy and Security, Pittsburgh, PA, USA, July 2005. Carnegie Mellon University (2005)
21. Pollach, I.: What's Wrong with Online Privacy Policies? In: Communications of the ACM archive, vol. 50, pp. 103–108. ACM Press, New York (2007)
22. W3C. Platform for Privacy Preferences (April 2002), `http://www.w3.org/TR/P3P/`
23. Warren, S.D., Brandeis, L.D.: The Right to Privacy. Harvard Law Review 4, 193–220 (1890)
24. Westin, A.: Privacy and Freedom. Atheneum, New York (1967)
25. Westin, A.F., Center for Social and Legal Research: Bibliography of surveys of the U.S. Public, 1970-2003. CSLR, Hackensack (2003)
26. Westin, A.F., HARRIS LOUIS & ASSOCIATES: Harris-Equifax Consumer Privacy Survey. Tech. rep., 1991. Conducted for Equifax Inc. 1,255 adults of the U.S. public (1991)

The Relationship between Data Protection Legislation and Information Security Related Standards

Martin Meints*

Unabhängiges Landeszentrum für Datenschutz Schleswig-Holstein,
Holstenstr. 98, 24103 Kiel, Germany
ULD61@datenschutzzentrum.de

Abstract. In the last 20 years standards in the context of information security rapidly developed and reached a high level of maturity. Information security also is an important task in the context of data protection, as outlined by the European Data Protection Directive 95/46/EC. However, this Directive does not explicitly relate to standards in the context of information security, security requirements are described quite generally. In this paper it is analysed how on a European level selected standards in the context of information security can be used to fulfill the security requirements described in the Directive 95/46/EC.

Keywords: Directive 95/46/EC, Data Protection Directive, ISO/IEC 27000 series, ISO/IEC 15408, CobiT, ISO/IEC TR 13335-3.

1 Introduction

In the Member States of the European Union national data protection legislation is based on the European Data Protection Directive 95/46/EC[1], hereafter called the Directive. Information security measures are referred to by the Directive as an important data protection principle. The Directive describes information security requirements in Recital 46 and Art. 17 only briefly. However, essential requirements for compliance of information security measures with the Directive can be derived from the Recital 46, Art. 17 and – because of special requirements in the case of sensitive data – Art. 8. This text analyses compliance requirements and describes how they can be fulfilled using various standards in the context of information security. In addition it is discussed how far adhering to these standards is necessary to achieve compliance with data protection legislation.

This text is structured as follows: In section 2 general considerations on the relationship between data protection and information security are made, followed by an overview of which security requirements are described in the Directive in section 3. Section 4 gives an overview on information security related standards mainly used in Europe. Section 5 describes which instruments introduced in the standards mentioned can be used to comply with the security requirements described

* The author wants to thank Diane Whitehouse for her valuable review comments.

[1] Available via http://ec.europa.eu/justice_home/fsj/privacy/law/index_en.htm

V. Matyáš et al. (Eds.): The Future of Identity, IFIP AICT 298, pp. 254–267, 2009.

in the Directive. Sections 6 and 7 analyse how these standards relate to state-of-the-art in information security, required by the Directive. The paper closes with a summary and conclusion section.

Please note that "state-of-the-art" in this context explicitly refers to information security in the context of the Directive and is understood as well accepted and established practices by security experts and practitioners. In other technical areas, e.g. operations of applications or operating systems, state-of-the-art may lead to established practices that are from a security point of view clearly not state-of-the-art.[2]

2 General Considerations on the Relationship between Data Protection and Information Security

Data protection and information security are two quite different domains when looking at targets and stakeholders (see e.g. [1]).

Information security mainly is driven by large organisations, with some support by national information security offices (such as U.S. National Institute of Standards and Technology (NIST) or German Federal Office for Information Security). Work in this domain mainly is carried out by technicians with some support by economists. The target of the activity is risk management / risk mitigation in and for *organisations* (governmental institutions/enterprises). As a consequence methodologies and measures developed in this domain are directed towards this target. Increasingly "good" and "best" practice is documented in international standards. In addition to catalogues of technical security measures over the last ten years approaches for integrated Information Security Management Systems (ISMS) and methods for risk assessment and risk treatment have been developed and standardised. These methods and catalogues of technical measures are also increasingly referenced by other domains, e.g. national legislation in the context of financial/tax management, data protection etc.

Data protection is about the protection of fundamental rights of citizens (so called data subjects) and driven mainly by lawyers (with a minor technical support). Risk assessment and mitigation is focused on *data subjects*, not organisations. The results of the risk assessment approaches of information security and data protection may well be conflicting.[3] However, security measures developed to protect the information of an organisation also may be effective to protect the data of data subjects and thus to support data protection. These two domains share analyses and understanding and at least sometimes take benefit from each others' experience.

---

[2] An example for this is erasure of data in the context of operating systems and security standards. While state-of-the-art of erasure in operating systems can mean that deleted data basically is hidden from the view of the user and can be restored easily with operating system internal tools or measures, secure erasure in the ISO/IEC 27002 refers to "incineration or shredding [of storage media], or erasure of data for use by another application […]". Indeed the state-of-the-art of secure erasure is not difficult to implement; however, the secure version of erasure is not widely distributed among standard operating systems and applications.

[3] A typical example for such a conflict is the handling of personal data in audit logs. While from the perspective of information security much data may be useful to analyse different types of attacks over a long period of time, the data minimisation principle asks for a limitation of the amount of personal data stored and the erasure as fast as possible.

3 Information Security Requirements of the Directive

Among lawyers there seems to be consensus to keep technical details outside European Union (EU) directives, EU regulations and national laws.[4] One important reason is frequent changes in technology requiring a regular update of the corresponding legislation. As security safeguards to a large extent are technically oriented and technically driven in their development, the Directive contains quite general requirements regarding information security. For guidance on concrete implementation data protection relies on other domains of knowledge, e.g. computer science and information security.

Art. 17 of the Directive states the targets of information security which are protection of "personal data against accidental or unlawful *destruction or accidental loss, alteration, unauthorised disclosure or access* [...] and against all other unlawful forms of processing". To fulfil this target, "the data controller must implement appropriate *technical and organisational measures* [...]". To achieve an appropriate level of information security, (technical) *state-of-the-art, costs*, data protection related *risks* and the *nature of personal data* processed need to be taken into account.

Art. 8 refers to the character of personal data. In this article *special categories of personal data* are described: Data referring to racial or ethnic origin, political opinions, religious or philosophical beliefs, membership in trade unions, health-related data, and data concerning the sex life of the data subject. In Art. 8 it is further stated that Member States shall generally forbid the processing of these data. Cases are described in which processing can be allowed and reference again to suitable safeguards in these cases is made (section 4).

Recital 46 explains Art. 17 and introduces many requirements also to be found later in Art. 17. However, one aspect not explicitly mentioned in Art. 17 is outlined in this Recital: The need to define technical and organisational security measures in a way that they cover the *lifecycles of procedures*[5] in which personal data are processed. Recital 46 refers to "the *time of design* of the processing system and [...] the *time of the processing* itself, particularly in order to *maintain security* [...]".

The Directive does not provide for a data protection or information security management system. The Directive also does not refer to existing standards. Legal requirements to be met are described, but with respect to the implementation there is much room for individualised approaches on a national and organisational level. For example the Directive does not suggest whether (a) an integrated management system for security and data protection is required or (b) two separate, but interacting management systems – one for security and one for data protection – can be used. In practice both implementations are commonly found.

The first approach (integrated management systems) seems to be used especially in the public sector and small private companies where security requirements in many

---

[4] See for example [2] for an internationally focused summary on this debate. In the still ongoing debate concerning the modernisation of the German Federal Data Protection Act the integration of concrete technical and management oriented security measures does not play a role at all, see e.g. [3].

[5] In this context a procedure is understood as a governmental or business procedure, covering one or more processes and relating Information and Communication Technology (ICT).

cases are mainly driven by compliance with data protection legislation and management resources are limited. This approach has the significant disadvantage of role conflicts between data protection and security management, disabling potentially quality assurance measures.[6,7] However, for small governmental organisations such as municipalities and small European member states this approach in future will remain relevant. The second approach (separate, but interacting management systems) seems to be implemented frequently predominantly by large organisations in the private sector, especially where security management needs to meet compliance requirements also from other legal or contractual sources (such as the U.S. Sarbanes-Oxley Act (SOX), EuroSOX, contracts with customers etc.).

The Directive also does not refer to other management systems relating to information security management such as Quality Management (e.g. based on the ISO 9000 series) or IT Service Management (e.g. based on the IT Infrastructure Library[8] (ITIL), partly also standardised as ISO/IEC 20000).

National data protection legislation may be more specific concerning security requirements. For example the German Federal Data Protection Act defines eight specific data protection related security goals in the annex to Art. 9.[9] National data protection legislation is not further analysed here as this would exceed the scope of this paper.

4 Information Security Related Standards – An Overview

Commonly international security standards refer to three main security goals, referred to as "CIA":

1. **C**onfidentiality,
2. **I**ntegrity (including authenticity and non-repudiation) and
3. **A**vailability.

These standards typically can be classified in three types, based on the orientation toward management or technology on the one hand and the area of application (organisations or products) on the other hand. Figure 1 shows the categorisation of most important standards according to information security:

---

[6] In the event of an integrated management system the manager in his data protection role states requirements, implements them in his role as security manager and finally checks in his role as data protection manager whether he himself implemented the requirements sufficiently – the result of this final check is highly predictable. However, this deficiency in the management system can be overcome by additional measures, e.g. regular external audits.

[7] Wherever in this text the masculine gender is used it is meant to encapsulate a person of both genders.

[8] ITIL (Information Technology Infrastructure Library; current version 3.0) is a good-practice Information Technology (IT) Service Management Framework maintained by the U.K. Office for Government Commerce (OGC). ITIL is available via http://www.ogc.gov.uk/guidance_itil.asp

[9] See http://www.bfdi.bund.de/nn_946430/EN/DataProtectionActs/Artikel/Bundesdatenschutzgesetz-FederalDataProtectionAct,templateId=raw,property=publicationFile.pdf/Bundesdatenschutzgesetz-FederalDataProtectionAct.pdf

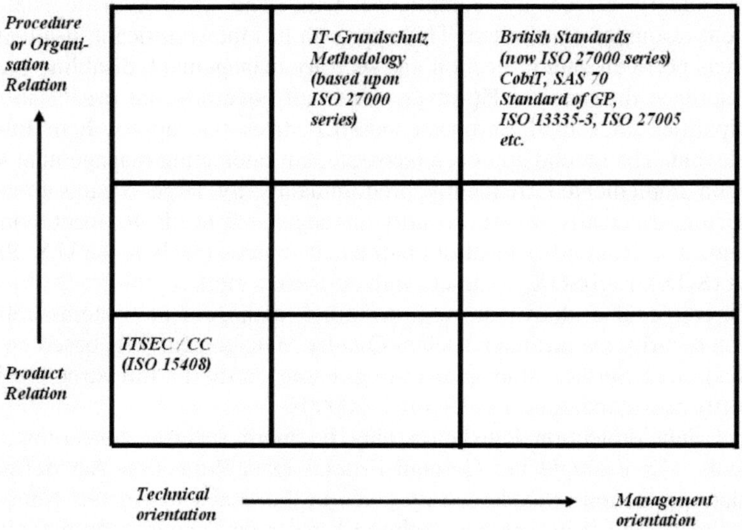

Fig. 1. Categorisation of information security related standards based upon [4][10]

Today the most important seem to be the three categories:

1. Information security management systems (ISMS, ISO 27000 series, Standard of Good Practice for Information Security[11], SAS 70[12] etc.), IT Governance Frameworks (CobiT[13]) and methodology standards (especially ISO TR 13335-3 and 27005 for risk assessment and treatment); these standards are kept general with respect to technical security measures.

   This means that e.g. the targets of technical and organisational security measures are described in so called "Controls", but the specific technical implementation for operation systems etc. and good practice processes are not specified.

   With respect to processes and functional structures ISMS heavily rely on principles and good practice developed in the context of quality management (standardised in the context of the ISO 9000 series). This includes process design (e.g. the use of the Deming cycle[14] for continuous quality assurance

---

10 Boxes in the middle are to be understood as "as well category 1 as category 2".

11 The "Standard of Good Practice for Information Security" is being developed by the Information Security Forum (ISF). The standard is available free of costs via https://www.isfsecuritystandard.com/SOGP07/index.htm

12 SAS 70 (Statement on Auditing Standards No. 70) is a certificate for service organisations developed by the (U.S.) American Institute of Certified Public Accountants (AICPA). The certificate contains controls relating to information technology and information security. See http://www.sas70.com/about.htm

13 Control Objectives for Information and related Technology, currently Version 4.1. CobiT is available free of costs via http://www.isaca.org

14 The Deming cycle has been established in the context of quality management for more than 50 years, in the context of environment management for more than 15 and in the context of information security management for more than 10 years. All information security management related standards analysed in this text refer to the Deming cycle.

and improvement and life cycles of information and communication (ICT) products and procedures and hierarchal process structures containing core and supporting processes), process documentation and improvement (e.g. by use of Key Performance Indicators, KPI).

2. Information Security Management Systems based on ISO 27000 series equipped with a catalogue of technical security measures (e.g. the IT-Grundschutz Methodology of the German Federal Office for Information Security (BSI))[15].
3. Product related security standards with a strong technical orientation (e.g. ITSEC and Common Criteria (ISO 15408)); the Common Criteria contain a number of Security Functions in different classes and families which are to be taken into consideration in product development and operation. Though these Security Functions are described independent of existing implementations, they can be implemented quite concretely.

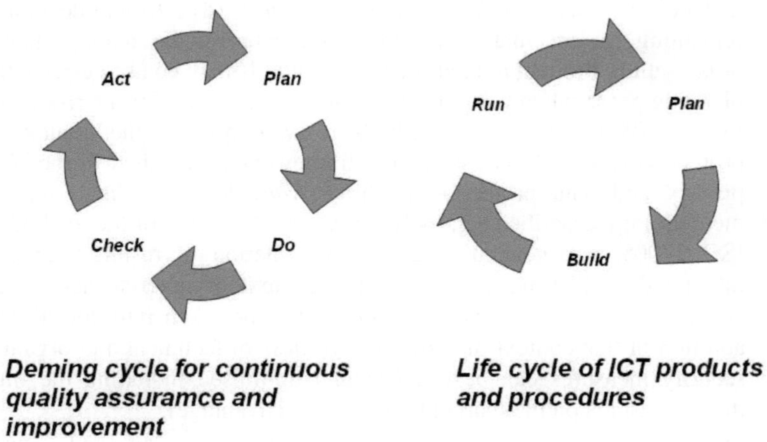

Fig. 2. Cyclic good practice process used in the context of ISMS

5 Standards and Data Protection Requirements

Generally speaking, the standards mentioned are suitable to match the security requirements of the Data Protection Directive. How this could look like in detail, is described in this section.

The security goals referred to in the standards (confidentiality, integrity, availability) are well within the scope of the *security goals* outlined in the Data Protection Directive. To meet the other requirements the approach of two separate but

[15] The IT-Grundschutz Methodology contains three BSI standards (BSI 100-1 to 100-3; a fourth standard dealing with business continuity management is in preparation) describing the methodology which is compliant with ISO 27001 and 27005, and the IT-Grundschutz Catalogues (compliant with ISO 27002). These documents are accessible free of costs via http://www.bsi.de/gshb/intl/index.htm

interacting management systems seems to be most suitable [5]. The standards mentioned cover three levels of acting in organisations, namely the strategic (horizon of planning three to five years), tactical (horizon of planning six months to three years) and operational level (horizon of planning up to six months). The following instruments described in the standards mentioned seem especially relevant:

- On the strategic level an *ISMS* covering security aspects of procedures in each phase of the lifecycle. This includes an effective management structure (hierarchy) and good-practice cyclic processes (Deming cycle and lifecycle). Special emphasis in the standards is put on the personal take over of the responsibility for effectiveness of the ISMS by the management of the organisation and *quality assuring measures* (audits). Essential information about the ISMS shall be published in a *security policy.*
- On the tactical level a *security concept* for each procedure, containing (a) a description of the procedure and related ICT (a *network plan* and a *list of assets*[16]), (b) a *risk assessment* and (c) a *risk treatment plan* containing *technical and organisational security measures* (d) a formal declaration that remaining (or residual) risks are taken over by the management of the organisation. Product related security standards may be used especially in the planning phase when hard- and software are selected. For the risk assessment ISO 27005 provides two methods relevant also in the context of data protection risks. A risk assessment framework established in the context of privacy and data protection is the *Privacy Impact Assessment (PIA),* a methodology described e.g. by Roger Clarke [6]. Parts of the methodology of ISO 27005, e.g. generation and documentation of results, can easily be integrated in PIA framework. In the context of the risk assessment also *special categories of personal data* need to be taken into consideration. In addition in this context the *cost effectiveness* of technical and organisational security measures can be checked and optimised including the impact of these measures on the market (competitive advantage).
- On the operational level an *implementation plan* and *operational documentation* of implemented measures. This documentation is essential as a reference for internal and external security and data protection audits.

6 Security Standards in Relation to State-of-the-Art

State-of-the-art in accordance with the Directive 95/46/EC in the context of information security is difficult to describe. The reasons for this are mainly:

- The Directive does not refer to standards.
- Changes in the environment in which information is processed, especially the technology used, threats to and vulnerabilities in systems, and

[16] Assets are understood as anything of value in the context of information processing to the organisation. Assets may contain hardware, software licences, documents and even personal experience, if the information inside people's heads is taken into consideration.

requirements and targets of organisations do not allow a long term stable evaluation of practice.

- Requirements and abilities of organisations vary largely so that good practice in or for one organisation does not necessarily suit another. In this context in addition to other influencing factors such as (legacy) system infrastructures etc., the size of an organisation is closely linked to its abilities. Large organisations typically can spend more resources on information security compared to small organisations. In addition it has to be taken into consideration that international standardisation mainly is driven by large organisations that are able to spend resources on this task. Existing standards differ in targets. While some of them, especially certification standards, aim at "best practice" and "excellence" and may exceed state-of-the-art, others summarise "good practice" and state-of-the-art. Important differences between good practice standards and certifications standards are e.g., an explicit (and provable) management commitment, an effective management system containing function bearers able to enforce security, sufficient resources and effective processes, application of a risk assessment methodology compliant to ISO 13335-3 or 27005, and completeness and quality in covering the security controls (or security functions) listed in the standards.

As a result there can be no general and homogeneous judgement as to how standards relate to state-of-the-art. In this section an attempt to classify the most relevant standards relating to information security as "is state-of-the-art" or "is exceeding state-of-the-art" is presented.

6.1 The ISO 27000 Series

The ISO 27000 series contain a number of standards with different targets. As shown in Fig. 3, the standards in the ISO 27000 series can be categorised[19] in three classes (see white boxes):

1. Terminology (aiming at a standardised vocabulary),
2. Requirements containing standards for certification (ISO 27001: ISMS in organisations) and accreditation (ISO 27006: requirements auditors have to meet in order to get certified and licenced with a certification body),
3. Guidance standards, containing good practice and methodologies (currently ISO 27002 "Code of Practice", containing control objectives and controls together with guidance relating the implementation of the controls and ISO 27005 "Information Security Risk Management", describing essential elements of a risk management process and related tasks. In addition ISO 27005 describes how qualitative and quantitative risk assessment can be carried out and provides examples for the application of these risk assessment methods.)

While the standards in dark grey boxes already exist, the standards in light grey boxes are still in preparation.

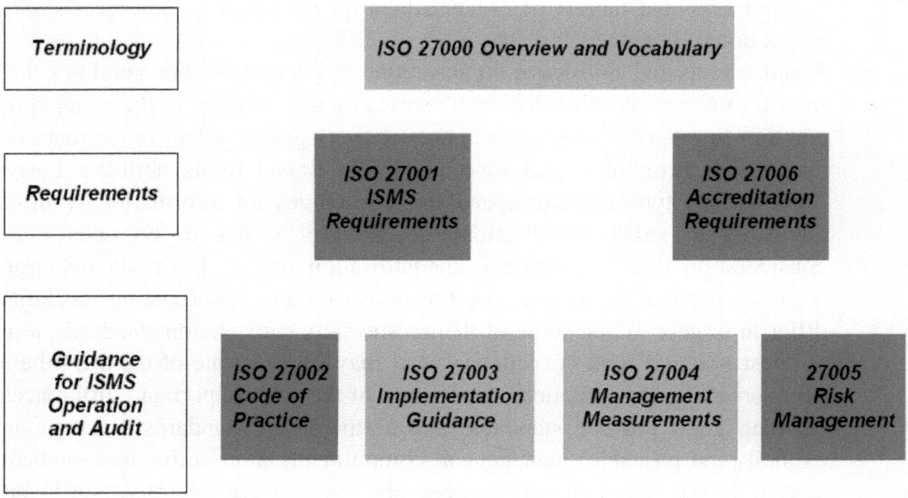

Fig. 3. Overview on existing and planned standards in the ISO 27000 series (non-comprehensive overview)[17]

The standards in the categories 1 (terminology) and 3 (guidance) aim at "good practice" and state-of-the-art. They allow an adaptation of the implementation of technical measures and methods to the specific requirements of different types of organisations.

The standards in the category 2 (requirements) aim at certificates and "best practice". They exceed partially state-of-the-art (e.g. ISO 27001 in the completeness of documentation and the implementation of controls), while other parts, especially the design and implementation of ISMS, clearly describe "good practice". However, partial implementation of the ISO 27001, especially when carried out by small organisations, still can be state-of-the-art.

6.2 IT-Grundschutz Methodology

The IT-Grundschutz[18] Methodology consists of three important parts:

- The description design an operation of an ISMS in compliance with the ISO 27001,
- A specific risk assessment approach based on qualitative risk assessment as described in ISO 27005,
- The IT-Grundschutz Catalogues, a collection of risks and technical and organisational security measures. This catalogue is based on ISO 27002, but

[17] This categorisation was presented by the German Federal Office for Information Security in the ISO 27001 auditors training 2007 and 2008 (documentation not publically accessible).

[18] The IT-Grundschutz Methodology, formerly and unclearly translated as baseline protection methodology, is an approach to start the development of a security concept with an initial set of security measures, covering for a "standardised" organisation a related set of initial risks sufficiently. The concretely needed security level for a "real", existing organisation is derived from this initial security level in a qualitative risk assessment.

exceeds this standard in technical concreteness and reference to existing implementations e.g., concerning operating systems and applications.

The reference to the IT-Grundschutz Methodology and the content of the IT-Grundschutz Catalogues can be considered to be state-of-the-art.

For the IT-Grundschutz Methodology also a certificate issued by the German Federal Office for Information Security is available, based on ISO 29011 and ISO 27006. This certificate again aims at "best practice" and exceeds state-of-the-art.

6.3 CobiT

CobiT is designed as an IT governance framework and currently does not support the certification of organisations. CobiT essentially is a collection of relevant control objectives and controls exceeding the scope of the ISO 27002 by integrating aspects of IT service management and quality management. Full and partial implementation of CobiT also can be considered to be state-of-the-art.

6.4 ISO 13335-3, Now ISO 27005

This standard was withdrawn in June 2008, as the security standards were being restructured by ISO and the content was modernised and shifted to ISO 27005. Both standards describe different methods for carrying out risk assessments and risk treatment. This includes three methods for risk assessment for organisations:

- qualitative,
- quantitative risk assessment, and
- the baseline protection approach.

The qualitative risk assessment contains the evaluation of risks for an organisation based on a qualitative estimation (e.g. based on a scale from 1 to 5) of potential impact and likeliness or frequency of occurrence. Based on an organisation specific risk policy, a decision is made whether the risks analysed are acceptable or not (in the latter case they need to be dealt with).

The quantitative risk assessment provides a method to evaluate risks as an Annual Loss Expectancy (ALE). In case these losses are not acceptable, a treatment of the corresponding risks is required.

The baseline protection approach in the originally described way is not supported in ISO 27005 any more. The successor methodology, the IT-Grundschutz Methodology, is a qualitative risk assessment approach.

In the event that risks are not acceptable, four different treatment options can be chosen:

- Reduction of risks by technical and organisational security measures aiming at the reduction of the likeliness to occur or the reduction of the impact in case an incident happens until the remaining risk is acceptable;
- Avoidance of risks e.g. by redesigning the system to avoid existing threats or vulnerabilities;
- Transfer of risks, typically by insuring them; or
- Acceptance, in which the risk turns into a remaining or residual risk.

In practice these options also can be combined. Frequently risks are reduced by implementing organisational and technical security measures and then the remaining risk is transferred e.g. to an insurance company.

The application of the described risk assessment methods can be considered to be state-of-the-art in security. However, these methods also can be applied in the context of specific privacy and data protection risks and can be used in the context of the Privacy Impact Assessment (PIA, [6]) as well.

6.5 Common Criteria (ISO 15408)

The Common Criteria (CC)[19] are designed as a certification standard for information security related products. Today relatively few products are certified only, so that the existence of CC certificates cannot be considered to be state-of-the-art. In addition the manufacturer applying for a CC certificate has a significant influence which security functions are assessed on which level in the certification process. As a result the sheer existence of a CC certificate does not mean that the product is suited for any thinkable application in the area of certification. More precisely, CC certificates need be evaluated carefully when looking for security solutions. Nevertheless, if suited to the purpose for which they are meant to be used, CC-certified products should be preferred in the context of procurement procedures.

The CC also provides an overview on security functions categorised in so called classes and families relevant for certified products. One example for this is the family FAU_GEN summarising security requirements for audit logging in applications [7]. These security functions also can be used in the context of procurement or development of own solutions. They can be classified as state-of-the-art.

6.6 Summary

The following table sums up how the standards analysed relate to state-of-the-art:

Table 1. Overview of the categories of standards analysed

Standard	**Content and remarks**	**Considered to be state-of-the-art in security**	**Considered to exceed state-of-the-art in security**
ISO/IEC 27001	Information Security Management Systems (ISMS)	X (partial implementation, especially concerning hierarchy and processes of the ISMS)	X (certificates)
ISO/IEC 27002	Code of Practice, catalogue of generic information security measures	X	

[19] Currently (November 2008) CC version 2.3 are standardised as ISO/IEC 15408 while the current version 3.1 still is in the standardisation process at the International Organization for Standardization (ISO).

Table 1. *(continued)*

ISO/IEC 27005	Information Security Risk Management	X (risk assessment methods also can be applied in the context of data protection risks and the Privacy Impact Assessment (PIA))	
ISO/IEC 27006	Accreditiation Requirements; covering certificates for auditors and requirements for Certification Bodies (CBs)		X (certificates)
ISO/IEC TR 13335-3	Risk Assessment Methodology; withdrawn in June 2008	X (see ISO/IEC 27005)	
IT-Grundschutz Methodology	Three BSI-Standards and the IT-Grundschutz Catalogues	X (ISMS, risk assessment methodology and security measures in the Catalogues)	X (certificates)
CobiT V4.1	IT governance framework	X	
ISO/IEC 15408	Security certificates and protection profiles for ICT products	X (security functions)	X (certificates)

7 State-of-the-Art in Relation to Security Standards

One question in the relationship between state-of-the-art and security standards is still open: Can state-of-the-art be fulfilled without – possibly unwittingly – making use of the content of these standards? The answer clearly is no. Today there seems to be no good technical or management practice that completely does not either relate to or map with the standards mentioned. This is also true for security white papers concerning products, manufacturers, or vendors' issues for their customers, as they refer at least implicitly to standards. The reference in many cases is quite explicit when looking into the IT-Grundschutz Catalogues, as reference to established products in the context of operating systems and applications is made. Examples which come from the white papers can be found for example in the context of networking equipment, operating systems or multi-purpose printing devices.[20] But in

[20] See e.g. https://secure.sophos.de/security/whitepapers/index.html (Virus protection solutions by Sophos), http://www.microsoft.com/Downloads/details.aspx?FamilyID=90ec8abb-08c7-4706-b730-9a1f9fcf2d9f&displaylang=en (Microsoft Windows Vista, especially the integrated "Windows Security Center") and http://www.cisco.com/en/US/products/hw/switches/ps708/products_white_paper09186a008013159f.shtml (VLAN Security White Paper for Cisco networking devices).

some cases the link to the standards mentioned is not made explicitly in the security white papers. It is often up to the readers to establish these links.

8 Summary and Conclusions

Regarding information security, the Data Protection Directive 95/46/EC contains general requirements only. The international standards for information security and related management systems investigated here can be used to implement these requirements. However, as the Directive does not refer to standards, the fulfilment of the security requirements listed in the Directive is possible without directly and explicitly referring to information security related standards. In addition, standards aiming at certification of management systems or products exceed state-of-the-art when they are implemented completely, as they aim at "best practice". Today these certificates are not requested by Data Protection Commissions as a proof of compliance with security requirements set up in relation to the Data Protection Directive.

Nevertheless, explicit or implicit reference of security measures implemented to proceedings and guidance provided by international standards can be considered to fulfil the state-of-the-art requirement of the Directive. On the other hand, the state-of-the-art implementation of the Directive in complete avoidance or violation of the content of these standards today seems to be impossible.

So far a Europe wide harmonised guidance on how to use information security related standards in the context of the implementation of the Directive does not exist. In the interest of the harmonisation of the European market this could well be a worthwhile task. But how could it be achieved?

In the context of harmonisation of the implementation of data protection in Europe the Article 29 Data Protection Working Party (Art29DPWP)[21] is important; it is composed of national Data Protection Commissions and other authorities (e.g. on a federal state level). Harmonised guidance on the application of data protection legislation typically is given in so called "Working Papers". A Working Paper on the application of information security related standards could help to give the guidance missing so far. This paper could serve as a contribution to such a Working Paper. Clearly, this issue (and thus the Working Paper) needs to be reconsidered regularly, as standards (and, of course, the technical background) change.

Another approach currently is taken in the European initiative "EuroPrise"[22], offering a European Privacy Seal for products and services. In this context a catalogue of technical criteria was developed based on information security related standards. Targets of Evaluation (ToE) need to fulfil the requirements of this catalogue in order to gain the privacy seal. The maintenance of this catalogue is planned to be supported by the so called "European Privacy Seal Board". To guarantee European coverage and acceptance of this seal the establishment of this board in close connection to the Art29DPWP, e.g. as a sub-working group, could be a good approach which would ensure the coherence of this catalogue with the suggested Working Paper and other European standardisation approaches in the area of data protection.

---

[21] See http://ec.europa.eu/justice_home/fsj/privacy/workinggroup/index_en.htm for an introduction, an overview on current members and adopted Working Papers.

[22] See https://www.european-privacy-seal.eu/

References

1. German Federal Data Protection Commission (ed.): Data Protection Module for the IT-Grundschutz Catalogues, Berlin (2007), http://www.bsi.de/gshb/baustein-datenschutz/index.htm
2. Dumortier, J.: Hat das Fachgebiet "Recht und Informatik" noch Zukunft? In: Taeger, J., Wiebe, A. (eds.) Informatik – Wirtschaft – Recht; Regulierung in der Wissensgesellschaft, pp. 59–70. Nomos Verlag, Baden-Baden (2004)
3. Roßnagel, A., Pfitzmann, A., Garstka, H.: Modernisierung des Datenschutzrechts. Opinion by order of the German Federal Ministry of Interior, Berlin (2001), http://www.computerundrecht.de/media/gutachten.pdf
4. Initiative D21, IT-Sicherheitskriteriensysteme im Überblick, Bonn, Germany (2001)
5. Müller, G., Wohlgemuth, S. (eds.): FIDIS Deliverable D14.2: Study on Privacy in Business Processes by Identity Management, pp. 42–47. Frankfurt a.M. (2007), http://www.fidis.net/fileadmin/fidis/deliverables/fidis-wp14-del14.2-study_on_privacy_in_business_processes_by_identity_management.pdf
6. Clarke, R.: Privacy Impact Assessment, Canberra, Australia, An updated version of this text is available via (1998), http://www.anu.edu.au/people/Roger.Clarke/DV/PIA.html
7. Meints, M., Thomsen, S.: Protokollierung in Sicherheitsstandards. Datenschutz und Datensicherheit 31(10), 749–751 (2007)

Investigating Anonymity in Group Based Anonymous Authentication

Daniel Slamanig[1,2] and Christian Stingl[1]

[1] Carinthia University of Applied Sciences,
Medical Information Technology – Healthcare IT & Information Security Group,
9020 Klagenfurt, Austria
[2] University of Klagenfurt, Computer Science – System Security Group,
9020 Klagenfurt, Austria
{d.slamanig,c.stingl}@cuas.at

Abstract. In this paper we discuss anonymity in context of group based anonymous authentication ($\mathcal{GBAA}$). Methods for $\mathcal{GBAA}$ provide mechanisms such that a user is able to prove membership in a group $\mathcal{U}' \subseteq \mathcal{U}$ of authorized users $\mathcal{U}$ to a verifier, whereas the verifier does not obtain any information on the actual identity of the authenticating user. They can be used in addition to anonymous communication channels in order to enhance user's privacy if access to services is limited to authorized users, e.g. subscription-based services. We especially focus on attacks against the anonymity of authenticating users which can be mounted by an external adversary or a passive verifier when $\mathcal{GBAA}$ is treated as a black box. In particular, we investigate what an adversary can learn by solely observing anonymity sets $\mathcal{U}'$ used for $\mathcal{GBAA}$ and how users can choose their anonymity sets in case of $\mathcal{U}' \subset \mathcal{U}$. Based on the information which can be obtained by adversaries we show that the probability of user identification can be improved.

1 Introduction

The Internet is nowadays used by a permanently increasing number of people. Their actions comprise on the one hand private activities, e.g. using it as a source of information, doing online banking, communicating with other persons, reading their newspapers, participating in electronic auctions. On the other hand people use it for business related activities. Obviously, the collection of information divulged and exchanged during these activities may represent an extensive picture of a person and covers many topics related to ones privacy. For example, these information may be highly valuable for providers hosting online services when analyzing user's behavior [20,35]. In this context there are tools available for free, e.g. Google Analytics, which provide a huge set of functionalities for aforementioned purposes, even for unaware and casual users. Nevertheless, users may also benefit from these methods by means of Web personalization, i.e. the customization of delivered Web content with respect to the user's preferences. However, privacy issues are very often neglected, which questions the before

V. Matyáš et al. (Eds.): The Future of Identity, IFIP AICT 298, pp. 268–281, 2009.

discussed advantages. This can be illustrated by a user who queries a health information service to obtain information on a serious disease. Recent studies show that 80 percent of health searchers seek the information for themselves and 60 to 80 percent of Americans have already used the Internet to find health information [32]. Hence, if any other party is able to link these information to the user, then it may be possible to draw compromising conclusions.

The aforementioned threats are in our opinion highly realistic, since protocols used in Internet communication do not explicitly provide mechanisms to preserve the anonymity of users. Additionally, we are confronted with a phenomenon denoted as privacy myopia [19]. This means, that people often are not aware of dangers related to privacy and sell or give away their data without reflecting on potential negative consequences. For instance, in context of the Internet this means that users reveal IP-addresses which enable third parties to link several actions and may enable third parties to identify the physical users behind their computers. Furthermore, users often easily give away person related information to third parties which exceeds the amount of information necessary. The latter aspect is the subject of privacy enhanced identity management and has experience major research interest in recent years (cf. [5]).

In this paper we will discuss anonymity aspects related to group based anonymous authentication ($\mathcal{GBAA}$), which provides anonymity for users if access to services is limited to an authorized set of users. If a user needs to authenticate to a service provider by means of traditional authentication mechanisms, in general the identity of the user is known by the service provider. By means of $\mathcal{GBAA}$, the server solely learns the membership of the authenticating user in the set of authorized users, but does not learn the exact identity. This can be valuable for users, if the sole knowledge of service accesses, i.e. the frequency of access, may lead to compromising conclusions. The applications we have in mind for $\mathcal{GBAA}$ are any kind of Internet services that require user authentication, but users want to hide their behavior from the service provider. Thereby, the main advantage of $\mathcal{GBAA}$ schemes is that they can be build upon existing and widely deployed public key infrastructures based on X.509 certificates (PKIX) and user registration for services solely requires the user to provide a valid X.509 certificate to the service provider. This results on the one hand in higher security compared to widely used username/password authentication schemes and on the other hand in a privacy improvement for the user. For instance, consider a Internet service which provides access to an electronic health record (EHR) of a person, whereas the EHR represents a life-long documentation of the medical history of a person. In this context, even the knowledge of the frequency of access to the EHR may enable a third party to draw compromising conclusions about the state of health of the person. Additionally, the use of $\mathcal{GBAA}$ schemes, which are based on public key certificates, prevents users from identity theft by means of password guessing, dictionary attacks or other threats.

The remainder of this paper is organized as follows: In section 2 we discuss aspects of anonymity that are important for Internet based services. In the subsequent section 3 we will briefly introduce $\mathcal{GBAA}$, attack models and scenarios as well as some problems related to $\mathcal{GBAA}$. Section 4 discusses the choice of anonymity sets used for authentication and provides a detailed analysis. Finally, section 5 concludes the paper and discusses some future aspects.

2 Different Aspects of Anonymity

Anonymity aspects of users in the context of Internet services are twofold. Firstly, the anonymity of a user may be revealed by the communication channel itself. Consequently, users need to hide their identity when sending messages over the communication channel. This can be achieved by means of anonymous communication channels. Secondly, identities of users may be revealed at higher network layers, i.e. the application layer. This is especially of interest if services require user authentication at the application layer. Subsequently, we will briefly discuss the aforementioned aspects.

2.1 Communication Anonymity

Mechanisms that provide anonymity and unlinkability of messages sent over a communication channel are denoted as anonymous communication techniques and have been intensively studied in recent years, see [12] for a sound overview. There are several implementations available for low-latency services like Web browsing, e.g. Tor [15], JAP [18], as well as high-latency services like E-Mail, e.g. Mixminion [13].

These anonymous communication channels help to improve the privacy of users in context of eavesdroppers and curious communication partners. Especially, regarding the latter one anonymity can be preserved if electronic interaction does not rely on additional identifying information at higher network layers, i.e. the application layer. For example, a user who queries a public web page using an anonymous communication channel may remove all identifying information from higher network layers and thus will stay anonymous.

In our considerations we assume that we have a communication channel that guarantees perfect anonymity and unlinkability. Then a user is connected to a service provider (server) via a kind of *"magic channel"* that leaks no information on the identity of the user at the communication layer. Clearly, this is a somewhat idealized consideration, since real world anonymous communication channels do not realize perfect anonymity resp. unlinkability (cf. [30]) and there may exist additional side channels, e.g. online-behavior of users, which can be used to improve the probability of identification of communicating parties.

2.2 Anonymity at Higher Layers

However, if service providers offer their services only to authorized sets of users, e.g. subscription-based services, closed communities, they require identification of users which in general takes place at higher layers by means of entity authentication mechanisms. In entity authentication or identification protocols the holder of an identity usually claims a set of attributes including an identifier and interactively proves the possession of the claimed identity to a verifier. This identifier is usually unique within a specific context, e.g. application, but may be a pseudonym, which is not linkable to the physical identity of a person. But there usually exists a party which is aware of this link and additionally, actions conducted under the same pseudonym can be linked. Nevertheless, there exists anonymous credential systems which can be used to anonymously prove the possession of attributes of credentials while preserving unlinkability of different showings of a credential and anonymity of the holders (cf. [4,7,8,24]). These approaches are especially suitable in a multi-provider setting, where users obtain credentials for a pseudonym from one provider and are able to show these credentials under different pseudonyms to other providers. Nevertheless, there are also known attacks (cf. [21,27]) against unlinkability and anonymity of anonymous credential systems when using them in a real world context. We do not consider the aforementioned approaches, since we are interested in a single-provider and "ad hoc" setting. However, the aforementioned mechanisms can also be used to realize anonymous authentication (cf. [6]), but in general they do not provide "ad hoc" mechanisms as discussed below, i.e. they rely on a proprietary setup with every user. Therefore, we will subsequently discuss an alternative approach based on cryptographic primitives like ring signatures [31], which we call group based anonymous authentication ($\mathcal{GBAA}$), that provides mechanisms to perform anonymous authentications based on "ad hoc" groups, i.e. without relying on interaction with other group members and without any additional proprietary setup.

3 Group Based Anonymous Authentication

Group based anonymous authentication ($\mathcal{GBAA}$) aims to provide a somewhat paradoxical solution to enhance user's privacy in context of authentication. It provides mechanisms such that a user is able to prove membership in a group $\mathcal{U}' \subseteq \mathcal{U}$ of authorized users $\mathcal{U}$, whereas the verifier does not obtain information on the identity of the authenticating user. The set $\mathcal{U}'$ will also be denoted as the anonymity set [29]. Clearly, anonymous communication systems are a prerequisite for providing anonymity in the context of anonymous authentication.

A naive approach to realize $\mathcal{GBAA}$ would be to give a copy of a secret k to every user $u \in \mathcal{U}$, which could be used in conjunction with a traditional authentication scheme. Obviously, the revocation of a single user u_i would result in a reinitialization and thus in reissuing a fresh secret k' to every remaining user $u \in \mathcal{U} \setminus u_i$. Hence, this approach is far from being practical. Improved techniques for $\mathcal{GBAA}$ were explicitly treated in [3,23,28,33,37] and additionally with special properties like being anonymous as long as the number of authentication is beyond a threshold [36], the ability to detect fraudulent users [6,11] and with the ability to revoke the anonymity of users [3,22]. They can be be realized by means of group signatures [1,9, etc.], witness indistinguishable signatures [10], ring signatures [16,31, etc.] or similar concepts as (deniable) ring authentication [26].

The latter two classes of signature and authentication schemes are preferable to group signatures in the context of large and dynamic groups, as it is the case with Internet services, since they can be generated "ad hoc" without depending on an explicit setup phase or reinitialization in case of dynamic groups. Thereby "ad hoc" means that an authenticating user does not need the knowledge, consent or assistance of the remaining members of an ad hoc group to perform an authentication. Furthermore, in general they do not require a proprietary setup and do only rely on standard public key certificates, i.e. X.509 certificates, which are widely deployed and available. It must be mentioned that there are already attempts to integrate group, ring and traceable signatures, which can be used for $\mathcal{GBAA}$, into the PKIX framework [2].

There are three important properties that $\mathcal{GBAA}$ mechanisms need to provide (cf. [23,33]):

1. **Anonymity:** The verifier is not able to determine the identity of an authenticating user with probability higher than $1/|\mathcal{U}'|$.
2. **Unlinkability:** It is impossible to link k, $k > 1$, instances of the $\mathcal{GBAA}$ protocol of one (anonymous) user $u_i \in \mathcal{U}'$.
3. **Security:** Only authorized users $u \in \mathcal{U}$ should be able to pass the $\mathcal{GBAA}$.

The properties we are focusing on in this paper are anonymity and unlinkability, and in particular we investigate strategies to construct groups used for $\mathcal{GBAA}$. This is especially of interest in context of large groups, since the computational effort in $\mathcal{GBAA}$ protocols usually grows (linearly) with the size of the anonymity set, i.e. the cardinality of $\mathcal{U}'$. Thus, a large set of authorized users may force a user to prove his membership using a subset of all authorized users for efficiency purposes. It must be mentioned that we do not explicitly discuss technical details on the construction of methods for $\mathcal{GBAA}$ and will treat them as a black box in the remainder of this paper.

The question that comes up is, whether a verifier or even an observer is able to reduce the anonymity and consequently unlinkability by continuously observing anonymity sets, although the underlying $\mathcal{GBAA}$ method and communication channel provides perfect anonymity and unlinkability.

3.1 Attacker Model

As mentioned above, we are not considering anonymity provided by the $\mathcal{GBAA}$ itself and the communication channel. Consequently, we assume that the $\mathcal{GBAA}$ methods provide perfect anonymity, unlinkability and security and the communication channel provides perfect anonymity and unlinkability ("magic channel"). Clearly, these assumptions are very strong with respect to the real world and thus the results presented in this paper, i.e. the reduction of anonymity of users, may even be improved enormously by substituting the perfect $\mathcal{GBAA}$ and communication channel by actually deployed methods.

The attack model used in this paper considers the following adversaries.

- **Honest but curious (passive) verifier:** An insider who is able to monitor all actions inside the verifier's system, but does not actively manipulate messages which are exchanged during the $\mathcal{GBAA}$.

- **Eavesdropper:** Anyone who is able to monitor the inbound traffic of the verifier. As above, the eavesdropper solely behaves passive, i.e. does not manipulate exchanged messages.

Passive attacks conducted by an eavesdropper can easily be prevented by means of encrypted communication, i.e. a communication channel which provides confidentiality and integrity of transmitted messages. However, it must be mentioned that an external adversary may run a denial of service (DoS) attack against the verifier's system in order to deter authentications of users anyway. We do not consider active attackers, since there exist measures incorporated into $\mathcal{GBAA}$ protocols to detect a cheating verifier (cf. [23]), which are outside the scope of this paper. Furthermore, in practice an actively cheating verifier may leak out some day and will consequently not be trustworthy anymore.

An adversary may mount the subsequent attacks, whereas we focus on the first one in this paper and the latter one will only be stated for the sake of completeness.

- **Anonymity sets only:** An adversary is clearly able to record all information which are shown to him during any instance of a $\mathcal{GBAA}$. Thus he can count the occurrences of users in anonymity sets. The adversary will try to reduce the anonymity of single users solely by means of the aforementioned information.
- **Behavioral heuristic:** Since unlinkability is a required property, every action inside the system requires a single $\mathcal{GBAA}$ protocol. Thus, authentications of a single user are likely to occur cumulative since in general at least a few operations are conducted within the verifier's system.

3.2 Some Problems Related to $\mathcal{GBAA}$

One inherent problem in "ad hoc" $\mathcal{GBAA}$ is, that the physical person which holds a digital identity, irrespective of the representation, e.g. X.509 certificates, is not directly known to a user. Consequently, a user may not be able to distinguish "real" from "fake" identities. Especially in large groups, a verifier may be able to forge identities of "authorized users" which look valid to all other users. This is crucial, if verifiers set up their system (parameters) autonomous, i.e. issue credentials or certificates on their own, and do not involve a commonly trusted party, e.g. a trusted certification authority which issues public key certificates. It must be stressed, that this attack is an active one which can be conducted by malicious verifiers to reduce the anonymity of users. However, we assume that the verifier is honest but curious in our attack model. This fake-user insertion attack can be somewhat compared to the sybil attack [17], which has been investigated in a somewhat similar context [25]. But, in our case the verifier creates a set of forged identities on his own and integrates them into the system. Consequently, the effective anonymity set for $\mathcal{GBAA}$ will be reduced by users unawarely including fake identities in their anonymity sets.

Another problem in this context is that the authenticating user needs to be sure, that all actually chosen users are indeed authorized users at the point of time of authentication. We want to emphasize, that the task of determining authorized users, i.e. to check if a user is authorized and the respective certificate is valid, is a time consuming and non-trivial task, but is inherent to all certificate based $\mathcal{GBAA}$ protocols. However, we will not consider this problem in detail in this paper since it does not affect our investigations.

4 Analysis

In this section we firstly analyze strategies to construct anonymity sets and secondly propose methods that can be used by an adversary to improve the probability of identification of users.

4.1 Group Construction Strategies

In the following we will discuss the strategies to construct anonymity sets for $\mathcal{GBAA}$. Thereby, we consider the two possible scenarios, i.e. on the one hand the entire group and on the other hand a subgroup of authorized users.

Entire Group. If a user chooses the entire group $\mathcal{U}$ for $\mathcal{GBAA}$, the probability of user u_i being the one who actually authenticates in any anonymity set is $p_{u_i} = 1/|\mathcal{U}|$. Hence, this approach guarantees perfect anonymity [14,34]. This strategy is immune against fake-user insertion attacks, since always all users are chosen. However, it must be emphasized that for actual available protocols for $\mathcal{GBAA}$ the computational effort grows at least linearly with the size of the anonymity set. Hence, in case of a large set of authorized users, this approach is impractical.

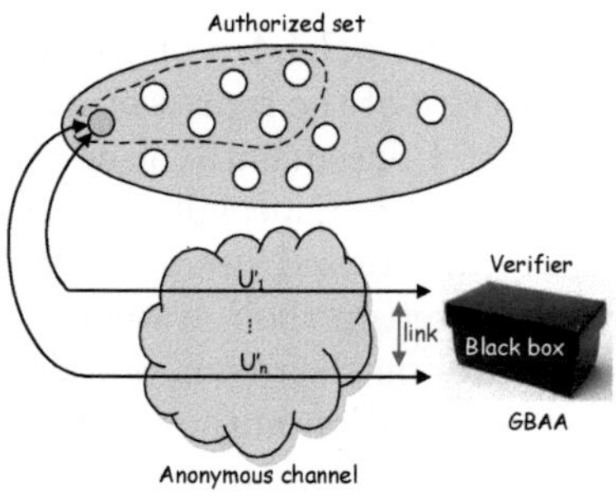

Fig. 1. Static subgroup approach from the point of view of the prover

Subgroup. This alternative approach is characterized by choosing a subset $\mathcal{U}' \subset \mathcal{U}$ for $\mathcal{GBAA}$, whereas we assume that $|\mathcal{U}'| \ll |\mathcal{U}|$. Therefore, users need to construct subgroups following some specific strategy. The obvious method for a user u_i to construct an anonymity set of size k is, to independently choose $k-1$ users uniformly at random from $\mathcal{U}$ and to subsequently integrate himself into the anonymity set. This approach is prone to a fake-user insertion attack, since the verifier may include faked "authorized" users into the set of all authorized users. Consequently, the level of security depends on the fraction of "fake" users.

Considering the subgroup-approach we distinguish between static subgroups and dynamic subgroups.

Static Subgroup. In case of static subgroups, a user $u_i \in \mathcal{U}$ initially chooses $k-1$ users uniformly at random from $\mathcal{U}$ and forms his static anonymity set by adding himself to this set. Subsequently, he uses his initial chosen anonymity set for every $\mathcal{GBAA}$. If $\mathcal{U}$ is large, e.g. $|\mathcal{U}| = 200$, and the size of the anonymity set is smaller than the size of $\mathcal{U}$ ($\mathcal{U}' \approx 100$), it is very unlikely that two distinct users choose exactly the same anonymity set, i.e. $\approx 1/\binom{|\mathcal{U}|}{|\mathcal{U}'|}$. Hence, if a user applies this strategy all $\mathcal{GBAA}$s are in general linkable. Additional, with side channel information, e.g. user's behavior, it may be easier to identify a single user. As a consequence we want to point out that this approach is in our opinion not appropriate.

Dynamic Subgroup. In case of dynamic subgroups a user $u_i \in \mathcal{U}$ constructs his anonymity set $\mathcal{U}'$ independently for every single authentication. Thus unlinkability is guaranteed and with respect to the above strategies in our opinion it is the preferred strategy in context of large sets of authorized users. Nevertheless,

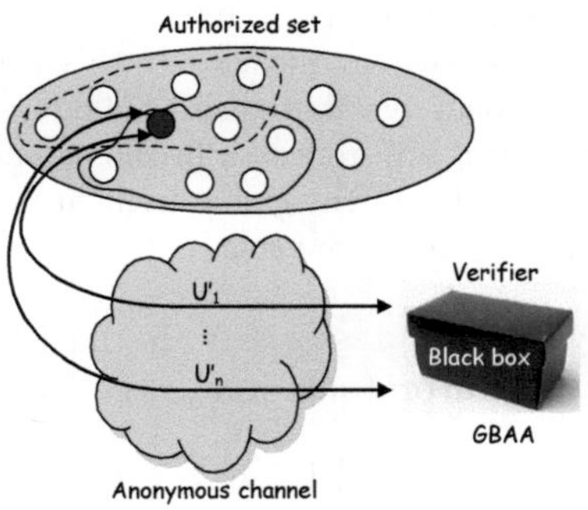

Fig. 2. Dynamic subgroup approach from the point of view of the prover

we will subsequently examine potential weaknesses of this dynamic subgroup approach which can be used by an adversary to improve the probability of identifying authenticating users.

4.2 Anonymity Sets Only Attack

As mentioned above, we are now focusing on anonymity sets independent of the protocol used for $\mathcal{GBAA}$. Furthermore, we assume that these information can be monitored by an adversary, e.g. the verifier or an eavesdropper. In particular, we introduce methods to analyze the anonymity sets and derive measures to improve attacks against anonymity. In order to compute these measures a $|\mathcal{U}| \times N$ history

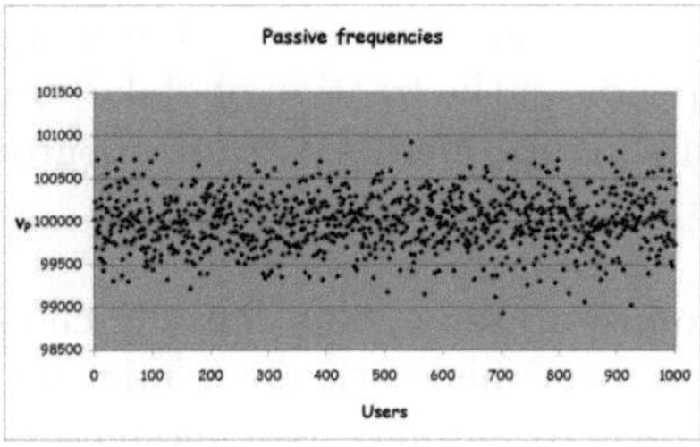

(a)

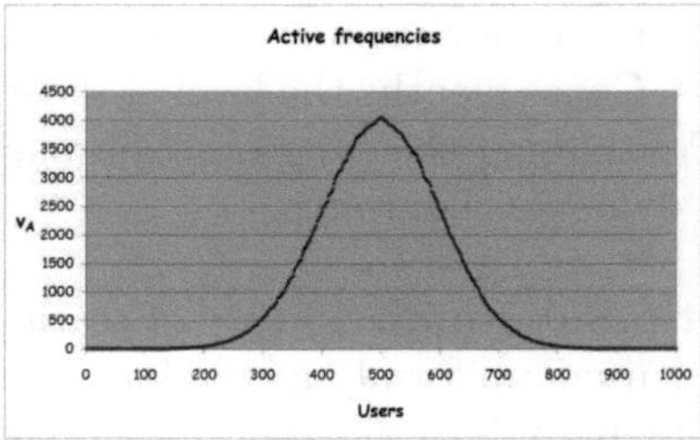

(b)

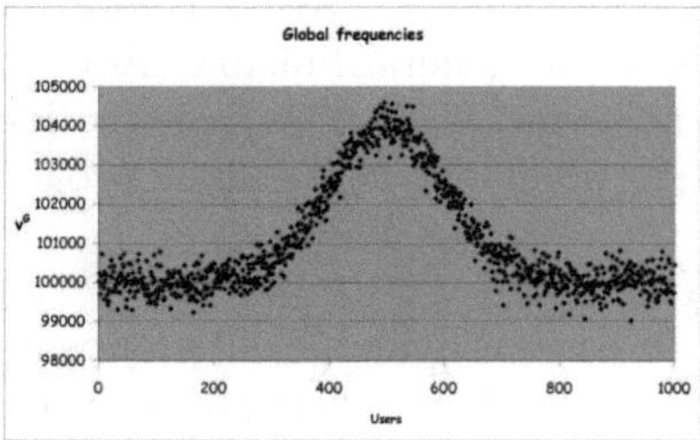

(c)

Fig. 3. The setting for this example is: $|\mathcal{U}| = 1000$, $N = 10^8$. Subfigure (a) illustrates the uniform distribution of the passive frequencies. In this example it was assumed that the active frequencies are Gaussian distributed (b). Subfigure (c) shows that the distribution of the active frequencies is still reflected in the global frequency. Furthermore, it can be conjectured that the value of the global frequency is directly "connected" to the value of the active frequency and vice versa.

matrix $\mathcal{H}$ will be used, where $\mathcal{U}'_j$, $1 \leq j \leq N$, is the j-th anonymity set and N is the overall number of $\mathcal{GBAA}$ protocol runs.

$$\mathcal{H}(i,j) = \begin{cases} 1, & \text{if } u_i \in \mathcal{U}'_j, \\ 0, & \text{else.} \end{cases}$$

Put differently, the matrix represents the collection of all anonymity sets which were used in $\mathcal{GBAA}$s and the element $\mathcal{H}(i,j)$ contains the value 1 if and only if user u_i occurred in the respective anonymity set $\mathcal{U}'_j$. Based on this matrix, we are defining the global frequency $\nu^G_{u_i}$ of user u_i which is the sum of the i-th row. The global frequency of a user u_i itself consists of an active part $\nu^G_{u_i,\mathcal{A}}$, i.e. the number of actual authentications of the user, and a passive part $\nu^G_{u_i,\mathcal{P}}$, i.e. other users choose u_i in their anonymity sets. Obviously, an adversary can solely determine the sum $\nu^G_{u_i} = \nu^G_{u_i,\mathcal{A}} + \nu^G_{u_i,\mathcal{P}}$ of the users frequency from the history matrix. The two subsequent facts can easily be obtained.

$$\sum_{i=1}^{|\mathcal{U}|} \nu^G_{u_i,\mathcal{A}} = N \tag{1}$$

$$\sum_{i=1}^{|\mathcal{U}|} \nu_{u_i,\mathcal{P}}^{G} = \sum_{i=1}^{N} (|\mathcal{U}_i'| - 1) \tag{2}$$

Considering the above mentioned method to create subgroups one can conclude that the passive frequencies are uniformly distributed and the average of all passive frequencies is $\bar{\nu}_{\mathcal{P}} = \sum_{i=1}^{N}(|\mathcal{U}_i'| - 1)/N$. In contrast, the distribution of the active frequencies is in general unknown, but it is very unlikely that the distribution is uniform in real world scenarios. At this point the following question arises: What kind of information can be obtained about the global frequency? A first observation is, that the sum of the passive frequencies is much greater then the sum of the active frequencies. For instance, if the size of the anonymity set is constant then $\sum \nu_{\cdot,\mathcal{P}} / \sum \nu_{\cdot,\mathcal{A}} = |\mathcal{U}'| - 1$. Secondly, we know that the passive frequencies are uniformly distributed and thus we are able to derive a confidence interval α for the expected value. Hence, all passive frequencies will lie in the confidence interval with probability p (see table 1). Based on the global frequency of a single user u_i it is possible to derive an interval for the active frequency of this user (see figure 4). The parameter (α) determines the lower and upper bound of the confidence interval. By subtracting these bounds from the global frequency one obtains an interval for the active frequency which holds with probability p.

$$max(\nu_{u_i}^{G} - \bar{\nu}_{\mathcal{P}}(1+\alpha), 0) \leq \nu_{u_i,\mathcal{A}}^{G} \leq max(\nu_{u_i}^{G} - \bar{\nu}_{\mathcal{P}}(1-\alpha), 0) \tag{3}$$

Table 1. Confidence interval α, probability p and number of outliers

Authorized users $\lvert\mathcal{U}\rvert$	Anonymity set $\lvert\mathcal{U}'\rvert$	Number of auth. N	α	p	Outliers
1000	100	1000.000	0.005	≈ 0.8863	≈ 113
1000	100	1000.000	0.01	≈ 0.9984	≈ 2
1000	100	1000.000	0.02	≈ 1	≈ 0

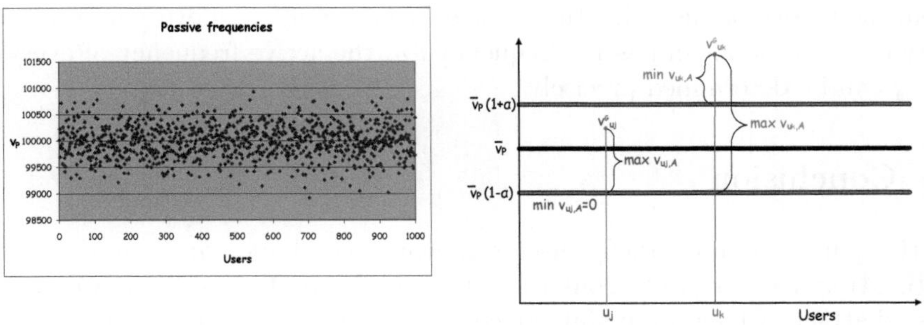

(a) (b)

Fig. 4. In subfigure (a) an exemple confidence interval is shown. Based on this confidence interval ranges for the active frequency of two users are derived (b).

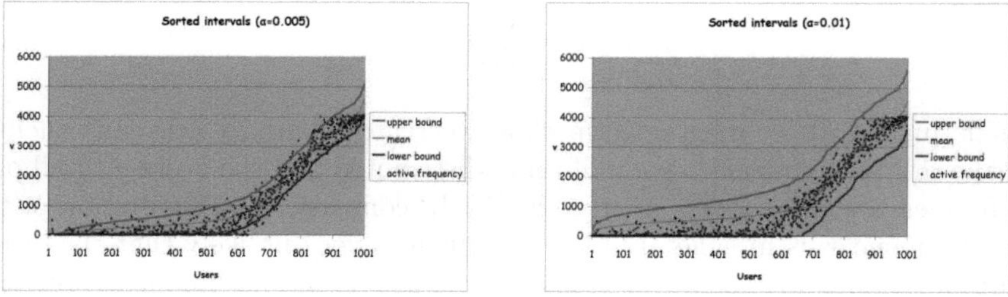

(a) (b)

Fig. 5. Upper and lower bounds for active frequencies for two choices of the parameter α; (a): $\alpha = 0.005$; (b): $\alpha = 0.01$

Note that the lower α the more precise are the lower and the upper bound for the active frequency. But, the number of passive frequencies which are not inside the confidence interval will grow and consequently the number of active frequencies which do not satisfy equation (3). From equation (3) it is possible to derive the maximum size of the interval $\delta_{\mathcal{A}}$, whereas $\delta_{\mathcal{A}} \leq 2\alpha\nu_{\mathcal{P}}$. This is also reflected in figure 5 where $\nu_{\mathcal{P}} = 100.000$ and $\alpha = 0.005$ ($\alpha = 0.01$). Consequently, $\delta_{\mathcal{A}} = 1000$ (2000) which can also be seen in figures 5. Considering two users u_i and u_j where the upper bound of user u_i is significantly smaller then the lower bound of the user u_j, then $\nu^G_{u_i,\mathcal{A}}$ is also significantly smaller than $\nu^G_{u_j,\mathcal{A}}$. These information can prospectively be used to improve the probability of identification of u_j in comparison to u_i.

It must be mentioned, that this estimation is independent of the distribution of the active frequencies. Furthermore, we have evaluated a number of random number generators (RNG) provided by standard libraries of different programming languages and most of them behave as the probability theory predicts and clearly was the basis for our investigations. However, we have also encountered a few RNGs that provide "better" results than expected and consequently more precise bounds could be obtained. Put differently, RNGs that behave "better" than the theory predicts, i.e. the passive frequency $\nu^G_{u_i,\mathcal{P}}$ of every user u_i will be very close to the mean passive frequency $\bar{\nu}_{\mathcal{P}}$, the active frequency of every user $\nu^G_{u_i,\mathcal{A}}$ can be determined precisely.

5 Conclusion

In this paper we have briefly discussed group based anonymous authentication ($\mathcal{GBAA}$) and strategies to construct anonymity sets. Furthermore, we have discussed attacks which can mainly be conducted by passive adversaries and finally we have pointed out how to estimate the number of authentications per user. This result can be used to reduce the anonymity of authenticating users. Additional side-channel information, e.g. user's behavior, can be used to further improve the efficiency of the proposed approach. We conclude, that $\mathcal{GBAA}$, even considered as a black box, leaks information on authenticating users over a period of time. One important fact is, that the approximated active frequencies of users are more precise the greater the number of protocol runs. In order to counter this kind of attack we recommend to significantly reduce the number of $\mathcal{GBAA}$s. This can be achieved by a combination of $\mathcal{GBAA}$ and token based anonymous transactions, which is topic to current and future research.

Acknowledgements

The authors would like to thank the anonymous referees for their valuable comments and Michael Reiner for providing the simulation results to us.

References

1. Ateniese, G., Camenisch, J., Joye, M., Tsudik, G.: A Practical and Provably Secure Coalition-Resistant Group Signature Scheme. In: Bellare, M. (ed.) CRYPTO 2000. LNCS, vol. 1880, pp. 255–270. Springer, Heidelberg (2000)
2. Benjumea, V., Choi, S.G., Lopez, J., Yung, M.: Anonymity 2.0 - X.509 Extensions Supporting Privacy-Friendly Authentication. In: Bao, F., Ling, S., Okamoto, T., Wang, H., Xing, C. (eds.) CANS 2007. LNCS, vol. 4856, pp. 265–281. Springer, Heidelberg (2007)
3. Boneh, D., Franklin, M.: Anonymous Authentication with Subset Queries. In: Proc. of the 6th ACM conference on Computer and communications security, pp. 113–119 (1999)
4. Brands, S.: Rethinking Public Key Infrastructures and Digital Certificates: Building in Privacy. MIT Press, Cambridge (2000)
5. Camenisch, J., Shelat, A., Sommer, D., Fischer-Hübner, S., Hansen, M., Krasemann, H., Lacoste, G., Leenes, R., Tseng, J.: Privacy and Identity Management for Everyone. In: DIM 2005: Proceedings of the 2005 workshop on Digital identity management, pp. 20–27. ACM, New York (2005)
6. Camenisch, J., Hohenberger, S., Kohlweiss, M., Lysyanskaya, A., Meyerovich, M.: How to Win the Clone Wars: Efficient Periodic n-Times Anonymous Authentication. In: Proceedings of the 13th ACM conference on Computer and communications security, CCS 2006, pp. 201–210. ACM, New York (2006)
7. Camenisch, J., Lysyanskaya, A.: An Efficient System for Non-transferable Anonymous Credentials with Optional Anonymity Revocation. In: Pfitzmann, B. (ed.) EUROCRYPT 2001. LNCS, vol. 2045, pp. 93–118. Springer, Heidelberg (2001)
8. Chaum, D.: Security without identification: transaction systems to make big brother obsolete. Commun. ACM 28(10), 1030–1044 (1985)
9. Chaum, D., van Heyst, E.: Group signatures. In: Davies, D.W. (ed.) EUROCRYPT 1991. LNCS, vol. 547, pp. 257–265. Springer, Heidelberg (1991)
10. Cramer, R., Damgård, I., Schoenmakers, B.: Proofs of Partial Knowledge and Simplified Design of Witness Hiding Protocols. In: Desmedt, Y.G. (ed.) CRYPTO 1994. LNCS, vol. 839, pp. 174–187. Springer, Heidelberg (1994)
11. Damgård, I., Dupont, K., Pedersen, M.Ø.: Unclonable Group Identification. In: Vaudenay, S. (ed.) EUROCRYPT 2006. LNCS, vol. 4004, pp. 555–572. Springer, Heidelberg (2006)

12. Danezis, G., Diaz, C.: A Survey of Anonymous Communication Channels. Technical Report MSR-TR-2008-35, Microsoft Research (January 2008)
13. Danezis, G., Dingledine, R., Mathewson, N.: Mixminion: Design of a Type III Anonymous Remailer Protocol. In: SP 2003: Proceedings of the 2003 IEEE Symposium on Security and Privacy, Washington, DC, USA, pp. 2–15. IEEE Computer Society, Los Alamitos (2003)
14. Diaz, C., Seys, S., Claessens, J., Preneel, B.: Towards Measuring Anonymity. In: Dingledine, R., Syverson, P.F. (eds.) PET 2002. LNCS, vol. 2482, pp. 54–68. Springer, Heidelberg (2003)
15. Dingledine, R., Mathewson, N., Syverson, P.: Tor: The Second-Generation Onion Router. In: Proceedings of the 13th USENIX Security Symposium, p. 21 (2004)
16. Dodis, Y., Kiayias, A., Nicolosi, A., Shoup, V.: Anonymous Identification in Ad Hoc Groups. In: Cachin, C., Camenisch, J.L. (eds.) EUROCRYPT 2004. LNCS, vol. 3027, pp. 609–626. Springer, Heidelberg (2004)
17. Douceur, J.R.: The Sybil Attack. In: Druschel, P., Kaashoek, M.F., Rowstron, A. (eds.) IPTPS 2002. LNCS, vol. 2429, pp. 251–260. Springer, Heidelberg (2002)
18. Federrath, H.: Privacy Enhanced Technologies: Methods, Markets, Misuse. In: Katsikas, S.K., López, J., Pernul, G. (eds.) TrustBus 2005. LNCS, vol. 3592, pp. 1–9. Springer, Heidelberg (2005)
19. Froomkin, M.: The Death of Privacy? Stanford Law Review 52(5), 1461–1543 (2000)
20. Joshi, A., Joshi, K., Krishnapuram, R.: On Mining Web Access Logs. In: Proceedings of the 2000 ACM SIGMOD Workshop on Research Issues in Data Mining and Knowledge Discovery, pp. 63–69. ACM, New York (2000)
21. Kesdogan, D., Pham, V., Pimenidis, L.: Information Disclosure in Identity Management. In: Proceedings of 12th Nordic Workshop on Secure IT-Systems, Reykjavik, Iceland, October 11-12 (2007)
22. Kilian, J., Petrank, E.: Identity Escrow. In: Krawczyk, H. (ed.) CRYPTO 1998. LNCS, vol. 1462, pp. 169–185. Springer, Heidelberg (1998)
23. Lindell, Y.: Anonymous Authenticaion. Whitepaper Aladdin Knowledge Systems (2007), http://www.aladdin.com/blog/pdf/AnonymousAuthentication.pdf
24. Lysyanskaya, A., Rivest, R.L., Sahai, A., Wolf, S.: Pseudonym Systems. In: Heys, H.M., Adams, C.M. (eds.) SAC 1999. LNCS, vol. 1758, pp. 184–199. Springer, Heidelberg (2000)
25. Martucci, L.A., Kohlweiss, M., Andersson, C., Panchenko, A.: Self-Certified Sybil-Free Pseudonyms. In: Proceedings of the first ACM conference on Wireless network security, WiSec 2008, pp. 154–159. ACM, New York (2008)
26. Naor, M.: Deniable Ring Authentication. In: Yung, M. (ed.) CRYPTO 2002. LNCS, vol. 2442, pp. 481–498. Springer, Heidelberg (2002)
27. Pashalidis, A., Meyer, B.: Linking Anonymous Transactions: The Consistent View Attack. In: Danezis, G., Golle, P. (eds.) PET 2006. LNCS, vol. 4258, pp. 384–392. Springer, Heidelberg (2006)
28. Persiano, P., Visconti, I.: A Secure and Private System for Subscription-Based Remote Services. ACM Trans. Inf. Syst. Secur. 6(4), 472–500 (2003)
29. Pfitzmann, A., Köhntopp, M.: Anonymity, Unobservability, and Pseudonymity - A Proposal for Terminology. In: Federrath, H. (ed.) Designing Privacy Enhancing Technologies. LNCS, vol. 2009, pp. 1–9. Springer, Heidelberg (2001)
30. Raymond, J.-F.: Traffic Analysis: Protocols, Attacks, Design Issues, and Open Problems. In: Federrath, H. (ed.) Designing Privacy Enhancing Technologies. LNCS, vol. 2009, pp. 10–29. Springer, Heidelberg (2001)

31. Rivest, R.L., Shamir, A., Tauman, Y.: How to Leak a Secret. In: Boyd, C. (ed.) ASIACRYPT 2001. LNCS, vol. 2248, pp. 552–565. Springer, Heidelberg (2001)
32. Sarasohn-Kahn, J.: The Wisdom of Patients: Health Care Meets Online Social Media (April 2008), http://www.chcf.org
33. Schechter, S., Parnell, T., Hartemink, A.: Anonymous Authentication of Membership in Dynamic Groups. In: Franklin, M.K. (ed.) FC 1999. LNCS, vol. 1648, pp. 184–195. Springer, Heidelberg (1999)
34. Serjantov, A., Danezis, G.: Towards an Information Theoretic Metric for Anonymity. In: Dingledine, R., Syverson, P.F. (eds.) PET 2002. LNCS, vol. 2482, pp. 41–53. Springer, Heidelberg (2003)
35. Srivastava, J., Cooley, R., Deshpande, M., Tan, P.-N.: Web Usage Mining: Discovery and Applications of Usage Patterns from Web Data. SIGKDD Explor. Newsl. 1(2), 12–23 (2000)
36. Teranishi, I., Kurukawa, J., Sako, K.: k-Times Anonymous Authentication. In: Lee, P.J. (ed.) ASIACRYPT 2004. LNCS, vol. 3329, pp. 308–322. Springer, Heidelberg (2004)
37. Tzeng, W.-G.: A Secure System for Data Access Based on Anonymous Authentication and Time-Dependent Hierarchical Keys. In: Proc. of the ACM Symp. on Information, computer and communications security, pp. 223–230. ACM, New York (2006)

Author Index

Author Index

MIX
Papier aus verantwortungsvollen Quellen
Paper from responsible sources
FSC® C105338

If you have any concerns about our products,
you can contact us on
ProductSafety@springernature.com

In case Publisher is established outside the EU,
the EU authorized representative is:
Springer Nature Customer Service Center GmbH
Europaplatz 3, 69115 Heidelberg, Germany

Printed by Libri Plureos GmbH
in Hamburg, Germany